Air Power and the Evacuation of Dunkirk

Air Power and the Evacuation of Dunkirk

The RAF and Luftwaffe during Operation Dynamo, 26 May – 4 June 1940

Harry Raffal

BLOOMSBURY ACADEMIC
LONDON • NEW YORK • OXFORD • NEW DELHI • SYDNEY

BLOOMSBURY ACADEMIC
Bloomsbury Publishing Plc
50 Bedford Square, London, WC1B 3DP, UK
1385 Broadway, New York, NY 10018, USA
29 Earlsfort Terrace, Dublin 2, Ireland

BLOOMSBURY, BLOOMSBURY ACADEMIC and the Diana logo are trademarks of
Bloomsbury Publishing Plc

First published in Great Britain 2021
Paperback edition published 2023

Copyright © Harry Raffal, 2021

Harry Raffal has asserted his right under the Copyright, Designs and
Patents Act, 1988, to be identified as Author of this work.

For legal purposes the Acknowledgements on p. vii constitute
an extension of this copyright page.

Cover design: Terry Woodley
Cover image: A Junkers Ju 87 dropping bombs over allied troops awaiting evacuation from
the beaches of Dunkirk, 26 May – 4 June 1940. De Luan/Alamy Stock Photo

All rights reserved. No part of this publication may be reproduced or
transmitted in any form or by any means, electronic or mechanical,
including photocopying, recording, or any information storage or retrieval
system, without prior permission in writing from the publishers.

Bloomsbury Publishing Plc does not have any control over, or responsibility for,
any third-party websites referred to or in this book. All internet addresses given
in this book were correct at the time of going to press. The author and publisher
regret any inconvenience caused if addresses have changed or sites have ceased
to exist, but can accept no responsibility for any such changes.

A catalogue record for this book is available from the British Library.

Library of Congress Cataloging-in-Publication Data
Names: Raffal, Harry, author.
Title: Air Power and the Evacuation of Dunkirk: The RAF and Luftwaffe during Operation
Dynamo, 26 May – 4 June 1940 / Harry Raffal.
Description: London ; New York : Bloomsbury Academic, 2021. | Includes bibliographical
references and index. |
Identifiers: LCCN 2021001939 (print) | LCCN 2021001940 (ebook) | ISBN 9781350180499
(HB) | ISBN 9781350180468 (ePDF) | ISBN 9781350180475 (eBook)
Subjects: LCSH: Dunkirk, Battle of, Dunkerque, France, 1940–Historiography. | World War,
1939-1945–Aerial operations. | Great Britain. Royal Air Force. | Germany. Luftwaffe.
Classification: LCC D756.5.D8.R34 2021 (print) | LCC D756.5.D8 (ebook) | DDC
940.54/21428–dc23
LC record available at https://lccn.loc.gov/2021001939
LC ebook record available at https://lccn.loc.gov/2021001940

ISBN:	HB:	978-1-3501-8049-9
	PB:	978-1-3502-2998-3
	ePDF:	978-1-3501-8046-8
	eBook:	978-1-3501-8047-5

Typeset by Integra Software Services Pvt. Ltd.

To find out more about our authors and books visit www.bloomsbury.com
and sign up for our newsletters.

Contents

List of Figures and Tables	vi
Acknowledgements	vii
Abbreviations	ix
Introduction	1
1 The two forces	25
2 The Luftwaffe's attacks, 29 May and 1 June	79
3 The suspension of daylight evacuations	97
4 The Luftwaffe's attacks on Dunkirk before 29 May	119
5 The Luftwaffe's attacks on Dunkirk on 30–31 May	137
6 Results, limitations and potential of Luftwaffe night attacks and mine operations	157
7 RAF and Luftwaffe fighter operations during Dynamo	173
8 The operations of Coastal Command	223
9 The operations of Bomber Command	251
Conclusion	293
Appendices	304
Bibliography	312
Index	331

Figures and Tables

Figures

1	Comparison of various forms of air attack	40
2	Percentage of hits likely to be attained by a level-bombing attack on a destroyer (underway at 10 knots) on basis of average bombing error and theoretical height of attack needed to attain the average bombing error in ideal conditions	129
3	Fighter Command and Luftwaffe aircraft losses over Dunkirk caused by the enemy air force	174
4	Bomber sorties despatched [Left Axis] and bomb tons dropped [Right Axis]	252
	See also: Appendix I Map of the Routes to Dunkirk and the Beaches	304

Tables

1	Number of authorized crews compared to number considered fully operational in the Luftwaffe, August 1938	42
2	Number of troops embarked from Dunkirk by ship type	85
3	Number and location of LMA and LMB mines reported as dropped in May and June 1940 by the Luftwaffe at ports or channels associated with Allied evacuations	163
4	Luftwaffe minelaying sorties, May–June 1940	164
5	Fighter Command sorties, number of patrols and the average strength of patrols during Operation Dynamo	182
6	Number of Fighter Command aircraft made available for daylight air cover of Dunkirk	202
7	Number of Fighter Command squadrons made available for daylight air cover of Dunkirk	204
8	Number of Fighter Command sorties, total number of hours of air cover and average flight time during Operation Dynamo	204
9	Aircraft available for operations and number of sorties made by 2 Group during Operation Dynamo	257

Acknowledgements

This work owes much to the generosity of the Sir Richard Stapley Educational Trust, which provided several bursaries during the course of my PhD and greatly eased the financial pressures of completing this research. A bursary from the Royal Air Force Museum supported the final year of writing and I am also thankful for bursaries and grants from the Royal Historical Society and the Princess Royal Trust.

I have always had the great fortune to have been supported by excellent history teachers and I am conscious of the debt I owe to all of them but particularly to Jonathan Taylor and Matthew Fergusson. During my PhD at the University of Hull the guidance of Dr David Omissi provided me with the ambition and confidence to answer questions I would not even have considered at the outset of this work. His feedback has consistently pushed me to enhance my ideas and explore further areas of research. Following my PhD, I benefited from the advice of Dr Ross Mahoney and Professor Robin Pearson, from the suggestions of reviewers, and from discussions regarding air power with a number of academics whilst at the Royal Air Force Museum.

I owe a particular debt to Dr James Corum who provided a large number of relevant Luftwaffe documents which were of great value to this work. The willingness to freely offer these documents was remarkably generous. I would also like to thank Stephen Walton, the senior curator of the documents section at the Imperial War Museum Duxford, for his advice on the museum's Enemy Document Section. I am grateful to the staff of the Institute of Historical Research library, where much of this work was written, and to Melanie Ransom, the Royal Historical Society Administrative Secretary, for her help with reimbursements. My thanks go to who proofread various drafts of this work, in particular Suzy Hickmet, Reginald Raymond, Lawrence Fitzrovia, Ellie and Hilary Haralampous.

Over the eight years it has taken to complete this work I have been aided by the help, advice and criticism of a great many people. My father has been a constant sounding board, mainly willingly, for the ideas within this work as they were developed whilst my mother has been an unstinting source of encouragement, support and assistance. Joe Bryan provided two outstanding contributions shortly before the completion of this book. Various friends have had to endure lengthy conversations regarding Operation Dynamo and these discussions have improved this work in many ways. To those of my friends who have escaped a similar fate but have always been available to provide a distraction I am no less grateful. Of all those who have helped me during the course of this work, none has been more important than Ellie Haralampous who has listened to me obsess over the minutia of Operation Dynamo without complaint and whose insightful comments have pushed me to consider various aspects of the topic from new perspectives. Above all Ellie was the crutch I leant on when disheartened, the first person I shared the excitements of my day with and on whose honest opinion I could always trust. What ever value the reader finds in this work, they find enhanced by her unfailing contribution and support.

Despite all the help I have received any errors that remain are my own.

Abbreviations

AASF	Advanced Air Striking Force
AFVs	Armoured Fighting Vehicles
AHB	British Air Historical Branch
A.K.	*Armeekorps*
A.M.W.R.	Air Ministry War Room
A.R.	Artillerie-Regiment
AOC	Air Officer Commanding
AOC-in-C	Air Officer Commander-in-Chief
AOK	*Armee Ober Kommando*
ASU	Aircraft Storage Unit
BAFF	British Air Forces in France
BEF	British Expeditionary Force
C-in-C	Commander in Chief
CAC	Churchill Archives Centre, Cambridge
CO	Commanding Officer
EDS	Enemy Documents Section
FS	French Ship
FTS	Flying Training School
GC&CS	Government Code and Cypher School
GRT	Gross Registered Tons
HF	High Frequency [radio]
HMHS	His Majesty's Hospital Ship

HMS	His Majesty's Ship
Ia	*Erster Generalstabsoffizier*
IWM	Imperial War Museum
Jafü	*Jagdführer*
JG	*Jagdgeschwader*
KG	*Kampfgeschwader*
LHCMA	Liddell Hart Centre for Military Archives, King's College, London
LTF5	F5 *Lufttorpedo*
LMA	Luftmine A
LMB	Luftmine B
(mot)	Motorized
MV	Motor Vessel
NARA	National Archives and Records Administration, Washington, DC
N.L.O.	Naval Liaison Officer
OIC	Admiralty Operational Intelligence Centre
OKH	*Oberkommando des Heeres*
OKL	*Oberkommando der Luftwaffe*
ORB	Operations Record Books
ORP	Okret Rzeczypospolitej Polskiej
PoW	Prisoner of War
RAF	Royal Air Force
RNLB	Royal National Lifeboat
R/T	Radio Transmissions
SNO	Senior Naval Officer
SS	Steamship

StG	Sturzkampfgeschwader
TNA	The National Archives, Kew
TNMDA	The National Meteorological Digital Archive
TsAMO RF	Central Archive of the Ministry of Defence of the Russian Federation
USAF	United States Air Force
USNWC	USA Naval War College
VA	Vice Admiral
VHF	Very High Frequency [radio]
W/T	Wireless Transmissions
ZG	Zerstörergeschwader

Introduction

Operation Dynamo, the evacuation of the Allied armies from the French port of Dunkirk, has been widely studied. There has, however, been little analysis of the operations conducted by the Royal Air Force (RAF) and the Luftwaffe during the evacuation. This work considers the air forces at Dunkirk, their application of air power and their military effectiveness.

On the evening of 26 May 1940, the evacuation of Dunkirk and the surrounding beaches began with the hope that it would be possible to defend the port for forty-eight hours and allow 45,000 troops to be rescued. On 19 May, as the scale of the forthcoming defeat was becoming obvious, General Edmund Ironside, Chief of the Imperial General Staff, had confided to Anthony Eden, Minister for War, that the loss of the troops of the British Expeditionary Force (BEF) would mean the end of the British Empire.[1] Major General Ismay, Churchill's Chief Staff Officer, believed that 'the flower and also the seed-corn of our Army seemed almost certain to be lost'.[2] By the time Dynamo was concluded on the morning of 4 June, over 338,000 Allied troops had been evacuated.[3] Although the majority of the BEF's vehicles, artillery and heavy equipment had been abandoned, Britain was able to use those troops rescued from Dunkirk to rebuild its military capabilities and continue the war.[4]

Despite marking the culmination of a catastrophic military defeat for the Allied campaign in France and the Low Countries, the rescue of the BEF from Dunkirk was regarded as a 'miracle of deliverance' in Britain.[5] Accounts from Dunkirk were cultivated by the British authorities to produce an uplifting national myth. The 'Dunkirk Spirit' – which remains to this day a deeply ingrained part of the British cultural landscape and lexicon – fortified the nation's will to fight at a point when British military fortunes were at their nadir.[6] The myth of the little ships collected from British ports and crewed by citizen sailors crossing the Channel to rescue the nation's soldiers held an idealism almost ready-made to appeal to the American public. Even before the evacuation was complete

R. L. Duffus penned an editorial in *The New York Times* which helped convey what Dunkirk promised for the future arguing that:

> So long as the English tongue survives, the word Dunkirk will be spoken with reverence. For in that harbour, in such a hell as never blazed on earth before, at the end of a lost battle, the rags and blemishes that have hidden the soul of democracy fell away. There, beaten but unconquered, in shining splendour, she faced the enemy ... It was not so simple a thing as courage, which the Nazis had in plenty. It was not so simple a thing as discipline ... It was the common man of the free countries ... This shining thing in the souls of free men Hitler cannot command, or attain, or conquer ... It is the great tradition of democracy. It is the future. It is victory.[7]

The success of Operation Dynamo was not, however, achieved without cost. From a French perspective the evacuation was, as General Weygand perceived it, 'certainly not a victory' but rather 'the least unfortunate resolution of what could have been a catastrophe'.[8] Over 35,000 troops of the French rearguard, whose resistance had allowed the BEF to escape, were captured and the evacuation elicited much resentment in France.[9] The fleet involved in the evacuation suffered heavy losses in their efforts to extricate the Allied forces at Dunkirk. The Royal Navy alone lost six destroyers and six minesweepers, with another nineteen destroyers and seven minesweepers damaged.[10] The total loss of named ships and vessels during Dynamo exceeded 190 of which 45 were definitely the result of air attack. Many ships were lost in situations where air attack was the probable, but not definite, cause. Other ships were lost or damaged owing to 'misadventure' in circumstances where air attack can be considered a contributing factor.[11] These losses came despite attempts by the RAF to protect the evacuation which saw Fighter Command alone fly over 2,200 sorties.[12] Despite these efforts, both military and naval personnel involved in the evacuation were highly critical of the RAF's air operations over Dunkirk.

Such was the extent of the antipathy towards the RAF during the course of Operation Dynamo that some RAF personnel took the precaution of disguising their uniform before reaching the beaches.[13] Soldiers returning from Dunkirk directed considerable hostility towards the RAF, with incidences between British Army and RAF personnel continuing for some time afterwards.[14] Criticism regarding the lack of air support at Dunkirk was also made by French soldiers. Denis Barlone, a Captain in the French 2nd North African Division, recorded that the French troops 'joined together in roundly cursing the total lack of aeroplanes ... the officers agree'.[15] Aware of the importance that Fighter Command would play in the forthcoming Battle of Britain, Winston Churchill was quick to extoll the virtues of the RAF at Dunkirk and to claim that the success of the evacuations from Dunkirk proved the limits of German airpower.[16] In rebutting criticisms of the RAF Churchill argued that fighting inland, out of sight of the beaches, Fighter Command had 'decisively defeated' the Luftwaffe and won 'a victory inside this deliverance'.[17]

The narrative that Churchill established to dispel criticism of the RAF has shaped the subsequent historiography of the RAF at Dunkirk.[18] The RAF's official history used Churchill's defence to rebut criticisms of the air cover made in the report on the evacuation by Vice Admiral Ramsay (Vice Admiral – Dover) who had organized and directed Operation Dynamo.[19] Churchill's speech and subsequent history of the Second World War have had such influence that many veterans evacuated from Dunkirk comment that they were wrong to criticize the RAF and reference Churchill's defence when doing so. Geoffrey Stewart has noted, however, that 'Churchill and the British authorities exaggerated the damage inflicted on the Luftwaffe for propaganda purposes, anxious to serve up a victory of some sorts.'[20] Nevertheless, historians of Operation Dynamo have often uncritically accepted Churchill's narrative regarding the RAF victory over the Luftwaffe in the air battle at Dunkirk. Instead of asking what the RAF accomplished historians have previously satisfied themselves with demonstrating that the RAF was at Dunkirk. The aim of this book is not to repeat that exercise – Fighter Command's 2,200 sorties during the nine days of the evacuation demonstrate the RAF were attempting to provide air cover for Operation Dynamo.[21] Cecil James, reviewing Fighter Command's operations over Dunkirk in 1944, argued that:

> The extreme view – that the RAF did nothing – is of course, absurd. ... The view of the other extreme – that the RAF alone made the evacuation possible – is no less untenable. ... That the RAF contributed to the result is, therefore, certain. ... To what extent however, is a question that cannot yet be answered finally.[22]

Although the RAF and Luftwaffe are discussed in the histories of the military and naval aspects of Operation Dynamo, there has been little serious analysis of the air operations at Dunkirk.[23]

The lack of attention given to the operations of the RAF and Luftwaffe is significant because it has created misconceptions regarding the application and value of air power during the evacuation. Air power during the Dunkirk evacuation can be understood as the use of air capabilities to influence the behaviour of adversaries, allies and the course of events.[24] Two core aspects of air power shaped the operating environment within which the evacuation of

Dunkirk took place: attack and control of the air.[25] A tendency to consider the operations of the air forces from the British perspective (which views Dynamo as a success) has, however, meant that only a limited analysis has taken place of how air power was applied and influenced the evacuation. It is necessary to consider the operations of both air forces, and the cause of each side's successes and failures, in order to establish the influence of air power on the evacuation of Dunkirk. In doing so, it will also be possible to understand the military effectiveness of both the RAF and the Luftwaffe during Dynamo, which – as well as being their first true clash of the Second World War – was the prelude to their contests against one another in the Battle of Britain. The military effectiveness of the air forces at Dunkirk can best be understood as their respective abilities to produce a favourable military outcome from their available resources.[26] This work brings these concepts together to assess the extent to which the air forces influenced the behaviour of adversaries, allies and the course of events during Dynamo to realize the military outcome they wished to accomplish.

Considering the successes and failures of the Luftwaffe's air operations is essential. The inability to prevent the evacuation of the majority of Allied troops from Dunkirk, the military outcome the Luftwaffe wished to achieve, represented the Luftwaffe's first serious failure in the war and has been characterized as both a psychological and material defeat.[27] The failure to prevent the evacuation of the BEF certainly represented a defeat for the Luftwaffe; however, it does not inevitably follow that the Luftwaffe's overall failure was the product of the RAF's operations. It is necessary to consider what factors prevented the Luftwaffe from halting the evacuation. The successes that the Luftwaffe accomplished also need to be considered. As will be discussed, the Luftwaffe forced the RAF to change how it defended the evacuation, they inflicted heavy losses on the evacuation fleet, and they came close to halting the operation whilst British forces remained at Dunkirk. Furthermore, the extent to which it was the Luftwaffe which prevented the evacuation of over 30,000 French troops needs to be established when considering how both air forces contributed to the result of Operation Dynamo.

The failure to understand the RAF and Luftwaffe air operations during the Dunkirk evacuation has also had an impact on the historical understanding of events during the Battle of Britain. By considering 11 Group's operational use of wing patrols during the evacuation, it is possible to develop a fuller understanding of the subsequent tactical decision in the Battle of Britain not to employ wing patrols.[28] The clashes between the two forces during the Battle of Britain are better understood by appreciating the results of air operations during the evacuation and the factors which influenced these results. The Royal Navy's capacity to prevent a German invasion of Britain without air cover has been questioned and used to argue for the importance of the RAF's victory in the Battle of Britain.[29] The Luftwaffe's ability to apply air power and undertake anti-sea operations against surface vessels during an attempted invasion of Britain is, however, better understood by considering how effective the Luftwaffe was in attacks on the ships involved in the evacuation.

Previous works on the Dunkirk evacuation are also characterized by a lack of consensus relating to the capabilities of the air forces, the context in which they operated during the evacuation, and factors which affected their operations during Dynamo. The numbers available to each side and the proximity to Dunkirk of the bases that the forces were operating from were both critical in determining what each side could accomplish during Dynamo. There has been a general consensus that Fighter Command fought the battle with the disadvantage of 'numerical inferiority' with writers variously describing them as 'always outnumbered', 'hopelessly outnumbered' and 'heavily outnumbered'.[30] The capability of the Luftwaffe to achieve the aim of halting all evacuations from Dunkirk given the losses they had already entailed has, however, also been questioned.[31]

Furthermore, there has been no consensus as to which sides air bases were located the greatest distance from Dunkirk and therefore permitted less combat time over Dunkirk. The RAF has frequently been considered to have been operating at a distinct disadvantage during the evacuation of Dunkirk – because the Luftwaffe was operating from advanced airfields whilst Fighter Command's bases were located in south-east England – and that this in part accounted for the success that the Luftwaffe was able to achieve.[32] The belief that the Luftwaffe were significantly closer to Dunkirk than the RAF has remained part of the historical narrative and has been casually accepted in cultural accounts, most recently in 2017 in the film *Dunkirk* where a British fighter pilot is required to take 'desperate risks with fuel'.[33] Historians who have focused on the Luftwaffe have opposed this position.[34] Williamson Murray has suggested that 'the Germans fought at a disadvantage' as 'British bases on the other side of the channel lay closer to [the] evacuation beaches. ... Consequently, British fighters possessed more loiter time in the combat zone.'[35] Robin Prior has noted that the 'bulk of the Luftwaffe ... would have further to fly than the RAF squadrons based in south-eastern England'.[36] In considering the evacuation of Dunkirk, Ronald Atkins has argued that 'it was the RAF which generally found itself operating from bases closer to the aerial combat'.[37] Hans-Adolf Jacobsen has asserted that the Stukas in particular were too far from Dunkirk so that only a small effort could be made against the evacuation whilst shortages of fuel and bombs at the advanced airfields worsened the situation.[38]

The lack of historical consensus regarding the capabilities and strengths of the RAF and Luftwaffe has extended to the capabilities of the aircraft and aircrews of the two sides. Proponents of the RAF have argued that, despite being numerically inferior, Fighter Command defeated the Luftwaffe at Dunkirk because of a qualitative superiority.[39] By contrast Nicholas Harman has asserted that 'the British had begun to claim … that the RAF over Dunkirk established its "qualitative superiority" over the Luftwaffe. This was eyewash, mere propaganda.'[40] The concept that RAF held a qualitative superiority over the Luftwaffe is referenced in works on Dynamo in relation to the respective side's fighters; the British types in particular are frequently eulogized without discussion of the notable flaws which affected their performance during the evacuation.[41] Works on the Battle of Britain have widely discussed the capabilities of the two sides' aircraft.[42] The strengths and limitations of the aircraft in respect to providing air cover during the Dunkirk evacuation rather than the Battle of Britain have, however, received less attention.[43]

Despite suggestions that the RAF achieved a victory over Dunkirk because of its qualitative superiority, works contrasting the RAF and the Luftwaffe maintain that the majority of German pilots were more experienced – in both individual pilots and combat leaders – and enjoyed superior combat training and tactics than the pilots of Fighter Command.[44] There are some notable exceptions. Karl-Heinz Frieser has argued that 'probably one of the most stubborn myths … is the superiority of the Luftwaffe' and that 'another cliché involves the superiority of the German pilots. On average, those pilots were considerably more poorly trained than the Allied pilots.'[45] Further to this, David Isby has noted that German fighter pilots 'lacked sufficient instrument flying skills. An emphasis on "blue sky" flying proved costly when blue skies were few and far between.'[46] Issues regarding the Luftwaffe's training and capabilities, in relation to the tasks it was required to fulfil at Dunkirk, have also been raised.[47] Karl Larew has asserted that 'the Germans were neither trained nor equipped to attack fast-moving, highly manoeuvrable naval targets such as destroyers'.[48] This view was shared by *Generalmajor* Wilhelm Speidel, Chief of Staff of *Luftflotte* 2 during Dynamo, who believed that Dunkirk 'was a completely new kind of mission beyond either the capabilities of its [the Luftwaffe's] equipment or the training of the units concerned'.[49] Despite some discussion relating to the threat posed to ships by German dive-bombers – and limitations of Luftwaffe's medium bombers in this regard – there remains a lack of understanding as to the extent of the Luftwaffe's dependence on dive-bombers to conduct effective strikes against ships during Dynamo.[50] The divergent views regarding the capabilities to the two forces – both in relation to each other's fighters and regarding their ability to achieve their individual objectives during Dynamo – are a significant limitation in the current understanding of the air operations during the Dunkirk evacuation.

The bombing operations of the Luftwaffe are one of the most discussed aspects of the air forces' activities during the Dunkirk evacuation. The attacks, however, are not analysed to consider the Luftwaffe's successful application of air power on 29 May, when the evacuation was almost halted because of losses incurred to the evacuation fleet, and 1 June, when daylight evacuations were suspended after heavy losses to air attack. The bombing of Dunkirk is instead examined chronologically with the perspective not on what the air force achieved, and how they achieved it, but instead on how Allied troops were successfully evacuated.[51] The decision to suspend daylight evacuations on 1 June, however, followed heavy losses to the evacuation fleet, primarily as a result of air attacks.[52] On 1 June, and temporarily on 29 May, the Luftwaffe successfully employed air power to deny the Allied naval forces, principally the Royal Navy, control of the sea in the vicinity of Dunkirk. On both days the Luftwaffe influenced Allied maritime operations and the course of events. The results that the Luftwaffe's bombing achieved, and how this should influence questions as to the Luftwaffe's wider – as well as Fighter Command's suggested – success have received little detailed consideration.[53] Following Churchill's claim that it was Fighter Command which defeated the Luftwaffe, the operations of the Luftwaffe are recounted in works on Dunkirk alongside the patrols of Fighter Command with the narrative often drawing on exciting combat reports which are not always representative of the wider air operations. As a result, a deterministic reading of the Luftwaffe's failure has been established, centred on the notion that the success of Dynamo was the result of Fighter Command's air cover of the evacuation.[54] The notion that the Luftwaffe suffered a clear defeat at Dunkirk has, however, been disputed by Williamson Murray who has argued that despite their efforts to dominate the battle area facing 'insurmountable obstacles' the result of the air battle was 'inconclusive; neither side had won a clear-cut victory'.[55] Murray does, however, go on to state that the 'RAF won an important victory by preventing unhindered use of the Luftwaffe's capability'.[56] The question of why the Luftwaffe's bombing failed to halt daylight evacuations before 1 June, and failed entirely to prevent Dynamo proceeding during the hours of darkness, has not been addressed in detail. Within this gap in the literature the limitations of the Luftwaffe's bombing in the face of anti-aircraft defence have also received little attention, often because of the perceived limitations of the Royal Navy's anti-aircraft armament.[57] The causes of the Luftwaffe's failure to prevent the evacuation of Dunkirk have not been fully explored, and the extent of this defeat has not been established; this is a significant gap in the historical knowledge of Operation Dynamo.

There is a significant gap in the historical literature on Dynamo as to the decision to halt daylight evacuations on 1 June with a lack of consensus as to the extent to which German artillery fire on the evacuation routes (see Appendix I) influenced this decision. Ramsay's despatch shows that whilst artillery influenced the cessation of daylight evacuations this was 'in conjunction with the result of enemy air attack'.[58] Although Ramsay appeared to believe that artillery had begun to 'menace' the point where Route X entered the Dunkirk Roads by the evening of 1 June, his report on Dynamo indicates that it was 'the scale of enemy air attack' on 1 June which 'was primarily responsible for the suspension of daylight evacuation'.[59] This 'menacing' artillery fire is given greater prominence by the RAF's official historian Denis Richards, who suggests that artillery fire which prevented ships from travelling to and from Dunkirk along Route X was a primary cause for the decision to suspend daylight evacuation. Richards states that it was only when 'confronted with this prospect of heavy losses from both aircraft and artillery' that Ramsay felt himself bound to call a halt to evacuation in daylight.[60] Richards also helped draft the RAF's response to Ramsay's despatch in which he argued that on 1 June the decision to suspend evacuation during the daylight hours was necessitated as much by enemy shelling of the approach channel as by air attack.[61] Historians have typically accepted that artillery fire on 1 June either caused or significantly contributed to the suspension of evacuation during full daylight.[62] Richard Collier, a former RAF pilot, has argued that 'all three approach routes were under lethal gunfire' and that this forced Ramsay to accept that suspending further daylight evacuations 'the only sane plan'.[63] The lack of analysis regarding the decision to suspend daylight evacuations on 1 June has skewed the present historical debate as to the Luftwaffe's failure at Dunkirk and the RAF's success. If the German artillery was the primary cause for the daylight evacuation of Dunkirk being halted then the RAF could rightfully claim that it had prevented the Luftwaffe from halting the evacuation. Bomber Command's missions against German artillery positions after 1 June also assume greater importance. However, if the Luftwaffe forced the daylight evacuation of Dunkirk to be halted, a decision which played a crucial part in the failure to evacuate 35,000 men of the French rearguard, then Fighter Command's contribution to the evacuation must be considered in a more negative light. This point is also crucial in establishing the Luftwaffe's influence on the Dunkirk evacuation. Whilst the Luftwaffe is generally considered to have lost the air battle over Dunkirk, if daylight evacuations were halted because of artillery fire then the Luftwaffe's role must be regarded as a total failure.

The fighter operations of the two air forces have been discussed in greater detail in accounts of Dunkirk than other applications of air power.[64] There have, however, been only two studies of the fighter clash between the Luftwaffe and Fighter Command during Dynamo both of which primarily rely on air combat reports and follow the traditional narrative established by Churchill.[65] There are no works which relate solely to the Luftwaffe or the other commands of the RAF during Dynamo. There is also an absence of detailed discussion relating to Dynamo in studies of the air forces and air power during the Second World War.[66] The discussion of fighter operations in wider accounts of Dynamo has to a large extent focused on refuting accusations from those at Dunkirk that Fighter Command was largely absent. Historical discussion of Fighter Command has noted that some of the effort for the support of the evacuation was exerted out of sight of the beaches.[67] The disadvantage Fighter Command faced having to operate standing patrols whilst the Luftwaffe, holding the initiative, could choose when to attack, and so saturate the area, has also been discussed. There has, however, been no analysis as to how effective British and German fighter operations were in securing their respective aims during Dynamo. Both sides changed the method by which they attempted to achieve – or in the case of the RAF deny – air superiority during the operation. From 29 May, Fighter Command chose to operate patrols in greater strength with the consequence of this change being larger gaps between patrols and so longer periods where there was no British air cover over the evacuation. Cecil James records that 'the new methods enjoyed fair success' with only really damaging attacks succeeding on 1 June in 'unavoidable intervals between patrols'.[68] Peter Gray has argued that by 'flying "big wings" over Dunkirk at key times' 11 Group were 'able to achieve air superiority limited in time and space and a modicum of air parity for the remainder'.[69] This is an area of significance; the pre-war fighter defence concepts of the RAF related to the concentration of the maximum fighter force possible against the enemy bomber formation. Following Dunkirk the tactic of concentrating forces in 'big wing' formations caused considerable controversy.[70] The change in Fighter Command's attempts to contest air superiority over Dunkirk has not, however, been analysed in relation to the results achieved against the Luftwaffe and the progress of Dynamo.[71] John Harris has maintained that although 'heavy fighter sweeps were being made … assembling the squadrons took time and it was in the gaps between them that the heaviest losses had occurred'.[72] The Luftwaffe's fighter operations have not been considered from the perspective that they forced Fighter Command to alter their method of contesting air superiority. Luftwaffe bombers suffered heavy losses on 27 May; their losses were lower on 29 May and 1 June, however, despite conducting a greater number of sorties. The extent to which this was a consequence of effective fighter cover by the Luftwaffe has not been discussed in histories of Operation Dynamo.

There is also a lack of consensus regarding Fighter Command's commitment to the air protection of Operation Dynamo and whether the resources provided to 11 Group were appropriate for the task it had been assigned. The number of Fighter Command squadrons which became involved in providing air cover during Dynamo is frequently used to suggest that Fighter Command's support for the evacuation was extensive.[73] Nonetheless, a greater measure of air cover could have been provided to the evacuation had Air Chief Marshal Hugh Dowding, AOC-in-C Fighter Command, provided 11 Group with a greater number of squadrons at the outset of Dynamo. The full strength of Fighter Command was at no point totally committed to the air cover of Dunkirk which Walter Lord believes was due to Dowding 'already thinking ahead to the defence of Britain'.[74] Indeed, Dowding has been accused of 'miserliness … with his warplanes, particularly Spitfires' by Ronal Atkin and has been criticized by Robin Prior as being 'parsimonious to the point of danger'. Atkin goes as far as to argue that restricting the squadrons committed to Dynamo caused the RAF to lose the air battle over Dunkirk but to subsequently win the Battle of Britain.[75] Dowding's concerns as to heavy losses over Dunkirk are understandable given the casualties the RAF had suffered during the earlier fighting in France.[76] Several factors, in addition to Dowding's fear of further losses, influenced Fighter Command's initial disposition: a number of Fighter Command's squadrons had already provided air cover over France, others were not adequately equipped at the outset of the evacuation, and Fighter Command was also required to provide for the air defence of Britain. However, there is little exploration within the historical literature studying Fighter Command or Dunkirk as to whether, having been ordered to provide maximum assistance to Operation Dynamo, the number of squadrons Fighter Command committed to the battle from the outset could have been higher and, if so, whether it ought to have been.[77]

Works considering Coastal Command, the Fleet Air Arm (FAA) and Bomber Command either ignore the period of Dynamo or merely provide a brief narrative of the relevant operations without considering their wider significance to the evacuation.[78] This is despite the praise these forces received for their efforts during the evacuation.[79] Histories of Dynamo, as well as those on naval operations in 1940, provide few details of the significance of Coastal Command's operations.[80] Incidences of Coastal Command's air patrols engaging in air combats with German aircraft are occasionally recorded but the general importance of these patrols is not assessed. In particular the threat from German motor torpedo boats (E-Boats) and the counter-sea operations – involving direct air action in the maritime domain – that Coastal Command undertook to reduce this threat have been under-represented in histories of both the evacuation and the RAF's operations during this period.[81] In addition to applying air power in anti-surface operations – to detect and engage German maritime surface forces – Coastal Command also undertook anti-submarine operations during Dynamo to locate and attack German submarines (U-Boats).[82] The RAF also undertook a range of air strikes during Dynamo with squadrons from both Coastal and Bomber Command engaging in close air support, air interdiction and strategic attacks. Close air support – undertaken to disrupt, degrade, deny or destroy enemy activity or capabilities which are in close proximity to land forces – for the Dunkirk perimeter receives more frequent mention in works on Dynamo but again the wider significance of these operations to the success of the evacuation is largely absent.[83] Air interdiction strikes – the action taken to disrupt, degrade, deny or destroy an adversary's capabilities before they can be used against friendly forces – undertaken during Dynamo targeted enemy personnel, lines of communication, logistics and headquarters.[84] These attacks have been largely ignored in previous works on Dynamo despite their potential importance to the defence of Dunkirk. Histories of Dynamo are also largely mute on the operations, and impact, of the RAF's night bombers in both the tactical roles discussed above and their strategic attacks which were aimed at industrial targets thought to be of fundamental importance to the German war effort.[85] Both the supporters and detractors of Bomber Command have criticized their operations during this period, either in wider studies of the campaign, the war or the Command itself. Supporters of Bomber Command have criticized the diversion of part of their effort to attacks against tactical targets believing that, given the small force available, the maximum force should have been concentrated on carefully selected objectives of decisive importance.[86] During Dynamo, Bomber Command attempted to use strategic attacks to achieve a coercive effect which would influence the Luftwaffe to change the use and distribution of its own air power assets.[87] As will be discussed, Bomber Command anticipated that its attacks on German industries would lead to a redistribution of the Luftwaffe's fighters and anti-aircraft units to air defence roles in Germany whilst also causing German bombers to be redirected to targets in Britain. Bomber Command has been criticized, however, for having too great a focus on strategic objectives.[88] Eden was largely fulsome in his praise of the RAF's effort in the Battle of France; however, he believed that the 'employment at this time of the heavy bombers remains open to criticism'.[89] The RAF's strategic conceptions were, in the word of the official military history, 'radically at fault'.[90] Ironside recorded in his diary that the Air Staff strategic conceptions 'ignored the question of the Army' and that the RAF acted 'very much by themselves'.[91] The question of what Bomber Command accomplished during Dynamo has either been ignored or considered as part of the wider Battle of France.[92] Robert Jackson, for instance, has stated that 'Bomber Command's contribution, whole hearted though it may have been, failed to influence the outcome of the Battle of France in the slightest'.[93] There is therefore a significant gap in the understanding of Bomber Command's effect on the Dunkirk evacuation.

This work utilizes a wide range of sources relating to the development of the RAF and its operations during the evacuation of Dunkirk. Reports, memoranda and correspondence relating to the progress of training and development provide a detailed insight into how the RAF believed its pre-war development occurred.[94] These are supplemented by personal accounts of pilots who underwent training during this period and their reflections on its strengths and flaws given their subsequent war experience.[95] The air operations over Dunkirk similarly draw on both archive documents produced by the RAF and personal accounts of RAF personnel.[96] The use of oral histories and personal recollections provides an important supplement to official records. They provide a different perspective on historical events than the one allowed through the use of official documents alone. Nevertheless, personal recollections must also be used judiciously. Individual recalling events in both the immediate and distant past can misremember an event for a number of reasons, not least to enhance their own importance in actions that took place or to conform their recollection to details they were subsequently provided.[97] Details regarding the evacuation have been researched using the voluminous reports submitted to the Admiralty in the immediate aftermath of Dynamo.[98] The Naval Staff History produced by W. Gardener is an authoritative account of Operation Dynamo; its appendices provide copies of several telegrams that have subsequently been lost from the official Admiralty file.[99] The personal papers of naval figures involved in the evacuation and accounts of individuals who participated in the evacuation have provided a further layer of detail.[100]

Whilst this work enjoys an abundance of source material where it relates to the RAF, the surviving German records for this period are limited and incomplete. Shortly before the end of German resistance the *Oberkommando der Luftwaffe* ordered the destruction of unit war diaries and other documents to prevent their capture – an order which was in general obeyed and has left fewer than 5 per cent of the Luftwaffe's original documents in existence.[101] Surviving Luftwaffe records from the Bundesarchiv-Militärarchiv, Freiburg, and copies of captured records in American, British and Russian archives have been used to provide evidence of Luftwaffe development and training; these have been supplemented by Allied reviews of the Luftwaffe's development and relevant secondary sources which have considered specific aspects of the Luftwaffe's training and development.[102] From the point of view of operations the diary of *Generalmajor* Wolfram von Richthofen, commander of *Fliegerkorps* VIII, has been of considerable value.[103] Although almost no unit records survive, a captured copy of the Luftwaffe's situation report for the period provides a general oversight of the Luftwaffe's operations during the evacuation.[104] Supplementing these documents are German Army records and diaries which contain numerous references to the progress of the evacuation and German air operations. The individual accounts of the period by Luftwaffe personnel are useful, but limited in number and brief in relation to the Dunkirk evacuation.[105] Previous historical research on the operations of specific Luftwaffe units based on surviving documents and interviews with German veterans has been considered in conjunction with information from primary material to fill gaps relating to the details of operations. In addition to these there are considerations of air operations prepared by the German Air Historical Branch during the war as well as the historical studies on the Luftwaffe produced for the United States Air Force (USAF).[106] The war diaries of the *Oberkommando der Kriegsmarine* Operations Division and the *Führer der Torpedoboote* provide useful details relating to the operation of E-Boats which would otherwise be lacking.[107] Details of German air operations during the Dunkirk evacuation have also been established from British documents. Reports detailing information from Enigma decryptions, plain language interceptions and interpretations of traffic analysis have allowed for a greater understanding of the Luftwaffe's operations.

The files of Luftwaffe Flak units suffered considerable destruction because of this policy, and files for individual German artillery units are also scarce. In the case of the German artillery the use of files captured by the Allied powers and retained by American, British and Russian forces have been consulted and German Army records and war diaries have been used to trace the co-operation of artillery units to the extent that remains possible. Reports of officers commanding ships involved in the evacuation have also been considered to determine how far artillery affected the evacuation. These reports – submitted to the Admiralty immediately after the conclusion of Operation Dynamo – have been qualitatively and quantitatively analysed to determine whether German artillery did indeed play a primary role in suspending daylight evacuation. Patterns within the reports were established through close reading and content analysis with variables within the reports analysed – on the basis of both a deductive and inductive coding technique – for events relating to air operations or artillery fire.[108] The decision process which led to the suspension of the evacuation has been established on the basis of existing Admiralty records, reports and telegrams which were made between Captain Tennant, Senior Naval Officer (SNO) – Dunkirk, and Vice Admiral Ramsay.[109]

To understand the impact that the Luftwaffe and RAF had on Operation Dynamo it is necessary to first provide an in-depth assessment of the air forces relating to their numerical strength and airbase situation as well as making a qualitative analysis of their capacity to undertake the operations assigned to them during the evacuation. Having established the conditions under which the operation took place, the operations of the Luftwaffe will be examined in detail. The successful German air attacks on 29 May and 1 June will be analysed first to understand why the Luftwaffe was able to effectively apply air power on both days. Having done this, the decision to suspend daylight evacuation on 1 June and the extent to which the suspension was solely the result of air attacks will be considered. This work will then consider the German air operations before 29 May, and then separately those between 29 May and 1 June, to understand why German air power did not successfully halt daylight evacuations from Dunkirk before 1 June. The potential and limitations of German night attacks will then be established to consider whether the Luftwaffe had the capability to halt all major embarkations had they halted daylighted evacuations before 1 June. The operations of both sides' fighters will be considered and the extent to which the RAF and Luftwaffe were able to achieve their respective objectives for air cover over Dunkirk will be established. Finally, the operations of Coastal Command (including the FAA) and Bomber Command will each be considered separately to assess what operations they undertook, the impact they achieved and their influence on the outcome of Operation Dynamo. This exercise is important beyond establishing the effectiveness of the air forces at Dunkirk. By considering the air operations over Dunkirk it is possible to understand whether the RAF did achieve the 'decisive victory' claimed for it by Churchill or if Britain's ability to continue the war against Nazi Germany was the result of good fortune, the Royal Navy's endurance and the Luftwaffe's errors.

Notes

1. Anthony Eden, *The Reckoning* (London: Cassell, 1965), p. 105.
2. General Hastings Lionel Ismay, *The Memoirs of Lord Ismay* (London: Heinemann, 1960), p. 132.
3. Vice Admiral B. H. Ramsay, 'The Evacuation of the Allied Armies from Dunkirk and Neighbouring Beaches', *London Gazette*, 17 July 1947, pp. 3295, 3299, 3316.
4. Major-General Sir Edward Spears, *Assignment to Catastrophe, Vol. I: Prelude to Dunkirk, July 1939–May 1940* (London: William Heinemann, 1954), p. 302; Field Marshal Bernard Law Montgomery, *The Memoirs of Field Marshal Montgomery* (Barnsley: Pen & Sword, 2010), p. 67.
5. Winston S. Churchill, Prime Minister, Hansard, HC Deb. (Series 5) Vol. 361, Col. 790 (4 June 1940).
6. Mark Connelly, *We Can Take It: Britain and the Memory of the Second World War* (London: Routledge, 2014), p. 88; Anthony Eden, 'The Spirit of the BEF', *The Listener*, Issue 595, 6 June 1940 (London: British Broadcasting Corporation), n.p.; Nicholas Harman, *Dunkirk: The Necessary Myth* (London: Hodder & Stoughton, 1980), pp. 246–8; Lucy Noakes and Juliette Pattinson (eds.), *British Cultural Memory and the Second World War* (London: Bloomsbury, 2014), pp. 12–14; Penny Summerfield, 'Dunkirk and the Popular Memory of Britain at War, 1940–58', *Journal of Contemporary History*, Vol. 45, No. 4 (2010), p. 788.
7. *New York Times*, 'Dunkerque', 1 June 1940.
8. Commandant Pierre-Jean Lyet, *La Bataille de France Mai–Juin 1940* (Paris: Payot, 1947), p. 113; General Maxime Weygand, *Mémoires: Rappelé au Service* (Paris: Flammarion, 1950), p. 132.
9. Jean Beaux, *Dunkerque: 1940* (Paris: Presses Pocket, 1969), pp. 310–11, 315; Dominique Lormier, *La Bataille de Dunkerque, 26 Mai–4 Juin 1940: Comment l'Armée Française a Sauvé l'Angleterre* (Paris: Tallandier, 2011), p. 190; Patrick Oddone, *Dunkirk 1940: French Ashes, British Deliverance, The Story of Operation Dynamo*, (trans.) Malcolm Hall (Stroud, Gloucestershire: Tempus, 2000), pp. 106–7; Max Schiavon, 'Les Relations entre Hauts Commandements Français et Britannique en 1939–1940', *Revue Historique des Armées*: No. 264 (2011), p. 70.
10. W. J. R. Gardner, *The Evacuation from Dunkirk: Operation Dynamo, 26 May–4 June 1940* (London: Routledge, 2000), pp. 158–61.
11. The National Archives, Kew (hereafter TNA): ADM 199/793 – HM Ships lost During the Evacuation of Troops from Dunkirk; Gardner, *Evacuation*, pp. 158–61;

Captain S. W. Roskill, *The War at Sea, 1939–1945*, Vol. I, *The Defensive* (London: HMSO, 1954), p. 226.
12. TNA: AIR 25/193 – Operations Record Books (hereafter ORB): 11 Group; TNA: AIR 25/219 – ORB: 12 Group; TNA: AIR 27 – ORB: Fighter Command Squadrons, May–June 1940.
13. Imperial War Museum (hereafter IWM): Audio/7336 – Arthur Taylor, Reel 3.
14. IWM: Audio/6365 – Colin Merriam Glover, Reel 3; IWM: Audio/11036 – Eric Francis Chandler, Reel 2; IWM: Audio/11103 – Alan Geoffrey Page, Reel 1; IWM: Audio/11449 – Peter Derrick Macleod Down, Reel 1; IWM: Audio/12405 – John Beville Howard Nicholas, Reel 1; IWM: Audio/12611 – Norman Percy Gerald Barron, Reel 2; Ismay, *Memoirs*, p. 135; Squadron Leader Kenneth Butterworth McGlashan and Owen Zupp, *Down to Earth: A Fighter Pilot's Experience of Surviving Dunkirk, the Battle of Britain, Dieppe and D-Day* (London: Grub Street, 2007), pp. 30–1.
15. D. Barlone, *A French Officer's Diary: 23 August 1939 to 1 October 1940*, (trans.) L. V. Cass (New York: Macmillan, 1943), p. 64.
16. Churchill cited in Spears, *Prelude to Dunkirk*, p. 297; Broadcast by Winston S. Churchill, 'This Was Their Finest Hour', *The Listener*, Issue 597, 20 June 1940 (London: British Broadcasting Corporation), n.p.
17. Churchill Archives Centre, Cambridge (hereafter CAC): CHAR 9/140A/9–28 – Typescript Copy of Notes for House of Commons Speech Addressing the Fall of Belgium and the Evacuation of the British Expeditionary Force from Dunkirk, 4 June 1940, p. 18; Churchill, Hansard, HC Deb. (Series 5) Vol. 361, Col. 791 (4 June 1940).
18. Winston S. Churchill, *The Second World War*, Vol. II, *Their Finest Hour* (London: Cassell, 1949), pp. 91–2.
19. Denis Richards, *The Royal Air Force 1939–1945*, Vol. I, *The Fight at Odds* (London: HMSO, 1953), pp. 132–3.
20. Geoffrey Stewart, *Dunkirk and the Fall of France* (Barnsley: Pen & Sword, 2008), p. 116.
21. TNA: AIR 25/193 – ORB: 11 Group; TNA: AIR 25/219 – ORB: 12 Group; TNA: AIR 27 – ORB: Fighter Command Squadrons, May–Jun. 1940.
22. T. C. G. James, *The Growth of Fighter Command, 1936–1940*, (ed.) Sebastian Cox (London: Frank Cass, 2002), p. 96.
23. Barker, *Dunkirk*; Lieutenant-Colonel Ewan Butler and Major J. S. Bradford, *The Story of Dunkirk* (London: Arrow, 1955); Robert Carse, *Dunkirk: 1940* (New Jersey: Prentice-Hall, 1970); Chatterton, *Epic*; Divine, *Nine Days*; Hans-Adolf Jacobsen 'Dunkirk 1940', in H. A. Jacobsen and J. Rohwer (eds.), *Decisive Battles of World War II: The German View*, (trans.) Edward Fitzgerald (London: André Deutsch, 1965), pp. 29–69; Robert Jackson, *Dunkirk: The British Evacuation, 1940* (London: Cassell, 2002); Thompson, *Dunkirk*; Patrick Turnbull, *Dunkirk: Anatomy of Disaster* (London: Batsford, 1978).

24 Directorate of Air Staff, *AP3000* [4th Edition] (London: Ministry of Defence, 2009).
25 Reconnaissance and intelligence played a more limited role and will be discussed where relevant.
26 Allan R. Millett, Williamson Murray and Kenneth H. Watman, 'The Effectiveness of Military Organizations', in Allan R. Millett and Williamson Murray (eds.), *Military Effectiveness, Vol. I, The First World War* (Cambridge: Cambridge University Press, 2010), pp. 2–4.
27 Mathew Cooper, *The German Air Force, 1933–1945: An Anatomy of Failure* (London: Jane's, 1981), p. 119; John Harris, *Dunkirk: The Storms of War* (Newton Abbot: David & Charles, 1988), p. 126; Robert Jackson, *Air War over France: 1939–40* (London: Ian Allan, 1974), p. 121; Williamson Murray, *Strategy for Defeat: The Luftwaffe 1933–1945* (Royston: Eagle, 2000), p. 38; Richard Overy, *Goering: The 'Iron Man'* (London: Routledge, 1984), p. 103.
28 Peter Gray, *Air Warfare: History, Theory and Practice* (London: Bloomsbury, 2016), p. 59.
29 Richard Overy, *The Battle of Britain: Myth and Reality* (London: Penguin, 2010), pp. ix–x; Cooper, *German Air Force*, p. 130.
30 A. J. Barker, *Dunkirk: The Great Escape* (London: Dent, 1973), p. 73; John Buckley, *Air Power in the Age of Total War* (London: University College London Press, 1999), p. 130; Butler and Bradford, *Dunkirk*, pp. 132–9; E. Keeble Chatterton, *The Epic of Dunkirk* (London: Hurst & Blackett, 1940), p. 217; Harris, *Dunkirk*, p. 54; John Killen, *The Luftwaffe: A History* (Barnsley: Pen & Sword, 2013), p. 116; Leo McKinstry, *Spitfire: Portrait of a Legend* (London: John Murray, 2008), p. 187; Richards, *Fight*, p. 135; John Terraine, *The Right of the Line* (London: Wordsworth, 1998), p. 154; Thompson, *Dunkirk*, p. 228; John Williams, *The Ides of May: The Defeat of France, May–June, 1940* (New York: Alfred A. Knopf, 1968).
31 E. R. Hooton, *Luftwaffe at War, Vol. II, Blitzkreig in the West, 1939–1940* (Hersham, Surrey: Ian Allan, 2007), pp. 69–70; Murray, *Strategy*, p. 41; Hans Umbreit 'The Campaign in the West', in Militärgeschichtliches Forschungsamt (ed.), *Germany and the Second World War, Vol. II, Germany's Initial Conquests in Europe*, (trans.) Dean S. McMurry and Edwald Osers (Oxford: Clarendon Press, 1991), p. 291.
32 Patrick Bishop, *Battle of Britain: A Day-to-Day Chronicle, 10 July 1940–31 October 1940* (London: Quercus, 2010), p. 46; Norman Franks, *Air Battle for Dunkirk: 26 May–3 June 1940* (London: Grub Street, 2006), p. 34; Harman, *Dunkirk*, p. 202; Jackson, *Dunkirk*, p. 130; Alain Marchand and Claude Huan, 'Dunkerque: Opération "Dynamo"', *La Fana de l'Aviation*, No. 248 (1990), pp. 40–3; Overy, *Battle*, p. 8; Richards, *Fight*, pp. 135, 142.
33 Bradshaw, Peter, 'Dunkirk Review', *The Guardian* (17 July 2017), [https://www.theguardian.com/film/2017/jul/17/dunkirk-review-christopher-nolans-apocalyptic-war-epic-is-his-best-film-so-far, accessed 23 February 2018].

34 Cajus Bekker, *The Luftwaffe War Diaries: The German Air Force in World War II* (London: Corgi, 1969), pp. 158–9; Hans-Ekkehard Bob, 'Memories of a German Veteran', in Paul Addison and Jeremy A. Crang (eds.), *The Burning Blue: A New History of the Battle of Britain* (London: Pimlico, 2000), p. 124; Cooper, *German Air Force*, pp. 118–19; William Green, *Warplanes of the Third Reich* (London: Macdonald and Jane's, 1979), p. 543; Henry Probert, *The Rise and Fall of the German Air Force, 1933–1945* (Poole: Arms & Armour Press, 1983), p. 72; Murray, *Strategy*, p. 41.

35 Murray, *Strategy*, p. 41; Williamson Murray, 'The Luftwaffe against Poland and the West', in Benjamin Franklin Cooling (ed.), *Case Studies in the Achievement of Air Superiority* (Washington, DC: US Air Force, 1994), p. 95.

36 Robin Prior, *When Britain Saved the West: The Story of 1940* (New Haven, CT: Yale University Press, 2015), p. 133.

37 Ronald Atkin, *Pillar of Fire: Dunkirk 1940* (Edinburgh: Birlinn, 2000), p. 149.

38 Hans-Adolf Jacobsen, *Dünkirchen* (Neckargemünd: Kurt Vowinckel, 1958), p. 194.

39 Chatterton, *Epic*, p. 217; Air Marshal Joubert de la Ferte, 23 May 1940, 'Broadcast "War in the Air: Air War in Brief"', *Flight*, 30 May 1940, p. 491; David Masters, *So Few: The Immortal Record of the R.A.F* (London: Eyre & Spottiswoode, 1941), pp. 13, 236; Thompson, *Dunkirk*, p. 228; Williams, *Ides*, p. 260.

40 Harman, *Dunkirk*, pp. 156, 202–3.

41 Buckley, *Air Power*, pp. 130–1; H. Montgomery Hyde, *British Air Policy between the Wars: 1918–1939* (London: Heinemann, 1976), p. 419; David Isby, *The Decisive Duel: Spitfire vs 109* (London: Little, Brown, 2012), pp. 108–9; Chris Lee-McCloud, 'Spitfire!', *Journal of Museum Ethnography*, No. 17 (2005), pp. 166–7; Marchand and Huan 'Dunkerque', p. 45; Overy, *Battle*, p. 39.

42 Bishop, *Battle*, pp. 33, 100, 338; Stephen Bungay, *The Most Dangerous Enemy: A History of the Battle of Britain* (London: Auram, 2000), p. 80; Len Deighton, *Fighter: The True Story of the Battle of Britain* (New York: Alfred A. Knopf, 1978), pp. 72, 81–2, 108; James Holland, *The Battle of Britain: Five Months That Changed History, May–October, 1940* (London: Corgi, 2011), pp. 537, 663, 673–9; Isby, *Decisive*, pp. 108–9, 119–25; Overy, *Battle*, pp. 52–3; John Ray, *The Battle of Britain: Dowding and the First Victory, 1940* (London: Cassell, 2000), pp. 29, 47, 67, 190; Derek Wood and Derek Dempster, *The Narrow Margin* (Barnsley: Pen & Sword, 2003), pp. 46–7, 55–6, 206–7.

43 Douglas C. Dildy, *Dunkirk 1940: Operation Dynamo* (London: Osprey, 2010), p. 34; Franks, *Air Battle*, p. 167; Walter Lord, *The Miracle of Dunkirk* (Ware, Hertfordshire: Wordsworth, 1998), p. 134.

44 Bob, 'Memories', p. 124; Richard Collier, *The Sands of Dunkirk* (Glasgow: Fontana, 1974), p. 89; Cooper, *German Air Force*, p. 134; Anthony J. Cummings, *The Royal Navy and the Battle of Britain* (Annapolis, MD: Naval Institute Press, 2010), p. 60; Len Deighton, *Blitzkrieg: From the Rise of Hitler to the Fall of Dunkirk*

(London: Jonathan Cape, 1979), p. 193; Dildy, *Dunkirk*, pp. 30, 89; Franks, *Air Battle*, p. 44; Norman Gelb, *Dunkirk: The Incredible Escape* (London: Michael Joseph, 1990), p. 107; Isby, Decisive, pp. 87, 124–5; Vincent Orange, *Park: The Biography of Air Chief Marshal Sir Keith Park* (London: Grub Street, 2010), p. 89; Overy, *Battle*, p. 54; Ray, *Battle*, pp. 38–9, 48.

45 Karl-Heinz Frieser, *Blitzkrieg Legend: The 1940 Campaign in the West* (Annapolis, MA: Naval Institute, 2012), pp. 44, 49.
46 Isby, *Decisive*, pp. 107–8.
47 Gregory Blaxland, *Destination Dunkirk: The Story of Gort's Army* (London: William Kimber, 1973), p. 346.
48 Karl G. Larew, 'The Royal Navy in the Battle of Britain' *The Historian*, Vol. 54, No. 2 (1992), p. 244.
49 Wilhelm Speidel, 'The German Air Force in France and the Low Countries 1939–1940', Vol. III, 'Fall Gelb: Part 2B', USAF Historical Study No. 152 (1958), pp. 340, 474.
50 Geirr Haar, *The Battle for Norway: April–June 1940* (Barnsley: Pen & Sword, 2010), p. 12; Hooton, *Blitzkreig*, pp. 67–74; Alfred Price, *The Luftwaffe Data Book* (London: Greenhill, 1997), p. 178; Peter C. Smith, *Stuka Spearhead: The Lightening War from Poland to Dunkirk, 1939–1940* (London: Greenhill Books, 1998), pp. 56–7; John Ward, *Hitler's Stuka Squadrons: The Ju 87 at War, 1936–1945* (St. Paul, MN: MBI, 2004), pp. 82–9.
51 Barker, *Dunkirk*; Blaxland, *Destination*; Dildy, *Dunkirk*; Hugh Sebag-Montefiore, *Dunkirk: Fight to the Last Man* (London: Viking, 2006); Lord, *Miracle*; Thompson, *Dunkirk*.
52 Cooper, *German Air Force*, p. 119; Deighton, *Blitzkrieg*, p. 291; Harris, *Dunkirk*, p. 126; Lord, *Miracle*, pp. 228–9; Roskill, *Defensive*, p. 226.
53 Buckley, *Air Power*, pp. 130–1; Gray, *Air Warfare*, pp. 59, 121; Killen, *Luftwaffe*, p. 116; Overy, *Air War*, p. 30; Terraine, *Right of the Line*, p. 154.
54 Churchill, 'This Was Their Finest Hour', n.p.; Franks, *Air Battle*, p. 160; Klaus A. Maier, 'The Operational Air War until the Battle of Britain', in Militärgeschichtliches Forschungsamt (ed.), *Germany's Initial Conquests in Europe*, p. 339; Jochen Prien et al., *Die Jagdfliegerverbände der Deutschen Luftwaffe 1934 bis 1945: Teil 3, Einsatz in Dänemark und Norwegen, 9.4. bis 30.11.1940, Der Feldzug im Westen 10.5. bis 25.6.1940* (Eutin, Schleswig-Holstein: Struve´s Buchdruerei und Verlag, 2002), p. 5–7; Thompson, *Dunkirk*, p. 228.
55 Murray, *Luftwaffe*, pp. 85–7.
56 *Ibid.*, p. 87.
57 Cummings, *Royal Navy*, p. 30; James Goldrick, 'The Problems of Modern Naval History' *Great Circle*, Vol. 18, No. 1 (1996), p. 55; Probert, *Rise and Fall*, p. 64; Alan Raven and John Arthur Roberts, *British Battleships of World War Two: The Development and Technical History of the Royal Navy's Battleships and*

Battlecruisers from 1911 to 1946 (Annapolis, MD: Naval Institute Press, 1976), p. 348; Jon Tetsuro Sumida, '"The Best Laid Plans": The Development of British Battle-Fleet Tactics, 1919–1942', *International History Review*, Vol. 14, No. 4 (1992), pp. 691, 698–9.

58 Ramsay, 'Despatch', p. 3296, col. 2.
59 TNA: ADM 199/792 – Report of Vice Admiral Sir Bertram H. Ramsay, Vice Admiral Dover on Operation Dynamo.
60 Richards, *Fight*, p. 140.
61 TNA: AIR 2/7934 – RAF Comments on Despatch by Flag Officer Commanding Dover on the Evacuation of the Allied Armies from Dunkirk and Neighbouring Beaches, 26 May–4 June 1940; TNA: ADM 1/19997 – Evacuation of Allied Armies from Dunkirk: Comments on Report by Flag Officer Dover before Publication as supplement to London Gazette.
62 Allen Andrews, *The Air Marshals: The Air War in Western Europe* (New York: William Morrow, 1970), p. 83; W. S. Chalmers, *Full Cycle: The Biography of Admiral Sir Bertram Home Ramsay* (London: Hodder and Stoughton, 1959), p. 90; Churchill, *Finest Hour*, p. 100; Dildy, *Dunkirk*, p. 75; Jacobsen, *Dünkirchen*, p. 169; James, *Growth*, p. 95; Orange, *Park*, p. 87.
63 Collier, *Sands*, p. 238.
64 Franks, *Air Battle*, p. 70; Lord, *Miracle*, pp. 56–7, 220–2; Gelb, *Dunkirk*, pp. 105–8, 130–41, 220; Thompson, *Dunkirk*, pp. 228, 257–8.
65 Franks, *Air Battle*; Simon W. Parry and Mark Postlethwaite, *Dunkirk: Air Combat Archive* (Walton-on-Thames: Red Kite, 2017).
66 Buckley, *Air Power*, pp. 130–1; Gray, *Air Warfare*, pp. 59, 121; Killen, *Luftwaffe*, p. 116; Overy, *Air War*, p. 30; Terraine, *Right of the Line*, p. 154.
67 Blaxland, *Destination*, p. 206; Butler and Bradford, *Dunkirk*, p. 164; Churchill, *Finest Hour*, p. 91; Sholto Douglas, *Years of Command* (London: Collins, 1963), p. 81; Franks, *Air Battle*, p. 157; Gardner, *Evacuation*, p. 123; Gelb, *Dunkirk*, p. 108; James, *Growth*, p. 95.
68 James, *Growth*, p. 95.
69 Gray, *Air Warfare*, p. 59.
70 H. R. Allen, *Who Won the Battle of Britain* (London: Arthur Baker, 1974), p. 97; Bill Newton Dunn, *Big Wing: The Biography of Air Chief Marshal Sir Trafford Leigh-Mallory* (Shrewsbury: Airlife, 1992), pp. 67–76; John Ferris, 'Fighter Defence before Fighter Command: The Rise of Strategic Air Defence in Great Britain, 1917–1934', *Journal of Military History*, Vol. 63, No. 4 (1999), p. 872; Niall Mackay and Christopher Price, 'Safety in Numbers: Ideas of Concentration in Royal Air Force Fighter Defence from Lanchester to the Battle of Britain', *History*, Vol. 96, No. 3 (2011), p. 305; Vincent Orange, 'Review, The Battle of Britain, New Perspectives: Behind the Scenes of the Great Air War by John Ray', *Journal of Military History*, Vol. 59, No. 2 (1995), pp. 348–9; John Ray, *The Battle of Britain, New Perspectives: Behind*

the Scenes of the Great Air War (London: Brockhampton, 1994), pp. 64, 76–80; Dilip Sarkar, *Bader's Duxford Fighters: The Big Wing Controversy* (Worcester: Ramrod, 1997), pp. 83, 129–36, 146–53; John Frayn Turner, *The Bader Wing* (Barnsley: Pen & Sword, 2007), p. 59.

71 Martin Marix Evans, *The Fall of France: Act with Daring* (Oxford: Osprey, 2000), p. 116; Franks, *Air Battle*, p. 157; Gelb, *Dunkirk*, pp. 140–1; Lord, *Miracle*, p. 221; Malcolm Smith, 'The RAF', in Addison and Crang (eds.), *Burning Blue*, pp. 33–4.

72 Harris, *Dunkirk*, p. 126.

73 Colin Gray, 'Dowding and the British Strategy of Air Defence, 1936–40', in Williamson Murray and Richard Hart Sinnreich (eds.), *Successful Strategies: Triumphing in War and Peace from Antiquity to the Present* (Cambridge: Cambridge University Press, 2014), p. 271; Wing Commander R. E. Havercroft cited in Nettle, *Dunkirk*, p. 120; Ray, *Battle*, p. 29; Smith, 'The RAF', p. 34.

74 Lord, *Miracle*, pp. 221–2; Peter C. Smith, *Stuka at War* (London: Ian Allan, 1980), p. 45.

75 Atkin, *Pillar of Fire*, p. 205; Prior, *When Britain*, p. 133.

76 Terraine, *Right of the Line*, pp. 154–5.

77 M. Kirby and R. Capey, 'The Air Defence of Great Britain, 1920–1940: An Operational Research Perspective', *Journal of the Operational Research Society*, Vol. 48, No. 6 (1997), p. 563.

78 Max Hastings, *Bomber Command* (London: Pan, 1999), p. 63; Andrew Hendrie, *The Cinderella Service: Coastal Command, 1939–1945* (Barnsley: Pen & Sword, 2007), pp. 19–23, 60–1; Terence Horsley, *Find, Fix and Strike: The Work of the Fleet Air Arm* (London: Eyre and Spottiswoode, 1943), p. 10; Air Chief Marshal Sir Philip Joubert de la Ferte, *Birds and Fishes: The Story of Coastal Command* (London: Hutchinson, 1960), p. 141; H. W. Koch, 'The Strategic Air Offensive against Germany: The Early Phase, May–September 1940', *The Historical Journal*, Vol. 34, No. 1 (1991), pp. 128–31; Gordon Thorburn, *Bomber Command, 1939–1940: The War before the War* (Barnsley: Pen & Sword, 2013), p. 156.

79 TNA: ADM 199/792 – Report of Vice Admiral Ramsay; TNA: AIR 20/4447 – Air support of the BEF in France, Letter from Major General D. Johnson to Lieutenant General B. Fisher on Bomber Action at Nieuport, 8 June 1940; *Daily Telegraph*, 'RAF Defence of Dunkirk', 3 June 1940, p. 3; *The Times*, 'RAF's Great Help', 29 May 1940, p. 6; *Manchester Guardian*, 'Bombers' Efforts in Support of Troops', 31 May 1940, p. 3.

80 Cummings, *Royal Navy*, p. 30; Gardner, *Evacuation*, pp. 100, 115, 188; Roskill, *Defensive*, pp. 216–28; Jackson, *Dunkirk*, p. 127; Bernd Stegemann, 'The First Phase of the War at Sea', in Militärgeschichtliches Forschungsamt (ed.), *Germany and the Second World War, Vol. II Germany's Initial Conquests in Europe*, (trans.) Dean S. McMurry and Edwald Osers (Oxford: Clarendon Press, 1991), pp. 169–71.

81 Andrew Bird, *Coastal Dawn: Blenheims in Action from the Phoney War through the Battle of Britain* (London: Grub Street, 2012), pp. 80–9; Andrew Hendrie, *Seek and Strike: The Lockheed Hudson in World War II* (London: William Kimber, 1983), p. 67; Horsley, *Find*, p. 10; Jackson, Dunkirk, p. 152; Basil Liddell-Hart, 'The Second World War', in C. L. Mowat (ed.), *The New Cambridge Modern History*, Vol. XII [2nd Edition], *The Shifting Balance of World Forces, 1898–1945* (Cambridge: Cambridge University Press, 1968), p. 754; Marchand and Huan 'Dunkerque', p. 46.
82 Development, Concept and Doctrine Centre, *Joint Defence Publication 0-30: UK Air and Space Power* [2nd Edition] (Shrivenham: Ministry of Defence, 2017), p. 34.
83 Atkin, *Pillar of Fire*, p. 184; Barker, *Dunkirk*, p. 72; Development, Concept and Doctrine Centre, *Joint Defence Publication 0-30*, p. 4; Jackson, Dunkirk, pp. 126–7; Peter C. Smith, *Skua! The Royal Navy's Dive-Bomber* (Barnsley: Pen & Sword, 2006), pp. 164–5; Stewart, Dunkirk, p. 108.
84 Development, Concept and Doctrine Centre, *Joint Defence Publication 0-30*, p. 33.
85 Barker, *Dunkirk*, p. 72; Gelb, *Dunkirk*, p. 220; Divine, *Nine Days*, p. 266; Jackson, Dunkirk, pp. 126–7; Thompson, *Dunkirk*, p. 91.
86 Air Ministry, *Bomber Command: The Air Ministry Account of Bomber Command's Offensive Against the Axis, September, 1939–July, 1941* (London: HMSO, 1941), pp. 52–3; Arthur Harris, *Bomber Offensive* (Barnsley: Pen & Sword, 2005) pp. 40–1; Max Hastings, *Bomber Command*, p. 63; John Slessor, *The Central Blue: Recollections and Reflections* (London: Cassell, 1956), pp. 296–7.
87 Development, Concept and Doctrine Centre, *Joint Defence Publication 0-30*, p. 4.
88 Barker, *Dunkirk*, p. 72; Robert Jackson, *Before the Storm: The Story of Royal Air Force Bomber Command, 1939–42* (London: Arthur Baker, 1972), p. 234; W. A. Jacobs, 'Air Support for the British Army, 1939–1943', *Military Affairs*, Vol. 46, No. 4 (1982), pp. 178–80; Mathew Powell, *The Development of British Tactical Air Power, 1940–1943: A History of Army Co-operation Command* (London: Palgrave Macmillan, 2016), pp. 52–4.
89 Eden, *Reckoning*, p. 105.
90 L. F. Ellis, *The War in France and Flanders, 1939–40* (London: Her Majesty's Stationary Office, 1953), p. 314.
91 Field Marshal Sir Edmund Ironside, *The Ironside Diaries: 1937–1940* (eds.) Roderick Macleod and Denis Kelly (London: Constable, 1962), p. 316.
92 Hastings, *Bomber Command*, p. 63; Koch, 'Strategic Air Offensive', pp. 128–31; Thorburn, *Bomber Command*, p. 156.
93 Jackson, *Air War*, p. 109.
94 TNA: AIR 2/2058 – Bomber Command Training Policy; TNA: AIR 6/60 – Preliminary Statement to the Air Council by the Air Member for Training on Training Arrangements Generally, 23 July 1940; TNA: AIR 10/5551 – Flying Training, Policy and Planning, p. 97; TNA: AIR 14/54 – Factors Affecting

Operational Training in Units; TNA: AIR 14/57 – Bomber Command Annual Training Report: 1938; TNA: AIR 14/920 – Air Fighting Committee, Air Staff Paper on General Review of Training in Expansion, *c*.1938; TNA: AIR 32/14 – History of Flying Training: Training of Pilots, 1914–1945.

95 IWM: Audio/10152 – Charles Brian Fabris Kingcombe, Reel 1; IWM: Audio/27074 – Cyril Bamberger, Reel 7; IWM: Audio/12674 – Gerald Richmond Edge, Reels 1–2; IWM: Audio/11616 – George Binmore Johns, Reel 2; Hugh Dundas, *Flying Start: A Fighter Pilot's War Years* (Barnsley: Pen & Sword, 2011), pp. 28–9; Richard Hillary, *The Last Enemy* (London: Vintage, 2010) pp. 26–40.

96 IWM: Audio/2803 – John William Maxwell 'Max' Aitken, Reel 1; IWM: Audio/10119 – Norman Patrick Watkins Hancock, Reel 1; IWM: Audio/11510 – David George Samuel Richardson Cox, Reel 1; IWM: Audio/11534 – Desmond Vincent-Jones, Reel 1; IWM: Audio/14368 – John Bidsee, Reel 1; IWM: Audio/31394 – Jack Hubert Hoskin, Reel 1; TNA: AIR 20/2765 – Notes on interview with Flight Lieutenant Tuck of 92 Squadron; Dundas, *Flying*, pp. 28–9; Ian Gleed, *Arise to Conquer* (London: Grub Street, 2010), p. 43; Charles Lamb, *War in a Stringbag* (London: Cassell, 2001), p. 65.

97 Lynn Abrams, *Oral History Theory* (Abingdon: Routledge, 2010), p. 85.

98 TNA: ADM 199/786–94 – Operation Dynamo: Evacuation of Troops from Dunkirk, Vol. I–IX.

99 Gardner, *Evacuation*, pp. 162–94.

100 CAC: RMSY 8/10 – Admiral Sir Bertram Home Ramsay's Papers Relating to the Evacuation from Dunkirk, 1940; IWM: Audio/2803–31394 – Interviews with Participants of Operation Dynamo; IWM: Documents/11483a (LVM/3, Box No. P65) – Private Papers of Admiral Sir Vaughan Morgan; TNA: ADM 199/788A – Report of Rear Admiral Wake-Walker on Operation Dynamo; TNA: ADM 199/789 – Reports of Captain Tennant, Commander Richardson and Commander Elwood on Operation Dynamo; TNA: ADM 199/792 – Report of Vice Admiral Ramsay.

101 Horst Boog, 'German Air Intelligence in the Second World War', *Intelligence and National Security*, Vol. 5, No. 2 (1990), p. 350; Price, *Luftwaffe*, p. 194.

102 James S. Corum, 'Defeat of the Luftwaffe, 1935–1945', in Robin Higham and Stephen J. Harris (eds.), *Why Air Forces Fail* (Lexington, KY: University Press of Kentucky, 2016), pp. 207–30; Wilhelm Deist, 'The Rearmament of the Wehrmacht', in Militärgeschichtliches Forschungsamt (ed.), *Germany and the Second World War, Vol. I, The Build-Up of German Aggression* (Oxford: Clarendon Press, 2015), pp. 490–3; E. R. Hooton, *Phoenix Triumphant: The Rise and Rise of the Luftwaffe* (London: Brockhampton, 1999), p. 158; Barry Ketley and Mark Rolfe, *Luftwaffe Fledglings: 1935–1945: Luftwaffe Training Units and Their Aircraft* (Aldershot: Hikoki, 1996), pp. 3–39, 61–76; Werner Kreipe and Rudolf Koester, 'Technical Training within the German Luftwaffe', USAF Historical Study No. 169 (1955),

pp. 1–*ff*; Murray, *Strategy*, pp. 16–25; Probert, *Rise and Fall*, pp. 65–80; Richard Suchenwirth, 'The Development of the German Air Force, 1919–1939'. USAF Historical Studies No. 160 (1968), pp. 186–7.

103 Bundesarchiv-Militärarchiv, Freiburg (hereafter BA/MA): N 671/6 – Wolfram von Richthofen, Persönliches Kriegstagebuch.

104 TNA: AIR 20/9906 – German Air Force Situation Report on Western Front.

105 Werner Baumbach, *The Life and Death of the Luftwaffe* (Costa Mesa, CA: Noontide, 1991), p. 79; Adolf Galland et al., *The Luftwaffe at War, 1939–1945* (London: Ian Allan, 1972), pp. 40–2; Albert Kesselring, *The Memoirs of Field Marshal Kesselring* (London: Greenhill, 2007), pp. 58–60; Ulrich Steinhilper and Peter Osborne, *Spitfire on My Tail: A View from the Other Side* (Bromley: Independent Books, 2009), pp. 250–9.

106 TNA: AIR 20/7700–7711 – Translations of Captured German Air Historical Branch Studies and records of the Quartermaster General's Department of the German Air Ministry; Speidel, 'German Air Force'.

107 USA Naval War College (hereafter USNWC): Microfilm 354/Part A/Vol. 9–10 – Oberkommando der Kriegsmarine Kriegstagebuch der Seekriegsleitung, May–June 1940, (trans.) USA Office of Naval Intelligence, 1948; TNA: ADM 223/28 – Naval Staff – Tactical and Staff Duties Division – Foreign Documents Section, Summary of German E-Boat Operations in the English Channel and North Sea Based on Extracts from the War Diary of *Kapitän zur See* Büttow, *Führer der Torpedoboote*.

108 T. Jick, 'Mixing Qualitative and Quantitative Methods: Triangulation in Action', *Administrative Science Quarterly*, Vol. 24, No. 4 (1979), pp. 602–11; M. B. Miles and A. M. Hubermann, *Qualitative Data Analysis: An Expanded Sourcebook* [2nd Edition] (London: Sage, 1994), pp. 55–8.

109 TNA: ADM 199/786 to ADM 199/794 – Operation Dynamo: Evacuation of Troops from Dunkirk, Vol. I–IX; TNA: ADM 199/2206 – Naval War Diary; TNA: ADM 358/3241 – Operation Dynamo; Signals cited in Gardner, *Evacuation*, pp. 125–94.

1

The two forces

A consideration of the operations of the air forces during Dynamo requires an assessment of the factors which influenced the capabilities of both sides to exert air power over Dunkirk. The air battle above Dunkirk is often narrated as a story of an outnumbered, inexperienced, RAF facing the better trained, battle hardened, Luftwaffe and inflicting upon them a rebuff which ensured the success of the evacuation. Assumptions regarding the capabilities of the British and German air forces have, however, helped obscure the failings, and successes, of both air forces during the evacuation of Dunkirk. These assumptions have concealed how the RAF was supposedly able to overcome a superior enemy and why the Luftwaffe was unable to prevent the success of Dynamo. Before considering the air operations during Dynamo it is therefore important to assess the relative strengths and weaknesses of the two air forces and ascertain whether either side held a distinct advantage during in men, material or proximity to the battlefield.

The numbers available to each side and the proximity to Dunkirk of the bases that the forces were operating from were both critical in determining what each side could accomplish during Dynamo. The RAF was faced with the task of providing patrols above the evacuation fleet and bombing sorties in support of the Allied ground forces. The methods they employed to achieve these requirements were largely predicated on the number of aircraft which were available and the amount of time they could remain over the evacuation. The Luftwaffe's task, of bringing a complete halt to the evacuation and destroying the Allied resistance in the Dunkirk pocket, was much greater and required a sizeable force. Before attempting to understand why they failed to achieve their objective it is important to know what forces they had available for operations against the evacuation of Dunkirk. This chapter will then consider the location of the two sides' airbases. The use of advanced airfields allowed air forces to maximize their air time over the combat zone; if one side's air bases were considerably closer to Dunkirk than the other's it would have bestowed a considerable advantage. Wing Commander Cecil Bouchier, AOC RAF Hornchurch, asserted that Fighter Command's 'aircraft were outnumbered by those of the Luftwaffe, who were operating from nearby bases'.[1] Sholto Douglas, Deputy Chief of the Air Staff at the time of Dynamo, argued that Fighter Command was 'at a disadvantage because of the long-range at which the battles had to be fought'.[2] To address whether Fighter Command fought the air battle of Dunkirk at a disadvantage, as senior members of the RAF have claimed, the location of the air bases the two sides operated from will be analysed.

To understand the tactical and strategic decisions that came to be made during the battle it is also necessary to understand the advantages and limitations both sides held as a result of the men and material under their command. The aircraft that the two air forces employed during Dynamo presented limitations in how the air battle could be fought and influenced decisions made regarding the employment of forces during the evacuation. The individual training for the two sides' pilots, the experiences of combat they had gained and the leadership of air formations will then be assessed. These factors were enablers for the execution of air power during Dynamo. Establishing these factors is therefore important to determine the relative capabilities of the two forces and how this influenced their operations during Dynamo. In particular, it is important to consider the previous training and experience of the Luftwaffe in maritime and anti-shipping roles – functions into which its bombers were thrust during Dynamo – to understand the difficulties it faced halting the evacuation.

Numerical strength of the RAF and Luftwaffe

The Luftwaffe possessed a numerical advantage over the RAF during the evacuation of Dunkirk. This quantitative superiority, as opposed to any qualitative difference between the RAF and Luftwaffe, has previously been advanced as an explanation for the overall outcome of the air battle at Dunkirk and the manner in which the RAF chose to fight during the battle.[3] Fighter Command could call on some 600 modern single engine fighters, a third of which were available for the use of 11 Group, commanded by Air Vice-Marshal Keith Park, who were responsible for the fighter cover of the evacuation.[4] There is, therefore, an important distinction to be made between the aircraft available to 11 Group, and how it used this fixed number, and Fighter Command, who held additional resources. Dowding maintained the strength of 11 Group throughout the battle but he was unwilling to increase the frontline strength of Park's forces above this number (the reasons for this decision and the effect committing greater forces to the air battle may have had are considered in Chapter 7). Against the 200 aircraft of 11 Group, supplemented by aircraft from Coastal Command and the Fleet Air Arm, the Luftwaffe possessed a clear numerical advantage. In the last week of May the Luftwaffe possessed 820 Messerschmitt Bf 109 aircraft (typically designated as Me 109s by RAF pilots and referred to as such during the course of this book) which were operationally ready, close to 550 of which were available for operations from bases in Northern France and the Low Countries.[5] A proportion of these were, however, used in other sectors during Dynamo. For the majority of the air battle over Dunkirk the Luftwaffe seems to have conveniently drawn on a force of, at least, some 350 single engine fighters.[6] The twin engine Messerschmitt Bf 110 (hereafter referred to as the Me 110) increased the fighter forces available to the Luftwaffe. The Luftwaffe had begun the campaign in France with some 350 Me 110 aircraft and by the beginning of Operation Dynamo the number of operationally ready aircraft was probably in the region of 150.[7] Two weeks of combat losses in operations had sapped the strength of the Luftwaffe bomber forces and the use of forward airfields also had a serious consequence on serviceability rates. Forward staffs could not repair extensive battle damage and there was a shortage of spare parts. The intense fighting and the limitations of repair facilities at forward airfields had reduced some units to as low as 50 per cent serviceability.[8] Many bomber *Gruppen* were only able to call upon fifteen aircraft, out of an intended establishment of thirty. In KG 76, equipped with Dornier Do 17 bombers, the aircraft ready-for-action had been reduced by 40 per cent between 10 to 26 May, a serviceability rate which remained constant throughout Dynamo, whilst *Sturzkampfgeschwader* 2 were short of eighteen Junkers Ju 87s and three Do 17s on 28 May.[9] Nevertheless, a force of at least 300 bombers was available for operations against the evacuations from Dunkirk.[10] The numerical disadvantage 11 Group faced during Dynamo was compounded by the need to operate standing patrols whilst the Luftwaffe, holding the initiative, was able to strike when they wished and swamp the combat zone. The Luftwaffe's fighters, however, were not always able to operate in this manner, often having to provide escorts and, when co-ordination with bomber units was not possible, they also flew continuous patrols from Calais to Dunkirk as well as Boulogne-Lille-Ostend.[11] When the Luftwaffe bombers attacked the town of Dunkirk en masse on 27 May up to 300 aircraft were counted in the sky.[12] The limited resources of 11 Group were hard-pressed to break such formations up and fought at a disadvantage when trying to do so. The Luftwaffe's numerical advantage was, however, restricted. Adolf Galland, a fighter pilot in JG 52, would later recount that Dunkirk did not represent an all-out effort by the Luftwaffe because of the need for operations against French forces further south.[13] Although the extent to which this is representative of the Luftwaffe's operations throughout the evacuation of Dunkirk is debatable, coming as it does from a senior Luftwaffe figure – Galland was later *General der Jagdflieger* – attempting to excuse a significant defeat, Luftwaffe operations against French forces on the Somme did reduce the numbers available for much of Operation Dynamo.

The battle-weary formations of the Luftwaffe, who had been involved in continuous dawn-to-dusk operations for the previous two weeks, were also reduced in their combat potential because of fatigue. Luftwaffe fighter units had suffered heavily; I./JG 27 for instance had casualties of over 20 per cent of its initial establishment between 10 and 28 May.[14] The effects of tiredness and lack of sleep – perhaps accompanied by a fear of dying at the culmination of a campaign which promised a decisive German victory – were factors which effected the Luftwaffe's performance over Dunkirk. RAF fighter pilots would recount that many bombers showed little inclination to press home attacks in the presence of fighter cover, ditching their bombs and returning to base instead.[15] Operating in weakened formations, as a result of losses and damage, also reduced the military effectiveness of Luftwaffe's units.[16] Fatigue and accumulated losses, combined with the dissipation of forces caused by operations away from Dunkirk, reduced the effectiveness of the numerical superiority of the Luftwaffe over Dunkirk.[17]

Although the Luftwaffe enjoyed a numerical superiority over the RAF it was not a decisive one given the task at hand. Losses and fatigue had reduced both the size of the force and its effectiveness whilst conflicting demands reduced the number of aircraft available for continuous operations against the evacuation. Faced with the task of halting the evacuation, Kesselring, commander of *Luftflotte* 2, objected that the task was 'completely beyond the strength of my depleted forces'.[18]

Location of the RAF and Luftwaffe's airfields

The use of advanced airfields could bestow a considerable advantage to an air force as they reduced the fuel consumption of aircraft flying to the operational area so allowing them greater time over the combat zone. The air battle over

Calais, immediately before Operation Dynamo, had reinforced the need for the fighter aircraft of the Luftwaffe to be transferred further forward.[19] On 23 May *Generalmajor* Wolfram von Richthofen, commanding *Fliegerkorps* VIII, observed that his forces were at a disadvantage against the RAF operating from England as the Luftwaffe's airbases were based further back in Belgium and many had not advanced further than Antwerp.[20] On 24 May, *General der Flieger* Hugo Sperrle, commanding *Luftflotte* 3, complained that 'only the *Fliegerkorps* Richthofen can intervene in the attack, the associations of the other corps are so far behind that the situation on the front has already changed before they have the command to get started'.[21]

On 24 May, Richthofen looked ahead to the elimination of Allied forces at Dunkirk. To accomplish this, he felt he needed to advance both Stuka and fighter Staffeln to St. Pol, 70km from Dunkirk. Supply issues initially meant Richthofen considered it almost impossible to advance these units without the 'extreme exertions' of *Luftflotte* 3. By the beginning of Dynamo, despite encountering difficulties co-ordinating with fighter units, I./JG 1, I./JG 27 and III./JG 54 had been advanced to St. Pol.[22] This forward move was necessitated because Fighter Command, 'fighting close to its door', had achieved air superiority at Calais.[23] St. Pol became an important facility with a large proportion of the Me 109 force (120 aircraft) based at what became a congested advanced airfield. It appears, however, that St. Pol was, by 31 May, used as a base for forward reconnaissance as well as to refuel and rearm bombers – with the *Jagdgeschwader* moved to bases further back.[24] Other German fighters units had been advanced but not as close to Dunkirk and on 31 May commanders in the Luftwaffe ground-service organization were 'impatiently expecting a message as to when St. Leger-North and Pronville, Vitry-en-Artois (both located around Arras 90km and 105km from Dunkirk) would be ready for advanced fighter formations'.[25] On 27 May the length of the approach flight for *Jafü* 3's fighter cover of Dunkirk and Calais left little flight time over this area, estimated as being only ten to twenty minutes, and they were unable to provide fighter cover to bomber formations on their return to base because of a lack of fuel.[26] Furthermore, the German fighters which were located in West Belgium, 115km from Dunkirk, faced supply difficulties operating from temporary airfields.[27] Galland later recalled that as Dynamo commenced:

> The Luftwaffe entered a difficult period due to its extended lines of supply. Regrouping of squadrons at airfields close to the frontline was still too dangerous and, at the same time, operations from bases in the homeland were difficult because of the long distances involved.[28]

On 29 May, I./JG 20 moved to Ghent, 95km away from Dunkirk, operating from there against the evacuation on 1 June.[29] On 30 May, I. and II./JG 3, and the fighter group of *Lehrgeschwader* 2, were inspected at Montecouvez, 125km from Dunkirk, by *General der Flieger* Ulrich Grauert, Commander of *Fliegerkorps* I.[30] The majority of the Luftwaffe's units utilizing captured airfields were required to operate over 160km from Dunkirk from positions such as St. Aubin or Sovet in Belgium or Givet in France.[31] On 2 June, transport aircraft remained very active to Guise, Sissone and Evere.[32] These locations, all significantly further from Dunkirk than the bases available to Fighter Command, formed the primary forward hubs from which the Luftwaffe was operating.

Before Dynamo commenced the Luftwaffe's general shortage of fuel affected operations and delayed units being advanced forward.[33] *Fliegerkorps II* was unable to reinforce *Jafü* 3 because a shortage of fuel left it incapable of transferring a *Staffel* to Cambrai.[34] Both KG 26 and KG 77 reported shortages of fuel and on 26 May *Fliegerkorps* VIII reported that KG 77's operations had been 'hitherto hindered by fuel-shortage'.[35] The discovery of abandoned French aviation fuel in underground tanks at the airfield of Charleville greatly eased the situation faced by many units. At other airfields, however, problems remained even when fuel stocks were captured, because examination of certain stores led to instructions that captured aero-fuel was not utilizable in German aircraft before ethylization.[36] As well as the fuel captured and used at Charleville, however, definite use was made of stocks at Laon and captured aero-fuel eased the German supply situation at forward airbases during Dynamo.[37]

Shortly before the outset of Dynamo *Fliegerkorps* III and VIII were moving units to bases around Charleville and Guise, respectively 265km and 160km from Dunkirk.[38] These forward moves were required as experience during the campaign had shown the Luftwaffe that the effective operational range of the Ju 87B, with a full bomb-load, was limited to around 560km.[39] Richthofen's ambition to base Ju 87s at St. Pol was, however, unfilled and many dive-bomber *Gruppen* had limited time over Dunkirk.[40] On 25 May, StG 77 was operating from Rocroi, and having to undertake bombing sorties at the edge of the Ju 87's fuel range, and as late as 1 June Stab StG 77 was undertaking a 480km round flight from Rocroi to Dunkirk.[41] On 26 May Richthofen complained that he could do nothing against British destroyers shelling German positions at Calais because they were out of range of his Stuka forces.[42] When eight warships were observed off Calais at 14.40 on 25 May *Fliegerkorps* VIII did not have any aircraft available to attack them.[43] Earlier, at midday, aircraft flying over the coast from Calais to Boulogne were forced to return to their bases without attacking because of the extreme distance of operations.⁴⁴ Paul Temme, of JG 2, recalled providing fighter cover for a Stuka attack on Calais on 26 May flying '220km from Signy to the Channel Coast! There won't be much time for dog fighting when we get there'.⁴⁵ Richthofen's diary shows that on 28 May *Fliegerkorps* VIII had bombers at Guise and fighters at St. Pol. The situation, however, limited the operational time of Ju 87 units over Dunkirk – possibly to as low as twenty minutes.⁴⁶

During Dynamo, the Luftwaffe's medium bombers were able to operate from aerodromes in the Rhineland, although their home bases remained in Central and Southern Germany.⁴⁷ The German invasion of the Netherlands had provided few airfields suitable for medium bombers. Whilst the Luftwaffe quickly brought forward construction units to enlarge and extend the existing airfields, the majority of its medium bombers were still operating from bases in Germany at the time of Dynamo. A lack of suitable airfields for bombers also characterized the facilities the Luftwaffe captured in Belgium and Luxemburg. On 30 May III./KG 76, equipped with Do 17s, had orders to move forward to Sovet, in Belgium, over 200km from Dunkirk.⁴⁸ Airfields around Guise were utilized to refuel twin engine bombers. On 27 May Do 17s from a *Gruppe* of KG 77 landed at Guise fully loaded with bombs, refuelled, had a target assigned to them and were despatched against the evacuation to be replaced by another *Gruppe*.⁴⁹ Antwerp was used by KG 4, operating from Kirchellen some 325km from Dunkirk, on 27 May and 30 May as it made attacks on ships between Gravelines and Ostend. Three *Ketten* of KG 4 were called on to operate from Antwerp, where they were badly needed, shortly before midday on 27 May and at 03.30 on 31 May, two *Ketten* of KG 4 were ordered to land at Antwerp in order to pick up their fighter escort.⁵⁰ Despite the use of airfields, such as Antwerp and Guise, the distance the majority of Luftwaffe medium bomber force was operating from left them only able to make one attack on the evacuation a day.⁵¹ Variable weather between base and target also caused disruption. This would prove to be a limiting factor as the distances involved meant that if weather conditions were bad at the bombers base, on the flight route (including a forward airfield if they had to refuel on the return flight), or at Dunkirk, they could not complete their missions.

Captured advanced airfields also enabled Luftwaffe fighters to rearm and refuel for a second patrol without having to return to the airfield from which the unit was operating. Ulrich Steinhilper's unit, JG 52, operated from Charleville during Dynamo, and from 27 May they began to land at Cambrai after their first mission of the day in order to refuel and rearm and so be able to return for a second sortie. Forward airfields, however, had only a limited capacity even in this role and on 29 May JG 52 moved to the 'beautifully kept little airport' at

Laon, 190km from Dunkirk, in order to continue operations.[52] The shortage of forward airfields, however, is indicated by JG 52 being moved again, away from Laon, so that the airfield was available for a bomber *Gruppe*.[53] The Luftwaffe found that not only were there a limited number of suitable airfields from which they could operate from, but that those that they were able to use soon became grossly overcrowded.[54] On 24 May, II./JG 52 lost two Me 109s as the result of a collision whilst taxiing on the captured airfield at Sandweiler, Luxemburg, which continued to be used throughout Dynamo.[55] Fighter Command operated from a number of advanced airfields which, although they became crowded, were part of an established supply system. In contrast, the advanced airfields utilized by the Luftwaffe were ill prepared to deal with large and congested forces. The rapid advance of the Luftwaffe left its Airfield Maintenance Companies and transports overstretched, and those that were available were being primarily utilized to advance units closer to the French forces on the Somme rather than towards Dunkirk.[56] Possessing only a limited number of advanced airfields close to Dunkirk therefore placed considerable strain on the maintenance units available and, coupled with the airfields' own limitations, this in turn reduced the number of squadrons able to operate from these airfields. A subsequent study by the German Air Historical branch, in 1944, asserted the 'basic principle' that:

> technical efficiency is entirely dependent on the ground organisation and on the technical ground services, and that the mobility of a flying unit is limited by its technical resources. ... [During the campaigns in France] entire units or parts of units were repeatedly moved to airfields with totally insufficient technical equipment. This led to a decrease in the operational readiness and numerical strength of the flying units.[57]

The rough nature of many of the airfields and landing grounds pressed into service by the Luftwaffe also caused problems. The Me 109 had a weak undercarriage which could suffer damage on the advanced airfields which the Luftwaffe pressed into service. Such was the reputation of the Me 109's sensitive take-off and landing characteristics that, even on the maintained runways of the German fighter schools, it became known to its pilots as a 'crazy horse' and at Sissonne an Me 109 turned-over on landing and was completely written off.[58] The use of advanced airfields, the ground conditions of which were often far from ideal, posed problems for the Me 109, and a number were lost because of undercarriage failures. On 27 May, *Generaloberst* Milch, in his role as General Inspector of the Luftwaffe, criticized the ground-service organization for their choice of aerodrome at Philippeville and the number of fighter aircraft damaged during landing because of the poor condition of the airfield.[59] On 26 May, every aircraft of I./JG 52 was damaged during emergency landings in Belgium after they had become lost during their return from Dunkirk.[60] The improvised nature of some of the airfields pressed into service also caused problems during Dynamo. The heavy rain during the end of May softened the soil of the fields and plateaus and prevented some formations engaging in operations on crucial days of the evacuation.[61]

The RAF operated from a number of airfields in Britain during Dynamo. The use of air stations on the coast as advanced airfields from which aircraft could refuel placed Fighter Command's squadron much closer to the combat zone above Dunkirk.[62] RAF stations at Hawkinge and Manston were as close to Dunkirk as the furthest forward captured airfield being exploited by German fighters. The proximity of RAF Hawkinge, 80km from Dunkirk, allowed squadrons to patrol to Dunkirk during the morning, return, refuel and conduct a second sortie over the evacuation.[63] The squadron could then be replaced in the afternoon by a fresh squadron who would then enjoy similar benefits to their air cover over the evacuation. RAF Manston was 75km from Dunkirk and several squadrons of the RAF utilized the station as an advanced air base during Dynamo.[64] RAF Detling and Gravesend, 125km and 135km from Dunkirk respectively, were also used. Anthony Tuke, of 826 (FAA) Squadron, remembered that Detling was so full of fighter aircraft that pilots had to sleep in chairs at night whilst John Thompson, of 500 Squadron, recalled the airfield 'was really bulging at the seams with the variety of aircraft which were being housed there'.[65] Maintenance airmen were despatched to forward air bases to provide maintenance for other squadrons operating from them. This was the case with RAF Lympne, 90km from Dunkirk, where 613 Squadron despatched men to act in this capacity for three other squadrons during the evacuation.[66] Refuelling and rearming at stations such as Manston – but not having to transport the squadron's stores, supplies and personnel there to continue operating – allowed Fighter Command's squadrons to operate close to Dunkirk whilst not suffering from the disorganization and delays that often occurred when squadrons were required to move airfields.[67]

Fighter Command was able to utilize forward airbases in South-East England to reduce their flying time to Dunkirk to roughly twenty-five minutes.[68] The report of 11 Group noted that 'between sorties squadrons were refuelled and rearmed at advanced bases at Manston, Gravesend and Hawkinge' and that although occasionally it was possible to despatch squadrons from their normal bases this was only 'to undertake the shorter tasks on the French Coast'.[69] In instances when squadrons did operate from their permanent station during

Dynamo they typically took off from there to conduct an early morning sortie and landed at forward airfields such as Manston to refuel and rearm before their second sortie of the day.[70] Many squadrons, however, operated directly from advanced airfields. Pilots of 56 Squadron flew to the advanced airfield at Manston very early and would then be at readiness all day before returning to the squadron's home base, North Weald.[71] On 2 June, 92 Squadron flew to Martlesham Heath, 135km from Dunkirk, which appears to have been selected in this instance because the weather conditions at the station were more likely to allow the patrol to take off before dawn.[72] This was a further advantage of the RAF's bases. By drawing on a number of airfields at different points on the coast Fighter Command was able to maintain patrols over Dunkirk even when poor weather conditions prevented the use of certain airfields. With a more limited number of advanced airfields the Luftwaffe was hindered by local weather conditions.[73]

Furthermore, RAF squadrons operating from advanced airfields also had the advantage that their flight-route to Dunkirk allowed them to provide air cover above both Route Z and X. Fighter Command's patrol route crossed the channel to arrive over the French coast west of Calais before turning east to Dunkirk and then Belgium before returning to base or circling Dunkirk and returning via Calais.[74] Fighter Command's flight time to the evacuation therefore formed part of an effective patrol route, providing air cover over the evacuation routes, whilst the Luftwaffe's fighters were effective only once they had reached Dunkirk. Against this, the defensive perimeter surrounding Dunkirk – above which many of the air combats between the two air forces took place as Fighter Command attempted to prevent bomber formations reaching Dunkirk – was closer to the Luftwaffe's airfields. The combat time of the two sides' single engine fighters over the evacuation remained, however, in favour of the RAF.

Although the single engine interceptors of both forces had a relatively low range and endurance, the Me 109E was at a disadvantage to both the Hawker Hurricane and the Supermarine Spitfire in this regard. Placing an accurate figure on the differential between the RAF and Luftwaffe's single engine fighter's loiter time above the evacuation is complicated by questions of the height operated at, rate of climb and operating speed – all of which affected the range which could be achieved by the various types. The Me 109E had a fuel tank capacity of 400 litres and a lower operational flight time, 105 minutes, than either the Hurricane or the Spitfire.[75] Operating at altitudes above 14,000 feet would have limited its flying time to roughly ninety minutes.[76] Both these figures decreased as less economical speeds were demanded of the aircraft and reduced dramatically in combat. The Luftwaffe's flight routes to Dunkirk crossed through air space which remained contested and it is therefore unlikely that the Me 109 formations would have flown towards Dunkirk at lower, more economical, speeds. The Spitfire also had a limited range and endurance but could operate for over half an hour above Dunkirk allowing for ten minutes at full throttle when engaged in combat.[77] In exceptional circumstances, however, when not engaged and able to operate at their most efficient speeds, Spitfires managed to complete patrols with total flight times of two-and-a-half hours.[78] The Hurricane's endurance was slightly greater than that of the Spitfire but as George Johns, a pilot in 229 Squadron, recalled during operations over Dunkirk there was 'very little fuel: you couldn't stick around'.[79] The twin engine Me 110 fighter had a longer-range and operational endurance than the single engine types. It was, however, operating from airfields further back from Dunkirk than those of Fighter Command and did not shift the advantage of operational air time over the evacuation in favour of the Luftwaffe.

The advantage held by Fighter Command was, however, checked by its need to operate standing patrols. Flying standing patrols left Fighter Command having to distribute its air cover across the day. The Luftwaffe held the initiative, and could choose when to attack, which allowed it to concentrate its forces. The short loiter time of the Me 109, however, did restrict the fighter operations of German units over Dunkirk. This was particularly the case when German fighters were required to escort bomber formations attacking Dunkirk. The bombers did not usually arrive to rendezvous with their fighter escort at the appointed time and German fighters often had to withdraw just as the bombers arrived.[80]

Figures produced for Fighter Command's operational time over Dunkirk often build in the assumption of combat lowering the available figure. When Fighter Command's squadrons engaged in combat during Dynamo, however, they found that shortages of ammunition were as likely to force their early return as shortages of fuel were. On 26 May, pilots from 19 Squadron returned to base having used their entire allotment of ammunition in combat over the coast between Dunkirk and Calais. On 27 May, one pilot of 19 Squadron returned from combat with ammunition, citing fuel as a concern; however, the patrol had broken up by this stage and other pilots returned having used ammunition. Throughout Dynamo, RAF pilots who were forced to return to base following combat typically did so because they had expended all their ammunition rather than because of a shortage of fuel.[81] In considering Fighter Command's patrol, therefore, it is necessary to realize that whilst fuel was a limiting factor the effect that it had on Fighter Command's air cover of Dunkirk has been previously overestimated.

Aircraft of the RAF and Luftwaffe

It has been asserted that the superiority of their aircraft was one of the few areas in which the RAF held an advantage over the Luftwaffe. Montgomery Hyde has written that the Luftwaffe did not 'have anything to match the quality of the Spitfire and Hurricane eight-gun fighters'.[82] Even veterans of the Luftwaffe have, since the end of the Second World War, claimed the Spitfire was a 'much better aircraft' than the Me 109.[83] The Hurricane's performance was also very creditable and many Luftwaffe pilots were convinced that they had been shot down by a Spitfire rather than the less glamourous Hurricane they actually fell victim to.[84] Historians of the Luftwaffe have, however, adopted a very different position and maintained that at this point in the war the Luftwaffe Me 109E was superior to the Hurricane and at least the equal of the Spitfire.[85] The twin engines Me 110 has been much criticized by historians of the Battle of Britain because, operating as a close escort to bomber formations, it suffered heavy casualties to the more manoeuvrable fighters of the RAF.[86] The performance of the Me 110 at Dunkirk judged through this lens is unhelpful as it was able to provide an effective counterpunch to the British fighter force when possessing the advantage of height and speed. The performance of the various aircraft, and how they compared to one another, remained largely similar between Dunkirk and the Battle of Britain and is widely discussed elsewhere.[87] The majority of the two air forces' aircraft will not, therefore, be discussed here. It is, however, useful to briefly understand the capabilities of the single engine fighter aircraft and certain technical developments which affected course of the air battle during Dunkirk not least because Kesselring has since stated that 'it was the Spitfire which enabled the British and French to evacuate across the water'.[88]

The single engine fighters of the two sides were fairly evenly matched. The Spitfire Mk. I and Me 109E both had a similar top speed and were 'noticeably' faster than the larger Hurricane.[89] In combat the Spitfire and Hurricane, both equipped with eight Browning .303-inch machine-guns, were more manoeuvrable than the Me 109 which was, however, more heavily armed, with two 20mm MG FF cannon and two 7.9mm MG17 machine-guns.[90] The Me 109E's fuel injection Daimler-Benz DB 601A engine provided it with a further advantage allowing it to dive under negative G-forces without the engine cutting out whereas the atmospheric carburettors of the British types would flood under such conditions causing a momentary engine failure.[91] Peter Ayerst, of 73 Squadron, recalled that the Me 109:

could go into a steep dive and if they had a Hurricane on their tail they knew they could get away ... because in a Hurricane if you did that the ... the engine would cut ... with starvation of fuel to the carburettor.[92]

Hurricane pilots believed the fuel-injection engine was one of the few advantages that the Me 109 held over their aircraft.[93] There were, however, other advantages. The seating position in the Me 109 also allowed for higher G-force manoeuvres to be performed before the pilot blacked-out than was possible in either British type and it was also distinctly superior to either the Spitfire or Hurricane when operating at higher altitudes.[94]

The Spitfire also had a serious vulnerability which proved costly in the air battles over Dunkirk. Many of the Spitfire combat losses during Dynamo were the result of damage to the exposed header tank for the flammable Ethylene-Glycol coolant used in the Spitfire's radiator. This tank – located at the front of the Spitfire – was vulnerable to the fire of rear-gunners in bombers and, at the time of Dunkirk, was unarmoured.[95] For Peter Parrott, of 145 Squadron, whose coolant system was similarly damaged, the result was a crash-landing from which he emerged with his uniform 'absolutely soaked in Glycol'.[96] Alan Deere, of 54 Squadron, suffered similar damage to his coolant system whilst attacking a Dornier over Dunkirk and recalled that 'a bullet from the rear gunner went into my glycol tank ... that was my coolant system gone, that meant I was hors de combat. I had to come down'.[97] Deere would later describe the Spitfire as 'very vulnerable from a rear gunner because of the glycol header tank, which at that time wasn't armour-plated. That was the means of cooling your engine and if that went you'd had it'.[98] The vulnerability of the Glycol header tank caused many Spitfires to have to crash land in France or Belgium. These aircraft, although not seriously damaged, could not be recovered, repaired and reintroduced into Fighter Command's aircraft reserves.

Fighter Command's aircraft had a further weakness which was their lack of a self-sealing fuel tank.[99] From the end of April 1940 the Spitfire had begun to receive an upgrade to provide the fuselage fuel tanks with a fire-retardant coating and shielding. It was not until after Dynamo, however, that further efforts were made to provide the aircraft with a self-sealing fuel tank.[100] The Hurricane's lack of a self-sealing fuel tank was also a concern because the fuel tank in the forward fuselage was without protection and was positioned directly in front of the pilot whilst the wood construction and fabric covering of the rear fuselage allowed the rapid spread of fire. The lack of self-sealing fuel tanks produced losses which might otherwise have been avoided. This point is important beyond the losses themselves as a major factor influencing Dowding's decision to limit the exposure of his force was the fear that, operating over the Channel, losses of both men and material would be permanent.

A further concern which may have influenced Dowding's decision was that not all the fighters of his command were equipped with constant-speed propellers. Both the Hurricane and Spitfire were originally produced with two-speed variable pitch propellers before the constant-speed propeller was introduced.[101] The two-speed propeller had two pitch settings – fine and coarse – with which to control the blade angle of the propeller. At low speeds, the fine pitch setting was used so that the angle of the blade presented a large profile and provided a great deal of thrust. This setting, however, created significant amounts of drag so at high speed the pilot manually set the propeller pitch to coarse so that the blades presented a smaller profile. The performance of both the Hurricane and Spitfire increased significantly when they were equipped with a constant-speed propeller, which automatically adjusted the propeller's pitch to maintain the most efficient blade angle for the flight conditions and so maximized engine power.[102] Priority for the fitting of the Rotol constant-speed propellers had gone to the Hurricane (which benefited most from the boost in performance) whose pilots were greatly pleased by the resulting superior performance.[103] Whilst 54 Squadron was equipped with Rotol Spitfires in December 1939, with 19 Squadron having undertaken intensive reliability tests the previous month, Supermarine produced Spitfires that continued to be fitted with the De Havilland two-pitch propeller and only a few Spitfire squadrons engaged over Dunkirk had aircraft fitted with the Rotol propeller.[104] Some Hurricanes were also sent into operations over Dunkirk with variable-pitch propellers, greatly limiting their performance. After Dynamo, in response to urgent demands, De Havilland rapidly produced and began retrofitting a constant-speed propeller for the Spitfire. For 609 Squadron, whose Spitfires had fought over Dunkirk with the variable speed propeller, the results were 'astounding' transforming the Spitfire which 'now is an aeroplane'.[105]

Another important question is whether Fighter Command's types possessed rear armour during Operation Dynamo, with Norman Gelb asserting that they did not.[106] Rear armour had, however, been widely installed by this time. Certain Hurricane squadrons began to have rear armour installed shortly before the German invasion of France. Five squadrons had completed the installation by 10 May 1940, two more being expected to have completed installation by 12 May, but plans to install rear armour at further squadrons were retarded by the German offensive.[107] Rear armour was installed in the Hurricanes of 605

Squadron in time for patrols over Dunkirk, after their airmen worked all night to install it.[108] Kenneth McGlashan, of 245 Squadron, recalled that during one air battle over Dunkirk he 'totally neglected to look behind. The first indication I had of anything being wrong was when the armour plate behind my head began ringing like an alarm clock'.[109] The Spitfires of 611 Squadron fought over Dunkirk with 'armour plating recently fixed behind the pilot's seat' which saved the life of at least one member of the squadron.[110] In 609 Squadron rear armour plating was delivered after Dynamo had begun. Unceasing work by the airmen of the squadron over twenty-four hours ensured that thirteen Spitfires were retrofitted immediately before operations over Dunkirk on 30 May.[111] The Spitfire squadrons of 11 Group which had not had rear armour retrofitted were retained for home defence and were not involved in Dynamo.[112]

The Luftwaffe types also had vulnerabilities. The Me 109 began the war without a self-sealing fuel tank, despite the Germans possessing a very efficient design, and armour protection had not been installed on some of the Me 109s which fought over Dunkirk.[113] The Luftwaffe was, however, fighting closer to their own lines and crashed aircraft could be recovered. Whilst the recovery of damaged aircraft was not always accomplished – Richthofen would complain that not enough was done to rescue and repair crash landed aircraft before they became prey to souvenir hunters – they could, at least in theory, be repaired or have important parts salvaged and the pilots who survived were recovered.[114] The performance capabilities of the Me 109 suggest that at the very least it was the equal of Fighter Command's types. Kesselring's argument that the Spitfire 'enabled' the evacuation of the Allied forces cannot be accepted on the basis of it being a superior aircraft.

The Luftwaffe's attempt to halt the evacuation was, to a large extent, dependant on its diver bombers, in particular the Ju 87 – the Luftwaffe's most effective weapon against shipping.[115] A 1941 Royal Navy study, comparing the loss of vessels to various German aircraft, starkly demonstrated the greater success of the Ju 87 against all naval types and that it was able to achieve a very high degree of success against destroyers and other escort vessels.[116] The cast iron fittings of merchant ships, minesweepers and older destroyers used during Dynamo were particularly vulnerable to dive-bombers whose accuracy led not only to more direct hits but to more near-misses, the shock-effect of which was enhanced by the relative lightness of construction of these types.[117] The Luftwaffe's maritime successes during the Norwegian campaign, achieved through bombing, demonstrated that they were a serious threat provided their attacks were accurate.[118] The Ju 87 was effective because it could dive to a low-height and attain a greater degree of accuracy. The Junkers Ju 88 was an extremely robust medium bomber. Faster than both the Do 17 and Heinkel He 111 the Ju 88 also possessed dive-brakes, which allowed it to attack in a steep dive and accurately deliver bombs at a low-height; it was therefore a considerable threat to the evacuation.[119] Because of its dive-bomb capability the Ju 88 could accurately bomb shipping and had been used to equip units of *Fliegerkorps* X, which specialized in coastal and anti-shipping operations.[120] In May 1940, however, Luftwaffe crews felt that, on the basis of their experiences, successful attacks against destroyers, which were fast-moving and agile, required the more manoeuvrable Ju 87 and were not suitable targets for the Ju 88. This impression was borne out by the relative results the two aircraft achieved against shipping during the first two years of the war (see Figure 1). The Ju 88 was also considered limited against more manoeuvrable vessels because it was not able to dive as low as the Ju 87, which could dive down to 500 feet.[121] Robert Eunson, a seaman aboard HMS *Unicity*, recalled that the Ju 87 was able to dive so low that 'you could hear the click as they dropped the bombs.'[122] The Ju 87, however, was extremely vulnerable. Charles Kingcombe, of 65 Squadron, recalled that 'it was the dream of every RAF pilot to find them'.[123] Similarly Gerald Edge, of 605 Squadron, recognized that 'it was very, very easy to shoot down'.[124] The

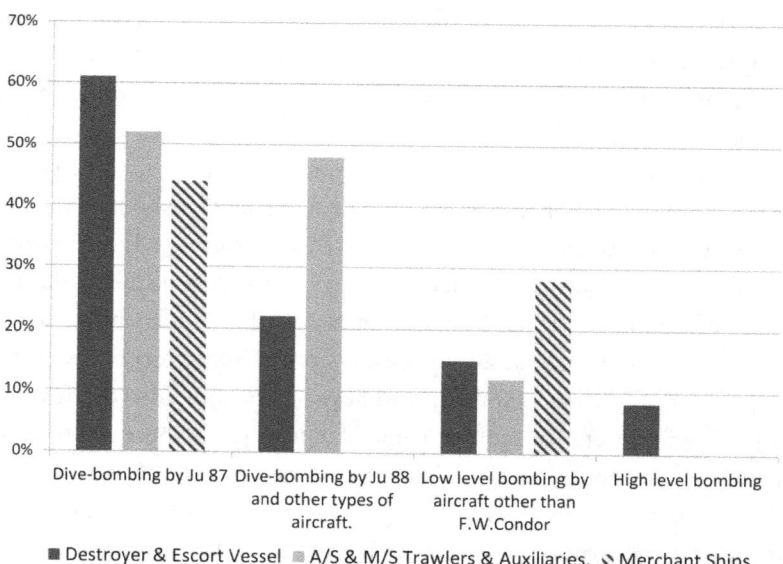

Figure 1 Comparison of various forms of air attack.[126]

Ju 88 provided a level of adaptability to both the weather conditions and the type of bombing operations the Luftwaffe faced at Dunkirk.[125] In considering the Luftwaffe's bombing it will be necessary to explore how effective different types of bombing attacks were at Dunkirk and the consequences this had on the Luftwaffe's attempts to halt the evacuation.

The inexperience and training of the two forces

Accounts of the air operations conducted by the Luftwaffe and RAF during 1940 have differed as to the advantage either side held with regard to training and experience. The Luftwaffe is often credited as holding an advantage in combat experience from previous operations in Poland and the Spanish Civil War; however, Geoffrey Stewart has taken the position that it is misleading 'to consider all the German pilots seasoned warriors'.[127] Criticism has also been made of the training German pilots received. Karl-Heinz Frieser has argued that on average Allied pilots were better trained than their German counterparts and David Isby has maintained that German fighter pilots were lacking in instrument flying skills which reduced their ability to operate when the weather was unfavourable.[128] Pilots in Fighter Command have presented a similar view and George Johns, of 229 Squadron, did not believe that Luftwaffe pilots 'were that much more experienced otherwise they'd have done a lot more damage'.[129] Despite such views, the general consensus regarding the RAF was that it was limited in its experience and at a disadvantage to the Luftwaffe's in regards to fighter tactics.[130] It is therefore important to assess the two forces' training and what impact it had on operations. It is also relevant to consider here the training that Bomber Command received both to contextualize the training of the Luftwaffe and to understand the Command's ability to conduct missions in support of Dynamo.

Flying training

From the outset of the Luftwaffe's expansion, training had been a priority. In August 1934, the Luftwaffe's armament programme had as a first phase a projected delivery of 3,021 aircraft – over half of which were to be used in training.[131] Generally efficient and well organized, the Luftwaffe's training programme delivered pilots to operational units with a greater number of hours undertaken in training, both in total flight time and in the aircraft they would fly, than was the case in the RAF at this time.[132] In 1939, German bomber and reconnaissance crews were usually posted to an operational unit having completed approximately 250 hours of flying, which typically lasted between eighteen and twenty-four months, whilst a fighter pilot could be trained roughly twice as fast and would have completed a total of some 200 hours flying training before being posted to an operational squadron where they would receive training on operational types which was often in the region of 100 hours.[133] In contrast Fighter Command pilots had to complete 200 hours of training with a further 60 to 75 hours completed on operational types, although the extent to which training on operational types was actually achieved varied.[134]

The main effort of operational units in the Luftwaffe from at least 1938 onwards, however, was directed towards war training with non-essential flight safety training set aside.[135] This had negative consequences for the overall training of these pilots and the training system itself had been weakened during this period. In 1936, shortly before the occupation of the Rhineland, a demand for an increase in the number of German fighter units was met by the simple expedient of disbanding the fighter training school at Schleissheim and organizing its instructors and better qualified advanced students into operational units.[136] Likewise the planned invasion of Czechoslovakia in 1938 saw instructors from the fighter school at Werneuchen staff a fighter group, the school being temporarily rendered useless for training.[137] These expedients to boost frontline strength had long-term effects on training, and in August 1938 the number of crews considered fully operational in the Luftwaffe was considerably lower than the authorized number (see Table 1).

The low level of fully operational crews must be placed in the context of the Luftwaffe's transition to more modern types, with more demanding performance levels; it does, however, indicate the strain on a system which needed to produce crews for new units, retrain existing personnel on new types, and produce an operational reserve to replace losses at the rate that would be incurred during hostilities. Bernd von Brauchitsch, at the time of Dunkirk a

Table 1 Number of authorized crews compared to number considered fully operational in the Luftwaffe, August 1938.[138]

	Bombers	Dive-Bombers	Fighters
Authorized crews	1,409	300	938
Crews considered fully operational	378	80	537

captain commanding a dive-bomber *Gruppe* and later chief-adjutant to Göring, reviewed the Luftwaffe's training in the following terms:

> It may be said without hesitation that the standard of training at the outbreak of war was inadequate. The few years that were available for the creation of the Luftwaffe did not suffice for training to reach a high average level. The efficiency of formations was repeatedly reduced by the creation of new units, thereby entailing a constant weakening of the standard of a unit each time its efficiency had been restored … These deficiencies were particularly prominent in fighter and bomber formations, while a more stable situation existed in the dive-bomber arm.[139]

At the outset of the war the Luftwaffe had to step up the pace of training as it had not built up a sufficient reserve of personnel whilst meeting the frontline needs of its rapid pre-war expansion.[140] By May 1940, Luftwaffe pilots were complaining about the 'ludicrously quick period of training'.[141] Certain Luftwaffe fighter units which operated during Dynamo were kept out of combat with Fighter Command's patrols unless they possessed an advantage, such as height, and outnumbered the enemy.[142] Shortcomings in the Luftwaffe's training programme therefore had direct consequences on its fighters operations during Dynamo.

Before 1935, the RAF was largely occupied with training. Flying Training Schools (FTS) provided the individual RAF pilot with the means to fly and a brief introduction to the military aspects of flying. The individual service training, however, was done almost wholly in the pilot's operational unit with the consequence that almost every operational unit was effectively turned into a small-scale training establishment. As pre-war expansion increased the RAF turned to civil aviation schools to help close the gap created by a shortage of trained instructors and suitable training aircraft.[143] The new training scheme, which was in force from 1936, included elementary flying training at a civil school and two stages of flying training at an RAF FTS. The first stage was intermediate training and was intended to teach pupils cross-country flying, flying in low visibility and night flying up to the stage of being able to make a solo landing at night. The second stage was advanced training for service work which was intended to include work in bombing and air gunnery as well as further instruction and experience in air navigation and map reading. From 1936 onwards the RAF's training offered the pupil less general service training but improved the pupil's skills for their individual flying role.[144] As the pace of expansion increased, the RAF's training began to move further towards quantity but given the shortage of trained instructors – a problem which was solved only by the expedient of training a proportion of new entrants as instructors – this was at the expense of the quality of the training provided.[145] Operational training in Bomber Command was handicapped during the early period of expansion because of the need to provide individual training to newly qualified pilots. This was particularly the case in the medium bomber squadrons; a November 1936 Bomber Command staff paper on training reached the assessment that in these squadrons 'operational training is practically non-existent owing to the prior needs of the new pilots ex-FTS'.[146] At the time of the Munich Crisis fewer than 50 per cent of the crews of Bomber Command's mobilizable squadrons would be fit for operations as judged by Bomber Command's peacetime standards.[147] Fighter Command's pilot situation was made difficult during this period because of the conversion to modern monoplanes whose higher performances also impaired the RAF's reserve position with only 200 reserve pilots fit to go into service.[148] To counter the difficulties of training pilots on modern fighter aircraft, Operational Training Units (OTUs) had been established in Spring 1939. The resources required for OTUs were, however, also needed to expand the number of operational squadrons. Expanding Fighter Command came at the cost of further improving the training establishment.[149] The situation regarding the training of personnel, particularly on operational types, was no better in Coastal Command, and Air Vice-Marshal Arthur Capel, then Director of Operational Training, remembered that 'Coastal Command, at the beginning of the war, had no real training organisation behind it, and in this respect was like Fighter Command.'[150]

The pre-war training programmes of both air forces managed to provide the pilots needed for both forces' rapid expansion. This accomplishment, however, was achieved by effectively using frontline squadrons as part of the training programme and came at the expense of building up a sizable reserve of pilots. Furthermore, both sides had deficiencies in their training schools and had dramatically increased the ratio of pupils to instructors which further diluted training standards and the creation of a reserve of pilots once the war had commenced.[151]

One expedient the Luftwaffe employed to build up a reserve of fighter pilots before the start of the offensive in France was to graduate pupils from the Advanced Fighter School after a comparatively short period of time and, by the end of May 1940, captured German fighter pilots observed that the advanced training of replacement personnel had in some cases decreased.[152] As Dynamo commenced on 26 May both sides had already sustained significant losses to their frontline strength and were utilizing pilots and aircrews from their reserves that lacked the experience of the men they replaced, and had typically not reached the same standards.[153]

During Dynamo it was noted in Bomber Command that the standard of formation flying in certain squadrons was 'not satisfactory', due to the presence of inexperienced pilots who had replaced personnel who had been lost on earlier operations, and that this had negative consequences for bombing operations.[154] The complaints of Luftwaffe bomber units echoed those voiced by Bomber Command; shortly before Dynamo commenced complaints regarding the critical shortage in reserve bomber crews became more frequent and caused significant apprehension in the Luftwaffe.[155] The limited number of reserve pilots was also a concern for the Luftwaffe.[156] The Luftwaffe had entered the war with an average personnel lag of 10 per cent in its bomber units, 12 per cent in its twin engine fighter units and 17 per cent in single engine fighter units. By January 1940 the lack of trained aircrews in reserve trained on the recently introduced Ju 88 was a particular problem.[157] The Luftwaffe fighters were also affected by combat losses – with a number of *außer Dienst* [retired] reserve officers recalled to service with JG 53 and ZG 2 by 30 May – it was, however, the RAF who experienced the most anxiety regarding their reserve of trained aircrew.[158]

The RAF's main concern lay not in its reserve of machines, for which it knew output was steadily increasing, but in the deficiency of trained pilots.[159] The conclusion of 43 Squadron, Fighter Command, was that the air battles in May had 'been remarkable for the steady drain of good pilots which have not been replaced' with the result that '43 Squadron cannot be considered to possess the same destructive possibility as when the month opened'.[160] At the outbreak of war the RAF Reserve, consisting of ex-service personnel, numbered fewer than 1,500 pilots, with 30 per cent unavailable for immediate mobilization because of their civilian occupations. The formation of the RAF Volunteer Reserve provided a further pool of pilots who, whilst not ready for immediate service, provided the RAF with an additional source of personnel. In August 1938, the strength of the RAF Volunteer Reserve stood at 1,870 pilots, of whom approximately half were qualified to fly solo on service aircraft. By 1 May 1939, the strength of the RAF Volunteer Reserve had almost doubled to 3,604 pilots, as well as 744 observers and 315 wireless operator air gunners.[161] The breathing space of the 'Phoney War' allowed the RAF to improve the training of these pilots.[162] The build-up of a reserve of personnel qualified on modern service types was, however, slow.[163] Concern within the RAF over the shortage of operationally ready pilots was a critical part in Dowding's decision to limit the squadrons of Fighter Command exposed to combat during Dynamo.[164] Only through understanding that the RAF training system had not produced a sufficient surplus of pilots to comfortably replace its losses is it possible to understand the context behind the strategy Dowding pursued during Dynamo.

Combat tactics and training

The formations and method of attack developed by Fighter Command left it at a distinct disadvantage during Operation Dynamo. The tactics developed by Fighter Command before the Second World War were based on the belief that they would largely be attacking unescorted German bombers. David Cox, of 19 Squadron, described the training in Fighter Command as 'out of date; the Air Ministry had never envisaged bombers coming with a fighter escort'.[165] Fighter Command's training dictated a series of rigid Fighter Area Attack patterns. The Fighting Area Attacks were complex, with six standard attacks each with variations intended to cover all eventualities – but derived in such detail that each attack variation was for a specific circumstance. The Fighter Area Attacks were developed between their original conception, in 1936, and use, in 1940, but the six standard attacks can be considered as taking the following form: Fighter Attack No. 1 – Section (three aircraft) of fighters attack in line astern against a single enemy bomber. Fighter Attack No. 2 – Section of fighters attack, in sequence, from directly below a single enemy bomber. Fighter Attack No. 3 – Section of fighters attacks in Vic formation from dead astern of an enemy bomber formation. Fighter Attack No. 4 – A section of fighters attacks a formation of bombers from below (similar in execution to Fighter Attack No. 2). Fighter Attack No. 5 – Section of fighters moves into line abreast, to attack in unison a large formation of bombers by targeting a smaller number of the enemy on the flank, before breaking away and reforming the Vic. Fighter Attack No. 6 – conducted with a whole squadron of fighters attacking nine bombers by a process of sections deploying in line astern, then subsequently altering the direction of flight by 90° to bring the squadron in dead astern before being deployed into line abreast for the attack.[166] These attack patterns required the unit to maintain a tight formation and, designed for use against unescorted bombers, these attack patterns proved unrealistic in combat conditions.[167] During Dynamo many Fighter Command squadrons flew in tight Vic formation, which limited the freedom of observation of most of the pilots as everyone apart from the leader of the Vic concentrated on their alignment. As well as requiring restrictive formation flying simply knowing which attack pattern and variation to apply required detailed knowledge whilst the time required to manoeuvre and engage in a pre-determined attack pattern left the formation vulnerable to attack from enemy fighter escorts.[168] Training for fighter-on-fighter combat was minimal and the majority of practice interceptions were formation attacks on bombers.[169]

The lack of dog fighting training and the combat inexperience in Fighter Command often caused their patrols over Dunkirk to become drawn into unprofitable battles or lured into air traps. Gerald Edge recalled 605 Squadron 'engaged a sole enemy aircraft [during Dynamo] and got split up and then six Me 109s started chasing me'.[170] Even when Fighter Command squadrons found themselves with the advantage of height during Dynamo they failed to utilize it the fullest extent possible. Fighter Command's squadrons did not attempt to break up enemy formations by using 'dive and zoom' tactics, where the aircraft dived down to attack and then used the speed gained in the dive to regain their initial position from which they could either engage the target again or threaten another target.[171] Instead, in instances where squadrons found they were above enemy formations, they typically dived down, attacked and then remained on the same level as they sought to engage the enemy in prolonged dog fights. The poor combat tactics of the RAF often reduced their ability to break up enemy formations even when they possessed superior numbers. Paul Temme records 'a vicious free-for-all' developed when eight Me 109s of *Jagdgeschwader* 2 were engaged by twenty Spitfires as they covered a Stuka attack on 26 May but, despite repeated attempts to break the Me 109 cover and reach the Stukas, the Spitfires were kept well at bay.[172] These failings in combat tactics were directly attributable to the pre-war training of Fighter Command. As will be seen when discussing Fighter Command's patrols in Chapter 7 one of the handicaps to providing effective air cover over Dunkirk was the willingness of fighter squadron to break formation when attacking German aircraft. This resulted in air patrols either being fragmented, or more commonly ended, even after small combats, with British fighters often having to return to base, to refuel and rearm, leaving no further air cover over the evacuation.

Geoffrey Page, of 56 Squadron, recalled that 'later on in the war we copied the German tactics ... they were ahead of us in the way they flew their fighter formations'.[173] The Luftwaffe had developed and honed their formation patterns during the Spanish Civil War and they were far more effective at allowing observation and providing cover for all the aircraft in the formation than the more rigid RAF flight formations. The Luftwaffe basic air unit was two aircraft, the *Rotte*, operating in a formation of four, the *Schwarm*. When operating as a *Staffel* (the equivalent of the RAF squadron), the *Schwarm* which comprised the *Staffel* would be stepped at different altitudes.¹⁷⁴ By flying in this formation each aircraft was able to scan the sky for enemy aircraft as well as help ensure the mutual protection of the formation. By spacing the aircraft of the formation further apart, as opposed to the close Vic employed by Fighter Command, greater speeds could also be maintained and the manoeuvrability of the aircraft maximized.

The Luftwaffe's experience of aerial combat in the Spanish Civil War provided the crucible in which tactics and formations could be perfected. Although the combat experiences provided by the Spanish Civil War were gained by a limited number of personnel, they were incorporated into the Luftwaffe's fighter training with members of the Condor Legion often serving as training instructors on their return to Germany.¹⁷⁵ In this way the lessons learnt in the Spanish Civil War were disseminated across the force. Walter Krupinski, who underwent basic training in 1940 before serving in JG 52, argued that the benefit of the Spanish Civil War 'was not the experience of these pilots in the group', rather it was that the lessons which had been had 'learnt were brought into the units and even into the schools, the fighter schools'.¹⁷⁶ The Polish campaign provided further experience of combat for some of the Luftwaffe's fighter pilots. These experiences benefitted the Luftwaffe and gave it an advantage over Fighter Command. Fighter pilots in the Luftwaffe had typically gained combat experience – or had been trained by a pilot who had combat experience – or were led by officers who had seen combat.

The shortcomings in Fighter Command's tactical training were worsened by the lack of experienced combat leaders in the force. Fighter Command's squadrons fought Dynamo whilst being led by officers with little, or no, combat experience. In the Luftwaffe, it was recognized as a general rule that only 'young men' who were adaptable and capable of withstanding the strains of modern air war could be of real use in building up a successful fighter arm.¹⁷⁷ By contrast, Fighter Command retained pilots and squadron leaders trained in the biplane era on types incapable of the speed and performance of either the Hurricane or Spitfire, for which new air tactics were required. David Isby has argued that 'many experienced pilots lacked air combat and gunnery skills or the aggressive instinct of a successful fighter pilot' as 'the pre-war RAF had not inculcated these'.¹⁷⁸ One of the consequence of being poorly led over the evacuation is that squadrons often struggled to intercept the enemy. Hugh Dundas, of 616 Squadron, recalled that a little under half the time his squadron operated over Dunkirk they did not engage the Luftwaffe in part because of the squadron's inexperience but also because they were poorly led.¹⁷⁹

I dare say that if we had had a more experienced leader things would have seemed – and probably would have been – different. But my chief memory and impression of the Dunkirk patrols is of their nightmarish quality. We seldom seemed, some-how, to be in the right place at the right time … Often we were engaged in a short, sharp action, usually resulting in the squadron becoming split up into sections or individual aircraft. On other occasions we returned to Rochford without having fired our guns.[180]

Inexperienced leadership increased Fighter Command's losses during the battle. John Bidsee recalled that 609 Squadron had 'very, very bad losses at Dunkirk. We lost about half the squadron largely because we had a commanding officer who, frankly, was not up to it'.[181] The commanding officer of 19 Squadron was shot down the first time he led the squadron in action. David Cox recalled that the commanding officer's inexperience also led to a number of losses after:

he made a stupid error of climbing at about 140 miles an hour into a formation of German bombers with the escort Me 109s sitting above. The result was the squadron lost about three or four. … He was actually an ex-Flying School instructor, who were brilliant pilots but being a brilliant pilot doesn't make you a good fighter pilot.[182]

The inexperience of Fighter Command's squadron leaders reduced the overall military effectiveness of Fighter Command's efforts during Dunkirk and results in a greater number of casualties than might otherwise have been the case.

The standardized formations and attack patterns of Fighter Command also dictated gun harmonization – the point at which the bullets from all the guns converged. The typical harmonization employed during Dynamo gave a large pattern of bullets, known as the 'Dowding spread', at a range of some 400 yards because it was felt that an average pilot would achieve a greater number of hits at this range with this widespread pattern.[183] On the basis of experience in France, however, a number of squadrons had their guns harmonized to give a tighter spread intended for use at a range of 250 yards.[184] The belief that machine-guns should be harmonized to give a large 'shot-gun' pattern was important, however, because it led to too little attention being devoted to gunnery instruction and, as a consequence, the average standard of shooting in Fighter Command was low.[185] Anthony Cummings has argued that the RAF 'could not produce enough well-trained graduates able to fly their aircraft well and to shoot straight' and that there was a 'complete inadequacy of gunnery training in 1940'.[186] The experience, or lack of it, that Gerald Edge had in air gunnery prior to combat demonstrates the inexperience in Fighter Command at this time:

We had not the faintest idea what would happen when we pressed the button and fired the rounds, we asked and asked but never got permission. When we did get permission to fire 100 rounds we got quite a rocket back from Group. They said they meant 100 rounds [in total] not 100 rounds a gun! ... We had not had any practice and I was the only one to fire 100 rounds in our squadron for quite a long time.[187]

The air firing exercise Richard Hillary experienced involved being 'given a few rounds in each gun and sent off to fire them into the Severn'.[188] George Johns, of 229 Squadron, recalled that he had 'never been trained really in deflection shooting' and that the secret for most combat victories at the time was that the pilot 'got in so close they couldn't miss'.[189] The low standard of gunnery inevitably hindered Fighter Command's attempts to shoot down bombers and break up formations over Dunkirk. Norman Hancock, of 1 Squadron, remembered being 'highly inexperienced' and that 'the He 111 which I had the temerity to attack was a damn site better shot than I was'.[190] Cyril Bamberger, of 610 Squadron, recalled that when he was posted to the squadron he 'didn't know anything about combat ... [or] anything about shooting'.[191] Bamberger also noted that across Fighter Command this inexperience manifested itself in a tendency to open fire on enemy aircraft before they were in range. The shortcomings of Fighter Command's pilot's gunnery skills reduced their opportunity for air victories and lowered the results they were able to achieve over Dunkirk.[192]

The gunnery training of the German fighter arm could also produce pilots whose skills fell short of the ideal, particularly after the war began. Krupinski started training in 1939 and studied gunnery skills but entered service 'suffering from bad shooting'.[193] The lack of advanced gunnery training – during Krupinski's weapon training he only fired once on a ground target and he did not fire on an air target at all – resulted in pilots struggling to achieve victories until they had gained experience in combat.[194] Weapons training received greater emphasis shortly before the Second World War and Werner Kreipe, Luftwaffe General Chief of Staff from 1942 to 1944, considered that at that time 'the guidance of the student's aggressiveness into the proper channels and the insistence upon the perfect mastery of gunnery techniques were two of the most vitally important aspects of a fighter pilot's training'.[195] Nevertheless, as with similar shortcomings in Fighter Command, the military effectiveness of the fighters over Dunkirk was reduced by pilots who were inexperienced in firing on air targets.

A criticism of the Luftwaffe which frequently emerges in the historiography of the Battle of Britain was the inability of their fighters to adequately escort, and protect, their bomber force.[196] Raymond Proctor has asserted that lessons from the Spanish Civil War were erroneously learnt regarding the need for fighter escorts, with fighters turned loose on free-hunts, and that from '1938 until well into the Battle of Britain this erroneous thinking about [free-hunts] was dominant in the minds of the Luftwaffe planners, so much so that there was practically no training between bomber and fighter pilots'.[197] Bernd von Brauchitsch has similarly argued that 'it was evident that training in operational collaboration was not adequate, the result being that bomber and fighter Geschwader approached the target as separate formations and frequently did not succeed in assembling over the target area'.[198] It is notable, however, that units such as JG 2 who operated in escort roles more frequently were able to provide such cover for bombers effectively at Dunkirk. British Air Intelligence concluded during Dynamo that 'the tactics of escort fighters accompanying short-range bombers by day have obviously been well practiced ... Escorting fighters stick to their task and do not get drawn off into dog fights when attacked by British fighters'.[199] Galland has asserted that one of the difficulties in escorting the bombers during Dynamo was that the bombers did not usually rendezvous with their fighter escort at the appointed time and that German fighters often had to withdraw from the combat area just as the bombers arrived.[200] This suggests that the problem the Luftwaffe faced in providing escorts at Dunkirk was perhaps not one of insufficient training or preparation in fighter escorts but rather relates to the previously discussed issue of their lack of 'loiter-time' over the evacuation. In considering the role of the German fighters at Dunkirk in Chapter 7 it is necessary to consider how successful they were in protecting bomber formations both by escorting the bombers directly and in conducting fighter sweeps. In considering Fighter Command's operations during Dynamo it is necessary to examine the extent to which the methods employed by the Luftwaffe's fighters forced Fighter Command to alter its own tactics and what effect this had on the British air cover of the evacuation.

The interwar training programme of the Luftwaffe produced a generation of flyers who, whilst being well led and fully versed in the more advanced fighter tactics the Luftwaffe had developed, individually were no more skilled in flying technique than their individual rivals in the RAF.[201] The RAF's pilots were not, however, as well trained or experienced in air combat techniques and tactics as the majority of those in the Luftwaffe. Despite this, the difference was not so great that it represented an overwhelming advantage for the German pilots. There was also a sizeable minority of the Luftwaffe's pilots whose training was not as advanced as has often been considered to have been the case because, in the rapid pre-war expansion and the drive to produce operational crews between the start of the war and May 1940, training fell short of producing a cadre of personnel trained to a universally high standard.[202] In the same way as the advantages of the superior Luftwaffe training should not be overstated, claims regarding deficiencies must be restrained. The Luftwaffe used operational squadrons to supplement the training of pilots before the launch of Fall Gelb and these squadrons went into a frenzy of training in the spring of 1940 ahead of their offensive in May. Furthermore, by the end of Dynamo the RAF had rotated inexperienced squadrons into the battle who were below the level of training Fighter Command would have wished them to have attained before first experiencing combat. Although the individual flying training of pilots in the Luftwaffe did not exceed that of Fighter Command, their pilots did hold an advantage in air combat skills. The Luftwaffe's air formations, combat tactics and the experience of its flight leaders were also superior to those of Fighter Command. These factors influenced the military effectiveness of the two sides' fighter operations over the Dunkirk evacuation.

Instrument and navigation training in the two forces

The weather conditions during Dynamo were often unfavourable, with poor visibility and low cloud cover. These conditions represented a challenge for both the RAF and the Luftwaffe to maintain the intensity of their operations and achieve their respective objectives. The Luftwaffe also faced the additional challenge of having to navigate to Dunkirk across unfamiliar territory. The capacity of the Luftwaffe to conduct this navigation, particularly in poor weather, was an important aspect behind the number of missions they were able to undertake during Dynamo most notably for their medium bomber force. It is also an important point to establish because, had the Luftwaffe succeeded in halting daylight evacuations at the outset of Dynamo, the Royal Navy would have continued to embark men from Dunkirk by night. To establish the Luftwaffe's capability to halt a night evacuation it is important to consider their bomber crews' ability to navigate to Dunkirk outside daylight hours. Bomber Command also operated at night and it is necessary to consider whether the targets they attacked were dictated by limitations to their night-time navigational abilities.

Instrument training in the fighter arms of the RAF and Luftwaffe

Instrumental flying in unfavourable conditions was required by Fighter Command during Dynamo to ensure they were able to provide air cover for the evacuation and for squadrons to maintain formation on patrol. During the pre-war period, great efforts were made to improve instrumental flying. Pilots were instructed on the use of instruments at FTS and Fighter Command's types were equipped with a panel of instruments which included an artificial horizon, directional gyro and a Turn and Slip indicator.[203] Training in this regard, however, still left a great deal to be desired. The consequences of errors made in training were often fatal. Richard Hillary's experiences at FTS shortly after the war had begun reveal the deficiencies that had been produced by the RAF's rapid expansion, with pilots learning the skills of blind-flying as much through trial and error as through a formulated training programme. Hillary recalled that he would:

> never forget the first time I flew really high, and looking down, saw wave after wave of white undulating clouds that stretched for miles in every direction ... Soon I could see nothing and had to rely solely on my instruments. I did a slow roll. This was extremely stupid ... My speed fell off alarmingly. I pushed the stick forward: the speed fell still further and I nearly went into a spin. I could not tell whether I was on my back or right way up, and felt very unhappy. I lost about 2000 feet and came out of the cloud in a screaming spiral, but still fortunately a long way above the earth. I straightened up and flew home with another lesson hard learned.[204]

Hillary survived his 'moment of blind panic' but during his subsequent night training a fellow pupil lost his life in a similar incident.[205] It is fair to conclude, however, that, despite limitations in the navigation standards Fighter Command's pilots faced few problems because operating from Britain, navigation to France and back was straightforward and, with the oil tanks at Dunkirk having been set ablaze, the towering smoke columns from the port allowed an easy point of reckoning.

The Luftwaffe's training has been criticized for largely failing to prepare German air crews for operation in unfavourable weather conditions; indeed the deficiencies in training were such that the Luftwaffe was primarily a fair weather force in 1940.[206] This is directly relevant to the ability of the Luftwaffe to halt the evacuation of Dunkirk. During Dynamo, the Luftwaffe's attempts to impede the evacuation were greatly handicapped by the low visibility and weather conditions. Pre-war fighter training in the Luftwaffe was not intensively focused on instrumental training or the skills necessary for blind-flying. The training programme of the *Jagdschule* (Fighter School) contained aerial combat practice under varying cloud conditions. Aspects of specialized training required for flying in difficult weather conditions suffered, however, because of the need to produce pilots for operational units.[207] During Dynamo the Luftwaffe's efforts to provide fighter cover to their bombers were frustrated in unfavourable condition by the difficulties pilots had navigating to the rendezvous point.[208] The Me 109 itself lacked a blind-flying panel and although an altimeter was provided the absence of an artificial horizon was to the detriment of its pilot's ability to operate in heavy cloud cover.[209] Although the smoke columns over Dunkirk aided the Luftwaffe in identifying the evacuation the return flights to unfamiliar advanced bases could prove problematic in unfavourable conditions and instances of Me 109 losses during Dynamo can be attributed to low standards of navigation. A number of JG 52's Me 109s had to be written off following emergency landings in Belgium after pilots had become lost in bad weather on their return from operations over the evacuation.[210] One must also question whether units who were not confident in their navigational abilities left the combat zone earlier than might otherwise have been necessary in order to ensure they had sufficient fuel to compensate for errors in navigations that might be made during return to operational airfields. Pilots of the Me 110 received more thorough training in instrument flying and navigation.[211] Despite the enhanced instrumental training of the Me 110 pilots, however, their operations were still restricted during Dynamo by bad weather conditions at their air bases and when unfavourable conditions prevailed on the flight routes to Dunkirk.[212] In the difficult weather conditions which prevailed over North France and the Low Countries for much of Dynamo, the deficiencies in instrumental training and navigation skills in the Luftwaffe's fighter force reduced the operations they were able to fly over Dunkirk. Most significantly it impeded the timely rendezvous with bomber formations reducing the escort cover these could be provided.

Instrument training in the bomber arm of the Luftwaffe

German aviation development in the interwar period, particularly the experience gained in long-distance flying, navigation and instrumental flying within the German civil aviation sphere, led to the integration of all-weather blind-flying training schools (*Blindflugschulen*) into the Luftwaffe training programme.²¹³ The Luftwaffe's experience in Spain has also been credited with aiding the development of the skills required for night and bad weather flying. James Corum has argued that this experience left the Luftwaffe 'better trained in the fundamental navigation and flying skills required for strategic bombing' which meant that at the outset of the Second World War it was the only force in Europe that 'was even moderately competent at night flying and bad weather navigation'.²¹⁴ Williamson Murray has also noted that during bombing missions in Spain the Luftwaffe discovered the difficulties in finding and hitting targets at night which convinced them of the necessity for navigational aids for bad weather and night operations.²¹⁵ Murray, however, questions the extent of achievements in this direction observing that in 1939 'Kesselring admitted that even given a high level of technical competence, he doubted whether the average bomber crew could hit their target with any degree of accuracy at night or in bad weather'.²¹⁶ Although by September 1939 there were five *Blindflugschulen*, and instrumental training for bomber pilots had grown in prominence, the skills required for night flying were often underdeveloped.²¹⁷ Every bomber pilot went through a blind-flying course lasting three-and-a-half weeks; the pressure to deliver pilots to meet the need of the Luftwaffe's rapid pre-war expansion, however, resulted in some pilots and crews being rushed through courses in order to send them to operational units, undermining a training syllabus which was, in theory, comprehensive.²¹⁸ Blind-flying training was particularly susceptible to being curtailed to boost the number of pilots sent to operational units as it was part of the most expensive, longest and complicated aspects of the German training programme.²¹⁹ Navigational training over the North Sea was undertaken by some operational Luftwaffe units in an effort to develop general navigation, instrumental flying and navigation over the sea without fixed landmarks.²²⁰ Efforts to improve the standard of navigational training at operational units were, however, limited because of a focus on essential combat skills.²²¹

The Luftwaffe's bombers were equipped with the necessary instruments for blind-flying.²²² Given the average standard of instrumental flying in the Luftwaffe's bomber force at this time unfavourable conditions during the improvised operations conducted against Dunkirk therefore had a pronounced effect. The weather at their bases could impede operations because it prevented safe take-offs, or landings on return. The weather at Dunkirk could prevent bombing and the route-weather could handicap navigation and restrict operations.²²³ Flying over unfamiliar territory in poor weather conditions, which could prevent observation of visual landmarks on the ground, the difficulties of navigation were magnified by a lack of known landmarks, routes and railways (a method known as Bradshawing in Bomber Command). The navigation skills of the Luftwaffe's bomber force were therefore an important aspect of their ability to effectively attack the evacuations from Dunkirk during days where unfavourable weather conditions prevailed.

The limitations of the instrumental and navigational training of certain units in the Luftwaffe's bomber force are well illustrated by a bombing attack made on 10 May 1940. Three He 111s of a larger formation of III./KG 51 lost their bearings whilst blind-flying in bad weather on a mission to attack Dijon. The aircraft dropped below the heavy cloud cover when flight time calculations suggested the aircraft should have reached Dijon and the inexperienced lieutenant leading the formation mistakenly identified the German town of Freiburg as a French city and dropped their bombs before returning to land at Landsberg.[224] During the Battle of Britain, on 27 September 1940, a lack of instrument training in I. and II./KG 77 led to the bomber formations being broken up when flying through thick cloud and the delay in reforming and rendezvousing with their fighter escort led to disastrous losses.[225]

The issue of navigation and blind-flying is also important in the context of Dynamo because if the Luftwaffe had successfully halted daylight evacuation before 1 June they may have had to operate against Dunkirk at night. The Luftwaffe had practised night attacks during pre-war exercises and was able to conduct night attacks in support of tactical objectives.[226] The relative failure to inflict losses on the evacuation fleet, or even significantly disrupt the evacuation, at night will be discussed in Chapter 4. It should, however, be cautioned that the Luftwaffe was conducting large-scale attacks by day and therefore the resources to conduct night attacks were limited. Had daylight evacuations been halted earlier, and the need for large-scale night operations arisen, it is possible that better results against the evacuation could have been achieved. Having halted daylight evacuations on 1 June, strong air attacks were to be carried out by *Fliegerkorps* IV from dark on 1 June until after dawn on 2 June, their mass attacks being aimed against the port installations of Dunkirk and the inland approaches leading to these points.[227] The port installations were to be targeted from 21.00 on 1 June until 02.00 on 2 June, with the night attacks then conducted on ground targets south-east of Dunkirk until 05.00.[228] The Luftwaffe support of ground forces on the Dunkirk perimeter on the night of 1–2 June was consistent with their objectives throughout Dunkirk. Pre-war training and large-scale exercises underpinned the efficiency achieved between air and ground forces and co-operation between reconnaissance and bomber units in identifying and attacking particular objectives, such as rail targets.[229] Heavy bombing of positions on the perimeter in close proximity to the German Army would, however, have been difficult and these operations were conducted towards dawn to aid the accuracy of the strikes. Accurately attacking shipping by night was not, however, something the Luftwaffe had prepared for and it did not possess the capacity to carry out large-scale sustained night flying operations. Sustained and effective bombing of the evacuation at night would therefore have been difficult had the Luftwaffe succeeded in halting evacuations earlier.[230] If large-scale night attacks had been made against shipping in Dunkirk harbour they would have been aided by the burning fuel tanks in the port which silhouetted ships as well as providing a recognizable, and easily located, navigational feature.[231] Previous attacks on shipping by bomber formations had been directed to the target by a reconnaissance aircraft repeatedly transmitting a wireless signal for the bombers to home in on.[232] Returning to base would have posed a challenge for bomber crews but not one which would have precluded operations (as demonstrated by the attacks during the night of 1 June discussed above). Bases in Germany possessed the Lorenz blind-landing aid and aircraft operating from forward airfields could have had their sorties timed to reach these bases shortly after dawn, thus aiding landing.[233] During the Dunkirk evacuation these methods were not utilized because the need did not exist. Had the operational situation been different, however, the Luftwaffe may have been able to effectively bomb the evacuation port and, to some extent, target shipping at night.

Instrument training in Bomber and Coastal Command

The unfavourable weather conditions and low visibility also affected Bomber and Coastal Command during Dynamo. Furthermore, night-flying was required by both Commands during their operations in support of the evacuation. The RAF's instrumental training, however, left its pilots ill prepared for blind-flying or navigation at night.[234]

The RAF's training syllabus afforded night flying little attention prior to 1934. Indeed, the skills required for navigation, even by day, were accorded a low priority before 1935 and Frederick Richardson – who would retire from the RAF a Group Captain and authored AP1234 'Air Navigation' in 1941 – later described ignorance of navigation as 'endemic in the RAF' at this time.[235] By 1936 the situation had barely improved; night flying was often limited in training to a total of six hours flying – involving take-offs and landing after a circuit of the airfield – and one 30km flight flown from the airfield and back.[236] In comparison crews of Bomber Command were required to navigate a round trip of 1,400km on certain missions during Dynamo.[237] On 1 March 1937, Air Vice-Marshal Playfair, AOC 3 Group Bomber Command, wrote that only forty-four pilots, from the fourteen night flying squadrons in the Group, could be considered as competent to carry out operational exercises by day and night and that it had only been possible to reach this number by including pilots with as little as sixteen hours night flying experience.[238] The low priority afforded to night flying is well-illustrated by a memorandum from Bomber Command, drafted in July 1937, on the various tactical problems arising from the introduction of new medium bomber types which took the view that 'night flying should be treated as experimental'.[239] Although the description of night flying as 'experimental' was objected to by Air Commodore Sholto Douglas, then Director of Staff Duties, as 'inappropriate' and likely to lead to night flying being placed too low in the scale of importance, the situation in training hardly improved.[240] In 1938 FTS continued to do little more than 'ensure that every pilot has flown at night'.[241] As late as February 1939 the Bomber Command Training Regulations stated that 'there must be no tendency to assume that night flying training now given at FTS is necessarily sufficient to ensure that a newly joined pilot of an operational squadron is capable, without further instruction, of flying by night on the type with which the unit is equipped'.[242]

Training for bad weather flying was almost entirely impractical at the FTS because they were not equipped with wireless direction-finding aids to help pilots safely return if they became lost. The result was that all pilots had to remain below cloud level and in sight of the ground on cross-country flights whilst instrumental flying could only be practised under the hood (in which the cockpit would be covered by a hood and the trainee would fly dependent on their instruments alone).[243] A lack of wireless facilities in training aircraft meant pilots were not permitted to fly in clouds or in conditions of bad visibility and in March 1939 cross-country night flights were cancelled because of the risk involved.[244] These conditions greatly inhibited the ability of newly trained crews to operate as effective members of their squadrons with the result that operational squadrons were burdened with instructing newly trained personnel in instrumental and navigational flying whilst also attempting to improve their general flying skills.[245] The training of Coastal Command squadrons intended for long-distance reconnaissance had a greater focus on long-range navigation. The lack of equipment, particularly navigational aids, at service squadrons in both Bomber and Coastal Command, however, made it difficult to give newly trained pilots continued practice in bad weather flying or blind-flying.[246] At the end of 1937 Air Chief Marshal Edgar Ludlow-Hewitt, AOC-in-C Bomber Command, characterized his new command as 'unable to operate in anything but fair weather' and 'entirely unprepared for war' which meant that the British bomber force was 'judged from a war standard, practically useless'.[247] By the time of the German invasion of France the situation had only marginally improved. A more comprehensive navigational curriculum had been introduced, but the report of 4 Group, Bomber Command, cautioned that the training achieved in the flight schools was 'not what it purports to be on paper'.[248] By May 1940, OTUs had started producing crews trained to a 'satisfactory standard'.[249] Positive reports also began to be made during Dynamo regarding the 'high standard' of navigation and night flying.[250] Air Vice-Marshal Norman Bottomley, Senior Air Staff Officer Bomber Command Headquarters, cautioned, however, that although 'little trouble has been experienced in navigating to the area of the target' he had little optimism regarding the ability of Bomber Command crews to accurately strike targets at night and that:

> even the most experienced crews have found it extremely difficult to pin-point their position and find their allotted target … Some of the less experienced crews have little or no knowledge of map reading and consequently stand even less chance of finding their target.[251]

Despite Denis Richards championing the 'ambitious programmes of night training' at the outset of the war, Bomber Command was not capable of the accuracy necessary to undertake night operations against German positions in close proximity to Allied troops on the Dunkirk perimeter.[252] During Dynamo, 3 Group recorded that navigation 'to and from the Low Countries was almost entirely by dead reckoning with map reading over enemy territory'.[253] The use of dead reckoning and W/T loop bearings did not lead to highly accurate navigation results over enemy territory. The necessity of weaving to afford the gunners a better view, changes in wind direction and changes in speed all reduced the accuracy of navigation by dead reckoning, the effects of which were multiplied during long-range bombing missions.[254] Other navigational methods such as Astro-navigation could be used only by a small percentage of RAF crews and the necessary conditions for its use were rare during Dynamo. Accurate map reading was therefore an important requirement in the navigation to bombing targets but proved a constant limitation.[255] Weather conditions could also restrict Bomber Command's operations and on the night of 29–30 May four Vickers Wellington bombers were lost because of fog over their home bases.²⁵⁶ The British official history of the strategic air offensive against Germany concluded that, in 1939, 'Bomber Command was not trained or equipped … to find its target areas, let alone its targets, by night'.²⁵⁷ The situation was not aided by the navigation of bombers frequently being conducted by pilots rather than air observers (later classified specifically as navigators) who had been trained in, and were meant to hold primary responsibility for, aircraft navigation. The explanation for this lies, partly, in the initial low regard for the observer's role and the lack of importance generally attached to navigation at this time within the RAF. Undoubtedly, however, part of the problem lay in the observer's navigation training which, owing to a shortage of resources, was often insufficient and left pilots unwilling to delegate the navigational responsibility to them.²⁵⁸

The above factors all restricted the night operations in support of Dynamo. Nevertheless, the close proximity of targets in the German rear areas meant that Bomber Command was able find and strike a number of targets in support of the evacuation. The probability of accurately navigating to a target decreased, however, the further the target was from the crew's base of operations.²⁵⁹ The limitations in navigation were less serious for Coastal Command, because many were following patrol lines parallel to the coast. Coastal Command aircraft operating at any distance from the coast, particularly off the Hook of Holland, could be provided with direction-finding bearings by W/T.

The Luftwaffe's anti-shipping training and maritime aviation capabilities

The Luftwaffe's lack of training and equipment to undertake effective attacks against ships was a significant shortcoming during Dynamo. Over-water navigation and maritime air operations garnered little attention in the training syllabus at the main Luftwaffe training schools partly because aircrews of the *Seeluftstreitkräfte* (the German Naval Air Arm) were trained separately.²⁶⁰ Whilst the Luftwaffe's advanced officer training included some study of naval warfare it was limited, and ground operations received greater focus with such operations studied down to the battalion level.²⁶¹ The lack of attention regarding naval matters extended into the Luftwaffe's short training courses. During the winter of 1937–8 of nearly one hundred short training courses scheduled only four were dedicated to matters relating to naval aviation.²⁶² The absence of any real emphasis on naval aviation explains why, despite the excellent co-ordination it was able to achieve against ground targets and with units of the German Army, the Luftwaffe struggled when supporting naval operations.[263] The Luftwaffe's pre-war operational training had studied the problems presented in bombing naval facilities and harbours – and had included plans for strikes against Dunkirk and other Channel ports – it had not, however, prepared adequately for the challenges of striking naval targets at sea.[264] Despite this lack of training dive-bombers were able to inflict considerable losses on the evacuation fleet which, given the narrow confines of the harbour and the channels leading to it, were often restricted in their freedom of manoeuvre. The Luftwaffe's level-bombers enjoyed less success, however, and the lack of anti-shipping training proved a serious impediment to its attempts to halt the evacuation.

The Luftwaffe's lack of an air torpedo was a particular shortcoming in its anti-maritime capabilities. As Anthony Cummings has noted 'while dive-bombing was effective in good weather against smaller warships it was still less effective than torpedo bombing … [which] was a significant weakness in the Luftwaffe's capability'.[265] The torpedo in service was the ineffective F5 *Lufttorpedo* (LTF5) a 45cm diameter aerial torpedo which was over 5 metres long.[266] During trials in 1939 German air torpedoes showed a failure rate of 49 per cent and the LTF5 had a range of limitations.[267] Aerodynamic difficulties meant the torpedo suffered from poor flight stability when released from the aircraft and coupled with the LTF5's inadequate structural strength this necessitated a low level release at low speed.[268] The drive mechanism was also extremely sensitive with both ignition and steering being susceptible to technical failure.[269] There were also faults in the depth control and fusing of the torpedoes.[270] The Luftwaffe's experience with the LTF5's fusing pistols, which detonated the torpedo, was not entirely removed from the naval torpedo. So serious were the deficiencies in the German naval torpedo's pistol that Dönitz believed that never before 'in the history of war have men been sent against the enemy with such a useless weapon'.[271] German plans for air attacks on British naval targets and harbour facilities, prepared towards the end of 1939, had stressed the need for a better torpedo; however, no improvements were achieved.[272] The problems that the Luftwaffe encountered with the *Lufttorpedo* were, in part, a reflection of the difficulties the Luftwaffe and Kriegsmarine had in co-operating in the sphere of maritime air operations. Tensions between the Luftwaffe and Kriegsmarine, which largely stemmed from the former's desire to control all German air assets, restricted the sharing of research knowledge and limited the collaboration between the two services whilst the Kriegsmarine was developing the *Lufttorpedo*.[273] The capabilities of the LTF5 were so poor that during 1940 production was halted. The decision was later reversed but the halt of production is testimony to how negative the German experience of air torpedoes had been.[274] Attacking at low altitude, at a precise speed range and typically at a 90° angle to the target, was essential to undertake a successful horizontal torpedo attack. Errors in either altitude or speed would lead either to the torpedo exploding on contact with the water or plunging to too low a depth. The typical view the Luftwaffe held up to 1940 regarding aerial torpedoes was reflected in a statement made by Major Storp during a meeting regarding further air torpedo development: 'why should I drop a bomb into the water when I can just drop them onto the deck with dive-bombers?'[275] One of the significant factors effecting successful torpedo attacks by aircraft was, like dive-bombing, good visibility. In the case of torpedo attacks good visibility was necessary to determine and predict the course of a target. There were days at Dunkirk where low visibility would have made torpedo operations difficult. However, had the Luftwaffe possessed an effective torpedo capability it would have had greater flexibility to attack shipping during Dynamo.

The Luftwaffe also lacked the aircraft to conduct successful torpedo operations at Dunkirk. A considerable number of floatplanes capable of carrying torpedoes were available for coastal defence in Germany before the start of the war, but these were mostly obsolete.[276] He 111 aircraft had begun to be used to drop air torpedoes with elements of III./KG 26 starting to receive aircraft equipped with torpedo releasing gear at the start of 1940. The He 111s performance as a torpedo-bomber – with a torpedo which was largely inadequate – was, however, faltering and He 111s were not declared fully operational in this role until the end of 1940.[277] Fliegerkorps X had begun to receive the Ju 88 for its anti-maritime role but, despite Admiral Raeder pressing for the Naval Air Arm to be equipped with this type, it had to make do with relatively obsolete, low performance seaplanes.[278]

The failure to develop and train the aerial torpedo arm, along with the absence of even an adequate aerial torpedo, placed near-total reliance on the German dive-bombers and level-bombers.[279] Level-bombers were able to deliver a respectable bombload; however, the level-bombing of agile warships was seldom successful. As the height from which a ship was attacked increased the probability of achieving a hit on that ship decreased. Because attacks from higher altitudes increased the effect of errors in bomb aiming, with the distance from which the bomb fell from the target increasing in relation to the height of attack. Attacks from higher altitudes also increased the time available to ships to take effective evasive action and level-bomber crews needed to be trained in attacks on ships to accurately hit them.[280] When HMS *Vivacious* had her first experience of being bombed off Holland, shortly after the German invasion of the Low Countries, sub-lieutenant Gilhespy felt that the German He 111 bomber pilot 'was as scared as ourselves and dropped his bombs all well clear of us'.[281] The training in naval operations of anti-shipping units in *Fliegerkorps* X was more systematic and thorough than in the main body of the *Luftwaffe*.[282] The personnel of *Fliegerkorps* X were provided with special training in maritime operations which prepared them to a certain extent for operations against naval targets.[283] Bombers from *Fliegerkorps* X undertook a number of attacks on British ports during the early stages of the war with some success, and, during the invasions of Denmark and Norway, these units were able to inflict notable losses on British naval forces.[284] Units of Fliegerkorps X had not, however, been sufficiently trained in conditions of low cloud, poor visibility or high wind.[285] Furthermore, during Dynamo units trained in a maritime capacity represented a minority of the participating Luftwaffe units. Crews of KG 30 were involved in attacks on Dunkirk; however, other specialist anti-shipping units were not used against the evacuation and remained in action against Allied shipping off Norway and in the North Sea.[286] The majority of Luftwaffe units operating against the evacuation were largely untrained in the skills required to undertake effective attacks against naval targets. This was a serious limitation to the Luftwaffe's operations against the evacuation of Dunkirk.

Conclusion

The Luftwaffe possessed a numerical advantage over Fighter Command. Despite this, the Luftwaffe was not always able to maximize the effect of its numerical advantage because it was also supporting the German Army as it continued its campaign against French forces on the Somme. Furthermore, whilst some of the Luftwaffe's advanced airfields were as close to Dunkirk as the RAF's bases in South-East England not all of the Luftwaffe units had been advanced into close proximity of Dunkirk. Combined with the smaller fuel capacity of the Me 109 the Luftwaffe's fighters were at a disadvantage compared to those of Fighter Command in the time they could operate over Dunkirk. This reduced the effect of the Luftwaffe's numerical superiority although Fighter Command remained at a disadvantage because the Luftwaffe held the initiative. At various times during Dynamo the Luftwaffe was able to concentrate its forces over Dunkirk and overwhelm Fighter Command's air cover. The German Me 109E-3 was superior to the Hurricane and at least the equal of the Spitfire during Dynamo. The flying training that the average Luftwaffe pilot received did not give them an advantage over their RAF counterparts. The RAF did possess an effective and capably trained fighter force, although the Luftwaffe's superior combat experience and fighter formations were a considerable benefit. The leadership of the Luftwaffe's fighter units in combat was also markedly better than many of the squadrons of Fighter Command at this time. These factors influenced the contest for control of the air over Dunkirk but as will be seen in Chapter 7 they did not decisively determine how either side attempted to achieve this aspect of air power. The Luftwaffe's bomber force, however, was either vulnerable to air interception or ill-equipped to strike shipping – a factor worsened by the lack of training in anti-shipping attacks. Attacks on enemy harbour facilities had received attention pre-war; the Luftwaffe was, however, ill prepared for maritime operations of the nature encountered during the Dunkirk evacuation. Both Bomber and Coastal Command squadrons had received sufficient training to undertake operations which did not require long-distance navigation by night. This was sufficient to allow Coastal Command to effectively discharge its various responsibilities during Dynamo. Bomber Command was, however, restricted in its ability to accurately find and attack specific targets which required any long-distance navigation.

Notes

1. Cecil 'Boy' Bouchier, *Spitfires in Japan: From Farnborough to the Far East – A Memoir* (Folkestone: Global Oriental, 2005), p. 192.
2. Sholto Douglas, 'Fighter Command', *Flying and Popular Aviation*, Vol. 31, No. 3, (1942), p. 65.
3. Barker, *Dunkirk*, p. 73; Buckley, *Air Power*, p. 130; Butler and Bradford, *Dunkirk*, pp. 132–9; Chatterton, *Epic*, p. 21; Harris, *Dunkirk*, p. 54; Killen, *Luftwaffe*, p. 116; Richards, *Fight*, p. 135; Terraine, *Right of the Line*, p. 154; Thompson, *Dunkirk*, p. 228; Williams, *Ides*, p. 260.
4. TNA: AIR 16/352 – 11 Group Report, Operations over France during May–June 1940, 8 July 1940; Basil Collier, *A History of Air Power* (London: Weidenfeld and Nicolson, 1974), pp. 157–8.
5. TNA: AIR 20/7703 – AHB, Statistics of German Aircraft Losses for period September 1939–December 1940, Compiled from Captured records of the Quartermaster General's Department of the German Air Ministry; TNA: AIR 22/71 – Directorate of Air Intelligence, Air Ministry Weekly Intelligence Summary, No. 39, 30 May 1940; TNA: AIR 22/168 – A.M.W.R. Daily Report for Summary, No.

311, 25 May 1940; Prien, *Jagdfliegerverbände*, p. 66; Collier, *History of Air Power*, pp. 157–8.
6   TNA: AIR 22/107 – Air Ministry Daily Telegraphic Intelligence Summaries, 8 June 1940.
7   TNA: AIR 20/7703 – AHB, Statistics of German Aircraft Losses for period September 1939–December 1940, Compiled from Captured records of the Quartermaster General's Department of the German Air Ministry; TNA: AIR 40/1270 – Frontline Strength of the German Air Force at 3 monthly periods during the European War, 1939–1945, A.I.3 (b) (Compiled from Official German Records), October 1945.
8   Kesselring cited in Harman, *Dunkirk*, p. 30; Hooton, *Blitzkrieg*, p. 70.
9   TNA: HW 5/2 – GC&CS, German Section, Reports of German Army and Air Force High Grade Machine Decrypts (hereafter GC&CS Decrypts), CX/JQ/2, CX/JQ/14.
10 Bekker, *Luftwaffe*, p. 158; Gelb, *Dunkirk*, p. 106; TNA: AIR 22/168 – Air Ministry War Room (hereafter A.M.W.R.) Daily Report for Summary, No. 316, 31 May 1940.
11 TNA: AIR 22/107 – Air Ministry Daily Telegraphic Intelligence Summaries, 1 June 1940; TNA: AIR 22/168 – A.M.W.R. Daily Reports for Summaries No. 313–14, German Air Force Operations, 28–29 May 1940.
12 Oddone, *Dunkirk*, p. 88.
13 Liddell Hart Centre for Military Archives, King's College, London (hereafter LHCMA): LIDDELL HART 15/15/22 – Adolf Galland, 'The Birth, Life and Death of the German Day Fighter Arm', 1945.
14 TNA: HW 5/2 – GC&CS Decrypts, CX/JQ/3.
15 TNA: AIR 16/352 – 11 Group Report, 8 July 1940.
16 Speidel, 'German Air Force', p. 314.
17 *Ibid.*, p. 484.
18 Kesselring cited in Bekker, *Luftwaffe*, p. 159.
19 Speidel, 'German Air Force', p. 198.
20 IWM: EDS/AL/1429 – 4. Armee Ia, Kriegstagebuch, 23 May 1940.
21 *Ibid.*, 24 May 1940.
22 BA/MA: N 671/6 – Richthofen, Kriegstagebuch, 24–25 May 1940; BA/MA: RL 10/538 – Jagdgeschwader 27, Kriegstagebuch, Frankreich Feldzug, 25 May 1940; TNA: HW 5/1 – GC&CS Decrypts, CX/FJ/101.
23 BA/MA: N 671/6 – Richthofen, Kriegstagebuch, 25 May 1940.
24 BA/MA: N 671/6 – Richthofen, Kriegstagebuch, 28 May 1940; TNA: AIR 24/217 – Bomber Command Intelligence Report No. 633, 31 May 1940; TNA: HW 5/1 – GC&CS Decrypts, CX/FJ/114; TNA: HW 5/2 – GC&CS Decrypts, CX/JQ/2, CX/JQ/4, CX/JQ/10; Prien, *Jagdfliegerverbände*, p. 417.
25 TNA: HW 5/2 – GC&CS Decrypts, CX/JQ/11.
26 TNA: HW 5/1 – GC&CS Decrypts, CX/FJ/108, CX/FJ/113.
27 TNA: HW 5/2 – GC&CS Decrypts, CX/JQ/2–14.

28 Galland, *Luftwaffe*, p. 42.
29 AIR 16/1081 – Air Intelligence, Aerodromes in Belgium, Holland and France in Use by German Air Force Units, 31 May–6 June 1940, 31 May 1940; TNA: HW 5/2 – GC&CS Decrypts, CX/JQ/12A.
30 Jochen Prien et al., *Jagdeschwader 3 'Udet' in World War II*, Vol. II, *II/JG in Action with the Messerschmitt Bf 109* (Atglen, Pennsylvania: Schiffer, 2003), p. 13.
31 TNA: AIR 22/168 – A.M.W.R. Daily Report for Summary, No. 313, 28 May 1940.
32 TNA: AIR 22/169 – A.M.W.R. Daily Report for Summary, No. 320, 4 June 1940.
33 BA/MA: RL 10/538 – Jagdeschwader 27, Kriegstagebuch, Frankreich Feldzug, 25 May 1940, 20 May 1940.
34 TNA: HW 5/1 – GC&CS Decrypts, CX/FJ/108.
35 TNA: HW 5/1 — GC&CS Decrypts, CX/FJ/109.
36 TNA: HW 5/2 – GC&CS Decrypts, CX/JQ/24.
37 Steinhilper, *Spitfire on my Tail*, p. 259.
38 TNA: HW 5/1 – GC&CS Decrypts, CX/FJ/102, CX/FJ/104.
39 Speidel, 'German Air Force', p. 177.
40 BA/MA: N 671/6 – Richthofen, Kriegstagebuch, 24–28 May 1940.
41 Peter C. Smith, *Stuka Squadron: Stukagruppe 77 – The Luftwaffe's 'Fire Brigade'* (Wellingborough, Northamptonshire: Patrick Stevens, 1990), pp. 57–8.
42 BA/MA: N 671/6 – Richthofen, Kriegstagebuch, 26 May 1940.
43 IWM: EDS/AL/1399 – 10. *Panzer-Division* Ia, Extract from War Diary, 25 May 1940; TNA: HW 5/1 – GC&CS Decrypts, CX/FJ/102.
44 TNA: HW 5/1 – GC&CS Decrypts, CX/FJ/106.
45 Paul Temme cited in John Weal, *Jagdgeschwader 2 'Richthofen'* (Oxford: Osprey, 2000), p. 39.
46 BA/MA: N 671/6 – Richthofen, Kriegstagebuch, 28 May 1940; Collier, *Sands*, p. 134.
47 TNA: AIR 22/10 – A.M.W.R. Daily Summary, No. 317, 1 June 1940.
48 TNA: HW 5/2 – GC&CS Decrypts, CX/JQ/4.
49 TNA: HW 5/2 — GC&CS Decrypts, CX/JQ/3.
50 TNA: HW 5/1 – GC&CS Decrypts, CX/FJ/111; TNA: HW 5/2 – GC&CS Decrypts, CX/JQ/5–8.
51 Jacobsen, *Dünkirchen*, p. 195.
52 Steinhilper, *Spitfire on my Tail*, pp. 256–61.
53 TNA: AIR 24/217 – Bomber Command Intelligence Report No. 633, 31 May 1940.
54 BA/MA: N 671/6 – Richthofen, Kriegstagebuch, 24–28 May 1940; TNA: HW 5/2 – GC&CS Decrypts, CX/JQ/2–11; Hooton, *Blitzkreig*, p. 68.
55 John Weal, *Jagdgeschwader 52: The Experten* (London: Bloomsbury, 2012), p. 23.
56 Prien, *Jagdeschwader 3*, p. 15.

57　TNA: AIR 20/7700 – Translations of Captured German Air Historical Branch Study, 'Basic Principles Underlying the Technique of Air Warfare, with Illustrations from Experiences between 1939 and 1944', 4 October 1944.
58　IWM: Audio/11388 – Walter Krupinski, Reel 1; TNA: CAB 106/1206 – AHB, German Losses based on Returns to Luftwaffe Quarter Master General; TNA: HW 5/1 – GC&CS Decrypts, CX/FJ/112; TNA: HW 5/2 – GC&CS Decrypts, CX/JQ/1–23.
59　TNA: HW 5/1 – GC&CS Decrypts, CX/FJ/112.
60　Steinhilper, *Spitfire on my Tail*, p. 204.
61　IWM: EDS/AL/1429 – 4. Armee Ia, Kriegstagebuch, 28 May 1940.
62　TNA: AIR 16/352 – 11 Group Report, 8 July 1940.
63　IWM: Audio/2803 – Aitken, Reel 1.
64　TNA: AIR 27/2082 – ORB: 604 Squadron; Jonathon Falconer, *RAF Fighter Airfields of World War 2* (Shepperton, Surrey: Ian Allan, 1993), p. 61.
65　IWM: Audio/28766 – Anthony Montague 'Steady' Tuke, Reel 2; IWM: Audio/15985 – John Thompson, Reel 1.
66　TNA: AIR 27/2117 – ORB: 613 Squadron.
67　Allen, *Who Won*, p. 84; Lamb, *War*, p. 65.
68　IWM: Audio/10152 – Kingcombe, Reel 1.
69　TNA: AIR 16/352 – 11 Group Report, 8 July 1940.
70　TNA: AIR 27/1315 – ORB: 213 Squadron.
71　IWM: Audio/11103 – Page, Reel 1.
72　TNA: AIR 27/743 – ORB: 92 Squadron.
73　BA/MA: N 671/6 – Richthofen, Kriegstagebuch, 30–31 May 1940; IWM: EDS/AL/1429 – 4. Armee Ia, Kriegstagebuch, 28 May 1940.
74　IWM: Audio/11103 – Page, Reel 1.
75　TNA: AIR 20/7707 – Captured Enemy Documents, Adolf Galland, 'The Battle of Britain'; Messerschmitt AG, *L.Dv.556/3 (Entwurf) Bf 109 E Flugzeughandbuch* (Berlin: Reichsminister der Luftwaffe, 1939), Teil 9 Anlagen; Willy Radinger and Walter Schick, *Messerschmitt Me 109: Das Meistgebaute Jagdflugzeug der Welt. Entwicklung, Erprobung und Technik. Alle Varianten von BF (Me) 109A bis 109E* (Oberhaching, Bavaria: Aviatic Verlag, 1997), pp. 95–110.
76　Messerschmitt, *Bf 109 E Flugzeughandbuch*, Teil 9, Anlagen; Messerschmitt AG, *Betriebs und Rüstanleitung Me 109 mit Motor DB 601* (Berlin: Reichsminister der Luftwaffe, 1941); E. R. Hooton, *The Luftwaffe: A Study in Air Power, 1933–1945* (London: Classic, 2010), p. 77.
77　IWM: Audio/10152 – Kingcombe, Reel 1.
78　TNA: AIR 27/743 – ORB: 92 Squadron.
79　IWM: Audio/11616 – Johns, Reel 1.
80　LHCMA: LIDDELL HART 15/15/22 – Galland, German Day Fighter Arm, 1945.
81　TNA: AIR 50/10/15, 23, 28, 37 – Combat Reports, Sergeant Jennings, Pilot Officer Lyne, Flying Sergeant Potter, Flying Sergeant Unwin, 26 May–1 June 1940;

TNA: AIR 50/16/24 – Combat Report, Pilot Officer Smyth, 2 June 1940; TNA: AIR 50/19/70 – Combat Report, Flying Sergeant Ottewill, 1 June 1940; TNA: AIR 50/22/18 – Combat Report, Flight Lieutenant Coghlan, 27 May 1940; TNA: AIR 50/33/7 – Air Combat Report, Flying Sergeant Cartwright, 27 May 1940.
82 Hyde, *British Air Policy*, p. 419.
83 IWM: Audio/11388 – Krupinski, Reel 1.
84 TNA: AIR 22/71 – Directorate of Air Intelligence, Air Ministry Weekly Intelligence Summary, No. 39, 30 May 1940.
85 Harman, *Dunkirk*, pp. 156, 202–3; Price, *Luftwaffe*, pp. 152–3.
86 Wood and Dempster, *Narrow Margin*, pp. 284, 459; Overy, *Battle*, p. 53; Ray, *Battle*, p. 47.
87 Bishop, *Battle*, pp. 33, 100, 338; Holland, *Battle*, pp. 537, 663, 673–9; Isby, Decisive, pp. 108–9, 119–25; Wood and Dempster, *Narrow Margin*, pp. 46–7, 55–6, 206–7.
88 Kesselring, *Memoirs*, p. 59.
89 IWM: Audio/30001 – Peter Ayerst, Reel 8.
90 IWM: Audio/11388 – Krupinski: Reel 1; Green, *Warplanes*, p. 549; David Owen, *Dogfight: The Supermarine Spitfire and The Messerschmitt BF 109* (Barnsley, Pen & Sword, 2015), p. 159.
91 Allen, *Who Won*, p. 79.
92 IWM: Audio/30001 – Ayerst, Reel 8.
93 IWM: Audio/12217 – Maurice Equity Leng, Reel 3.
94 Green, *Warplanes*, p. 549; Owen, *Dogfight*, p. 159.
95 Jonathon Glancey, *Spitfire: The Biography* (London: Atlantic, 2006), p. 40.
96 IWM: Audio/13152 – Peter Lawrence Parrott, Reel 2.
97 IWM: Audio/10478 – Alan Christopher Deere, Reel 1.
98 Franks, *Air Battle*, p. 62.
99 IWM: Audio/10159 – Hugh Spencer Lisle Dundas, Reel 1.
100 Isby, *Decisive*, p. 121; Eric B. Morgan and Edward Shacklady, *Spitfire: The History* (London: Guild, 1989), p. 72.
101 IWM: Audio/30001 – Ayerst, Reel 5; Isby, *Decisive*, p. 119.
102 Curtiss-Wright Corporation, Propeller Division, *Propeller Theory* (Caldwell, NJ: Curtiss-Wright Corporation, 1944), pp. 13–14.
103 AIR 14/100 – Reports to Bomber Command on Matters of Tactics Resulting from Operations; AIR 27/1/17 – ORB: 1 Squadron, 18 April 1940.
104 TNA: AIR 27/252 – ORB: 19 Squadron; TNA: AIR 27/511 – ORB: 54 Squadron; Isby, *Decisive*, p. 119; Morgan and Shacklady, *Spitfire*, p. 72.
105 TNA: AIR 27/2102/11 – ORB: 609 Squadron.
106 Gelb, *Dunkirk*, p. 107.
107 TNA: AIR 2/3353 – Minute from Officer of the Directorate of Operations and Intelligence, with responsibilities for the Air Defence of Great Britain and

Operational Questions in Europe, to Director of Military Co-Operation, Regarding Progress of Fitting Rear Armour to Hurricanes and Spitfires, 10 May 1940; TNA: AIR 20/2061 – Air Ministry to Fighter Command, Confirming Retrofitting of Rear Armour in Hurricanes and Spitfires.

108   IWM: Audio/12674 – Edge, Reel 1.
109   McGlashan, *Down to Earth*, pp. 8–9.
110   TNA: AIR 27/2109 – ORB: 611 Squadron.
111   TNA: AIR 27/2102 – ORB: 609 Squadron.
112   TNA: AIR 16/352 – 11 Group Report, 8 July 1940.
113   TNA: CAB 65/2/41 – War Cabinet, Conclusions of Meeting No. 107, 7 December 1939; Messerschmitt, *Bf 109 E Flugzeughandbuch*, Teil 9, Anlagen.
114   TNA: HW 5/1 – GC&CS Decrypts, CX/FJ/109.
115   Cummings, *Royal Navy*, p. 32.
116   TNA: ADM 199/1189 – Tactical Summary of Bombing Attacks by German Aircraft on HM Ships and Shipping from September 1939 to February 1941.
117   *Ibid.*
118   Chris Goss, *Sea Eagles*, Vol. I, *Luftwaffe Anti-Shipping Units, 1939–41* (Hersham, Surrey: Classic, 2005), p. 22.
119   Kreipe and Koester, *Technical Training*, p. 142.
120   Goss, *Luftwaffe*, pp. 20–2; Probert, *Rise and Fall*, p. 129.
121   TNA: AIR 40/3070 – Information from PoWs, M.I.1.H. Interrogation, SRA 84, 6 May 1940.
122   IWM: AUDIO/13663 – Robert William Eunson, Reel 1.
123   IWM: Audio/10152 – Kingcombe, Reel 1.
124   IWM: Audio/12674 – Edge, Reel 2.
125   Wolfgang Dierich, *Die Verbände der Luftwaffe 1935–1945: Gliederungen und Kurzchroniken, eine Dokumentation*, (Stuttgart: Motorbuch, 1995), p. 93.
126   Based on data in TNA: ADM 199/1189 – Tactical Summary of Bombing Attacks by German Aircraft on HM Ships and Shipping from September 1939 to February 1941. The percentage of success equates to ships of each class sunk or seriously damaged as a percentage of the total attacks of that method which had been recorded on each shipping category. In the case of dive-bombing attacks by Ju 88s on merchant ships, and high altitude level-bombing on trawlers and merchant ships, no attacks were recorded
127   Stewart, *Dunkirk*, p. 118.
128   Frieser, *Blitzkrieg Legend*, pp. 44, 49; Isby, *Decisive*, pp. 107–8.
129   IWM: Audio/11616 – Johns, Reel 1.
130   Bob, 'Memories', p. 124; Collier, *Sands*, p. 89; Cooper, *German Air Force*, p. 134; Dildy, *Dunkirk*, pp. 30, 89; Franks, Air Battle, p. 44; Overy, *Battle*, p. 54; Ray, *Battle*, pp. 38–9, 48.

131 Deist, Rearmament, p. 491.
132 Corum, 'Defeat of the Luftwaffe', p. 219; Ketley and Rolfe, *Luftwaffe Fledglings*, pp. 7–8.
133 TNA: AIR 14/1959 – German Air Force Training, Bomber Pilots; TNA: AIR 40/3070 – Information from PoWs, M.I.1.H. Interrogation, S.R.A. 140, 4 July 1940; James S. Corum, *The Luftwaffe: Creating the Operational Air War, 1918–1940* (Lawrence, KS: University Press of Kansas, 1997), p. 250; Corum, 'Defeat of the Luftwaffe', p. 219; Hooton, *Phoenix Triumphant*, p. 158; Kreipe and Koester, *Technical Training*, p. 175; Probert, *Rise and Fall*, pp. 31–2.
134 TNA: AIR 10/5551 – AHB, 'Flying Training, Policy and Planning', p. 97; Probert, *Rise and Fall*, p. 31.
135 BA/MA: RL 4/16 – Ausbildungsrichtlinien für das Sommerhalbjahr 1938, 15 February 1938.
136 Kreipe and Koester, *Technical Training*, pp. 174, 278.
137 *Ibid.*, p. 174.
138 Probert, *Rise and Fall*, p. 20.
139 TNA: AIR 20/7711 – AHB Translation of Captured Enemy Document, Oberst Bernd Von Brauchitsch, 'German Air Force Policy During the Second World War'.
140 Kreipe and Koester, *Technical Training*, p. 72.
141 TNA: AIR 40/3070 – Information from PoWs, M.I.1.H. Interrogation, S.R.A. 86, 9 May 1940.
142 Steinhilper, *Spitfire on my Tail*, p. 255
143 TNA: AIR 32/14 – Training of Pilots, pp. 14–17.
144 Air Vice-Marshal L. A. Pattinson, 'The Training of a Royal Air Force Pilot', *Journal of the Royal United Service Institute*, Vol. 83, No. 529, (1938), pp. 13–14.
145 TNA: AIR 32/14 – Training of Pilots, pp. 14–17; Hooton, *Phoenix Triumphant*, p. 158.
146 TNA: AIR 14/44 – Squadron Leader Victor Emmanuel Groom, 'Training in Heavy Bomber Squadrons', 13 November 1936.
147 TNA AIR 2/2584 – Meetings of the Mobilisation Committee, Minutes to Meeting No. 18, 15 September 1938; Hyde, *British Air Policy*, p. 429.
148 Hyde, *British Air Policy*, p. 430.
149 TNA: AIR 6/40 – Secretary of State's Progress Meetings on RAF Expansion Measures, Minutes to Meeting No. 187; TNA: AIR 10/5551 – AHB, 'Flying Training, Policy and Planning', p. 93.
150 TNA: AIR 19/183 – Air Vice-Marshal A. J. Capel, Minute to T.P., 9 October 1940.
151 TNA: AIR 10/5551 – AHB, 'Flying Training, Policy and Planning', pp. 61–3; TNA: AIR 20/7707 – AHB Translation of Captured Enemy Document, Adolf Galland, 'The Battle of Britain'; Hooton, *Phoenix Triumphant*, p. 158; Karl Ries, *Luftwaffen-Story: 1935–39* (Mainz: Dieter Hoffman, 1974), p. 32.

152 TNA: AIR 22/71 – Directorate of Air Intelligence, Air Ministry Weekly Intelligence Summary, No. 39, 30 May 1940; TNA: AIR 40/3070 – Information from PoWs, M.I.1.H. Interrogation, S.R.A. 140, 4 July 1940.
153 82 Squadron, for instance, had eleven out of twelve aircraft shot down on one day, 17 May 1940, during an attack on Gembloux. TNA: AIR 20/7703 – AHB, Statistics of German Aircraft Losses for period September 1939–December 1940, Compiled from Captured records of the Quartermaster General's Department of the German Air Ministry; TNA: AIR 27/681 – ORB: 82 Squadron; Suchenwirth, 'Development of the German Air Force', pp. 186–7.
154 TNA: AIR 14/676 – 2 Group Report on Operations during the Period 10 May–3 June 1940.
155 Kreipe and Koester, *Technical Training*, p. 296.
156 TNA: AIR 22/71 – Directorate of Air Intelligence, Air Ministry Weekly Intelligence Summary, No. 39, 30 May 1940; Kreipe and Koester, *Technical Training*, p. 178.
157 Kreipe and Koester, *Technical Training*, pp. 287–8.
158 TNA: HW 5/2 – GC&CS Decrypts, CX/JQ/6.
159 TNA: AIR 19/162 – Winston S. Churchill, to Archibald Sinclair, Secretary of State for Air, 'Shortage of Pilots', 3 June 1940; TNA: AIR 20/2064 – Air Vice-Marshal W. S. Douglas, Deputy Chief of the Air Staff, 'Note on the Despatch of Further Day Fighter Squadrons to France', 11 June 1940.
160 TNA: AIR 27/441 – ORB: 43 Squadron.
161 TNA: AIR 32/15 – History of Flying Training: Reserve and Auxiliary Forces, 1919–1947.
162 Hyde, *British Air Policy*, p. 476.
163 TNA: AIR 19/162 – Winston Churchill to Archibald Sinclair, 'Shortage of Pilots', 3 June 1940.
164 TNA: AIR 6/60 – Preliminary Statement to the Air Council by the Air Member for Training on Training Arrangements Generally, 23 July 1940.
165 IWM: Audio/11510 – Cox, Reel 1.
166 TNA: Air 16/41 – Fighting Area Attacks: Details and Diagrams.
167 IWM: Audio/10152 – Kingcombe, Reel 1
168 Bungay, *Most Dangerous Enemy*, p. 250.
169 IWM: Audio/11510 – Cox, Reel 1.
170 IWM: Audio/12674 – Edge, Reel 2.
171 TNA: AIR 14/176 – Fighter Command Tactical Memorandum No. 9, 'Operation of Fighter Forces by Day', 9 December 1940.
172 Paul Temme cited in Weal, *Jagdgeschwader 2*, p. 39.
173 IWM: Audio/11103 – Page, Reel 1.
174 Edward H. Sims, *Fighter Tactics and Strategy, 1939–1970* (New York: Harper & Row, 1972), p. 92.

175 BA/MA: RL 2-II/283 – Jagdflieger Anleitung. – Entwurf, September 1939; Murray, *Strategy*, p. 24; Probert, *Rise and Fall*, p. 14; Raymond L. Proctor, *Hitler's Luftwaffe in the Spanish Civil War* (London: Greenwood, 1983), p. 255.
176 IWM: Audio/11388 – Krupinski, Reel 2.
177 Kreipe and Koester, *Technical Training*, p. 177.
178 Isby, *Decisive*, p. 124.
179 IWM: Audio/10159 – Dundas, Reel 1.
180 Dundas, *Flying*, pp. 28–9.
181 IWM: Audio/14368 – Bidsee, Reel 1.
182 IWM: Audio/11510 – Cox, Reel 1.
183 TNA: AIR 8/285 – Minutes of Air Ministry Meeting Discussing the Harmonisation of Guns and Fighting Range for Fixed Gun Fighters, 18 December 1939.
184 TNA: AIR 20/6296 – Professor Melville Jones to Air Vice-Marshal Douglas, 'Harmonisation of Cannon Guns in Fixed Gun Fighter Aircraft', 3 March 1940; Terraine, *Right of the Line*, pp. 155–6.
185 J. E. Johnson, *Full Circle: The Story of Air Fighting* (London: Cassell, 2001), pp. 129–30.
186 Anthony J. Cummings and Christina Goulter, 'Ready or Not? The RAF and the Battle of Britain', *BBC History Magazine*, Vol. 8, No. 11, (2007), pp. 22–3.
187 IWM: Audio/12674 – Edge, Reel 1.
188 Hillary, *Last Enemy*, p. 60.
189 IWM: Audio/11616 – Johns, Reel 2.
190 IWM: Audio/10119 – Hancock, Reel 1.
191 IWM: Audio/27074 – Bamberger, Reel 7.
192 *Ibid.*
193 Colin D. Heaton, 'Interview with Luftwaffe Ace Walter Krupinski', *Military History Magazine*, Vol. 15, No. 2, (1998), pp. 62–8.
194 IWM: Audio/11388 – Krupinski, Reel 1.
195 Kreipe and Koester, *Technical Training*, p. 179.
196 Bishop, *Battle*, p. 204; Deighton, *Fighter*, p. 174; Holland, *Battle*, p. 558; Probert, *Rise and Fall*, p. 87; Overy, *Battle*, pp. 47, 67–8; Price, *Luftwaffe*, p. 153.
197 Proctor, *Hitler's Luftwaffe*, pp. 258–9.
198 TNA: AIR 20/7711 – AHB Translation of Captured Enemy Document, Oberst Bernd Von Brauchitsch, 'German Air Force Policy during the Second World War'.
199 TNA: AIR 22/71 – Directorate of Air Intelligence, Air Ministry Weekly Intelligence Summary, No. 39, 30 May 1940.
200 LHCMA: LIDDELL HART 15/15/22 – Galland, German Day Fighter Arm, 1945.
201 TNA: AIR 40/3070 – Information from PoWs, M.I.1.H. Interrogation, S.R.A. 86, 9 May 1940; James S. Corum, 'The Luftwaffe's Campaigns in Poland and the

West 1939–1940: A Case Study of Handling Innovation in Wartime', *Security and Defence Quarterly*, No. 1, (2013), p. 164.
202 Hooton, *Phoenix Triumphant*, p. 158.
203 TNA: AIR 14/920 – Air Fighting Committee, Air Staff Paper on General Review of Training in Expansion, c.1938.
204 Richard Hillary, *Last Enemy*, p. 32.
205 *Ibid.*, p. 40.
206 Isby, *Decisive*, pp. 107–8; Johannes Steinhoff, 'The German Fighter Battle against the American Bombers', in Lieutenant Colonel William Geffen (ed., trans.), *Command & Commanders in Modern Military History: Proceedings of the USAF Academy Second Military History Symposium, US Air Force Academy 2–3 May 1968* [2nd Edition] (Washington, DC: Office of Air Force History – Headquarters USAF, 1971), p. 318.
207 Kreipe and Koester, *Technical Training*, pp. 179–81.
208 TNA: HW 5/2 – GC&CS Decrypts, CX/JQ/1–14.
209 Messerschmitt AG, *BF 109 E: Lehrbildreihe Nr.42, Zelldias* (Berlin: Mathiesen, n.d.), p. 14; Owen, Dogfight, p. 220.
210 Steinhilper, *Spitfire on my Tail*, p. 204.
211 IWM: Audio/11247 – Wolfgang Julius Feodor Falck, Reels 2–3; Kreipe and Koester, *Technical Training*, p. 139.
212 TNA: AIR 22/169 – A.M.W.R. Daily Report for Summary, No. 317, 1 June 1940; Speidel, 'German Air Force', p. 358.
213 IWM: Audio/7462 – Frederick William Winterbotham, Reel 11; Murray, *Strategy*, p. 14.
214 Corum, *Luftwaffe*, p. 223.
215 Murray, *Strategy*, p. 16.
216 *Ibid.*
217 Hooton, *Phoenix Triumphant*, p. 158; Ketley and Rolfe, *Luftwaffe Fledglings*, p. 39.
218 TNA: AIR 40/1134 – Translation of Captured Enemy Documents and Interviews of Captured Personnel, Relating to the Organisation of German Air Force Training.
219 Hooton, *Phoenix Triumphant*, p. 158; Kreipe and Koester, *Technical Training*, p. 138.
220 TNA: AIR 16/261 – Air Chief Marshal Sir Cyril Newall, Chief of the Air Staff, to Air Chief Marshal Sir Hugh Dowding, AOC-in-C Fighter Command, 24 May 1940.
221 BA/MA: RL 4/16 – Ausbildungsrichtlinien für das Sommerhalbjahr 1938, 15 February 1938.
222 Aufklärungsfliegerschule (F) 3, Abt. I Technik, 'Merkblatt Ju88 A' [https://web.archive.org/web/20180620110914/http://www.germanluftwaffe.com/archiv/Dokumente/ABC/j/Junkers/Ju%2088/Ju_88__Aufklarungsfliegerschule.pdf];

Dornier-Werke, *Ersatzteil-Liste Do 17 E und F* (Friedrichshafen: Dornier, 1937).
223 TNA: AIR 16/1070 – Operations of Fighter Squadrons, Signals, 29–30 May 1940.
224 Anton Hoch, 'Der Luftangriff Auf Freiburg am 10 Mai 1940' *Vierteljahrshefte für Zeitgeschichte*: Jahrgang 4, Heft 2, (1956), pp. 124–37.
225 Christer Bergstöm, *The Battle of Britain: An Epic Conflict Revisited* (Oxford: Casemate, 2015), p. 239.
226 BA/MA: RL 2-II/835 – OKL, 3. Abteilung, Bericht Wehrmachtmanöver – Sonderdruck ziviler Luftschutz, c.1938.
227 IWM: EDS/AL/1433 – *Heeresgruppe* B Ia, War Diary No. 4, (trans.) Captain Hilton, 1 June 1940.
228 TNA: HW 5/2 – GC&CS Decrypts, CX/JQ/14.
229 BA/MA: RL 4/16 – Ausbildungsrichtlinien für das Sommerhalbjahr 1938, 15 February 1938; NARA: T321 R90 – Oberbefehlshaber der Luftwaffe, Ausbildungsverfügung für das Winterhalbjahr 1936–7, 17 September 1936, Frame 0000798.
230 Steinhoff, 'German Fighter Battle', p. 318.
231 TNA: AIR 35/189 – Wing Commander E. H. D. Spence, Air Liaison Officer to Admiral Nord, Dunkirk, to Air Marshal A. Barratt, AOC BAFF, Notes on the Evacuation of Dunkirk, c. June 1940.
232 TNA: ADM 1/12196 – Vice Admiral Commanding the First Cruiser Squadron, to the C-in-C Home Fleet, Organisation for Defence of Ships against Air Attack, 8 May 1940.
233 TNA: HW 5/2 – GC&CS Decrypts, CX/JQ/55; Horst Boog, 'The Strategic Air War in Europe and Air Defence of the Reich, 194–44', in Horst Boog, Gerhard Krebs and Detlef Vogel (eds.), *Germany and the Second World War*, Vol. VII, *Germany's Initial Conquests in Europe* (Oxford: Oxford University Press, 2006), p. 359; Corum, *Luftwaffe*, p. 223.
234 TNA: AIR 10/5551 – AHB, 'Flying Training, Policy and Planning', pp. 24–5, 63, 72–3.
235 Frederick Richardson, *Man Is Not Lost: The Log of a Pioneer RAF Pilot/Navigator, 1933–1946* (Shrewsbury: Airlife, 1997), pp. 64–5.
236 TNA: AIR 32/14 – Training of Pilots, p. 19.
237 TNA: AIR 25/109A – ORB: 5 Group.
238 TNA: AIR 14/44 – Air Vice-Marshal Playfair, AOC 3 Group, to Bomber Command Headquarters, 'Training of Twin Engine and Night Flying Bomber Pilots', 1 March 1937.
239 TNA: AIR 2/2058 – Headquarters Bomber Command, Memorandum to all Bomber Groups on 'Tactical Methods – Medium Bombers', 12 July 1937.

240　TNA: AIR 2/2058 – Air Commodore W. S. Douglas, Director Staff Duties, to Air Chief Marshal John Steele, AOC-in-C Bomber Command, Response to Bomber Command Memorandum on 'Tactical Methods – Medium Bombers', 4 August 1937; TNA: AIR 2/2058 – Minute 39, Air Commodore Douglas to Chief of the Air Staff (through Deputy Chief of the Air Staff), Regarding Bomber Command Memorandum on 'Tactical Methods – Medium Bombers', 19 July 1937.
241　TNA: AIR 32/14 – Training of Pilots, p. 35.
242　TNA: AIR 14/53 – Bomber Command Training Staff Instruction No. 56, BC/4517/TR, 9 February 1939.
243　TNA: AIR 14/57 – Bomber Command Annual Training Report, 1938; TNA: AIR 32/14 – Training of Pilots, p. 35.
244　TNA: AIR 32/14 – Training of Pilots, p. 36.
245　TNA: AIR 14/57 – Bomber Command Annual Training Report, 1938; TNA: AIR 32/14 – Training of Pilots, p. 18; Malcolm Smith, British Air Strategy between the Wars (Oxford: Clarendon, 1984), p. 274.
246　TNA: AIR 14/54 – Air Chief Marshal John Steele to Viscount Swinton, Secretary of State for Air, 'Factors Affecting Operational Flying', 1 September 1937.
247　TNA: AIR 2/2058 – Air Chief Marshal Ludlow-Hewitt, AOC-in-C Bomber Command, to Viscount Swinton, Report on Initial Inspection of Units on Bomber Command's readiness for War, 10 November 1937.
248　TNA: AIR 14/111 – Air Commodore Conigham, AOC 4 Group, to Air Chief Marshal Ludlow-Hewitt, Report on 'General Situation in Group', 9 December 1939.
249　TNA: AIR 14/673 – 3 Group Report on Operations during the Period 5–16 June 1940, 'Conclusions Drawn and Lessons Learnt from the Operation'.
250　TNA: AIR 14/676 – 4 Group Report on Operations during the Period 10 May–4 June 1940; TNA: AIR 14/676 – 5 Group Report on Operations during the Period 9 May–4 June 1940; TNA: AIR 14/676 – Air Marshal Portal, Dispatch on Bomber Command's Operations during the Period 9 May–16 June 1940.
251　TNA: AIR 14/67 – Air Vice-Marshal Bottomley, Senior Air Staff Officer – Bomber Command Headquarters, on Behalf of AOC-in-C Bomber Command, to Under-Secretary of State for Air, 14 June 1940.
252　Richards, Fight, p. 127.
253　TNA: AIR 14/676 – 3 Group Report on Operations during the Period 9 May–4 June 1940.
254　TNA: AIR 14/673 – 3 Group Report, 5–16 June 1940, 'Conclusions Drawn and Lessons Learnt from the Operation'.
255　Charles Webster and Noble Frankland, *The Strategic Air Offensive against Germany, 1939–1945*, Vol. I, *Preparations* (London: HMSO, 1961), p. 217.
256　TNA: AIR 14/676 – 3 Group Report, 9 May–4 June 1940.
257　Webster and Frankland, *Preparations*, p. 125.

258 Jeff Jefford, *Observers and Navigators: And Other Non-Pilot Aircrew in the RFC, RNAS and RAF* [2nd Edition], (London: Grub Street, 2014), pp. 146, 156, 176–84; Phillip Saxon, 'The Second World War', *Royal Air Force Historical Society Journal*, Vol. 17, No. 1, 'A History of Navigation in the Royal Air Force', (1997), pp. 53–4.
259 IWM: EDS/AL/1405 – Ab. Nr. T654/40g, Telegram Heeresgruppe B to Heeresgruppen A and C, 2 June 1940.
260 Ketley and Rolfe, *Luftwaffe Fledglings*, p. 74.
261 NARA: T321 R68 – Vorläufige Richtlinien für die Ausbildung der Offizieranwärter der Luftwaffe: Teil IV Gemeinsamer Luftkriegsschullehrgang, 1936, Frame 4818489–4818548.
262 BA/MA: RL 4/15 – Ausbildungsrichtlinien für das Winterhalbjahr 1938, 15 August 1937.
263 BA/MA: RL 2-II/280 – OKL, 3. Abteilung, Taktische Erfahrungen Nr. 2, Ausfertigung für Führungsstellen, c. November 1939.
264 BA/MA: RL 2-II/80c – Generalleutnant Erhard Milch, Wehrmachtsstudie 1935/1936, 28 November 1935; BA/MA: RL 2-II/154 – OKL, 3. Abteilung, Bericht Wehrmachtmanöver (Luftwaffe) 1937.
265 Cummings, *Royal Navy*, p. 33.
266 Friedrich Lauck, *Der Lufttorpedo: Entwicklung und Technik in Deutschland 1915–1945* (Munich: Bernard & Graefe, 1987), p. 24.
267 *Ibid.*, p. 23.
268 Probert, *Rise and Fall*, p. 109; Harold Thiele, *Luftwaffe Aerial Torpedo Aircraft and Operation in World War Two* (Crowsborough, East Sussex: Hikoki, 2004), p. 4.
269 TNA: AVIA 13/767 – Royal Aircraft Establishment, Report on Salvaged German Torpedo held at Royal Naval Torpedo Factory, 27 March 1940; TNA: HW 5/4 – GC&CS Decrypts, CX/JQ/243, CX/JQ/260
270 Lauck, *Der Lufttorpedo*, pp. 22–4; Probert, *Rise and Fall*, p. 109; Thiele, Luftwaffe Aerial Torpedo Aircraft, p. 4.
271 NARA: T1022, R3979 – Konteradmiral Karl Dönitz, Der Befehlshabers der Unterseeboote Kriegstagebücher (trans.) US Office of Naval Intelligence, 15 May 1940.
272 BA/MA, RL 2-II/24 – OKL, 1. Abteilung, Kurzstudie 'Luftkriegführung Gegen England', 22 November 1939.
273 Sönke Neitzel, 'Kriegsmarine and Luftwaffe Co-operation in the War against Britain, 1939–1945', *War in History*, Vol. 10, No. 4, (2003), p. 451.
274 Lauck, *Der Lufttorpedo*, p. 24.
275 *Ibid.*, p. 24.
276 TNA: ADM 1/9649 – Rear Admiral J. A. G. Troup, Director of Naval Intelligence, 'Foreign Development of the Torpedo as an Air Weapon', 17 May 1938.
277 Goss, *Luftwaffe*, pp. 16–17.
278 BA/MA: RM 7/168 – Letter from Admiral Raeder to Göring, 31 October 1939.

279 TNA: ADM 223/696 – Admiral Schniewind and Vice Admiral Schuster, Essay on 'The German Conduct of the War at Sea', 10 November 1946.
280 Geirr H. Harr, *The Gathering Storm: The Naval War in Northern Europe, September 1939–April 1940* (Barnsley: Seaforth, 2013), p. 232.
281 IWM: Audio/13933 – John Teague Gilhespy, Reel 10.
282 Asher Lee, *Goering: Air Leader* (London: Duckworth, 1972), p. 65.
283 Walter Gaul, 'Navy-Air Force Planning and Build-up of the Naval Air Forces; Their Disbandment, and the Transfer of Naval Air Commitments to the Operational Air Force', in *Essays by German Officers and Officials on World War II, Part II* (Wilmington, DE: Scholarly Resources, 1991), p. 9.
284 OKL, 8. Abteilung, January 1944, 'The Operational Use of the Luftwaffe in the War at Sea, 1939–43', in Isby (ed.), *The Luftwaffe and the War at Sea* (London: Chatham, 2005), pp. 124–5.
285 Oberst (i.G.) Walter Gaul, 'German Naval Air Operations in the First Six Months of the War', in Isby (ed.), *Luftwaffe*, p. 194.
286 TNA: ADM 199/2206 – Naval War Diary Summaries, 1 June 1940; TNA: HW 5/2 – GC&CS Decrypts, CX/JQ/9.

2

The Luftwaffe's attacks, 29 May and 1 June

It has been widely recognized that the Luftwaffe failed to prevent Operation Dynamo.[1] To understand the cause of the Luftwaffe's failure to halt Dynamo it is first necessary to consider the days that the Luftwaffe achieved significant success against the evacuation and the reasons for success on those days. On 29 May, the Luftwaffe temporarily suspended embarkations from Dunkirk and on 1 June it succeeded in halting all further daylight evacuation. This chapter will explore the Luftwaffe's operations on both days and the reasons that they were successful.

The success that the Luftwaffe was able to achieve during Dynamo is often considered in relation to the total number of ships, and vessels of all types, sunk or lost along the French and Low Countries coast from the evening of 26 May until the morning of 4 June. The number of vessels lost and sunk, often inflated, includes a wide variety of vessels sunk, lost or abandoned for various reasons. Winston Churchill placed the figure at 243 – with 170 of these being 'other small craft' – and this figure has been accepted in histories of Dynamo.[2] Any discussion of a figure higher than 200 has to be placed in the context that this involved a large number of craft and boats not considered to be naval vessels.[3] The Royal Navy lost six destroyers and twenty-four minor war vessels in Operation Dynamo with a further forty-five named types damaged.[4] Over 150 ships from other Allied countries, primarily French and Belgian, participated in Dynamo of which at least eighteen were lost.[5] In addition to these losses several French merchant ships, which were in Dunkirk harbour at the outset of the evacuation and whose lifting capacity could have made a contribution to the total number evacuated, were lost as a result of damage caused by the Luftwaffe's bombing. The total number of vessels sunk is, however, an inaccurate means of gauging the Luftwaffe's success or failure. It is necessary to consider instead the losses the Luftwaffe inflicted on the most significant vessels in the evacuation – the Destroyers and personnel vessels – as well as the minor war vessels which played an important ancillary role during Dynamo. The majority of the troops landed in England by British ships were lifted from Dunkirk either by Destroyer or personnel vessels, 96,000 and 87,000 respectively.[6] These types incurred heavy losses and by the end of evacuations on the night of 2–3 June only thirteen of the forty destroyers involved in Dynamo remained fit for service.[7]

To assess whether the Luftwaffe could have prevented the success of Operation Dynamo it is necessary to consider the losses the Luftwaffe was able to inflict on these vessels and how they achieved these successes. In taking this approach, two days stand out during Operation Dynamo – 29 May and 1 June. On 29 May twelve British ships were lost directly to air attack and the evacuation was almost halted, whilst on 1 June the Luftwaffe sank thirteen ships and further daylight evacuations from Dunkirk were suspended.[8] These successes demonstrate that the Luftwaffe was capable of halting the evacuation despite subsequent claims by senior Luftwaffe officers that it was beyond the force's capabilities.[9] To understand the effectiveness of the Luftwaffe to apply air power to influence Allied maritime operations and the course of the evacuation, it is necessary to consider the reasons for their success on 29 May and 1 June. Subsequent chapters will then consider the period before 29 May and then the events of 30 and 31 May in both cases assessing the German air attacks and the limitations which prevented the Luftwaffe halting the evacuation at an earlier date.

Operations on 29 May

During 29 May the Luftwaffe came close to halting the evacuation, with eight destroyers, five personnel ships and numerous other vessels either sunk or put out of action by air attack.[10] This success was largely due to the Luftwaffe effectively bombing vessels embarking troops at the eastern pier of Dunkirk Harbour, a breakwater which protected the outer harbour which was commonly referred to as the 'Mole', for the first time.[11] Seven of the ships which tied up alongside the Mole during the day were put out of action, five of them sunk.[12]

The Luftwaffe was active against the evacuation shortly after dawn; however, interference with the evacuation was limited because weather conditions interfered in planned operations, the early morning in particular seeing thick cloud coverage at both low and high altitude.[13] Attacks on shipping at Dunkirk had been planned for the morning with Do 17s of III./KG 76 prepared to use SC50 general-purpose bombs with a ricochet plate bolted to their nose, to ensure the bomb detonated above water when vessels were the target of attack.[14] *Kampfgeschwader* equipped with Ju 88s and He 111s were also active on 29 May, with He 111s of *Fliegerkorps* I ordered to carry out continuous attacks, supported by both Me 109 and Me 110 formations, against troops being embarked from the beaches east of Dunkirk.[15] Flying conditions were generally unfavourable during the morning but shortly after midday the weather had cleared sufficiently for the Luftwaffe to attack. In the clear conditions all three *Sturzkampfgeschwader* of *Fliegerkorps* VIII, some 180 Ju 87s, attacked ships at Dunkirk, as well as the town and port.[16]

At 12.15 a force of dive-bombers arrived over the Dunkirk roads. Six attacked the destroyer HMS *Jaguar* whilst the majority focused on the destroyer HMS *Gallant*; severe damage from a near-miss put *Gallant* out of action for the remainder of Dynamo.[17] Medium bombers of *Luftflotte* 2 continued the heavy air attacks against the evacuation during the mid-afternoon. The Luftwaffe's operations from this time on were heavy and continuous, producing significant losses. Lieutenant Commander Maud, commanding HMS *Icarus*, reported that air raids 'appeared to be coming over at hourly intervals with great regularity' with the raids typically lasting nearly thirty minutes.[18] The destroyer HMS *Verity* was continuously straddled for thirty-five minutes and embarkations aboard SS *Canterbury* were delayed amid heavy bombing aimed at ships alongside the Mole.[19] A heavy and accurate dive-bombing attack was then made on ships at the Mole which sank the trawler HMS *Calvi* and the destroyer HMS *Grenade* with HMS *Express* damaged by a near-missed.[20] The trawler HMS *Polly Johnson* was also damaged in this attack and later sank as a result.[21] A heavy and uninterrupted series of dive-bombing attacks developed on *Jaguar*, causing considerable damage to ship and personnel, and a near-miss damaged SS *Loch Garry*.[22] Neither ship would play any further part in Dynamo as a result of the damage sustained. SS *Clan Macalister* was abandoned after being hit and set on fire in an attack by thirteen dive-bombers.[23] The paddle minesweeper HMS *Gracie Fields* was then hit and abandoned shortly after leaving Dunkirk.[24] The destroyer HMS *Greyhound* was bombed as were the minesweepers HMS *Salamander* and *Sutton*.[25] *Sutton* straddled by a salvo whilst bomb splinters from two near-misses killed twenty men on *Greyhound*, wounded seventy others and caused serious damage in the engine and boiler room.[26] HMS *Sabre* was continually attacked by dive-bombers at Dunkirk harbour and HMS *Kellett* was attacked by dive-bombers near Nieuport buoy.[27] The trawler HMS *Nautilus* was straddled by bombs and had her engines and steering gear put out of action.[28] Several Belgian tugs which had been working at Dunkirk were sunk by the Luftwaffe as was the minesweeper FS *Joseph Marie*.²⁹ The beaches were also heavily bombed during the afternoon.³⁰ The minesweeper HMS *Oriole* – deliberately beached to allow troops to pass over her deck to other ships – was continually bombed and near-misses repeatedly doused her in water and sand.³¹ KG 4 was also in action during the afternoon providing air protection against gunfire from ships between Ostend, Nieuport and La Panne at the request of AOK 18.³²

The heavy air attacks continued into the evening of 29 May with over 200 aircraft attacking Dunkirk and Allied ground positions.³³ All three *Gruppen* of KG 77 attacked Dunkirk targeting the facilities of the inner harbour with a number of hits observed, some on gasometers and tanks which were seen to explode.³⁴ Luftwaffe bombers also reported both successful and unsuccessful attacks on transport vessels.³⁵ Dunkirk harbour and ships alongside the Mole were again heavily attacked with SS *Fenella* sunk and the Mole itself hit.³⁶ Shortly after 18.00 the paddle minesweeper HMS *Crested Eagle*, steering a course for Route Y, was hit by four bombs and beached.³⁷ As survivors from *Crested Eagle* were being rescued by HMS *Albury*, bombs were continually being dropped and two heavy machine-gun attacks were carried out.³⁸ The harbour was simultaneously attacked by numerous bombers and a significant attack, involving at least ten dive-bombers, developed on *Icarus*.³⁹ A further force of forty dive-bombers then arrived and attacks rapidly developed on all ships in the vicinity.⁴⁰ The continuous attacks temporarily made it impossible to enter the harbour, or remain in the vicinity, and orders were issued for ships to keep clear of the harbour.⁴¹

The evening also saw air attacks on the beaches intensify once more, with medium bombers making two large attacks from 17.00.⁴² At 17.30 ships off La Panne and the beaches east of Dunkirk experienced heavy dive-bombing attacks and smaller vessels were machine-gunned.⁴³ Between 18.00 and 19.00 numerous dive-bomb attacks were made on the minesweeper HMS *Pangbourne*, with fragments from several near-misses holing the hull on both sides and cutting the degaussing coil.⁴⁴ The sloop HMS *Bideford* was dive-bombed and had her stern blown-off amid the almost continuous air attacks made on Bray beach and the ships offshore during this period.⁴⁵ The destroyer HMS *Saladin* was attacked ten times and damage from near-misses left her unable to participate further in Operation Dynamo.⁴⁶ Off the beaches *Sabre* was severely shaken by near-misses and the proximity of the explosions in these attacks threw up columns of water – thick with oil fuel from ships previously hit – which covered the ship and blackened every man on deck. To the west of Dunkirk, He 111s attacked the personnel vessels SS *Normannia* and *Lorina*, both of which were hit and sunk, and HMS *Waverley* was also hit after enduring attacks for over ninety minutes.[47] Heavy air raids were also made on the channels to Dunkirk during the evening. The minesweeper HMS *Hebe* was targeted by three medium bombers whilst a large number of dive-bombers attacked ships arriving and leaving the Dunkirk area including HMHS *St Julien*, which had repeated attacks made on her.[48] *Canterbury* was attacked on the Dunkirk roads heading onto Route Y and was damaged by near-misses which put her out of action until repairs were completed on 3 June.[49] Between Middelkerke and La Panne HMS *Intrepid* was attacked by aircraft and was unable to take any further part in Dynamo after a bomb exploded alongside, causing considerable damage.[50] At 19.00 the Skoot *Fredanja* was damaged by a near-miss during an air attack east of Dunkirk.[51] The Armed Boarding Vessel SS *King Orry* was damaged by near-misses whilst attempting to get alongside the Mole at 19.30. *King Orry* received further damage from near-misses during a further attack on the Mole at 20.00 and sank at 00.30 on 30 May as a result of the damage sustained.[52] From 20.00 an air attack primarily directed at the ships lying off the beach developed with at least two ships hit, and embarkations slowed as medium bombers continued attacks until dark.[53] The weight of the Luftwaffe's attack during 29 May also caused destroyers involved in the evacuation to expend large quantities of anti-aircraft ammunition. The commander of HMS *Anthony* recorded that, along with other destroyers, *Anthony* was recalled shortly after 20.00 and that the decision was made in part because their anti-aircraft ammunition had been entirely depleted.[54]

Surviving Luftwaffe situation reports record that British fighter formations 'strove to cover the evacuation from the air and fierce air battles developed with German twin engined and single engined fighters which succeeded in maintaining air supremacy'.[55] On 29 May, therefore, the Luftwaffe did not just feel they had air superiority free from prohibitive interference from Fighter Command but believed they held complete control of air operations over Dunkirk. This does not fairly reflect the air cover provided by the RAF during 29 May. To provide air cover over Dunkirk, 11 Group – which was responsible for Fighter Command's efforts to protect the evacuation – had made the decision to operate patrols in greater strength but at less frequent intervals. The logic of that decision is considered separately; however, during periods of clear weather condition on 29 May the result was that aircraft from Fighter Command were either present in large numbers – and able to record notable casualties to the Luftwaffe – or, all too frequently, entirely absent. The Luftwaffe's bombing attacks were also launched after their fighters had swept Dunkirk with the aim of engaging, and clearing, Fighter Command's patrols. The Luftwaffe's tactics were not always successful; however, they did ensure that only two of the large bombing attacks on Dunkirk were met by British fighters.[56]

The Luftwaffe succeeded on 29 May in causing considerable damage and destruction to the ships at Dunkirk; the Luftwaffe's dive-bombers were the primary cause of this success. Richthofen recorded that the dive-bombers of *Fliegerkorps* VIII had performed excellently, sinking many ships.[57] The Dunkirk Mole itself was also hit and damaged by dive-bombers, although the damage was not sufficient to prevent further embarkations.[58] More significant were the eight destroyers put out of action and the loss of five personnel vessels; these types – with their capacity to transport large numbers of troops – were of vital importance to the evacuation (see Table 2).[59] The loss of so many destroyers caused considerable concern to the Admiralty and they withdrew the seven remaining modern destroyers from the operation as a result.[60] The decision regarding the withdrawal of the modern destroyers was later rescinded. It indicates, however, the concern that the Royal Navy felt regarding the mounting losses to air attack on 29 May and the 'grave risks attached to the operations at Dunkirk'.[61] If the decision to withdraw the modern destroyers had been maintained it would have left fifteen of the older types of destroyers, slower and capable of lifting fewer men, which without any further casualties could have been expected to maintain a flow of one destroyer per hour to Dunkirk; this would have limited their lift capability to 17,000 troops every twenty-four hours (Table 2).[62]

However, one of these older destroyers – *Verity* – would not sail for Dunkirk again because of the psychological effect of the Luftwaffe's attacks on 29 May. On return to the harbour men from *Verity*, which had been straddled continuously for thirty-five minutes on 29 May, broke out of the ship; those who were caught stated under interrogation that their nerves had given away and that they could not 'stand it' any further. A further member of the ship's company later attempted to commit suicide on the mess deck.[63] The air attacks of 29 May also caused concerns aboard other destroyers. *Windsor*, damaged on 29 May, sailed for Dunkirk on 30 May following repairs. *Windsor*'s commanding officer later reported that 'the nerves of my ship's company had been badly affected by the bombing' and that he was 'nervous as to what would be the reactions of my ship's company to further enemy action'.[64]

The air attacks also affected the civilian crews of a number of personnel vessels. An armed guard and several Royal Navy personnel had to be despatched to MV *Ngaroma* to stiffen the crew's resolve following 29 May.[65] The crew of SS *St Seiriol* did not sail for Dunkirk again following the ship's 'terrible' bombing. The 'strain and anxiety' had left all on board 'thoroughly shaken' and led the military doctor at Dover to decide, without hesitation, that the crew were unfit

Table 2 Number of troops embarked from Dunkirk by ship type.[73]

Type	Destroyer	Personnel vessel	Minesweepers	Skoots	Drifters
Ships involved in evacuation	39	45	36	39	51
Troops evacuated by ship type	96,000	87,000	46,000	22,000	12,000
Troops per type as percentage of total of troops evacuated	28%	26%	14%	7%	4%

to carry on any longer.[66] The scale of losses, and the damage to the Mole, also caused apprehension amongst the naval officers in charge of the evacuation. Following the fierce evening attacks, Tennant messaged Ramsay at 21.50 that whilst the harbour had not been blocked it was 'doubtful' if much more could be done during daylight hours if bombing resumed on the Mole.[67] Ramsay would later report that 'it was only by good fortune that the vital Dunkirk channel was not blocked by sinking ships at this early date'.[68] For a time during the evening of 29 May, it was feared that the channel into Dunkirk harbour was blocked and the Mole unusable.[69] Ramsay therefore made the decision to order all ships approaching Dunkirk not to approach the harbour but to proceed to the beaches instead, greatly slowing the rate of evacuation.[70] It was not until the morning of 30 May that large numbers of men were once more lifted from the Mole. The morning of 30 May was, as will be discussed, largely devoid of Luftwaffe attacks, and Ramsay believed that had the conditions at Dunkirk been accurately known ships with the capacity to embark a further 10,000 troops could have been made available with little impact on evacuations from the beaches.[71] Tennant in his report on the evacuation felt 'a great opportunity was missed' and 15,000 extra troops could probably have been embarked had ships arrived at the outer harbour.[72] At the end of 29 May therefore, the Luftwaffe had succeeded in using Air Power to inflict sufficient losses to the evacuation fleet to disrupt embarkations and temporarily force a change to the flow of traffic to Dunkirk.

Operations on 1 June

The Luftwaffe made use of the excellent flying conditions on 1 June to launch a sustained assault against vessels in Dunkirk harbour and off the coast in order to prevent further embarkations.[74] Shortly before dawn the Luftwaffe achieved the first of what would prove to be a long series of successes when the tug HMS *St Fagan* was shattered by a bomb whilst standing by in the Dunkirk Channel, level with the town.[75] Attacks then developed against ships alongside the Mole whilst fighters strafed the beaches and nearby ships.[76] These attacks were maintained during the early morning with Tennant reporting to Dover 'very heavy dive-bombing' attacks on ships.[77] During this initial wave of Luftwaffe attacks a four squadron patrol of Fighter Command intercepted part of the Luftwaffe formations. The Luftwaffe's fighters engaged the Fighter Command patrol but the RAF's air cover, coupled with naval anti-aircraft fire, limited the effect of the bomber's attacks on the evacuation. A further wave of Luftwaffe attacks arrived at 07.00. Fighter Command did not have a patrol over Dunkirk and – with the previous attack having left the evacuation fleet perilously low on, and in some cases without, anti-aircraft ammunition – the attacks began to inflict heavy losses.[78]

The destroyer *Keith* had been attacked a number of times during this period and by 06.00 had almost depleted its anti-aircraft ammunition; only two rounds remained for its four single-mounted 4.7-inch guns and 100 rounds of ammunition for two quick-firing 2-pounder autocannons.[79] At 07.37 *Keith* sighted a large bomber formation, with considerable fighter cover, and in the attack that followed a near-miss, from a delayed-action bomb dropped during a Ju 87 attack, jammed the steering gear. Shortly after 08.00 numerous dive-bombing attacks took place and *Keith* was straddled by a salvo which caused severe flooding and set the No. 2 boiler room on fire. Further dive-bombing attacks launched against the ship caused additional damage before *Keith* was finally sunk by a heavy salvo of bombs dropped by formation of fifty medium bombers. Shortly after the loss of *Keith* a medium bomber was seen returning towards the tug HMS *St Abbs*, which had helped rescue survivors from *Keith*. *St Abbs* was hit by a single bomb and sank rapidly.[80]

The minesweeper HMS *Skipjack* had survived repeated attacks during the morning; however, with little anti-aircraft ammunition remaining she was unable to evade an attack by ten Ju 88s. In this attack two bombs hit *Skipjack* causing damage which reduced the ships manoeuvrability and *Skipjack* was sunk in further attack.[81] During these morning attacks dive-bombers also severely damaged the destroyer HMS *Ivanhoe*, putting her out of action.[82] Sixty level-bombers, flying in three waves, then attacked as *Ivanhoe* was being escorted away from Dunkirk by the tug *Persia* and the War Ministry fast motorboat *Haig*. The anti-aircraft fire of *Haig* was able to prevent the medium bombers attacking at low level and *Ivanhoe* received no further damage.[83]

The destroyer HMS *Basilisk* was damaged by dive-bombers during the morning with one direct hit and six near-misses which buckled the ship's sides and upper deck. A second attack was then made on *Basilisk* by a formation of medium bombers; no hits were achieved but efforts to tow the *Basilisk* back to Britain were delayed. *Basilisk* was sunk later on 1 June by dive-bombers who pressed their attacks at low level.[84]

The attacks made during the early morning of 1 June had already succeeded in disrupting the evacuation and had sunk or damaged three destroyers and a minesweeper, all four attacks having involved dive-bombers. Watching these attacks by 'wave after wave of German bombers' one British unit which remained on the perimeter considered that, perhaps, they 'had been lucky to have been chosen for the rearguard' and were not being evacuated during the morning.[85]

The Luftwaffe planned a second large-scale air attack to arrive over Dunkirk from 09.00. During this period Do 17s of I./KG 76 made a number of attacks and claimed to have sunk a 3,000–5,000 tonne transport – the sinking of which saw *Feldwebel* Werner Schmidt awarded the Iron Cross – and achieved a direct hit on another.[86] A number of ships were lost during the attacks made from 09.00 onwards. The destroyer HMS *Havant* was badly damaged by a salvo of bombs dropped by a dive-bomber.[87] Amid incessant air bombardment, and numerous near-misses from delayed-action bombs, attempts by the minesweeper HMS *Saltash* to rescue *Havant* failed and she was abandoned.[88] The commanding officer of *Saltash* recalled that up to forty aircraft were overhead during this period and that:

> the ship was subject to heavy bombing and machine-gun attacks ... splinters from the bombs and spray from their splash fell on board frequently. It was very noticeable that nearly all the splinters were very small and far too light to do damage.[89]

Havant was, however, far too small to be the transport claimed by I./KG 76. The personnel vessel SS *Prague* was severely damaged and took no further part in the evacuation after three near-misses put the starboard engine out of action but the attack was made by dive-bombers as she returned to Dover.[90] During the heavy attack which damaged *Prague* the destroyer FS *Foudroyant* was hit by two consecutive salvo of bombs and blew up, sinking in two-and-a-half minutes.[91] The claims by I./KG 76 do not conform to either of these attacks and it is probable that Schmidt bombed one of the wrecks at Dunkirk, most likely that of *Clan Macalister* (examples of the numerous attacks on wrecks will be considered separately).

The morning attacks of 1 June demonstrate that the significant losses suffered by the evacuation fleet were almost wholly the result of dive-bombing. A formation of dive-bombers also sank *Brighton Queen*, fully loaded with troops, on Route X. *Brighton Queen* was not, however, the main target of the larger dive-bomber formation which was instead primarily directed against the personnel vessel SS *Scotia*. The Luftwaffe dive-bombers attacked in sections of four, with two aircraft strafing the ship to keep down anti-aircraft fire whilst the other two dropped bombs. *Scotia* was hit by at least four bombs and began to sink; dive-bombers dropped four more bombs on the sinking vessel and machine-gunned wreckage and survivors in the water.[92] The gunboat HMS *Mosquito* attempted to reach *Scotia* and rescue survivors but, during a further heavy attack, six dive-bombers from a larger flight targeted *Mosquito* obtaining a direct hit and sinking her.[93]

The sustained nature of the attacks in the morning of 1 June indicates that the Luftwaffe had secured air superiority. Fighter Command's air cover was unable to provide continuous cover of Dunkirk the reasons for which are fully discussed separately. The gaps in Fighter Command's air cover were, however, increased during the late morning and early afternoon by the Luftwaffe's fighters covering the area over Dunkirk, and the Channel, and engaging Fighter Command's patrols.[94] By operating in this manner the Luftwaffe was frequently able to draw the RAF air cover away from their primary task, which was to protect the evacuation from bombing. The Luftwaffe's air superiority was not continuous. The third Fighter Command patrol occurred during the late morning of 1 June. This patrol, involving thirty-seven Spitfires from four squadrons, was able to intercept an attack by an unescorted force of He 111s and Do 17s bombing from cloud level. The Fighter Command patrol inflicted heavy losses on the bomber formation. Despite these efforts, the heavy loss of shipping to the Luftwaffe during the morning of 1 June led to the decision to effectively suspend further daylight evacuations. Further shipping losses were, however, still to be experienced during 1 June. The destroyer *Worcester* ignored a signal from Ramsay to return to Dover, sent at 15.00, as she approached Dunkirk and was subsequently damaged by dive-bombers. The minesweeping trawlers FS *Denis Papin*, *Moussaillon* and *Vénus* were all lost to German dive-bombers on the approach to Dunkirk.[95] The destroyer *Harvester*; the corvette HMS *Kingfisher*; and the minesweepers HMS *Ross*, *Salamander* and *Westward-Ho* were also all damaged by dive-bombers, with only *Kingfisher* and *Westward-Ho* able to take further part in Dynamo.[96] In total, excluding smaller vessels such as barges and motorboats, 1 June saw twenty-one ships either lost or seriously damaged as a result of the Luftwaffe's attacks and only twelve personnel vessels were left in running order.[97]

The experiences of bombing on 29 May had shaken several crews and the intensity of the bombing on 1 June had a similar effect, with several personnel vessels refusing to sail for Dunkirk again. SS *Ben-My-Chree* refused to sail following 1 June with her crew having to be kept aboard by a guard with fixed bayonets. The captain and crew of SS *Tynwald* revolted and refused to return to Dunkirk as did the captain of SS *Manxman*.[98] The captain of SS *Malines* also refused to make any further trips to Dunkirk and sailed for Southampton without authorization later explaining that 'it seemed in the best interest of all concerned'.[99] A further ship, SS *Manx-Maid*, was supposed to sail for Dunkirk on three separate occasions but failed to complete a trip and was given up as 'hopeless'.[100] The tug *Contest* was also deliberately run aground to avoid carrying out naval orders following its experiences on 1 June. The effect of the heavy bombing on crews which had been to Dunkirk was not restricted to merchant ships. Lieutenant Commander Parish, Captain of *Vivacious*, was relieved due to nerves.[101] On *Hebe* one officer and twenty-eight members of the crew collapsed due to 'hysteria' and 'shock' brought about by the intense air attacks and constant strain.[102] By the end of 1 June the Luftwaffe's attack had brought several crews of the evacuation fleet to breaking point. Had the Luftwaffe been able to consistently replicate the intensity of its air attacks on 1 June and 29 May, which saw several crews buckle under the strain, the personnel involved in the evacuation would have been hard-pressed to maintain their operations.

Conclusion

On both 29 May and 1 June, the Luftwaffe's success against the evacuation came from the effective use of dive-bombers and the losses they inflicted, notably on ships which lifted the greatest number of troops from Dunkirk. That level-bombing failed to achieve greater results is unsurprising given that even the more accurate dive-bombers often failed to hit their targets. Arthur Joscelyne, serving aboard a Thames Barge, recalled a Stuka attack which he witnessed on a destroyer at Dunkirk:

> They roared down, and you could see the bombs drop out of them and this [destroyer] disappeared in a great mass of bubbles, huge bubbles coming up all round it. When the bubbles went down it was still there. I was amazed! It was incredible that they could have dropped these bombs all round [and not sunk it].[103]

Many of the more important vessels sunk during 29 May and 1 June were lost when their freedom to take rapid evasive manoeuvres was compromised which allowed more accurate attacks to be made. Similarly, successful attacks on 1 June were made when ships were short of anti-aircraft ammunition and there was no effective fighter cover, both of which allowed bombers to attack at low heights increasing the accuracy they achieved.[104] Nonetheless, the Luftwaffe demonstrated the ability to produce a favourable military outcome from their available resources.[105] The losses that the Luftwaffe inflicted on the evacuation fleet on 29 May and 1 June were prohibitive and the Royal Navy was obliged to suspend operations in daylight hours, temporarily in the case of 29 May, around Dunkirk. The Luftwaffe's success on 29 May and 1 June demonstrated that they could successfully apply air power, to shape the behaviour of Allied maritime forces and so disrupt the evacuation. It is necessary to consider why the Luftwaffe was unable halt the evacuation before 1 June. Before doing so, however, it is important to consider the decision which was made on 1 June to halt all further daylight evacuations from Dunkirk.

Notes

1 Cooper, *German Air Force*, p. 119; Harris, *Dunkirk*, p. 126; Jackson, *Air War*, p. 121; Murray, *Strategy*, p. 38; Overy, *Goering*, p. 103.
2 Churchill, *Finest Hour*, p. 90; Lord, *Miracle*, p. 269.
3 TNA: ADM 199/796A – Evacuation of BEF from France, Ships Used and Sunk.
4 TNA: ADM 199/793 – HM Ships Lost during the Evacuation of Troops from Dunkirk; TNA: ADM 358/3241 – Official Admiralty Communique, Evacuation from French Coast, 3 June 1940.
5 Gardner, *Evacuation*, p. 212.
6 Ibid.
7 TNA: ADM 199/360 – Dover Command, War Diary, 2 June 1940.
8 TNA: ADM 199/792 – Report of Vice Admiral Ramsay; Gardner, *Evacuation*, p. 158.
9 Adolf Galland, 'Defeat of the Luftwaffe', in Eugene M. Emme (ed.), *The Impact of Air Power* (Princeton, NJ: D. Van Nostrand, 1959), p. 251; Kesselring, *Memoirs*, p. 59.
10 TNA: ADM 199/792 – Report of Vice Admiral Ramsay.
11 Ibid.
12 TNA: ADM 199/787 – Report of Lieutenant R. Bill on Operations with Minesweeper Trawlers at Dunkirk on 29 May 1940; TNA: ADM 199/792 – Report of Vice Admiral Ramsay.

13 BA/MA: N 671/6 – Richthofen, Kriegstagebuch, 29 May 1940; TNA: ADM 199/786 – Commanding Officer of *Sabre*, Report of Activities during Operation Dynamo; TNA: ADM 199/787 – Commanding Officer of *Zeus*, Report of Activities during Operation Dynamo; TNA: ADM 199/788A – Master of *Maid of Orleans*, Report of Activities during Operation Dynamo; TNA: ADM 199/2205 – Naval War Diary Summaries, Evacuation of BEF, 29 May 1940; TNA: AIR 20/9906 – German Air Force Situation Reports on Western Front, 29 May 1940; TNA: AIR 27/1941 – ORB: 500 Squadron.
14 TNA: HW 5/2 – GC&CS Decrypts, CX/JQ/4.
15 TNA: AIR 22/168 – A.M.W.R. Daily Report for Summary, No. 316, 31 May 1940; TNA: HW 5/2 – GC&CS Decrypts, CX/JQ/1.
16 IWM: EDS/AL/1428 – *Heeresgruppe* A Ia, War Diary Part II, (trans.) Captain Hilton, 29 May 1940; TNA: ADM 199/786 – CO *Express* Report; TNA: ADM 199/786 – Commanding Officer of *Worcester*, Report of Activities during Operation Dynamo; Ward, *Hitler's Stuka Squadrons*, p. 86.
17 TNA: ADM 199/786 – Commanding Officer of *Gallant*, Report of Activities during Operation Dynamo; TNA: ADM 199/786 – Commanding Officer of *Jaguar*, Report of Activities during Operation Dynamo.
18 TNA: ADM 199/786 – Commanding Officer of *Icarus*, Report of Activities during Operation Dynamo.
19 TNA: ADM 199/786 – Commanding Officer of *Verity*, Report of Activities during Operation Dynamo; TNA: ADM 199/788A – Master of *Canterbury*, Report of Activities during Operation Dynamo.
20 TNA: ADM 199/786 – CO *Express* Report; TNA: ADM 199/786 – CO *Worcester* Report; TNA: ADM 199/786 – CO *Jaguar* Report; TNA: ADM 199/789 – Commander Minesweepers, Dover, Report on Operations of Dover Minesweepers during Operation Dynamo; TNA: ADM 199/791 – Commanding Officer of *Crested Eagle*, Report on the Loss of *Crested Eagle* during Operation Dynamo; TNA: ADM 199/792 – Commanding Officer of *Grenade*, Report on the Loss of *Grenade* during Operation Dynamo; TNA: ADM 199/793 – Report of Enquiry into the Loss of *Calvi* during Operation Dynamo; Gardner, *Evacuation*, p. 42. TNA: ADM 199/787 – Report of Lieutenant Bill.
21 TNA: ADM 199/793 – Report of Enquiry into the Loss of *Polly Johnson* during Operation Dynamo.
22 TNA: ADM 199/786 – CO *Jaguar* Report; TNA: ADM 199/788A – Master of *Loch Garry*, Report of Activities during Operation Dynamo.
23 IWM: Audio/1062 – F. C. Turner, Reel 1; TNA: ADM 199/786 – CO *Icarus* Report; TNA: WO 361/21 – Information Concerning Vessels Involved Operations Dynamo; Gardner, *Evacuation*, p. 41.
24 TNA: ADM 199/787 – Commanding Officer of Twente, Report of Activities during Operation Dynamo; TNA: ADM 199/792 – Commanding Officer of *Gracie*

Fields, Report on the Loss of *Gracie Fields* during Operation Dynamo; TNA: ADM 199/793 – Report of Enquiry into the Loss of *Gracie Fields* during Operation Dynamo; Gardner, *Evacuation*, p. 41.

25 TNA: ADM 199/786 – Commanding Officer of *Sutton*, Report of Activities during Operation Dynamo; TNA: ADM 199/786 – CO *Greyhound* Report.
26 *Ibid.*
27 TNA: ADM 199/786 – Commanding Officer of *Kellett*, Report of Activities during Operation Dynamo; TNA: ADM 199/786 – CO *Sabre* Report.
28 TNA: ADM 199/793 – Report of Enquiry into the Loss of *Nautilus* during Operation Dynamo.
29 Gardner, *Evacuation*, p. 161.
30 TNA: ADM 199/786 – CO *Malcolm* Report.
31 TNA: ADM 199/786 – Commanding Officer of *Oriole*, Report of Activities during Operation Dynamo.
32 TNA: HW 5/2 – GC&CS Decrypts, CX/JQ/4.
33 IWM: EDS/AL/1429 – 4. Armee Ia, Kriegstagebuch, 29 May 1940.
34 TNA: HW 5/2 – GC&CS Decrypts, CX/JQ/5.
35 TNA: AIR 22/168 – A.M.W.R. Daily Report for Summary, No. 315, 30 May 1940.
36 TNA: ADM 199/788A – Master of *St Seiriol*, Report of Activities during Operation Dynamo; Gardner, *Evacuation*, p. 43.
37 TNA: ADM 199/791 – CO *Crested Eagle* Report.
38 TNA: ADM 199/786 – Commanding Officer of *Albury*, Report of Activities during Operation Dynamo.
39 TNA: ADM 199/786 – CO *Icarus* Report.
40 *Ibid.*
41 TNA: ADM 199/786 – Commanding Officer of *Halcyon*, Report of Activities during Operation Dynamo; TNA: ADM 199/786 – Commanding Officer of *Saladin*, Report of Activities during Operation Dynamo; TNA: ADM 199/788A – Master of *Isle of Guernsey*, Report of Activities during Operation Dynamo; TNA: ADM 199/788A – Master of *St Julien*, Report of Activities during Operation Dynamo; TNA: ADM 199/792 – Report of Vice Admiral Ramsay.
42 TNA: ADM 199/787 – Commanding Officer of *Hilda*, Report of Activities during Operation Dynamo; TNA: ADM 199/787 – CO *Locust* Report; TNA: ADM 199/788A – Master *St Seiriol* Report.
43 TNA: ADM 199/786 – Commanding Officer of *Leda*, Report of Activities during Operation Dynamo; TNA: ADM 199/786 – Commanding Officer of *Salamander*, Report of Activities during Operation Dynamo; TNA: ADM 199/787 – Officer in Charge of Motorboat *Reda*, Report of Activities during Operation Dynamo; TNA: ADM 199/788A – Master of *Royal Sovereign*, Report of Activities during Operation Dynamo.

44 TNA: ADM 199/786 – Commanding Officer of *Pangbourne*, Report of Activities during Operation Dynamo.
45 TNA: ADM 199/786 – CO *Kellett* Report; TNA: ADM 199/788A – Officer in Charge of Motor Yacht *Elizabeth Green*, Report of Activities during Operation Dynamo.
46 TNA: ADM 199/360 – Dover Command, War Diary, 29 May 1940; TNA: ADM 199/786 – CO *Saladin* Report.
47 TNA: ADM 199/360 – Dover Command, War Diary, 29 May 1940; TNA: ADM 199/786 – CO *Sabre* Report; TNA: ADM 199/792 – Report of Vice Admiral Ramsay; TNA: ADM 199/792 – Commanding Officer of *Waverley*, Report of Activities and Loss of *Waverley* during Operation Dynamo; TNA: ADM 199/2205 – Naval War Diary Summaries, Merchant ship Casualties suffered during Evacuation, 31 May 1940; Gardner, *Evacuation*, pp. 42–5.
48 TNA: ADM 199/786 – Commanding Officer of *Hebe*, Report of Activities during Operation Dynamo; TNA: ADM 199/786 – CO *Kellett* Report.
49 TNA: ADM 199/788A – Master *Canterbury* Report.
50 TNA: ADM 199/786 – Commanding Officer of *Intrepid*, Report of Activities during Operation Dynamo.
51 TNA: ADM 199/787 – Commanding Officer of *Fredanja*, Report of Activities during Operation Dynamo.
52 TNA: ADM 199/789 – Commanding Officer of *King Orry*, Report of Activities during Operation Dynamo; TNA: ADM 199/793 – Report of Enquiry into the Loss of *King Orry* during Operation Dynamo.
53 TNA: ADM 199/786 – CO *Pangbourne* Report; TNA: ADM 199/786 – Commanding Officer of *Princess Elizabeth*, Report of Activities during Operation Dynamo; TNA: ADM 199/787 – Commanding Officer of *Jutland*, Report of Activities during Operation Dynamo; TNA: ADM 199/787 – Officer in Charge Motorboat *Reda* Report.
54 TNA: ADM 199/786 – CO *Sabre* Report.
55 TNA: AIR 20/9906 – German Air Force Situation Reports on Western Front, 29 May 1940.
56 *Ibid.*
57 BA/MA: N 671/6 – Richthofen, Kriegstagebuch, 29 May 1940.
58 TNA: ADM 199/789 – Report of Captain Tennant.
59 This figure does not include HMS *Wakeful* and *Grafton*, lost to enemy naval action on the night of 29 May 1940 in the number of Destroyers. The figure for personnel vessels includes SS *Normannia*, *Lorina*, *Fenella*, *Canterbury* and *King Orry*; excluded, however, are SS *Mona's Queen*, sunk by a magnetic mine, and SS *St Seiriol*, which took no further part in the evacuation because her crew were overwrought as a result of her experience. The SS *Clan Macalister* is also excluded from this figure – because it was not a personnel vessel – but its loss was significant.

60 TNA: ADM 199/360 – Dover Command, War Diary, 29 May 1940; Ramsay, 'Despatch', p. 3304, col. 2.
61 TNA: ADM 199/360 – Dover Command, War Diary, 29 May 1940.
62 TNA: ADM 199/792 – Report of Vice Admiral Ramsay.
63 TNA: ADM 199/786 – CO *Verity* Report.
64 TNA: ADM 199/786 – CO *Windsor* Report.
65 TNA: ADM 199/788B – Commodore Juke-Hughes, Principal Sea Transport Officer, Dover, to Vice Admiral Ramsay, 5 June 1940.
66 TNA: ADM 199/788A – Master *St Seiriol* Report; TNA: ADM 199/788A – Extract of Letter from Chairman of Liverpool and North Wales Steamship Company to Director of Sea Transport, 7 June 1940.
67 TNA: ADM 199/789 – Report of Captain Tennant; TNA: ADM 199/2205 – Naval War Diary Summaries, Captain Tennant to Vice Admiral Ramsay, 30 May 1940.
68 TNA: ADM 199/792 – Report of Vice Admiral Ramsay.
69 Ramsay, 'Despatch', p. 3304, col. 1.
70 TNA: ADM 199/360 – Dover Command, War Diary, 29 May 1940.
71 TNA: ADM 199/792 – Report of Vice Admiral Ramsay.
72 TNA: ADM 199/789 – Report of Captain Tennant.
73 Gardner, *Evacuation*, p. 212.
74 TNA: HW 5/2 – GC&CS Decrypts, CX/JQ/11.
75 TNA: ADM 199/793 – Report of Enquiry into the Loss of *St. Fagan* during Operation Dynamo.
76 TNA: ADM 199/792 – Report of Vice Admiral Ramsay; TNA: ADM 199/792 – CO *Keith* Report.
77 TNA: ADM 199/789 – Report of Captain Tennant.
78 TNA: ADM 199/792 – Report of Vice Admiral Ramsay; TNA: AIR 22/169 – A.M.W.R. Daily Report for Summary, No. 318, 2 June 1940; TNA: HW 5/2 – GC&CS Decrypts, CX/JQ/11; Gardner, *Evacuation*, p. 18.
79 TNA: ADM 199/792 – CO *Keith* Report.
80 Gardner, *Evacuation*, pp. 89–90.
81 TNA: ADM 199/792 – Commanding Officer of *Skipjack*, Report on the Loss of *Skipjack* on 1 June 1940.
82 TNA: ADM 199/360 – Dover Command, War Diary, 1 June 1940.
83 TNA: ADM 199/787 – Commanding Officer of *Patria* and *Haig*, Report of Activities during Operation Dynamo.
84 TNA: ADM 199/792 – Commanding Officer of *Basilisk*, Report on the Loss of *Basilisk* on 1 June 1940; Gardner, *Evacuation*, pp. 90–1.
85 TNA: WO 167/474 – 18th Field Regiment, Royal Artillery, War Diary, 1 June 1940.
86 TNA: HW 5/2 – GC&CS Decrypts, CX/JQ/13–15; *Der Adler*, 'Hölle Dünkirchen' Heft 13, 25 June 1940, p. 283.

87 TNA: ADM 199/793 – Report of Enquiry into the Loss of *Havant* during Operation Dynamo; Gardner, *Evacuation*, pp. 90–1.
88 TNA: ADM 199/360 – Dover Command, War Diary, 1 June 1940.
89 TNA: ADM 199/786 – Commanding Officer of *Saltash*, Report of Activities during Operation Dynamo.
90 TNA: ADM 199/360 – Dover Command, War Diary, 1 June 1940; TNA: ADM 199/788A – Master of *Prague*, Report of Activities during Operation Dynamo; TNA: ADM 199/791 – Master of *Lady Brassey*, Report of Activities during Operation Dynamo; Gardner, *Evacuation*, pp. 90–1.
91 Gardner, *Evacuation*, p. 92; McMurtie, *Jane's Fighting Ships*, p. 197.
92 TNA: ADM 199/786 – CO *Saltash* Report; Gardner, *Evacuation*, pp. 89–92.
93 TNA: ADM 199/360 – Dover Command, War Diary, 1 June 1940; TNA: ADM 199/792 – Commanding Officer of *Mosquito*, Report of Activities during Operation Dynamo.
94 TNA: AIR 20/9906 – German Air Force Situation Reports on Western Front, 1 June 1940.
95 Gardner, *Evacuation*, p. 93.
96 TNA: ADM 199/360 – Dover Command, War Diary, 31 May 1940; TNA: ADM 199/786 – Commanding Officer of *Ross*, Report of Activities during Operation Dynamo; TNA: ADM 199/786 – CO *Salamander* Report; TNA: ADM 199/786 – Commanding Officer of *Westward-Ho*, Report of Activities during Operation Dynamo; TNA: ADM 199/790 – Commanding Officer of *Kingfisher*, Report of Activities during Operation Dynamo.
97 TNA: ADM 199/360 – Dover Command, War Diary, 1 June 1940; Gardner, *Evacuation*, pp. 94–5.
98 TNA: ADM 199/788B – Commodore Juke-Hughes to Vice Admiral Ramsay, 5 June 1940.
99 TNA: ADM 199/788A – Master of *Malines*, Report of Activities during Operation Dynamo.
100 TNA: ADM 199/788B – Commodore Juke-Hughes to Vice Admiral Ramsay, 5 June 1940.
101 IWM: Audio/13933 – Gilhespy, Reel 10.
102 TNA: ADM 199/786 – CO *Hebe* Report; TNA: ADM 199/786 – Commanding Officer of *Whitshed*, Report of Activities during Operation Dynamo.
103 IWM: Audio/9768 – Arthur William Joscelyne, Reel 1.
104 TNA: ADM 199/788A – Master of *King George V*, Report of Activities during Operation Dynamo.
105 Millett et al., 'Effectiveness of Military Organizations', pp. 2–4.

3

The suspension of daylight evacuations

This chapter explores the decision to suspend daylight evacuations from Dunkirk on 1 June. As discussed in Chapter 2 the Luftwaffe achieved considerable success against the evacuation flee on 1 June, however, German artillery fire is also credited as playing an equal role in the decision to suspend daylight evacuations.[1] To determine the relative success or failure of the RAF and the Luftwaffe during Operation Dynamo it is essential to understand why daylight evacuations from Dunkirk were suspended. If artillery fire played a crucial role in the decision to suspend evacuations it reduces any claim of success that could be made for the Luftwaffe. Equally, if artillery fire was not an important factor in the decision to suspend daylight evacuations then it is necessary to recognize that the RAF failed to effectively provide air cover on 1 June.

German artillery fire had exerted an influence on the evacuation before 1 June. At the end of May, artillery batteries had advanced close enough to Dunkirk to heavily shell both Dunkirk harbour and the beaches at La Panne and Bray Dunes.[2] However, the artillery fire which is supposed to have ultimately halted the daylight evacuation of Dunkirk was not directed on the approach through Dunkirk harbour to the Mole, or against the adjacent beaches, but on the point Route X entered the Dunkirk Roads. There is therefore a distinction to be made between the heavy fire experienced in the town, the harbour and by the troops on the beaches, and the artillery fire on the shipping as it navigated its way along the coast West of Dunkirk. On 27 May artillery batteries on the coast east of Calais had forced Route Z to be abandoned during daylight hours. On 29 May artillery fire from Nieuport caused the use of Route Y to be suspended. In both cases daylight evacuation upon these routes was halted once artillery batteries had established positions on the coast parallel to the routes ships had to navigate along to reach Dunkirk. From these positions, the German artillery could bring observed and concentrated fire on the evacuation fleet whilst firing on a flat trajectory. These factors made the artillery fire a serious threat capable of halting ships navigating to or from Dunkirk.

This chapter will begin by discussing the capabilities of the various German artillery pieces, the limitations they faced when firing on shipping and their potential to halt daylight evacuations. The significance of artillery fire on Route X on 1 June and threat it posed to the evacuation will then be assessed. Finally, the decision to suspend further daylight evacuations will be considered. It will conclude that the suspension of further daylight evacuations from Dunkirk rested principally on the heavy losses to the Luftwaffe and that German artillery fire was not a primary factor in the decision.

Artillery types: Characteristics and limitations in an anti-shipping role

Artillery pieces of different calibres and type had different ranges and trajectories of fire which means that each piece had a very different effectiveness when used in an anti-shipping role. Before considering the types involved it is important to understand the technical difficulties which made some artillery pieces more suitable than others.

Meteorological factors had a significant impact on the accuracy of artillery fire on shipping; prevailing wind conditions had to be calculated but so too did the disruptive effect on ballistics of crossing the coast from a position over land to a target at sea. During this period, the barometric pressure exerted on the shell in flight would fluctuate making the atmospheric calculations necessary to obtain an accurate and repeatable fall of shot extremely difficult. Inaccurate calculations limited the value of observations of where the shot fell as corrections on range had to be made in isolation of how the different flight path of the projectile would be affected. The fall of shot correction method employed by German coastal artillery later in the war – as part of an established defensive system – involved fall of shot observations from two displaced observation posts. The observations were fed into a complicated series of calculations all of which were necessary to accurately correct fire against a target whose location and speed were variable.[3] The German artillery, and the spotters employed to correct the fall of shot of batteries which were not in visible range of their targets, had to adapt to these conditions for which, in the case of all but a few units, they were largely unprepared. The higher vertex height of a howitzer's trajectory increased the variability introduced by these meteorological factors whilst the flatter trajectory of field guns, and their higher muzzle velocity, resulted in these variables having a less pronounced effect on the fall of shot.[4] The carriage, and its recoil absorption, varied between different artillery pieces and this also had an important effect on the effectiveness of striking shipping off shore. What these limitations translate to is that artillery pieces positioned on the coast and firing on a flat trajectory had a greater chance of success when firing on ships and therefore posed a greater risk to the evacuation. In addition, the explosive force of the shell being used by different artillery pieces meant that the proximity to a ship a shell needed to land to cause damage varied. Indeed, near-misses were a major cause of damage particularly against older destroyers and merchantmen, whose brittle cast iron pipes and fittings were vulnerable to the shockwaves produced by explosions within close proximity of the ship.[5]

Historians who have dealt with the evacuation of Dunkirk have tended to omit any discussion of the type of artillery which fired on ships west of Dunkirk. It is quite common for the German artillery in use around Dunkirk to simply be described as 'heavy' artillery.[6] Where German artillery is discussed in greater detail it is not necessarily done with sufficient accuracy.[7] The absence of detail regarding German artillery is unfortunate because it has obscured the danger that particular types could have posed to the evacuation, and the limitations that they would have faced, were they to have been involved in the reported interdiction of Route X.

German heavy artillery could have posed a substantial threat to the evacuation. The 21cm-Mrs18 heavy howitzer fired a large high explosive shell weighing 113kg and could have brought accurate fire to bear on Route X.[8] However, the 16,700kg weight of the 21cm-Mrs18 and its size – the length of the barrel alone was 651cm – meant that it was not easy to manoeuvre or to conceal.[9] Had 21cm-Mrs18 pieces been located at the exposed positions on the coast, identified as the site of batteries firing on Route X, they would have been vulnerable to Allied air attack as well as to counter-battery fire.[10] Furthermore, whilst this type was involved in bombarding Dunkirk there were not many pieces available and the Germans preferred to use the 21cm-Mrs18 where its weight of fire was most telling.[11]

The Germans possessed several types of 15cm cannon such as the 15cm-K18. However, the same considerations which suggest the 21cm-Mrs18 was not used are applicable – in particular the relative scarcity of 15cm-K types and the unlikelihood of placing it in an exposed forward position. Preparations for the future offensive against the French also meant that it was unlikely that it was used in a role which a smaller calibre type could have fulfilled.

The s.10cm-K18, a 10.5cm calibre field gun, is also an unlikely candidate for the type firing on the evacuation on 1 June.[12] The long-range of the K18 makes it an unlikely candidate for the pieces which were positioned directly on the coast on 1 June. Instead, the s.10cm-K18 would have been used as the 'long arm' of the artillery, undertaking counter-battery work, harassing fire behind the Allied lines and fire support for units fighting on the perimeter.[13] During the Siege of Calais an s.10cm-K18 battery, of I./A.R.105, had opened fire on enemy ships as well as on the sea lanes, port and docks of Calais. However, I./A.R.105 struggled to combat the heavy shipping traffic en route to and from Calais as the firing positions they occupied were not directly on the coast.[14] There is one documented occasion of the K18 being used from coastal positions during the fighting at Calais. This occurred on 25 May when 10. *Panzer-Division* placed one *Zug* (two guns) of 10cm *Kanonen* in the dunes to counter naval movements. However, the Division's preference had been for Flak pieces to be used in this role because the weight and size of the K18 meant that it was ineffective in an anti-shipping role operating from the hastily emplaced positions in the dunes around Calais. Despite the presence of the 10cm artillery British destroyers were able to bombard German positions at Calais on 25 May.[15] The limitations the K18 faced at Calais would have been replicated at the positions utilized by artillery at Dunkirk on 1 June. Furthermore, preparations for *Fall Rot* led to the reallocation of heavy artillery from the formations besieging Dunkirk.[16]

In contrast, batteries of 15cm-s.F.H.18 were retained at Dunkirk in larger numbers because there were many such batteries within the German medium artillery regiments.[17] The 15cm-s.F.H.18 was a heavy howitzer with a maximum range of 10km when firing a standard high explosive shell, weighing 43.5kg.[18] The 15cm-s.F.H.18 possessed the capabilities to pose a serious threat to the evacuation. Batteries equipped with this type did fire on ships from positions east of Dunkirk near Nieuport and forced the suspension of shipping along Route Y.[19] Although a possible candidate for the fire on Route X from the west of Dunkirk on 1 June the positioning of this type on the coast would have been identifiable from aerial reconnaissance. British military intelligence concluded, however, that 'the absence of tracks and vehicles' at Le Clipon, from where Route X was being fired on, 'indicates that the guns are not of very heavy calibre'.[20] Given the ground conditions it was most unlikely that a heavy calibre battery, with its heavier weight of pieces, ammunition and extraneous equipment, would have been able to access this position, and fire from it, without leaving evident traces of its activity.

There is a further reason to suspect that the batteries accused of disrupting the evacuation on 1 June were not heavy artillery. During Dynamo, German heavy artillery batteries were tasked with bombarding the town and dock facilities at Dunkirk, so as to prevent the embarkation of troops, and had been engaged in fire support on the Dunkirk perimeter.²¹ These tasks – combined with operations at Lille and south of the Somme – had caused a serious ammunition shortage with forward units. Whilst this was the case for the 21cm-Mrs18, with units equipped with this type bemoaning the absence of the *munitionskolonne*, it was most serious at Dunkirk for the German 15cm artillery.²² As early as 25 May there were concerns regarding the shortage of ammunition for the 15cm-s.F.H.18 with XVI. *Armeekorps* noting that the shortage was 'severely noticeable' and had had an impact on its ability to engage heavily in counter-battery work.²³ On 25 May VIII. *Armeekorps* also reported that it 'desperately needed ammunition' and on 26 May reported the situation as 'catastrophic'.²⁴ On the same day the AOK 4 Quartermaster reported that the situation was 'undoubtedly a crisis'.²⁵ On 27 May XIX. *Armeekorps* artillery ammunition stocks were in a perilous situation and depleted to one-third of the initial issue.²⁶ On 28 May Colonel Zeitzler, Chief of Staff to General von Kleist, asked AOK 4 for the provision of further supplies of 'ammunition for l.F.H., s.F.H., 10cm Cannon and Anti-Tank'.²⁷ The situation was not one that prevented any further operations; *General der Artillerie* Franz Halder, Chief of the OKH General Staff, described it as an 'awkward but … temporary situation' that would soon remedy itself.²⁸ Resupplying the forces around Dunkirk was problematic, however, because of the planned offensive further south as well as logistical difficulties.

Whilst the 15cm-s.F.H.18 batteries of *Heeresgruppe* B were active against the evacuation fleet on 30 May, a shortage of high explosive ammunition meant that *Heeresgruppe* B was forced to request air support from *Luftflotte* 2 against British artillery firing from the stretch of dunes between Nieuport and Dunkirk.²⁹ As late as 17.00 on 31 May *Luftflotte* 2 was attacking an Allied artillery battery west of La Panne. On 2 June, after the daylight evacuation of Dunkirk had been halted, bombers returned to attacking Allied artillery positions around Dunkirk. Fifty-five per cent of *Luftflotte* 2's reported attacks on 2 June were directed against Allied artillery batteries and positions.³⁰

The shortage of ammunition also affected the artillery barrage on Dunkirk.³¹ On 30 May, only four 15cm batteries from *Heeresgruppe* A were firing on Dunkirk; even then, however, only so far as their ammunition allowed.³² The shortage of heavy artillery ammunition led to the 10.5cm-leFH18 and 8.8cm-Flak types (discussed below) being heavily drawn on to attack the town.³³ On the night of 30 May German Flak fired 3,000 shells into Dunkirk.³⁴ The need to use the 8.8cm-Flak in an artillery role was so pressing that its primary purpose of anti-aircraft defence was neglected with the result that, on the night of 31 May, complaints were made as to its inadequacy against British bombing attacks on German troops around the Dunkirk perimeter.³⁵

Despite heavy artillery pieces not having contributed to the shell fire on Route X, later credited as having contributed to the suspension of daylight evacuation, other types could have posed a threat. German anti-aircraft guns had the capabilities to damage, and indeed sink, shipping. The German 8.8cm-Flak pieces had been used within Germany for combined anti-aircraft and coastal defence duties.[36] Anti-aircraft gunnery demanded weapons with a high rate of fire, rapid fire-control calculation, fast tracking speeds and a high muzzle velocity. The 8.8cm-Flak was also equipped with a telescopic sight for direct firing. These factors greatly aided attacks on ships moving at speed off the coast and enabled 8.8cm-Flak pieces to achieve success against shipping during the Fall of France.[37] During the evacuation of Boulogne, on 24 May, an 8.8cm-Flak battery claimed to have sunk an Allied destroyer, in all probability FS *Chacal* – which as well as being attacked by anti-aircraft batteries was under fire from German tanks who also claimed credit for its loss – which was actually sunk by dive-bombers.[38] The accuracy of the claim to have sunk *Chacal* aside, 8.8cm-Flak batteries – positioned along the coast east of Calais 800 metres from the shore and spaced a little over 500 metres from one another – had successfully interdicted the daylight use of Route Z, sinking MV *Sequacity* and forcing several other ships to abandon the attempt and return to Dover.[39] During 29 May, 8.8cm-Flak batteries claimed to have sunk one patrol vessel and damaged five others, as well as damaging a further five large motorboats.[40] These claims do not conform with the reports from ships involved in the evacuation. The success achieved by 8.8cm-Flak batteries firing from coastal positions near Calais, however, demonstrates that they were capable of inflicting damage to the vessels being used to evacuate Dunkirk.[41] The use of 8.8cm-Flak over other artillery pieces at Calais also demonstrates the German Army's preference to use this type in an anti-shipping role.[42]

The distance ships reported being fired on, whilst navigating Route X on 1 June, also corresponds closely to the effective range of the 8.8cm-Flak, if limited for direct firing, the range of its tracer round, and the distance its crew would have been effectively trained to attack when using the gun on a horizontal firing plain.[43] Furthermore, Bomber Command sorties to attack artillery at Pointe de Gravelines found and attacked anti-aircraft batteries in good artillery positions in an area of scrub and sand dunes with good roads leading up to it 2.5 miles south-west of Le Clipon.[44] The topography of the positions near Le Clipon was similar to positions 8.8cm-Flak batteries were firing from east of Calais.

German anti-aircraft batteries were involved in the artillery fire against the evacuation and, during fighting along the coast which included actions before and after Dunkirk, claimed to have sunk more than twenty vessels of varying types.⁴⁵ *Flak-Regiment* 102 claimed to have hit three transport vessels during fighting at Dunkirk before it was withdrawn on 1 June. From 31 May preparations for future offensives against the remaining French forces on the Somme led to Flak batteries no longer deemed necessary to the fighting at Dunkirk were withdrawn.⁴⁶ Furthermore, surviving reports make no mention of ships sunk by Flak batteries during 1 June.

If 8.8cm-Flak batteries were not involved then the reported gunfire was most likely from a 10.5cm-leFH18 battery. The 10.5cm-leFH18 standard field gun-howitzer of the German divisional artillery at the start of the Second World War could achieve a range of up to 10.7km.⁴⁷ The 10.5cm-leFH18 was highly accurate and this, in conjunction with the ease with which the gun could be laid, meant that it was a good piece to fire against moving targets.⁴⁸ Batteries equipped with the 10.5cm-leFH18 had been advanced into artillery range of Dunkirk, and AOK 4 attempted to use its light artillery to fire into Dunkirk harbour from Fort-Mardyck, west of Dunkirk, during 30 May.⁴⁹ During Dynamo, ships were hit by what they believed were 10.5cm shells – although this fire did not always cause significant damage. On 31 May *Glen Gower* received a direct hit whilst alongside the Mole in Dunkirk harbour from what an artillery officer on board identified as a 10.5cm howitzer; whilst several men were killed the shell did not cause significant damage and *Glen Gower* remained in service.⁵⁰ The 10.5cm-leFH18 standard high explosive shell weighed 14.81kg. Although *Glen Gower*'s account suggests that the smaller calibre of the 10.5cm-leFH18 struggled for effectiveness when firing on a high trajectory – even when securing a direct hit – other accounts demonstrate that they could damage ships evacuating troops from Dunkirk.⁵¹ A limitation of the lower explosive charge of these shells compared to heavy artillery, however, was that near-misses caused less damage to the target. Artillery fire from pieces such as the 10.5cm-leFH18 therefore had to achieve greater accuracy to interdict the evacuation route.

The experience of several vessels at Dunkirk illustrates the challenge of hitting naval targets when they were under way. On 31 May the destroyer HMS *Express* was straddled by artillery firing from Gravelines; *Express* was not damaged in this attack, and no direct hits were secured against her.⁵² The Skoot *Friso* was also straddled by shells on 31 May and – despite only being able to make a top speed of 6 knots – was also able to avoid receiving a direct hit by cutting across sandbanks and so presenting the minimum target whilst opening the range as fast as possible.⁵³ Artillery units, who were not specialist in attacking targets underway at sea, struggled to bring effective artillery fire to bear.

Furthermore, shortages of high explosive ammunition resulted in the German artillery firing shrapnel in large quantities against ships employed in the evacuation.[54] The use of shrapnel reduced the German artillery's ability to halt the evacuation. On 29 May, SS *Killarney* was shelled by what it believed to be three 15cm batteries east of Calais; the absence of high explosives meant that despite being under fire for over thirty minutes *Killarney* received only light damage – although shrapnel killed eight men and injured a further thirty.[55] The experience of HMS *Snaefell* on the evening of 1 June – when artillery fire on Route X should have been at its most intense – reinforces the impression that there was not a surplus of high explosive ammunition for use against the evacuation fleet; *Snaefell* arrived off Dunkirk to 'bursts of shrapnel from enemy guns, which however fell short'.[56] HMS *Glen Gower* records that from 23.55 on 1 June she was continually under fire and that 'shrapnel was spraying the beaches and the ships. Shells were continually bursting overhead but the ship was very lucky and was hit only occasionally by pieces of shrapnel which did no damage.'[57] The experiences of motorboats and yachts at Dunkirk also suggest that a significant proportion of the artillery fire being directed against the beach and the ships standing off the shore was shrapnel.[58]

The scarcity of information on individual German artillery and Flak units means it is not possible to make a definitive conclusion as to which type was involved in firing from West of Dunkirk on 1 June. Although Flak batteries started to be withdrawn from Dunkirk before 1 June RAF attacks on these positions on 2 June reported anti-aircraft fire as coming from the location of the battery positions. Before 1 June, at positions near Calais the German Army had favoured the use of 8.8cm-Flak in the anti-shipping role.[59] Whichever type of German artillery was involved is evident that they were not heavy calibre batteries.

Nonetheless, concentrated fire on Route X could have had the capacity to threaten the continuation of Operation Dynamo. However, whether artillery fire was a threat on 1 June before daylight evacuations were halted is not clear. It is this which must be established before it is possible to determine whether artillery fire was a primary cause for the cessation of daylight evacuation or if the Luftwaffe alone was responsible for this feat.

The effects of artillery fire

The German artillery attempting to halt the evacuation concentrated the majority of its fire against the town, harbour and beaches surrounding Dunkirk.

Artillery fire had been directed against these targets from the early stages of the evacuation and was at times a severe impediment to the organized embarking of troops.[60] German artillery fire from Nieuport was particularly heavy throughout 31 May and was central to the decision made on the morning of 1 June to halt the lifting of troops from the beaches near La Panne. The evacuation fleet was instead concentrated on the Mole at Dunkirk which had proved capable of rapidly embarking large numbers of troops.[61] There is, however, no suggestion in the accounts relating to the decision to halt daylight evacuation on 1 June that artillery fire other than on Route X was a significant factor in that decision. This distinction is important because subsequent claims that artillery fire was a primary cause often draw on examples of artillery fire on the town and beaches rather than evidence of artillery firing on the channel where Route X exited onto the Dunkirk Roads amidst an area of treacherous sandbank. Importantly, there are few instances of artillery sinking ships after Route Z was abandoned (see the map of evacuation routes provided in Appendix I). The sinking of FS *Bourrasque* off Nieuport on 30 May, as it attempted to navigate Route Y, was an instance where artillery fire played a role in sinking a notable evacuation vessel. *Bourrasque* was not directly sunk by gunfire however, but instead struck a mine whilst attempting to avoid artillery fire.[62] Nor was this incident replayed to any great extent on 31 May or 1 June, and whilst several ships were forced off the evacuation route to evade gunfire, there were no significant losses as a result. Furthermore, the accounts of ship's captains involved in the evacuation of Dunkirk tend not to record artillery fire as the primary danger to their ships or assign any great significance to shore bombardment.

The reports of commanding officers of ships involved in Operation Dynamo record their crews persevering through the perils of shore bombardment and references to gunfire are typically incidental even where shelling was quite hazardous. This tends to be in stark contrast with the detail provided of air attacks during the evacuation. Such an account is that of Lieutenant J.A. Simson, commanding HMS *Lord Grey* and *Clythness*, for 31 May. Simson records several instances of heavy air activity over Dunkirk but only mentioned the artillery in terms of 'four or five colossal splashes, as of heavy shells, which fell round us soon after we had left'.[63] The captains of little ships involved in Operation Dynamo typically relate their experiences of artillery as a secondary, marginal, danger even in instances of exposure to artillery fire. B.A. Smith, one of only two civilian personnel from the Dunkirk Little Ships to receive a gallantry award, was working off the beaches of Dunkirk in the motor yacht *Constant Nymph* on 31 May and experienced the effect of artillery bombardment:

Jerry also had some big guns for which aeroplanes were spotting, and they dropped Very lights over the ships, but here again Jerry wasted ammunition without hitting anything. One of the crumps came as a nasty shock … she quivered all over but in the next moment she went on again and the noise of the crump followed the air push so I knew it was nothing serious.[64]

Smith's account also notes German aircraft spotting for artillery and other accounts of the evacuation similarly record aircraft spotting for artillery which went unmolested by the RAF.[65] Nor was the artillery spotting limited to aircraft. Observation balloons spotting for artillery were identified in use from 26 May and these were advanced further towards Dunkirk with artillery batteries.[66] HMS *Shikari* reported that on 30 May:

> On passing Nieuport Buoy came under fire from a battery behind Nieuport for seven minutes. It is thought that the fire was controlled by an observation balloon over Nieuport. This fact was reported by signal but the balloon was up for the next few days.[67]

Blackburn Skuas of 806 (FAA) Squadron observed an observation balloon spotting for four heavy guns 500 metres east of Nieuport on 31 May and the Skoot *Oranje* reported artillery shelling ships from this position 'using an observation balloon for spotting'.[68] Directed by observation balloons the shelling of La Panne caused considerable delays throughout 31 May and the decision was made early on 1 June to direct troops to use the Mole at Dunkirk and prevent further embarkation from the exposed beaches.[69] German observation balloons continued to be used to spot for the artillery and two were reported in the vicinity of Bergues on 1 June.[70] The threat caused Lord Gort to ask Ramsay, at 06.45 on 1 June, to inform the RAF that 'observation balloons must be seen off at once as they are causing a lot of damage'.[71]

The RAF, however, undertook little action against these observation balloons – a curious oversight if German artillery posed the serious threat that has since been claimed. Indeed, one of the criticisms of Fighter Command during this period was the apparent immunity with which these observation balloons operated.[72] Calls for action against the balloons did cause Fighter Command to order one squadron to attempt to attack the balloons at the end of their patrol but no fighter sweeps were undertaken with the specific instructions of bringing the balloons down and this minimal effort produced no result.[73] It is difficult to reconcile the attitude adopted by Fighter Command towards the observation balloons, or why more urgent requests regarding them were not made by the naval authorities, if observed artillery fire was threatening the continuation of the evacuation.[74]

There were relatively few ships lost to artillery fire during Dynamo and on 1 June artillery fire only accounted for the loss of HMS *Lord Cavan*. Incidences of damage caused by artillery fire on 1 June were also minimal. Nonetheless, it is important to establish whether artillery was playing a significant role in interdicting Route X. The reports submitted to the Admiralty by individual ships involved in the evacuation provide valuable evidence in this regard. Frequently, however, only those reports which provide the most dramatic extracts have been selected for inclusion in historical works. As a result, the typical experience of most ships involved in the evacuation has inadvertently been distorted. By qualitatively analysing the reports submitted to the Admiralty and identifying references to air attack or artillery fire and then quantitatively assessing the result, in comparison to one another, it is possible to identify a clear distinction between the threat of artillery fire and air attack on 1 June. Across these reports over twice as many references to air attack, as opposed to artillery, are recorded on 1 June. Separating the reports of British destroyers involved in the evacuation on 1 June shows a greater discrepancy. Twenty-one incidences of air attack are recorded compared to eight incidences of artillery fire – only four of which detail artillery fire on Route X. These four references do not suggest that British destroyers on Route X were in great danger as a result of artillery fire. In the case of *Shikari* only a few shots were fired at the ship, these occurring close to the navigation buoy 'No. 6 W'.[75] *Vivacious* left Dunkirk after dawn on 1 June and arrived at Dover without incident 'except for slight and inaccurate enemy gunfire at No. 5 buoy'.[76] None of the four references to artillery fire on Route X detail any hits, near-misses or damage caused to the ships. Furthermore, if these reports contain a discrepancy in the incidences of air attack or artillery fire on 1 June it is to under-represent the number of air attacks. Destroyers such as HMS *Keith*, lost to air attack on the morning of 1 June, are not represented in these figures as detailed reports were not submitted to the Admiralty. The reports submitted by minesweepers follow a similar pattern, with forty-one references to air attack and nineteen to artillery fire on 1 June. Of the nineteen references to artillery only four reference gunfire on Route X. The only minesweeper to record any damage from artillery fire was *Fitzroy* and this did not occur on Route X. Going beyond the frequency of references the language used is also significantly different between the artillery fire and air attacks experienced. When HMS *Windsor* suffered several near-misses and machine-gun attacks from dive-bombers her Captain reported that along with extensive damage to her ancillary equipment *Windsor*'s side was 'riddled like a pepperbox'.[77] The damage caused by artillery fire rarely elicited such descriptive language.

This analysis does not prove that German artillery was an incidental threat on 1 June, only that it was perceived as such by the authors of these reports when they composed the reports several days after the conclusion of Dynamo. There are reports from 1 June which do present artillery fire in a more dangerous light. The report of HMS *Kindred Star* and *Thrifty* records that, on arriving off Dunkirk at 14.30 on 1 June, they experienced 'shells falling very near from shore batteries' and an hour later 'several vessels were seen trying to enter Dunkirk Roads but all were driven back by [the] action of enemy aircraft and shore batteries. We altered course to bring us outside [of the] range of [the] shore guns'.[78] The record of *Kindred Star* and *Thrifty* does not, however, record the gunfire hitting any ships and their report records that they proceeded to Dunkirk via Route Y rather than Route X. Furthermore, the report suggests that the Luftwaffe was the main threat; at 15.30 on 1 June both ships were attacked by dive-bombers and radioed that they had been 'attacked by aircraft'. Neither this message nor the subsequent message sent by *Kindred Star* at 16.10, when the ships were again attacked by dive-bombers, made any reference to the fire from shore batteries.[79] This second air attack resulted in near-misses on both ships whilst nearby 'one trawler was seen to be badly hit by a bomb – afterwards sinking. Another unknown vessel was blown to pieces.' The near-misses fractured pipes in the boiler room of *Kindred Star* and forced both ships to leave Dunkirk whereupon, at 18.30, they experienced further air attacks.[80] By 20.44 on the evening of 1 June, Lieutenant Mead, in command of the Walton and Frinton RNLB, was advised against entering Dunkirk harbour but was able to do so and remain until 04.23 on 2 June. Lieutenant Mead was unfortunately killed by shrapnel whilst in Dunkirk harbour but the log that he maintained up until his death reveals that the primary threat to the evacuation fleet on 1 June was from air attack.[81] Soldiers and sailors did suffer from artillery fire at Dunkirk harbour; however, it did not prevent further embarkations by night following the suspension of 1 June. Sub-Lieutenant Yeatman, in command of the motorboat *Skylark*, reported that he 'found considerably greater risk from the movement of Allied craft than from Nazi shelling'.[82] This conclusion is borne out by the recommendations for good conduct submitted to the Admiralty for the crews of British destroyers during Dynamo with a disparity between recommendations for action involving air attack and recommendations involving artillery fire, ninety-one and six respectively.[83]

The decision to suspend daylight evacuation

The argument that artillery fire played an important part in the decision to halt daylight evacuation rests very largely on one crucial message. At 23.29 on 1 June Ramsay messaged the Admiralty:

> SNO Dunkirk 17.54/1 stating General concurs that evacuation for transports is to cease at 03.00. Channels to Dunkirk now all under fire of German batteries. New battery came into action this evening. Suspending traffic on only remaining daylight route namely X. Maintaining heavy barrage, sinking transports Mona's Isle and Brighton Queen and a Trawler in the fairway near No. 5 Buoy ... coupled with recent Naval losses ... have convinced me that any attempt to continue evacuation during the day is unwise.[84]

However, whilst Ramsay's message is an important source it is widely inaccurate and largely fails to reflect the reality of the situation. The message which Captain Tennant, SNO Dunkirk, sent, and to which Ramsay specifically refers, does not mention artillery. Instead Tennant places the responsibility for halting daylight evacuation on air attack.

> Things are getting very hot for ships. Over 100 bombers on ships here since 05.30. Many casualties. Have directed that no ship sail during daylight. Evacuation by transport therefore ceases at 03.00.[85]

Tennant's report on Dynamo also makes no reference to having called off daylight evacuation because of shore bombardment. Tennant's report confirms that the decision to halt daylight evacuation was made following the heavy losses suffered on the morning of 1 June and the heavy air attacks he witnessed later in the day against HMS *Worcester*.[86] Discussing these air attacks Tennant states that 'the heavy attacks on ships at sea compelled me to stop all sailings and arrivals during light'.[87] At 22.14, on 1 June, Ramsay had messaged Tennant and Major-General Alexander (Officer Commanding I Corps) that because of 'casualties to shipping by heavy artillery. All shipping has been ordered to withdraw before daylight tomorrow'.[88] Along with Ramsay's 23.29 message to the Admiralty it is clear that by end of the day Ramsay was crediting artillery fire with the decision to suspend daylight evacuation. Tennant's message to Ramsay, however, clearly shows that daylight evacuations had already been suspended.

   Ramsay's message was also inaccurate when he stated that German batteries which came into action in on the evening of 1 June were responsible for sinking HMS *Brighton Queen* and SS *Mona's Isle* as well as an unnamed trawler. The latter, *Lord Cavan*, was sunk by gunfire – the only loss to artillery on 1 June –

however, this did not occur on Route X.[89] Both *Lord Cavan* and SS *St Helier*, the only other ship of note to be seriously damaged by artillery fire on 1 June, were hit inside Dunkirk harbour.[90] SS *Mona's Queen* (erroneously identified as Mona's Isle in the message) was lost on 29 May, after striking a mine, whilst *Brighton Queen* was sunk by aircraft on 1 June in an attack which did not involve artillery. *Mona's Isle* had radioed that she was 'shelled off No. 5 Buoy, Dunkirk Channel'.[91] However, this message was received at 14.55 on 1 June before which, at 13.45, Ramsay had already recalled British destroyers from the evacuation.[92]

In addition to recalling ships from the evacuation ships at Dover were prevented sailing for Dunkirk before the German batteries Ramsay cited in his 23.29 message came into action on Route X. In the case of HMS *Malcolm*, having been unable to acquire instructions as to when to return to Dunkirk, her Captain decided to proceed to Dunkirk at 13.18. At the eastern entrance of Dover he was ordered by VA Dover not to depart.[93] In particular larger personnel vessels were halted and not despatched to Dunkirk until a point where they could arrive and operate after daylight.[94] At 13.16 on 1 June, as the scale of the losses to the Luftwaffe became apparent, Admiral Plunkett, C-in-C The Nore, responsible for guarding the East-Coast convoys and many of whose resources were being utilized in Operation Dynamo, pressed the Admiralty to limit the use of destroyers and only employ them 'for evacuation purposes in areas in which they can make use of their speed to evade air attacks'.[95] Admiral Taylor, who was organizing yachts and small craft during Dynamo, expressed alarm before midday on 1 June because vessels were 'being bombed and machine-gunned all the way to the North Goodwins'.[96] The scale of air attacks in the morning of 1 June led to the decision to prevent the ships of the evacuation which were unable to travel at speeds higher than 20 knots returning to Dunkirk during daylight.[97] This decision was also applied to the Dutch skoots which, manned with Naval personnel, were being used in the evacuation. The skoot *Cariba* reached Ramsgate at 09.00 on 1 June but received no further orders to sail to Dunkirk.[98] HMS *Locust*, a gunboat capable of a top speed of 17 knots, disembarked troops at Dover at 10.15 on 1 June but did not receive further orders until 20.00.[99] By 15.00 instructions were formally submitted that all vessels involved in the evacuation that evening arrive at Dunkirk harbour after 22.00.[100] These incidents represent a decision, if not to suspend, then to at least limit as far as possible further daylight evacuation; this was not a consequence of artillery fire but because of the losses suffered to air attack during the morning of 1 June. Whilst artillery batteries were firing on Route X during the morning it was successfully navigated by every ship which sailed out of Dunkirk before midday on 1 June and there was no suggestion that the entrance into Dunkirk had become unusable as a result of artillery fire.[101] HMS *Whitehall* reported the fire as coming from 'small guns' and artillery fire from shore batteries did not prevent the ships from successfully navigating the route at this time.[102] Indeed, Ramsay appears to have received no messages which suggested that artillery pieces at this location were of a large calibre or were preventing ships navigating to or from Dunkirk. The Admiralty, however, had become 'very distressed' at the losses suffered to air attack.[103] At 15.30 on 1 June, Dudley Pound informed the Chief of Staff Committee that:

> the present situation was that three destroyers, a minesweeper, and two transports, had been sunk by bombing attacks during the morning. He had given orders, therefore, that no more destroyers or other vessels should be sent in before dark ... evacuation would be suspended until 19.30, when it would continue until 03.00.[104]

Major-General Alexander, whom Ramsay cites in his telegram to the Admiralty at 23.29 on 1 June as concurring with the decision to suspend daylight evacuation, considered that the decision to halt daylight evacuation had been made because of the casualties suffered by the Royal Navy from 'enemy action'.[105] As the Navy's losses to enemy action on 1 June were almost exclusively the result of air attacks Alexander's account indicates that it was the aerial threat to the evacuation fleet which led to the decision to halt daylight evacuations and not the threat of artillery fire.

The impression that Ramsay suspended the daylight evacuation of Dunkirk primarily because of air attack is reinforced by the lack of action taken to counteract artillery batteries on 1 June itself.[106] The only counter-battery fire which was specifically ordered, against German artillery by a Royal Navy ship, was not against batteries firing on Route X. At 20.00 on 1 June HMS *Locust* began counter-battery fire against artillery supporting German infantry attacks and threatening shipping to the east of Dunkirk on Route Y.[107] Nor were instructions to make smoke whilst on Route X given to ships in order that they might screen their movements from enemy positions. Smoke screens could be created in a number of ways, including the vaporization of oil, and the Royal Navy possessed smoke-floats and chlorosulphonic acid projectors, both of which were used by destroyers during Dynamo.[108] For steamships an effective screen could be produced by the simple expedient of restricting air supply to the boiler and on 1 June *Killarney* avoided gunfire by producing as much smoke as possible.[109] The difficulty artillery faced in accurately striking a mobile target under way at sea and partially obscured by smoke was considerable. On 30 May, MV *Royal Daffodil* was 'shelled from shore and undoubtedly saved by one of HM destroyers putting up an effective smoke screen'.[110] A similar screen was produced by the destroyer HMS *Harvester* at 07.15 on 1 June to mask vessels from artillery fire from Nieuport.[111] On these occasions none of the ships involved reported any damage from artillery fire. During the course of 1 June, no Royal Navy ships were ordered to produce smoke screens to mask the areas which were vulnerable to artillery fire; a precaution one might reasonably assume would have been taken if artillery fire had been a significant cause for concern when the decision to suspend daylight evacuations was made. It is also important to note that the staff at Dover did not seek the co-operation of the RAF to attack the probable location of artillery batteries firing on Route X before daylight evacuations were halted on 1 June. Whilst Bomber Command undertook sorties against batteries at Gravelines from 2 June onwards, no attacks were made on these batteries by the RAF on 1 June itself.

Conclusion

The evidence from the ships logs and the chain of events reveal that it was the losses incurred as a result of air attack which halted daylight evacuation. The artillery fire which came to menace Route X was, at best, a contributing factor in the decision to suspend daylight evacuations. The Naval Staff History of the evacuation would later consider it 'impossible to resist the conclusion that ... the danger from enemy shell fire was magnified in the minds of those at Dover'.[112] Ramsay's staff was certainly exhausted by 1 June; Ramsay had written to his wife on 27 May that they were 'completely worn out' with 'no prospect at all of any let up'.[113] If temporary confusion and errors of facts emerged at Dover they were not, however, repeated elsewhere. The Admiralty Operational Intelligence Centre's report for 1 June made no reference to artillery but detailed 'heavy bombing reported ... from an early hour ... at all points on the coast'.[114] If German artillery held an exaggerated menace in the minds of those at Dover it was a consequence of the disruption and losses the Luftwaffe had inflicted and followed the decision to suspend evacuations because of the naval losses to air attack.

By establishing that Luftwaffe's application of air power halted daylight evacuations, without the additional support of German artillery, it is possible to look at their earlier operations through the prism of their success on 1 June. In doing so it will be possible to assess what differences in the Luftwaffe's approach, and the conditions they were fighting in, prohibited their success before 1 June. Similarly, establishing that Fighter Command was unsuccessful in protecting the evacuation on 1 June allows a new perspective from which to assess the strategy and tactics they pursued during Dynamo.

Notes

1. Ramsay, 'Despatch', p. 3296, col. 2; Richards, *Fight*, p. 140.
2. TNA: CAB 44/69 – War Cabinet Historical Section: Narrative, Section A, Part II (d), B.E.F. in France and Flanders: 31 May–4 June 1940.
3. TNA: WO 208/2986 – Illustrated Record of German Army Equipment, 1939–1945, Vol. II, Artillery; Part II.
4. TNA: WO 195/7824 – Study of Accuracy of Artillery Fire
5. TNA: ADM 199/1189 – Tactical Summary of Bombing Attacks by German Aircraft on HM Ships and Shipping from September 1939 to February 1941.
6. Carse, *Dunkirk*, p. 48; Jackson, *Dunkirk*, p. 170; Jacobsen, *Dünkirchen*, p. 169; Oddone, *Dunkirk*, pp. 90, 102.
7. One suggestion is the 17cm-K18, which only entered general service in 1941 and was not involved in the Battle of France.
    TNA: WO 208/2985 – Illustrated Record of German Army Equipment, 1939–1945; Dildy, *Dunkirk*, p. 75.
8. Ian V. Hogg, *German Artillery of World War Two* (London: Frontline Books, 2013), p. 95; Rudolf Witzel, *Mit Mörsern, Haubitzen und Kanonen: Aks Artillerieoffizier im Freiden und Krieg 1936–1945* (Würzburg: Flechsig, 2008), pp. 71.
9. TNA: WO 190/891 – Characteristics of Weapons Found in German Artillery Units, Military Situation Appreciations File; TNA: WO 208/2287 – Technical Reports Regarding Enemy Weapons: Technical Intelligence Summary 91, 4 November 1942; Witzel, *Mit Mörsern*, p. 71.
10. TNA: WO 167/474 – 18th Field Regiment Royal Artillery; *Unteroffizier* Martin, 'Tank Destroyers in the Dunkirk Blocking Force', in Alan Bance (ed., trans.), *Blitzkrieg in Their Own Words: First-Hand Accounts from German Soldiers, 1939–1940* (Barnsley: Pen & Sword, 2005), p. 169.
11. NARA: T78, R269-H 31/1 – OKH, 594. Generalstabs des Heeres/General der Artillerie (Ia) Nr. 1099/42 g.Kdos, 'Artilleristische Erfahrungen beim Angriff gegen einen in ständigen und feldmäßigen Befestigungen zur Verteidigung eingerichteten (Lehren aus dem Angriff auf Sewastopol, Mai/Juli 1942)', 12 August 1942.
12. TNA: WO 208/2968 – War Office Publication, Enemy Weapons.
13. Wolfgang Fleischer, *German Motorized Artillery and Panzer Artillery in World War II* (Atglen, PA: Schiffer, 2004), p. 52; Engelmann, *Deutsche Artillerie*, p. 119.
14. IWM: EDS/AL/1399 – 10. *Panzer-Division*, Extract from War Diary, 24 May 1940.
15. IWM: EDS/AL/1399 – 10. *Panzer-Division*, Extract from War Diary, 25 May 1940; TNA: ADM 199/786 – Commanding Officer of *Greyhound*, Report of Activities during Operation Dynamo.
16. Central Archive of the Ministry of Defence of the Russian Federation (hereafter TsAMO RF): Ф.500 оп.12451 д.50 – Pläne des OKH für die Fortführung der Operationen nach Abschluß der Kämpfe im Artois und in Flandern, 27–31 May 1940;

IWM: EDS/AL/1371 – *Heeresgruppe* A Ia, War Diary, Appendices, Ia Nr. 1150/40 g.Kdos, HeeresgruppenBefhel Nr.9, 31 May 1940; Jacobsen, *Dünkirchen*, p. 164.
17 TNA: WO 208/2960 – Notes on the German Army.
18 The maximum obtainable range when firing a standard high explosive shell with charge I was 4km.
    TNA: WO 208/2968 – War Office Publication, Enemy Weapons, Part IV: German Infantry, Heavy Anti-Aircraft and Divisional Artillery, February 1943; TNA: WO 219/1979 – Enemy Weapons and Equipment: Technical Intelligence Bulletin 3.
19 Credit for the closure of Route Y must be tempered, however, by the fact that Route X, which was faster, had become available.
20 TNA: WO 106/1644 – Military intelligence, Daily Intelligence Summaries and Maps.
21 IWM: EDS/AL/1372 – *Heeresgruppe* B Ia, War Diary, Appendices, Ab. Nr. 20131/40gk, Telegram from General Franz Halder, 25 May 1940.
22 Witzel, *Mit Mörsern*, p. 83; IWM: EDS/AL/1429 – 4. Armee I/a, War Diary, 24–30 May 1940.
23 IWM: EDS/AL/1407 – XVI. A.K. Ia, War Diary, 25 May 1940.
24 IWM: EDS/AL/1429 – 4. Armee I/a, War Diary, 25–26 May 1940.
25 *Ibid.*
26 TNA: CAB 146/452 – EDS Summary of XIX Corps War Diary, 27 May 1940.
27 IWM: EDS/AL/1429 – 4. Armee I/a, War Diary, 28 May 1940.
28 Generaloberst Franz Halder, *Kriegstagebuch: Tägliche Aufzeichnungen des Chefs des Generalstabes des Heeres, 1939–1942*, Vol. I, (ed.) Hans-Adolf Jacobsen (Stuttgart: W.Kohlhammer, 1962), p. 322.
29 IWM: EDS/AL/1433 – *Heeresgruppe* B Ia, War Diary, 30 May 1940.
30 TNA: AIR 20/9906 – German Air Force Situation Report on Western Front.
31 Ellis, *War in France*, p. 227; Jacobsen, *Dünkirchen*, p. 157.
32 IWM: EDS/AL/1429 – 4. Armee I/a, War Diary 30 May 1940.
33 *Ibid.*
34 *Ibid.*
35 IWM: EDS/AL/1405 – Ab. Nr. T 641/40g, Telegram Heeresgruppe B to Heeresgruppe A, 31 May 1940.
36 TNA: WO 208/2968 – War Office Publication, Enemy Weapons.
37 TNA: WO 208/3001 – German Anti-Aircraft Artillery, Military Intelligence Service, USA War Department, 8 February 1943; Adalbert Koch, *Die Geschichte der Deutschen Flakartillerie: 1935–1945* (Friedberg: Podzun-Pallas, 1982), p. 35.
38 TNA: HW 5/1 – GC&CS Decrypts, CX/FJ/101; Denys Cook, *Missing in Action: Or My War as a Prisoner of War* (n.p.: Trafford Publishing, 2013), p. 286; John Jourdan and Jean Moulin, *French Destroyers: Torpilleurs d'Escadre and Contre-Torpilleurs, 1922–1956* (Barnsley: Seaforth, 2015), p. 228.

39 IWM: EDS/AL/1429 – 4. Armee I/a, War Diary, 26–31 May 1940; TNA: ADM 199/2205 – Naval War Diary Summaries: Situation Reports, 27 May 1940; Gardner, *Evacuation*, p. 19.
40 TNA: AIR 20/9906 – German Air Force Situation Report on Western Front; IWM: EDS/AL/1429 – 4. Armee I/a, War Diary, 29 May 1940.
41 TNA: AIR 24/372 – Headquarters Coastal Command Narrative of Events, May. 1940.
42 IWM: EDS/AL/1399 – 10. *Panzer-Division*, Extract from War Diary, 25–27 May 1940.
43 Military Intelligence Division (USA War Department), 'Tactical Employment of Flak in the Field', *Intelligence Bulletin*, Vol. II, No. 3, (1943), pp. 28–9; TNA: CAB 146/395 – L. M. Yearsley, Director of Inspection of Armaments, to Miss Merrifield, Cabinet Office Historical Section, 15 March 1960.
44 TNA: AIR 14/1019 – Report on Bombing Operations, 2–4 June 1940.
45 Koch, *Geschichte der Deutschen Flakartillerie*, p. 35.
46 HW 5/2 – GC&CS Decrypts, CX/JQ/12.
47 TNA: WO 208/2968 – War Office Publication, Enemy Weapons.
48 TNA: WO 208/2968 – War Office Publication, Enemy Weapons; TNA: WO 208/2285 – M.I.10, Summary of Technical Reports regarding Weapons, War Industry and Transportation, No. 18, 6 July 1940.
49 IWM: EDS/AL/1429 – 4. Armee I/a, War Diary, 30 May 1940.
50 TNA: ADM 199/786 – CO *Glen Gower* Report.
51 TNA: ADM 199/786 – Commanding Officer of *Vivacious*, Report of Activities during Operation Dynamo.
52 TNA: ADM 199/786 – Commanding Officer of *Express*, Report of Activities during Operation Dynamo.
53 TNA: ADM 199/787 – Commanding Officer of *Friso*, Report of Activities during Operation Dynamo.
54 TNA: ADM 334/83 – Little Ships Club: Correspondence and Accounts of Dunkirk Evacuation.
55 TNA: ADM 199/788A – Master of *Killarney*, Report of Activities during Operation Dynamo.
56 TNA: ADM 199/786 – Commanding Officer of *Snaefell*, Report of Activities during Operation Dynamo.
57 TNA: ADM 199/786 – Commanding Officer of *Glen Gower*, Report of Activities during Operation Dynamo.
58 TNA: ADM 199/787 – Account of Walton and Frinton Life Boat' during Operation Dynamo.
59 TNA: AIR 14/1019 – Report on Bombing Operations, 2–4 June 1940; TNA: WO 106/1644 – Military intelligence, Daily Intelligence Summaries and Maps.
60 TNA: ADM 199/789 – Report of Commander Richardson, Report of Captain Tennant; TNA: WO 197/91 – Personal diary of Major R. Gordon-Finlayson, 10th Field Regiment Royal Artillery.

61 TNA: ADM 199/789 – Report of Captain Tennant.
62 Gardner, *Evacuation*, pp. 62–3.
63 TNA: ADM 334/83 – Lieutenant J. A. Simson, Dunkirk Notes.
64 TNA: ADM 334/83 – Dr B. A. Smith, Master of Motor Yacht *Constant Nymph*, Letter to Commander (Retd) W. B. Laurd on 'Dunkirk Operations'.
65 IWM: Audio/12780 – Victor Leslie Thomas Ayles, Reel 2.
66 TNA: AIR 14/1019 – Report on Bombing Operations, 2–4 June 1940.
67 TNA: ADM 199/786 – Commanding Officer of *Shikari*, Report of Activities during Operation Dynamo.
68 TNA: ADM 199/787 – Commanding Officer of *Oranje*, Report of Activities during Operation Dynamo; TNA: AIR 22/169 – A.M.W.R. Daily Reports for Summary.
69 TNA: AIR 25/301 – ORB: 16 Group, Summary of Events, 31 May 1940; TNA: ADM 199/2206 – Naval War Diary Summaries: Situation Reports 31 May–1 June 1940.
70 IWM: Audio/16056 – Eldred Porter Banfield, Reel 4; TNA: AIR 22/169 – A.M.W.R. Daily Reports for Summary; TNA: AIR 14/213 – Reports on Operations for Inclusions in Bomber Command Daily Bulletins; TNA: AIR 24/218 – Bomber Command Intelligence Reports.
71 TNA: AIR 35/305 – Back Violet, Record of Telephone Conversations.
72 IWM: Audio/7186 – Ian Alan Nethercott, Reel 2; TNA: CAB 44/64 – BEF Operations, II Corps: Part II, p. 469; TNA: ADM 199/792 – Commanding Officer of *Keith*, Preliminary Report of Proceedings for Period 30 May–1 June 1940; Lord, *Miracle*, p. 163.
73 TNA: AIR 35/305 – Back Violet, Record of Telephone Conversations; TNA: AIR 16/1072 – Operations of Fighter Squadrons, Signals, 1 June 1940.
74 TNA: WO 106/1673 – War Office Summary of Operations: Western Front.
75 TNA: ADM 199/786 – CO *Shikari* Report.
76 TNA: ADM 199/786 – CO *Vivacious* Report.
77 TNA: ADM 199/786 – Commanding Officer of *Windsor*, Report of Activities during Operation Dynamo.
78 TNA: ADM 199/791 – Officer in Charge of Kindred Star and Thrifty, Report of Activities during Operation Dynamo.
79 *Ibid.*
80 *Ibid.*
81 TNA: ADM 199/787 – Account of Walton and Frinton Life Boat.
82 TNA: ADM 199/787 – Officer in Charge of Motorboat *Skylark*, Report of Activities during Operation Dynamo.
83 TNA: ADM 199/786–795 – Operation Dynamo: Evacuation of Troops from Dunkirk; Vol. I–IX, Reports. The number of recommendations has been calculated on the number of action cited, in which multiple members of crew might be recommended for the same action, as opposed to citations for individuals. In the case of recommendations made which involved artillery the number of individuals

is fourteen. Across all ship types the ratio of air and artillery actions meriting recommendations is close to four to one.

84 TNA: ADM 358/3241 – Vice Admiral Ramsay to Admiralty, 2 June 1940.
85 Captain Tennant to Vice Admiral Ramsay, 17.45 1 June, cited in Gardner, *Evacuation*, p. 183.
86 TNA: ADM 199/789 – Report of Captain Tennant.
87 TNA: ADM 199/789 – Report of Captain Tennant, 'Appendix I: Activity of Enemy Aircraft'.
88 TNA: ADM 199/2206 – Naval War Diary: 1 June 1940, Message 22.14, Vice Admiral Ramsay to General Alexander and Captain Tennant.
89 Gardner, *Evacuation*, p. 98.
90 *Ibid.*
91 TNA: ADM 199/2206 – Naval War Diary, 1 June 1940.
92 *Ibid.*, Vice Admiral Ramsay Message 13.45, 1 June 1940.
93 TNA: ADM 199/786 – Commanding Officer of *Malcolm*, Report of Activities during Operation Dynamo.
94 TNA: ADM 199/788A – Reports of Masters of Personnel Vessels involved in Operation Dynamo.
95 TNA: AIR 20/6260 – ORB: Directorate of Operations (Naval Co-Operation), C-in-C The Nore, 13.16, 1 June 1940.
96 TNA: AIR 15/898 – N.L.O. Log, 1 June 1940.
97 IWM: Audio/10086 – Gerald Edward Ashcroft, Reel 1; ADM 199/787 – Operation Dynamo: Evacuation of Troops from Dunkirk; Vol. II.
98 TNA: ADM 199/787 – Commanding Officer of *Cariba*, Report of Activities during Operation Dynamo.
99 TNA: ADM 199/787 – Commanding Officer of *Locust*, Report of Activities during Operation Dynamo.
100 TNA: ADM 199/790 – Operation Dynamo: Evacuation of Troops from Dunkirk; Vol. V.
101 TNA: ADM 199/786 – Operation Dynamo: Evacuation of Troops from Dunkirk; Vol. I.
102 TNA: ADM 199/786 – Commanding Officer of *Whitehall*, Report of Activities during Operation Dynamo.
103 TNA: AIR 15/898 – N.L.O. Log, 1 June 1940.
104 TNA: CAB 79/4 – Chiefs of Staff Committee, 1 June 1940.
105 TNA: CAB 44/69 – War Cabinet Historical Section: Narrative, Section A, Part II (D), BEF in France and Flanders: 31 May–4 June 1940; TNA: CAB 44/62 – BEF Operations, I Corps: Part II.
106 TNA: AIR 41/40 – RAF Narrative, The RAF in the Bombing Offensive against Germany, Vol. II, Restricted Bombing, 1939 to 1941, pp. 95–6.
107 TNA: ADM 199/787 – CO *Locust* Report.

108 IWM: Film/ADM/5059 – Royal Navy Instructional Film, *Smoke Screens at Sea* (1944); TNA: ADM 199/786 – Reports of the Commanding Officers of *Harvester*, *Icarus* and *Ivanhoe* on Activities during Operation Dynamo.
109 TNA: ADM 199/788A – Master of *Killarney*, Report.
110 TNA: ADM 199/788A – Master of *Royal Daffodil*, Report of Activities during Operation Dynamo.
111 TNA: ADM 199/786 – Commanding Officer of *Harvester, Report* on Activities during Operation Dynamo.
112 Gardner, *Evacuation*, p. 98.
113 CAC: RMSY 8/10 – Ramsay's Letters to his Wife, Letter of 27 May 1940.
114 TNA: ADM 223/82 – Naval Intelligence Documents, OIC Daily Reports, 1 June 1940.

4

The Luftwaffe's attacks on Dunkirk before 29 May

The previous chapters have demonstrated that the Luftwaffe was able to inflict sufficient losses to the surface vessels engaged in Dynamo on 1 June, to halt further daylight evacuation. The attacks on 29 May also demonstrate that the Luftwaffe's effective use air power to disrupt the evacuation was not limited to 1 June. It is therefore necessary to consider those limitations which prevented the Luftwaffe halting further evacuations from Dunkirk before 29 May. This chapter will examine how the Luftwaffe employed air power against the evacuation before 29 May. It will explore how Dynamo was affected by the Luftwaffe's attacks on Dunkirk and the evacuation fleet and analyse the results of these operations to understand why the Luftwaffe was not able to prevent large-scale embarkations from Dunkirk.

Dunkirk had been bombed by the Luftwaffe from 16 May. An attack on the night of 18–19 May had damaged lock gates, set an oil tank and a cotton warehouse ablaze, and cut the power of the dock-cranes.[1] The main lock was, however, still working at this point, the channel was clear and lorries could still access most parts of the docks. On 20 May the Germans began to realize that along the Channel Coast, at Calais, Boulogne and Dunkirk, large-scale embarkations were occurring.[2] Subsequent attacks on Dunkirk, including those on 21 May when Ju 88s of KG 30 sunk a number of French ships in the docks, knocked out the power, gas and waterworks within the town.[3] A greater amount of fighter cover was considered essential at Dunkirk following heavy air attack immediately before Dynamo began.[4] In addition the minesweeper trawlers FS *La Jeannine*, FS *La Trombe II* and FS *Marguerite Rose* had been sunk off Dunkirk.[5] Before 26 May, however, the Luftwaffe was too far back to heavily bomb Dunkirk. Operational commitments at Calais and in support of German land forces also prevented the maximum strength of the Luftwaffe being directed against Dunkirk before this date. From 26 May, the Luftwaffe began to be able to concentrate large forces against Dunkirk.

26 May

A number of units from *Fliegerkorps* I and IV attacked the town and harbour of Dunkirk on 26 May whilst *Fliegerkorps* I was ordered to provide fighter cover in the area of Dunkirk and Calais from 07.00.[6] At 06.45 dive-bombing attacks were made on two destroyers but no hits were obtained.[7] The *Ngaroma*, loaded with stores, received some damage from near-misses during the afternoon, and at 15.00 SS *Maid of Orleans* reported a heavy raid and was forced to return to Dover without entering Dunkirk.[8] Attacks against vessels in the Calais roadstead were made during the day by both Ju 87 and Ju 88 aircraft.[9] Near Calais twelve Ju 88s were observed dive-bombing two trawlers, scoring near-misses which 'undoubtedly caused damage'.[10] During the afternoon HMHS *Worthing* and *Isle of Guernsey* and SS *Mona's Queen* were all unsuccessfully bombed off Calais on their way to Dunkirk.[11] At 19.30 the destroyer HMS *Wild Swan* was attacked by one aircraft whilst entering the Dunkirk channel, with four bombs falling 100 yards off.[12] The French cargo ship SS *Ceres* was also bombed and sunk as it made its way between Rouen and Dunkirk.[13]

The ships involved in embarking troops were, however, frequently able to operate without hindrance from the Luftwaffe whose bombing around Dunkirk was instead focused on the port.[14] The port was heavily bombed, with the railway and oil tanks left in flames, as were the entrances and exits to Dunkirk and British artillery positions covering the Dunkirk perimeter were also attacked by dive-bombers.[15] The majority of the Luftwaffe was, however, not committed against the evacuation.[16] Both *Fliegerkorps* I and VIII had orders to concentrate their attacks in the area east of, and between, Lille and Lens with the primary task of supporting AOK 8 and parts of AOK 2.[17] During the morning at least two important Stuka attacks were made in support of AOK 8 whose need for air support was acute because of a serious shortage of artillery ammunition.[18] *Fliegerkorps* IV had communicated with AOK 6 who wished for air support against Allied positions around Thielt and Meulebeke as well as long-range attacks against enemy movements west of a line Armentieres-Ypres-Thourout. *Heeresgruppe* B made clear to *Luftflotte* 2, however, that these priorities should remain only if they did not prevent sufficient numbers being employed to effectively attack embarkations from Ostend and Dunkirk.[19] *Fliegerkorps* IV did attack the Allied positions called for by AOK 6 and, together with KG 54, Allied columns in the area of Ypres.[20] Bombers from II./KG 27 – which British Air Intelligence considered to specialize in attacks on ports and harbours – also helped AOK 6 to the south-east of Ypres.[21] The evening saw a *Gruppe* of

KG 4 attack columns and artillery positions towards the Dutch frontier.[22] The Luftwaffe's lack of focus on Dunkirk during 26 May was not unreasonable; Dynamo only began in the evening and, even then, the Luftwaffe did have cause to think it possible that over 300,000 Allied troops would soon be evacuated from Dunkirk.

27 May

For the Luftwaffe 27 May was the first concerted attempt to halt Dynamo. *Fliegerkorps* I, II and VIII received orders for the 'destruction by bombing of all movements along the coast'.[23] The Luftwaffe's attacks on Dunkirk, made at hourly intervals, involved some 300 aircraft, which dropped over 250,000 kg of high explosives and 30,000 incendiary bombs.[24] Ships and port installations at Dunkirk and Ostend were targeted and the encircled Allied forces were attacked by waves of bombers.[25] The early attacks struck Dunkirk harbour causing considerable damage and sinking the French cargo ship SS *Aden*. SS *Côte d'Azur* was bombed in the inner harbour shortly after 07.00 and sank in shallow water – allowing her anti-aircraft armament to function until further bombing on 31 May.[26] By early morning the inner harbour was effectively blocked and a number of fires had broken out in the docks. At 09.04 *Windsor* drew alongside *Mona's Isle* who had been heavily machine-gunned whilst full of soldiers and escorted her back to Dover.[27] At 10.30 a heavy attack was made on *Vivacious* by twenty-five bombers, with 100 bombs being dropped on the ship.[28]

During the afternoon, there were continual air attacks and severe bombing of Dunkirk by relays of German bombers.[29] Shortly after 14.00 the SS *St Helier*, HMHS *St Andrew* and *St Julien* were attacked by two medium bombers whilst heading to Dunkirk on Route Y with bomb salvos falling close by.[30] At the same time the destroyer HMS *Wolfhound* received two near-misses after an attack by four Ju 87s. At 16.20 eight Ju 87s carried out a prolonged series of dive-bombing attacks on Dunkirk during which *Wolfhound* sustained minor damage.[31] Heavy air raids by medium bombers developed during the early evening; the Mole was hit during these attacks whilst *Wolfhound* was bombed again and took no further part in Dynamo as a result of the damage sustained.[32] The French naval authorities reported to Paris that Dunkirk had been 'bombed terribly' and further heavy bombing occurred at 19.30.[33] The weight of attacks saw ships ordered out of harbour, and the vicinity of Dunkirk, as it was considered 'impossible to remain'.[34] In addition to the almost continuous air raids on vessels in the harbour, the docks themselves and embarkations from the beaches other vessels reported constant bombing and machine-gun attacks whilst navigating to, and from, Dunkirk.[35]

The bombing of Dunkirk seriously impeded Dynamo during 27 May; however, limitations continued to reduce the scale of Luftwaffe's attacks.[36] Despite the increased focus on Dunkirk the German Army maintained its calls for air support against Allied forces to the south and massed bombing formations were used against Allied positions.[37] Dive-bombers were employed in close support of the German Army at the expense of a greater number of sorties against Dunkirk, with *Fliegerkorps* VIII obliged to send Ju 87s to Amiens to counter a reported British armoured counter-attack.[38] The Luftwaffe continued to attack forces in front of the German Army with Allied troops withdrawing towards Dunkirk being bombed and Stuka attacks on the perimeter at 06.00 and 06.30 following orders for the 'destruction of Gravelines with strong forces as early as possible'.[39] These attacks came at the expense of strikes against ships and troop embarkations. Furthermore, the dense smoke from the fires started in the inner harbour proved 'a blessing in disguise' and provided ships at Dunkirk with considerable cover from air attack.[40]

The air cover provided by Fighter Command on 27 May also impeded the Luftwaffe's efforts against the evacuation.[41] Losses amongst the Luftwaffe's bomber formations exceeded the total of the previous ten days combined and were close to a tenth of the total bomber force committed against Dunkirk during this day.[42] *Fliegerkorps II* lost twenty-three aircraft and sixty-four personnel over Dunkirk.[43] General Kesselring, the Commander of *Luftflotte* 2, later argued that 'it was the Spitfire which enabled the British and French to evacuate'.[44] The role of the British and Luftwaffe fighters will be considered separately; however, Fighter Command's efforts need to be considered as one of the limitations which prevented the Luftwaffe achieving greater success on 27 May. Fighter Command achieved this despite the limited resources they committed over Dunkirk, with the fighters of the Luftwaffe flying almost twice as many sorties on 27 May.[45]

Equally, the limitations achieved by the RAF should not be overstated. During 27 May the number of troops evacuated from Dunkirk was only 7,669 which was significantly lower than the British had hoped to recover during the first full operational day of Dynamo.[46] Furthermore, the Luftwaffe had caused sufficient damage to the facilities in Dunkirk harbour to prevent their use in embarking large numbers of men. The continuous bombing of Dunkirk had led Tennant to signal Ramsay that further embarkations were only possible from the beaches.[47] Embarking troops from the beach was a slow process and would have left little chance of evacuating the majority of the BEF. Following the heavy air attacks during the day Ramsay believed the night of 27 May appeared to be 'the last chance of saving' troops from the BEF.[48] The next twenty-four hours of the evacuation, however, proved critical. The Royal Navy began a remarkable extemporized use of the Dunkirk Mole to rapidly embark troops and the Luftwaffe, greatly hindered by bad weather, were unable to adequately interfere with Dynamo on 28 May.[49]

28 May

Operations against Allied embarkations at Dunkirk were limited on 28 May compared to the previous day.[50] In the absence of heavy bombing during the early morning conditions at Dunkirk were found to be practicable for embarkations and by 06.06 Ramsay was instructing destroyers to make for the Mole 'with all despatch'.[51] HMS *Mackay* embarked 600 troops in an hour from the Mole amid a series of air raids which occurred over Dunkirk from 10.00.[52] Air raids did intensify during the late morning and one attack was only driven off by the collective anti-aircraft fire of the destroyers alongside the Mole and batteries on shore. At 13.30 several unsuccessful bombing attacks were made on HMS *Javelin* while troops were being embarked.[53] The commanding officer of HMS *Montrose* reported that:

> The crash of exploding bombs and the thudding noise of anti-aircraft weapons was continuous ... the long pier jammed with troops made a particularly delectable target for enemy aircraft and it was very fortunate that they were prevented from machine-gunning the soldiers as the latter awaited embarkation.[54]

The raids against the Mole were, however, limited in size and frequency as were larger attacks on ships. The early morning saw only isolated attacks on vessels. At 04.15 the personnel vessel SS *Queen of the Channel* was attacked on Route Y and sunk by a single Ju 88.[55] The Skoots *Tiny*, *Twente* and *Hondsrug* and HMHS *St Andrew* were also all separately bombed by single aircraft during this period.[56] As with attacks on the harbour and town, the intensity increased during the late morning and afternoon, and at 11.45 the destroyer *Windsor* was attacked by fifteen Ju 88s. No direct hits were obtained but extensive damage was done to the ship by bomb splinters and strafing with *Windsor*'s starboard side 'riddled like a pepper box'.[57] Shortly afterwards two paddle minesweepers, HMS *Brighton Belle* and *Sandown*, were bombed as they returned to Ramsgate and, after striking wreckage whilst evading the attack, *Brighton Belle* sank.[58] At 12.35

HMS *Impulsive* was attacked and heavily bombed at low level by six He 111s on Route Y, off Kwinte Bank, with two pipes in the engine room fractured by the detonation of near-misses and further damage from strafing.[59] From 14.00 to 15.00 *Montrose, Sabre, Anthony* and *Worcester* were bombed and machine-gunned by forty-five medium bombers, attacking in groups of three, and the four destroyers' anti-aircraft establishment was heavily called upon.[60] Bray beach was also bombed during this period and attacks were made on the ships lying close inshore to the beach. Three Skoots *Kaap Falga, Abel Tasman* and *Alice* were attacked by twenty medium bombers, which also strafed the ships and troops on the beach; *Alice* later had to be abandoned because of damage sustained.[61] Numerous raids, involving large numbers of medium bombers, occurred during the evening but these did not focus on shipping.[62] Instead they heavily bombed the town of Dunkirk and by 23.00 it 'was in flames'.[63]

The Luftwaffe sank only two ships of note during 28 May and the weather undoubtedly played a part in this lack of success. During the early morning, intermittent rain showers and local mist on the French coast disrupted air operations.[64] The smoke over Dunkirk remained dense during the day of 28 May but some bombing became possible after a shift in the wind lifted much of the smoke away from where ships were embarking troops.[65] The weather deteriorated further, however, as the day progressed. Prolonged thunderstorms and heavy rain over the coast shielded the evacuation against further large-scale bombing attacks.[66] During the evening several Skoots took advantage of a rain squall to return to Britain and under its cover avoided the attention of German bombers in the area.[67] The storms over the coast also brought with them towering vertical cumulonimbus clouds; by the evening the base of these clouds was only several hundred feet from the ground in places and extended for several miles.[68] The low cloud base was a particular problem for the Luftwaffe's dive-bombers who were unable to fulfil a number of attacks requested by the German Army on this day.[69] The heavy rain inland over France and Europe also softened the ground at airfields with grass runways which further retarded the Luftwaffe's bombing efforts.[70] In the absence of large numbers of dive-bombers the evacuation suffered relatively few losses. The weather conditions alone, however, do not fully explain the low shipping losses of 28 May.

Analysis of operations before 29 May

Challenging weather conditions combined with a failure to maintain operational focus on Dunkirk, a failure to target the critical points of the evacuation and a failure to ensure the attacks that did occur were made as effectively as possible to collectively limit the effectiveness of the Luftwaffe's air attacks on 28 May. These failures were, however, in part a result of the success achieved on 27 May. The Luftwaffe had targeted the port facilities of Dunkirk's inner harbour before Dynamo commenced and following heavy attacks on 27 May the Royal Navy had concluded that the inner harbour was unusable for embarkations. The ships of the evacuation were instead embarking troops from the beaches at Bray Dunes and La Panne. The damage to these facilities was recognized by the Luftwaffe who assumed that large embarkations would not be possible as a result.[71] The town of Dunkirk was heavily damaged and air reconnaissance photographs clearly showed that Dunkirk port was out of action for large ships. These reports led to fewer operations being conducted than might otherwise have been the case.[72] The Allied defeat also appeared inevitable at the outset of the evacuation and this, combined with the belief that it would not be possible to lift large numbers of troops from Dunkirk, partially removed the impetus for the Luftwaffe to launch costly attacks against Dunkirk.[73] On 27 May *Fliegerkorps* I was, in the opinion of Richthofen, close enough to Dunkirk to launch an attack but *General der Flieger* Grauert vacillated and no attack materialized despite fighter support being made available for the attack.[74] On 28 May, whilst air operations against Dunkirk and other objectives along the coast were maintained, there was also a division of focus with operations against the defensive perimeter around Dunkirk and in support of German forces elsewhere.[75] On 28 May Richthofen discussed with his Chief of Staff, *Oberstleutnant* Hans Seidemann, the opportunity for action away near Humieres where there were both many targets and the opportunity to support German troops.[76] Dive-bombers were required for attacks on Allied armoured vehicles south of Amiens and the Luftwaffe also made raids at Dieppe and positions on the Somme.[77] *Fliegerkorps* I and VIII were instructed to be prepared to support AOK 4 whilst *Fliegerkorps* II and V were ordered to be ready to attack enemy movements near Amiens as well as bombing the Allied rearguard withdrawing towards Dunkirk.[78] A large number of German fighter sorties were also concentrated south of Amiens.[79] Towards midday there was an increased focus on the Allied evacuation but at ports other than Dunkirk. Belgian ports such as Zeebrugge and Ostend were a diversion for the Luftwaffe during this period and *Fliegerkorps* IV was instructed to attack all transports in the region of Nieuport and Ostend.[80] In the early morning of 28 May, Ju 88s of KG 30 operated over Ostend and operations continued there into the afternoon, during which the Luftwaffe inadvertently bombed German troops. The Luftwaffe maintained its air attacks on the harbour at Ostend until 29 May believing it to be involved in the Allied evacuation.[81] Harbour and rail installations, barracks, docks, locks and bridges were destroyed and large fires were caused in the town.[82] The bombing of Ostend was a diversion of resources at a critical junction in the evacuation of Dunkirk.[83] This was an important failure in operational intelligence which combined with unfavourable weather conditions to reduce the effectiveness of the Luftwaffe's attacks at an important point in the evacuation.

The Luftwaffe's attacks were also limited in the extent to which they targeted the most vulnerable points of the evacuation. These points were the Mole at Dunkirk, from which over 200,000 troops would be embarked, and the ships themselves, particularly those stationary alongside the Mole which were easier to hit.[84] The town of Dunkirk itself continued to be heavily bombed long after it had ceased to be a target worthy of the expenditure of such effort.[85] Whilst the town was reduced to ruins and many streets were blocked with rubble from collapsed buildings – which did complicate efforts to move troops to the harbour – Allied soldiers found the cellars of the buildings to be safe havens from the bombardment.[86] The large number of Allied motor vehicles abandoned outside of Dunkirk proved to be a target of considerable temptation for Luftwaffe crews and part of the bombing effort at the beginning of the evacuation was wasted against them.[87] The crowded troops on the beaches east of Dunkirk also appeared to offer the Luftwaffe an easy target; however, these attacks were far less profitable than the crews involved assumed.[88] The bombs dropped on the beaches, and the dunes behind them, buried themselves in the soft sand which absorbed much of their explosive force and fragmentation, greatly reducing the casualties they would otherwise have caused.[89] William Ridgewell, serving on *Grenade*, recalled that the Luftwaffe dropped 'most of their bombs on the beaches' and that one 'could see the sand being blown up'.[90] The Luftwaffe's attacks would have been more effective had they targeted ships involved in the evacuation, particularly those which had already embarked troops. Against these targets – frequently less manoeuvrable and unbalanced because of the large number of troops on board – the bombs were not only likely to cause greater loss of life but the loss of the vessel would have reduced the evacuation fleets carrying capacity. The bombing also failed to interdict troops trying to make their way to, and along, the outer Moles to be evacuated.[91]

The failure to focus on more critical targets during this period is understandable in the context that the Luftwaffe believed that, with the inner harbour destroyed, large-scale embarkations were no longer possible. In his diary entry for 28 May Richthofen described the evacuations from Dunkirk as being attempted with 'small vessels and rowing boats'.[92] At the beginning of the evacuation most of the troops embarked were being lifted off the beaches at La Panne and Bray and at one time there were some 20,000 soldiers awaiting embarkation. The shortage of small boats and launches, necessary to lift men off the beaches to larger vessels, caused great difficulties and the rate of embarkations was slow.[93] In such circumstances interference from the Luftwaffe, by both bombers and strafing fighter aircraft, caused much disruption and delay to the evacuation. It was, however, found to be practicable to bring ships alongside the Mole, allowing large numbers of troops to be quickly embarked directly on to ships; this greatly expedited the rate of embarkations. From this point disruption to the beach embarkations was largely insignificant compared to the effect that attacks on the Mole would have had. However, the Luftwaffe was slow to identify the importance of the Mole. In this the Luftwaffe's task was made harder by the smoke from burning oil tanks which helped to partially obscure the ships alongside the Mole and the number of men which were being embarked from it.[94] Such was the importance of smoke that on 29 May, when the wind had cleared much of the smoke from oil tanks away from the Mole, Commander Clouston, the pier master on the Mole, attempted, unsuccessfully, to have ships create an artificial smoke screen to cover embarkations.[95] The Mole, and shipping alongside it, was targeted on 29 May and the Luftwaffe caused heavy losses to the evacuation and temporarily halted further embarkations there. By 1 June the Luftwaffe's focus had decisively shifted and was concentrated against the ships of the evacuation fleet with the result that further daylight evacuations were halted.[96]

The factors above played a greater role in preventing the success of the Luftwaffe before 29 May than the air cover provided by the RAF. Fighter Command was, however, able to contest air superiority on 27 May and their patrols reduced the number of German bombers able to reach Dunkirk.[97] Nonetheless, the Luftwaffe was able to undertake attacks during the day and limit the number of troops evacuated from Dunkirk. If the targets the Luftwaffe selected were, with hindsight, not those that prevented further evacuations they were nonetheless able to effectively attack them. Dunkirk harbour was heavily bombed and the remaining dock facilities severely damaged.[98] Furthermore, the weight of bombing during the evening was such that larger ships were ordered out of the vicinity of Dunkirk as it was considered 'impossible to remain'.[99] On 28 May, the weather over Dunkirk limited the effective application of air power by either the Luftwaffe or the RAF. Fighter Command was not the primary cause of the limited results of German bombing. Patrols by Fighter Command attempted to contest air superiority against much larger Luftwaffe formations.[100] Fighter Command suffered heavily to achieve this – losing fourteen aircraft to the Luftwaffe's four. Had the RAF been entirely absent and the Luftwaffe faced no opposition, and without the prospect of losses on the scale recorded on 27 May, the Luftwaffe's attacks on 27 and 28 May would have been more effective. This was not, however, the main factor which limited the Luftwaffe successfully halting Dynamo through the application of air power.

Comparing the success of 29 May and 1 June to the operations before 29 May the greatest limitation the Luftwaffe faced was the absence of clear flying conditions. The main restriction that the unfavourable conditions placed on the Luftwaffe was that dive-bombers were not able to operate over the evacuation. The Ju 87 proved the most effective weapon against shipping and the Luftwaffe was not capable of halting the evacuation when its dive-bombers were unable to operate. Before 29 May the burden of halting the evacuation fell on the Luftwaffe's medium bombers; however, the effectiveness of these types was also reduced by the unfavourable weather conditions. The poor weather and smoke over Dunkirk forced the Luftwaffe's medium bombers either to fly low, where the limited anti-aircraft armaments of the ships involved in the evacuation were more effective, or stay at height, and accept severe limitations to the accuracy of their bombing.[101] As the altitude of an aircraft increased, errors made in bomb aiming were maximized and changes in air density and wind became factors. Bombing from higher altitude also increased the time of flight of the bomb; against moving targets – where the aiming point was not directly at the vessel at the time of bomb release but the point the vessel would be on impact – this led to a reduction in accuracy and allowed ships to take evasive action. These factors shaped the average bombing error – the distance from which the bomb would fall from the target aimed at. The average bombing error increased with the height from which bombs were dropped reducing the percentage of hits likely to arise from each attack (see Figure 2). Hits were more likely against stationary targets; however, even then accuracy was low when bombing from high altitude.

The bombing of Dunkirk's docks illustrates the difficulties of accurate bombing from high altitude; during attacks shortly before the commencement of Dynamo only 12 per cent of the bombs dropped on the docks hit their target.[103] The Mole, obscured at high altitude by smoke, was a harder target to hit than the facilities already destroyed. Successful attacks against the Mole and the ships alongside therefore needed to be made from lower altitudes. Many aircraft were deterred from effective low level attacks during the initial period of the evacuation because ships at Dunkirk often succeeded in concentrating their anti-aircraft fire effectively.[104] Wing Commander Spence, Air Liaison Officer – Dunkirk, recounted that 'as long as anti-aircraft ammunition was plentiful, the bombing by day was erratic'.[105] *Montrose* was attacked by successive waves

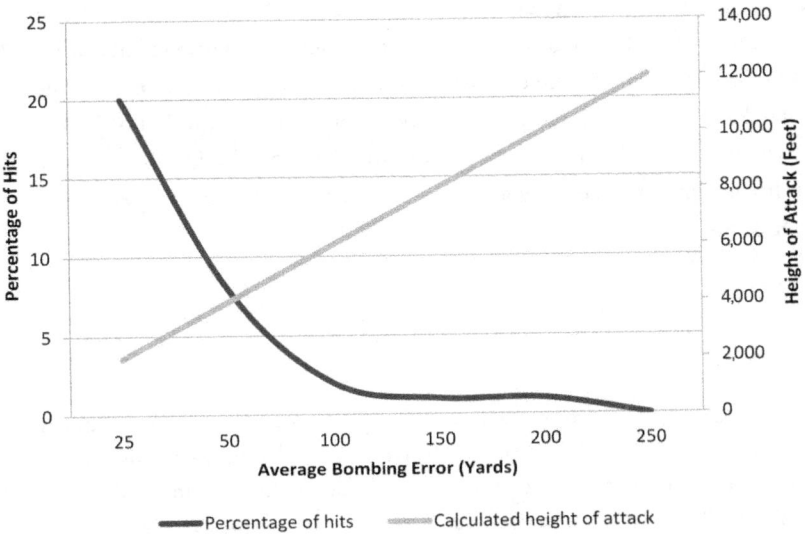

■■■ Percentage of hits   ■■■ Calculated height of attack

Figure 2 Percentage of hits likely to be attained by a level-bombing attack on a destroyer (underway at 10 knots) on basis of average bombing error and theoretical height of attack needed to attain the average bombing error in ideal conditions.[102]

of German bombers, a total of forty-five over the course of an hour, in the window in weather conditions during the afternoon of 28 May when low cloud cover had cleared sufficiently for attacks to be pressed at lower levels; however, anti-aircraft fire in the vicinity of Dunkirk ensured that bombers did not bomb *Montrose* at low level and the average height of attack was 8,000 feet.[106] However, despite the limitations of the bombing of ships at Dunkirk, the damage the Luftwaffe caused to the harbour facilities had prevented the Royal Navy from evacuating large numbers of troops. In discussing the period before 29 May, it must be realized that, whilst the Luftwaffe's attacks could have been more effective, before 28 May they had limited the number of Allied troops evacuated and large embarkations from the inner harbour of Dunkirk had been made impracticable. Retrospective criticism as to whether the Luftwaffe should have dedicated greater resources to attacks on Dunkirk needs to reflect the point that the Luftwaffe successfully achieved its initial aims of preventing the inner harbour being used for embarking large numbers of troops. On 27 May, 7,669 troops evacuated from Dunkirk were disembarked in Britain and on 28 May a further 17,804 troops had been recovered.[107] The number of troops evacuated increased from 28 May as the Royal Navy began to make effective use of the Dunkirk Mole. As discussed previously, however, on 29 May considerable success was achieved against ships alongside the Mole and the continuation of daylight evacuation from Dunkirk was imperilled. The explanation for the Luftwaffe's military effectiveness and successful application of air power on 29 May lay in the clear conditions for operations and the number of Ju 87 sorties against shipping. The next chapter will establish why the Luftwaffe was unable to achieve further success against the evacuation during the period between 29 May and 1 June.

Notes

1   TNA: AIR 22/71 – Directorate of Air Intelligence, Air Ministry Weekly Intelligence Summary, No. 39, 30 May 1940; TNA: AIR 35/189 – Wing Commander Spence to Air Marshal Barratt, Notes on the Evacuation of Dunkirk, c. June 1940.
2   IWM: EDS/AL/1428 – *Heeresgruppe* A Ia, War Diary Part II, 20 May 1940.
3   Georges Blond, *L'Epopée Silencieuse: Service à la Mer, 1939–1940* (Paris: Le Livre de Poche, 1970), p. 94; Peter C. Smith, *Dive Bomber!* (Mechanicsburg, PA: Stackpole, 2008), p. 188; *Der Adler*, 'Hölle Dünkirchen', p. 306.
4   LHCMA: LINDSELL 1/2 – War Diary of 'Q' Staff Command, Advance and Rear General Headquarters, 23 May 1940.
5   H. P. Willmott, *The Last Century of Sea Power*, Vol. II, *From Washington to Tokyo, 1922–1945* (Indianapolis: Indiana University Press, 2011), p. 291.
6   TNA: HW 5/1 – GC&CS Decrypts, CX/FJ/103.
7   TNA: ADM 199/786 – CO *Windsor* Report.
8   TNA: ADM 199/786 – Commanding Officer of *Wild Swan*, Report of Activities during Operation Dynamo; TNA: ADM 199/788A – Master of *Ngaroma*, Report of Activities during Operation Dynamo
9   IWM: EDS/AL/1399 – 10. *Panzer-Division*, Extract from War Diary, 26 May 1940; TNA: HW 5/1 – GC&CS Decrypts, CX/FJ/109.
10 TNA: AIR 22/168 – A.M.W.R. Daily Report for Summary, No. 312, 27 May 1940.
11 TNA: ADM 199/788A – Master *Isle of Guernsey* Report.
12 TNA: ADM 199/786 – CO *Wild Swan* Report.
13 TNA: ADM 199/2205 – Naval War Diary Summaries, Situation Report, Casualties and Defects, 26 May 1940; TNA: BT 389/35/91 – Allied Merchant Shipping Movement Cards, Ship *Ceres*.
14 IWM: Audio/13933 – Gilhespy, Reel 10.
15 IWM: Documents/17217 – Private Papers of Sydney Ball, The Diary of Gunner Sydney Ball, 26 May 1940; TNA: ADM 199/2205 – Naval War Diary Summaries, Situation Report, Dunkirk, 26 May 1940; TNA: HW 5/1 – GC&CS Decrypts, CX/FJ/107.

16 TNA: AIR 16/234 – Fighter Command Intelligence Summary No. 107, 26 May 1940; TNA: AIR 20/9906 – German Air Force Situation Reports on Western Front, 26–27 May 1940.
17 BA/MA: N 671/6 – Richthofen, Kriegstagebuch, 25–26 May 1940; IWM: EDS/AL/1399 – 10. *Panzer-Division*, Extract from War Diary, 26 May 1940; IWM: EDS/AL/1429 – 4. Armee Ia, Kriegstagebuch, 24–28 May 1940; TNA: HW 5/1 – GC&CS Decrypts, CX/FJ/108–109.
18 IWM: EDS/AL/1429 – 4. Armee Ia, Kriegstagebuch, 26 May 1940.
19 IWM: EDS/AL/1433 – *Heeresgruppe* B Ia, War Diary, 26 May 1940.
20 TNA: HW 5/1 – GC&CS Decrypts, CX/FJ/107.
21 TNA: AIR 22/168 – A.M.W.R. Daily Report for Summary, No. 315, 30 May 1940; TNA: HW 5/1 – GC&CS Decrypts, CX/FJ/107.
22 TNA: HW 5/1 – GC&CS Decrypts, CX/FJ/111.
23 *Ibid.*, CX/FJ/107, CX/FJ/110.
24 IWM: EDS/AL/1428 – *Heeresgruppe* A Ia, War Diary Part II, 27 May 1940; TNA: AIR 15/203 – Commander R. Bower, Naval Liaison Officer to Coastal Command, Air Support for the Evacuation of Dunkirk, 27 May 1940; TNA: AIR 20/9906 – German Air Force Situation Reports on Western Front, 27 May 1940; TNA: AIR 22/168 – A.M.W.R. Daily Report for Summary, No. 314, Part II, German Air Force Operations, 29 May 1940; Wolfgang Dierich, *Kampfgeschwader 51 'Edelweiss': The Complete History of KG 51 in World War II* (Atglen, PA: Schiffer, 2014), p. 30; Jackson, *Dunkirk*, p. 123.
25 IWM: EDS/AL/1428 – *Heeresgruppe* A Ia, War Diary Part II, 27 May 1940.
26 TNA: AIR 20/9906 – German Air Force Situation Reports on Western Front, 27 May 1940; TNA: BT 389/35/163 – Allied Merchant Shipping Movement Cards, Ship *Côte d'Azur*; Blond, *L'Epopée Silencieuse*, p. 100; Jackson, *Dunkirk*, p. 122.
27 TNA: ADM 199/786 – CO *Windsor* Report.
28 TNA: ADM 199/786 – CO *Vivacious* Report.
29 TNA: ADM 199/788A – Master of *St Andrew*, Report of Activities during Operation Dynamo; TNA: ADM 199/788A – Master *St Julien* Report.
30 TNA: ADM 199/786 – Commanding Officer of *Vimy*, Report of Activities during Operation Dynamo; TNA: ADM 199/788A – Master *St Andrew* Report; TNA: ADM 199/788A – Master of *St Helier*, Report of Activities during Operation Dynamo; TNA: ADM 199/788A – Master *St Julien* Report.
31 TNA: ADM 199/786 – Commanding Officer of *Wolfhound*, Report of Activities during Operation Dynamo.
32 TNA: ADM 199/786 – CO *Vimy* Report; TNA: ADM 199/786 – CO *Wolfhound* Report; TNA: ADM 199/788A – Master *St Helier* Report; Dierich, *Kampfgeschwader 51*, p. 30.

33 TNA: ADM 199/2205 – Naval War Diary Summaries, Dunkerque to Marine National, 27 May 1940.
34 TNA: ADM 199/788A – Master *St Andrew* Report; TNA: ADM 199/788A – Master *St Julien* Report.
35 TNA: ADM 199/786 – Commanding Officer of *Wolsey*, Report of Activities during Operation Dynamo; TNA: ADM 199/787 – Commanding Officer of *Brandaris*, Report of Activities during Operation Dynamo; TNA: ADM 223/127 – Naval Intelligence and OIC, Notes of Messages from Various Sources, 27 May 1940.
36 TNA: ADM 199/786 – CO *Wolfhound* Report.
37 TNA: AIR 20/9906 – German Air Force Situation Reports on Western Front, 27 May 1940; TNA: HW 5/1 – GC&CS Decrypts, CX/FJ/110.
38 BA/MA: N 671/6 – Richthofen, Kriegstagebuch, 27 May 1940; TNA: AIR 22/168 – A.M.W.R. Daily Report for Summary, No. 314, Part II, German Air Force Operations, 29 May 1940.
39 IWM: EDS/AL/1429 – 4. Armee Ia, Kriegstagebuch, 26 May 1940; TNA: HW 5/1 – GC&CS Decrypts, CX/FJ/107, CX/FJ/111; NARA: T315, R1689, Frame 382 – AOK 6, Armee-Befehl Nr. 14, 27 May 1940.
40 IWM: Audio/22132 – William George Ridgewell, Reel 2.
41 TNA: AIR 20/9906 – German Air Force Situation Reports on Western Front, 27 May 1940; TNA: CAB 106/1206 – AHB, German Losses based on Returns to Luftwaffe Quarter Master General.
42 LHCMA: LIDDELL HART 15/15/22 – Galland, German Day Fighter Arm, 1945; Eric Mombeek, *Jagdwaffe*, Vol I, Part 4, *Attack in the West, May 1940* (Crowborough, East Sussex: Classic, 2002), p. 36–37.
43 Herbert Mason, *Rise of the Luftwaffe: Forging the Secret German Air Weapon* (New York: Dial, 1973), p. 354.
44 Kesselring, *Memoirs*, p. 59.
45 TNA: AIR 22/107 – Air Ministry Daily Telegraphic Intelligence Summary, 8 June 1940; TNA: AIR 27 – ORB: Fighter Command Squadrons, May–Jun. 1940; Prien, *Jagdfliegerverbände*, p. 66.
46 Gardner, *Evacuation*, pp. 122, 215, 220.
47 TNA: ADM 199/2205 – Naval War Diary Summaries, Captain Tennant to Vice Admiral Ramsay, 20.05 27 May 1940.
48 TNA: ADM 199/2205 – Naval War Diary Summaries, Vice Admiral Ramsay to Ships *Grafton, Greyhound* and *Blyskawica*, 21.27 27 May 1940; Gardner, *Evacuation*, p. 162.
49 Prien, *Jagdfliegerverbände*, pp. 56–7.
50 TNA: ADM 199/789 – Report of Commander Richardson, Report of Captain Tennant; TNA: AIR 22/168 – A.M.W.R. Daily Report for Summary, No. 315, Part II, German Air Force Operations, 30 May 1940.

51 TNA: ADM 199/2205 – Naval War Diary Summaries, Vice Admiral Ramsay to Ships *Mackay, Sabre, Wolfhound, Worcester* and *Vega*, 06.06 28 May 1940.
52 TNA: ADM 199/786 – Commanding Officer of *Mackay*, Report of Activities during Operation Dynamo.
53 TNA: ADM 199/786 – Commanding Officer of *Javelin*, Report of Activities during Operation Dynamo.
54 TNA: ADM 199/786 – Commanding Officer of *Montrose*, Report of Activities during Operation Dynamo.
55 TNA: ADM 199/787 – CO *Oranje* Report; TNA: AIR 20/9906 – German Air Force Situation Reports on Western Front, 28 May 1940; Gardner, *Evacuation*, p. 29.
56 TNA: ADM 199/787 – Commanding Officer of *Hondsrug*, Report of Activities during Operation Dynamo; TNA: ADM 199/787 – Commanding Officer of *Tiny*, Report of Activities during Operation Dynamo; TNA: ADM 199/787 – CO *Twente* Report; TNA: ADM 199/788A – Master *St Andrew* Report.
57 TNA: ADM 199/786 – CO *Windsor* Report.
58 TNA: ADM 199/786 – Commanding Officer of *Sandown*, Report of Activities during Operation Dynamo.
59 TNA: ADM 199/786 – Commanding Officer of *Impulsive*, Report of Activities during Operation Dynamo.
60 TNA: ADM 199/786 – CO *Montrose* Report; TNA: ADM 199/786 – CO *Sabre* Report; TNA: ADM 199/786 – CO *Vimy* Report; TNA: ADM 199/786 – CO *Worcester* Report.
61 TNA: ADM 199/787 – Senior Officer of Skoots *Kaap Falga* and *Abel Tasman*, Report of Activities during Operation Dynamo; TNA: ADM 199/787 – Commanding Officer of *Alice*, Report of Activities during Operation Dynamo.
62 TNA: AIR 22/168 – A.M.W.R. Daily Report for Summary, No. 313, 28 May 1940.
63 TNA: ADM 199/788A – Commanding Officer of *Tilly*, Report of Activities during Operation Dynamo.
64 IWM: EDS/AL/1384/1 – 6. Armee Ia, Kriegstagebuch, 28 May 1940; TNA: ADM 199/2205 – Naval War Diary Summaries, Weather Report, 27 May 1940; TNA: AIR 27/1941 – ORB: 500 Squadron.
65 IWM: Audio/22132 – Ridgewell, Reel 2.
66 K. D. Anderson, 'Weather Service at War', *Royal Meteorological Society Occasional Papers on Meteorological History*, No. 7, (2009), p. 15.
67 TNA: ADM 199/787 – Senior Officer Skoots *Kaap Falga* and *Abel Tasman* Report.
68 TNA: AIR 27/1941 – ORB: 500 Squadron; Anderson, 'Weather Service at War', p. 15.
69 IWM: EDS/AL/1429 – 4. Armee Ia, Kriegstagebuch, 28 May 1940.
70 Ibid.

71 TNA: AIR 20/9906 – German Air Force Situation Reports on Western Front, 26–8 May 1940.
72 Harman, *Dunkirk*, p. 142.
73 BA/MA: N 671/6 – Richthofen, Kriegstagebuch, 24 May 1940; IWM: EDS/AL/1371 – *Heeresgruppe* A Ia Dairy, Ab. Nr.3211/40g, OKH, 'Tagesbefehl an Heeresgruppe A', 21 May 1940; IWM: EDS/AL/1429 – 4. Armee Ia, Kriegstagebuch, 27 May 1940.
74 BA/MA: N 671/6 – Richthofen, Kriegstagebuch, 27 May 1940.
75 IWM: EDS/AL/1428 – *Heeresgruppe* A Ia, War Diary Part II, 28 May 1940; IWM: EDS/AL/1433 – *Heeresgruppe* B Ia, War Diary, 28 May 1940; Jacobsen, *Dünkirchen*, p. 168.
76 BA/MA: N 671/6 – Richthofen, Kriegstagebuch, 28 May 1940.
77 TNA: AIR 22/168 – A.M.W.R. Daily Report for Summary, No. 313, 28 May 1940.
78 TNA: HW 5/1 – GC&CS Decrypts, CX/FJ/112.
79 *Ibid.*, CX/FJ/114.
80 IWM: EDS/AL/1384/1 – 6. Armee Ia, Kriegstagebuch, 28 May 1940; IWM: EDS/AL/1433 – *Heeresgruppe* B Ia, War Diary, 28 May 1940; TNA: HW 5/1 – GC&CS Decrypts, CX/FJ/107; TNA: HW 5/2 – GC&CS Decrypts, CX/JQ/3; Bekker, *Luftwaffe*, p. 166.
81 TNA: HW 5/1 – GC&CS Decrypts, CX/FJ/114.
82 TNA: AIR 20/9906 – German Air Force Situation Reports on Western Front, 26–8 May 1940.
83 Jacobsen, *Dünkirchen*, p. 196.
84 Gardner, *Evacuation*, p. 212.
85 Captain Basil Bartlett, *My First War: An Army Officer's Journal for May 1940, Through Belgium to Dunkirk* (London: Chatto & Windus, 1940), pp. 109–10.
86 Divine, *Nine Days*, p. 225.
87 *Der Adler*, 'Hölle Dünkirchen', p. 306.
88 AIR 27/1365 – ORB: 220 Squadron.
89 Bartlett, *My First War*, pp. 109–10, 117.
90 IWM: Audio/22132 – Ridgewell, Reel 2.
91 IWM: Audio/6462 – Leslie John Kearnes, Reels 2–3; IWM: Audio/6818 – James Louis Moulton, Reels 8–9.
92 BA/MA: N 671/6 – Richthofen, Kriegstagebuch, 28 May 1940.
93 TNA: ADM 199/360 – Dover Command, War Diary, 28 May 1940.
94 Jackson, *Dunkirk*, p. 125.
95 TNA: ADM 199/787 – Report of Lieutenant Bill.
96 TNA: CAB 79/4 – Chief of Staff Committee, Minutes of Meeting No. 162, 1 June 1940.
97 TNA: AIR 22/168 – A.M.W.R. Daily Report for Summary, No. 312, 27 May 1940.
98 TNA: ADM 199/2205 – Naval War Diary Summaries, Dunkerque to Marine National, 27 May 1940.

99 TNA: ADM 199/788A – Master *St Andrew* Report; TNA: ADM 199/788A – Master *St Julien* Report.
100 James, *Growth*, p. 94.
101 Brigadier T. F. J. Collins cited in Nettle, *Dunkirk*, p. 29.
102 This graph is based on the bombing results obtained by the FAA during moving target practice in 1938. TNA: AIR 14/108 – Memorandum on FAA Tactics of High Level-Bombing, September 1939.
103 TNA: AIR 35/189 – Wing Commander Spence to Air Marshal Barratt, Notes on the Evacuation of Dunkirk, *c.* June 1940.
104 TNA: ADM 199-/786 – CO *Express* Report; TNA: ADM 199/788A – Master *Loch Garry* Report; TNA: ADM 199/788A – Master *St Helier* Report; Private F. R. Farley cited in Nettle, *Dunkirk*, p. 61.
105 TNA: AIR 35/189 – Wing Commander Spence to Air Marshal Barratt, Notes on the Evacuation of Dunkirk, *c.* June 1940.
106 TNA: ADM 199/786 – CO *Montrose* Report.
107 Gardner, *Evacuation*, p. 220.

5

The Luftwaffe's attacks on Dunkirk on 30–31 May

This chapter will establish the results which were achieved by the Luftwaffe's attacks on the evacuation on 30 and 31 May and assess why the Luftwaffe was unable to halt the continual embarkation of troops from Dunkirk on either day. On both days, large numbers of troops were embarked from the Dunkirk Mole and from the beaches around Dunkirk. Over 120,000 troops were disembarked in Britain during the course of 30–31 May and by the time the Luftwaffe had halted further daylight evacuations on 1 June, the majority of the BEF had been evacuated. Having examined the Luftwaffe's operations before 29 May a range of factors reduced the effectiveness of the Luftwaffe's attacks on the embarkations at Dunkirk. Of those factors the weather conditions, which prevented use of the Ju 87 against targets around Dunkirk, were the most significant. The success the Luftwaffe achieved on 1 June, and its success on 29 May, was the result of favourable flying conditions which allowed the Ju 87 dive-bombers to inflict significant losses to the evacuation. After the success of 29 May, it is important to consider whether the reason the Luftwaffe did not achieve further success until 1 June was solely due to the prevailing weather conditions or if the Luftwaffe's application of air power was hindered by faults in target selection and a diversion of operational focus.

30 May

Heavy air attacks on Allied naval forces had been planned for the morning of 30 May and *Fliegerkorps* I, II and VIII were all ready for action.[1] Aircraft from three *Kampfgeschwader* which were standing by for operations in the vicinity of Dunkirk, with Me 110 fighter cover arranged for the formations, were unable to take off during 30 May because of low cloud cover over the Luftwaffe's bomber airfields.[2] With the exception of isolated aircraft, the morning, therefore, saw little German air activity of note.[3] By midday AOK 6 reported that Dunkirk was no longer being attacked by the Luftwaffe despite Allied evacuations continuing and forces across *Heeresgruppe* B desiring further air bombardment of Dunkirk.[4] Coastal Command aircraft reported a 'vast collection of vessels of all kinds between the Thames Estuary and Dunkirk entirely unmolested by enemy aircraft'.[5] *Vivacious* recorded that 'low misty weather made aircraft conditions difficult and 650 men were taken off the beach with hardly any embarrassment from the air'.[6]

As the morning ended, attacks on the evacuation started to increase. The Skoot *Despatch II* was attacked by a low-flying aircraft, the passenger launch *Silver Queen* was bombed, and the Skoot *Reiger* was subject to periodical strafing throughout the afternoon as it travelled to Dunkirk.[7] Throughout the afternoon there were several low level attacks on the beaches and by the end of the afternoon Dunkirk was subjected to air bombardment.[8] This activity was again, however, largely conducted by individual aircraft rather than by formations.[9] Operating individually Ju 88 aircraft seemed to avoid targets with even a modest anti-aircraft provision and destroyers and minesweepers had few accurate attacks directed at them during this period.[10] From 16.30 it was apparent to the Germans that large numbers of troops were being successfully evacuated. Orders were given for bombing anywhere in Dunkirk harbour and there were urgent demands for the Luftwaffe to disturb embarkations, with renewed orders issued at 17.45 for air attacks on Dunkirk and its surroundings.[11] The evening saw Dunkirk and the beaches east of it bombed.[12] From 20.00 onwards numerous ships reported heavier bombing by the Luftwaffe over the evacuation. The beaches, and the vessels working off them, were attacked by medium bombers.[13] At 20.45 the Skoot *San Antonio* was attacked and a delayed action bomb exploded under the stern. Damaged but still in service, the effect of this attack led to 'mutinous conduct' amongst the crew.[14] Attacks were also made on ships on the evacuation routes and the approaches to Dunkirk harbour during the late evening.[15] A single Ju 88 attacked *Anthony* at 22.00 and caused sufficient damage to put the destroyer out of action for the remainder of the evacuation.[16] For the majority of 30 May, however, the Luftwaffe found, according to a captured situation report, that 'extremely unfavourable conditions made it almost impossible to carry out the operations that had been planned against continued embarkations of enemy troops'.[17]

31 May

Weather conditions again interfered with the Luftwaffe's operations on 31 May – particularly those made shortly after dawn.[18] The intention for the attacks on 31 May had been for bombing to be delivered on the critical elements of the evacuation and reduce wasteful attacks on unprofitable targets such as the beaches. To this end *Fliegerkorps* I and VIII had been instructed not to attack the town or harbour of Dunkirk on 31 May but to instead concentrate on the transports and warships at sea or off the coast.[19] Conditions improved gradually as the morning progressed with the Luftwaffe able to conduct intermittent attacks – mainly by medium bombers at high level – on ships during the late morning.[20] The Luftwaffe's morning operations were, however, greatly affected by the extremely unfavourable weather conditions and it was not until 12.30 that the Luftwaffe had a notable success (when the minesweeper HMS *Devonia* was attacked off La Panne and suffered extensive damage to her hull from four near-misses).[21]

Bombing became more frequent from 14.00 onward with formations of medium bombers arriving at intervals, roughly half an hour apart, during the afternoon.[22] Bombing attacks on vessels returning to Dover were also made by individual aircraft during the afternoon.[23] During these attacks the Mole was bombed and shipping in the harbour was also unsuccessfully targeted. SS *Nephrite* was repeatedly attacked at the Mole by large formations of German aircraft, and *Nephrite* was also targeted by large formations on its return voyage.[24] SS *Levenwood* was repeatedly targeted off Bray beach.[25] Small boats were also targeted and forced away from the beaches with several damaged by bombs or run-aground during the air attacks with some suffering sufficient damage that they had to be abandoned.[26] However, with visibility restricted by the unfavourable conditions medium bombers also carried out attacks from high level on Bray beach as well as on the ships embarking troops there.[27] These attacks had little or no effect on the general evacuation.

A further series of bombing attacks began to be launched during the evening, and continued until dark. These attacks followed German Army reports that large numbers of ships were heading for Dunkirk, and that troops were continuing to be rapidly embarked, and succeeded in disorganizing further evacuations.[28] At 17.15 HMS *Ivanhoe*, *Whitehall* and *Express* were attacked off Dunkirk by fifty bombers.[29] *Hebe* was attacked off La Panne by four bombers and received slight damage from a near-miss close enough that her commanding officer considered it 'remarkable that great damage was not sustained'.[30] At 18.30 three medium bombers unsuccessfully attacked *St Helier* from 10,000 feet.[31] During the evening HMS *Venomous* observed sixty aircraft approaching Dunkirk which proceeded to attack ships in the harbour and approaching Dunkirk, including small craft, whilst the beaches near La Panne were bombed from high level by thirty He 111s.[32] The intense air bombardment of the beaches, combined with shelling from artillery batteries near Nieuport, caused smaller craft to abandon further embarkations and return to England and many of the power boats which had been brought over to Dunkirk returned to Dover.[33] This produced a shortage of craft used for towing boats and on 1 June Wake-Walker had to implore that they be sent back.[34] The outer harbour of Dunkirk also underwent a heavy bombing attack from formations of medium bombers during this time.[35] This attack forced ships to temporarily leave the Mole until the bombing, which was conducted from 5,000 feet, had concluded.[36] At 20.00 enemy bombers were still active with some ships bombed; the main weight of attack, however, fell on the town of Dunkirk.[37] In the evening light, with heavy smoke over Dunkirk harbour, many medium bombers attacked the town – despite earlier instructions that further attacks should not be made on it – because it was easily identifiable in the poor conditions.

Attacks were also made on Allied ground positions around Dunkirk from the afternoon of 31 May until the evening. From midday attacks were made against British positions in sand dunes east of Nieuport and these were followed, at 14.00, by attacks on artillery batteries west of La Panne. In the early evening, the Luftwaffe attacked troop positions on, and behind, the beaches at Bray Dunes; hits were reported on 'rafts, on roads and on anti-aircraft positions'. Later attacks again bombed anti-aircraft batteries around Dunkirk, with a direct hit reported on an anti-aircraft position in the vicinity of Dunkirk harbour. Between 18.30 and 22.00 high level attacks were also made on troops observed in Dunkirk as well as on Allied positions east of Dunkirk, near the villages of Bray, Coxyde and Zuydcoote.[38] The Luftwaffe's attacks on Allied positions primarily targeted artillery batteries. Sydney Ball, himself an artilleryman, watched the 19th Field Regiment, Royal Artillery, batteries 'blown to pieces … they lost about eight guns and lots of men'.[39] The attacks on British artillery batteries firing from positions to the east of Dunkirk had been requested by AOK 18 during the afternoon. They had been delayed, however, because of ground mist at the airfields of *Luftflotte* 2.[40] The air support missions which were flown in support of the German Army at Dunkirk, as well as other attacks made by *Luftflotte* 2 in support of the German Army near Abbeville, reduced the effort that could be made against the evacuation.⁴¹ Combined with unfavourable weather conditions this reduced the Luftwaffe's disruption of the evacuation. As a result, the disembarkations in Britain on 31 May proved to be the highest daily total of the whole operation, with 22,942 lifted from the beaches and 45,072 from the harbour. The total of 68,014 was achieved despite setbacks; beach embarkations had been handicapped by a breeze off the French coast during the late morning, which produced a slight popple of turbulence, and by increased artillery fire.⁴²

Target selection

The Luftwaffe's attacks on 30 and 31 May were characterized by a failure to concentrate its air attacks against the most important ships of the evacuation. It was noted by the Royal Navy before Dynamo that the Luftwaffe pilots did not appear to have been sufficiently trained in distinguishing between different types of vessels.⁴³ During Dynamo the Luftwaffe frequently targeted vessels which were of less importance to the evacuation than others in the vicinity.⁴⁴ The Luftwaffe's bombing effort was often expended against more manoeuvrable warships rather than the more vulnerable personnel vessels. HMS *Jaguar* was bombed heavily on 29 May but her commanding officer considered that 'enemy aircraft made a mistake in concentrating attacks on *Jaguar* when a large and fully loaded transport was astern' and that their 'misjudgement alone justifies the use of an overloaded destroyer as an anti-aircraft escort'.⁴⁵ Luftwaffe bombers also attacked small targets of insignificant value. During the afternoon of 31 May, the motorboat *Fervent* was heavily attacked by five He 111s which dropped over 120 bombs from low-height. The officer commanding Fervent considered it 'remarkable why the Heinkels used *Fervent* as their target when there were so very many large and small transports about'.⁴⁶ The heavy anti-aircraft fire near Dunkirk and larger ships frequently seems to have caused Luftwaffe pilots to seek 'softer' targets such as *Fervent*.⁴⁷ Many of the notable losses on 1 June were recorded against ships whose anti-aircraft ammunition had run low or been totally expended.⁴⁸ Whilst determined attacks were pressed in the face of naval anti-aircraft fire during Dynamo many bombers, particularly those acting individually, were held off by anti-aircraft fire.⁴⁹

The Luftwaffe also failed to effectively target the Dunkirk Mole during 30–31 May. From 29 May, the overriding concern and fear of British naval authorities organizing the evacuation in Dunkirk was that the Mole would be put out of action.⁵⁰ Even when bombing was not causing significant damage heavy air raids over the harbour led to the Mole being cleared for fear that the destruction of a ship alongside might prevent its further use for embarkations.[51] This caused considerable disorganization of the evacuation and inevitably slowed the process of embarkations. On 29 May five ships were sunk alongside the Mole and the evacuation was almost halted. Had this success been replicated on 30 or 31 May daylight evacuation would have been either suspended or significantly reduced. Air attacks on both these days were not, however, focused on the Mole and a large proportion of effort was focused on the troops embarked from the beaches. Captain Morgan, Chief Staff Officer to Vice Admiral Ramsay at Dover, would later write to Tennant that:

> It may be a brutal thing to say but I look on the beaches effort ... as chiefly helpful as being the draw and the camouflage that enabled Dunkirk Mole to carry on. Had it not been for the beaches which spread out the effort and absorbed an enormous amount of the German attack they would have concentrated on the Pier and soon put paid to it.[52]

Efforts were made to direct air attacks on the more vulnerable points of the evacuation. On 30 May *Luftflotte* 2 had instructions to only select ships in the harbour and along the moorings as targets for attack.[53] The Mole was, however, a difficult target to observe and accurately attack. From high altitude the Mole would have appeared a single strand of activity amidst a confused mass of shipping action, sunken vessels and burning warehouses. The wrecked inner harbour and beaches filled with Allied troops all provided a more obvious target. Calls were made for low level attacks, where it would have been practical to target more accurately, however, heavy anti-aircraft fire from the inner harbour area also discouraged low flying and reconnaissance as well as causing the Mole to be ignored in favour of targets with less effective defences.[54] Without clear intelligence detailing its significance, or unless a ship was alongside with large numbers of troops being obviously embarked, the Luftwaffe air crews frequently failed to realize the importance of the Mole. On 29 May, in weather conditions which permitted good visibility for bombers, extraordinary success was achieved against the Mole after the smoke, which had covered embarkations there, was cleared by a westerly wind. No longer obscured by smoke the large numbers of ships moored alongside the Mole made it a visible target and heavy bombing attacks were made against it. In the absence of favourable conditions for the Luftwaffe the importance of the Mole was often unobserved by its crews who failed to concentrate their bombing effort against it as a result. The Mole was struck several times and was targeted, by both aircraft and artillery, throughout its use. As well as being a comparatively difficult target to observe, however, it was a difficult target to destroy. The latticed concrete structure of the Dunkirk Mole was designed as a breakwater to withstand strong fluctuating forces and was capable of weathering varying high loads and stresses. This meant that only direct hits, or extremely near-misses, were capable of damaging the structure. The direct hits the Mole received did not prevent its continual use. Rudimentary repairs were quickly effected with planks of timber and this allowed men to cross over damaged sections. As well as being a difficult target to identify and destroy, however, it is evident that the Luftwaffe did not appreciate how vital the Mole was to the evacuation. That the Luftwaffe did not make a major effort to destroy the Mole after 1 June, which would have reduced the number of troops evacuated from the harbour by night, also indicates that its importance was never fully appreciated.

Luftwaffe crews also wasted considerable effort bombing the wrecks of ships which has already been sunk in the shallow waters in and around Dunkirk. The most notable of these wrecks was *Clan Macalister*, a 6787 GRT cargo ship.[55] On 29 May *Clan Macalister* was sunk close to the harbour mouth, settling in shallow waters on an even keel with her superstructure unsubmerged.[56] When a Coastal Command Lockheed Hudson flew over *Clan Macalister* on 1 June its crew were able to determine the ship had been abandoned.[57] However, in the days following *Clan Macalister*'s sinking the Luftwaffe crews, whether due to inexperience or less favourable visibility conditions, continued to bomb the wreck because it appeared to be an important target. The air attacks upon *Clan Macalister* permitted smaller craft still in operation to evade more concentrated hostile attention.[58] Tennant counted at least twenty-seven dive-bombing attacks on Clan Macalister and dive-bombers alone were observed to drop 180 bombs upon the wreck in the forty-eight hours after her sinking. Admiralty experts later estimated the presence of *Clan Macalister* saved Britain £1,000,000 worth of shipping.[59] Other wrecks also drew attention. The wreck of the destroyer FS *L'Adroit*, beached near Malo-Les-Baines, appeared to be afloat at high tides, until it was subjected to close scrutiny, and received a number of air attacks.[60] *Côte d'Azur*, a 3047 GRT French troopship, was sunk in Dunkirk's inner harbour on 27 May and continued to be bombed until the wreck received significant further damage on 31 May.[61] *Normannia*, a 1567 GRT Southern Railway steamer, was holed below the waterline on 29 May but was run aground in shallow water and settled on an even keel.[62] In much the same manner as *Clan Macalister*'s wreck *Normannia* served as a decoy and a considerable effort was expended on her by the Luftwaffe rather than ships still embarking and transporting troops from Dunkirk.⁶³ Attacks on wrecks at Dunkirk led the Luftwafe to believe it was inflicting sufficient losses to bring the evacuation to a halt. The Kriegsmarine, rather more circumspectly, believed such claims were exaggerated.⁶⁴

A frequent criticism of the Luftwaffe's target selection during Dynamo, and one not restricted to 30–31 May, was the failure to attack the British channel ports, where the majority of the troops which had been evacuated were disembarked.⁶⁵ Organizers of the evacuation expected attacks on Dover and great efforts were made to transport the returned troops away from disembarkation ports as soon as possible.⁶⁶ The war correspondent Bernard Gray who witnessed the scenes at Dover – and was informed by military authorities of the chaos that bombing could have caused there – considered the Luftwaffe's failure to bomb Dover as 'one of the major mysteries of the war'.⁶⁷ The Luftwaffe had undertaken reconnaissance of ports in the south-east of England and had planned attacks against them.⁶⁸ British intercepts indicated that an attack on the ports by a *Kampfgeschwader* had been planned on 29 May but that it had been postponed, and subsequently cancelled, because of unfavourable weather conditions.⁶⁹ The failure to bomb the disembarkation ports, or the railway headings behind them, when many targets – which had less chance to disrupt the evacuation – were attacked during the unfavourable conditions demonstrates that the bombing of these ports was not a priority for the Luftwaffe. The decision not to attempt to obstruct the disembarkation of troops by bombing ports such as Dover was a mistake. Before 29 May, however, the Luftwaffe did not conceive of the need for these strikes, which would have interfered with other operational requirements. Anthony Eden believed the failure to make 'any persistent attempt to bomb Dover' was because 'the Germans were chiefly concerned to ensure the defeat of the French armies'.⁷⁰ Following 29 May plans were made for such strikes but were abandoned because of unfavourable weather conditions.⁷¹ On 1 June air operations were designed to continuously attack Dunkirk to saturate the air defences by weight of numbers and halt the evacuation. Whilst the evacuation could have been disrupted by limited attacks on the disembarkation ports it is doubtful that meaningful disorganization could have occurred without a raid involving a large number of aircraft; such a raid would have deprived the attacks on Dunkirk on 1 June of significant resources.

Diversion of operational focus on 30–31 May

On both 30 and 31 May the Luftwaffe's application of air power against evacuations from Dunkirk was negatively affected by the need to provide close air support to German land forces. There was a continued dissipation of anti-surface operations and attacks on embarkations in favour of targets on the Dunkirk perimeter and the German southern front.[72] The German infantry, accustomed to the enemy having been softened up by air attack, as well as to total air superiority above them, became reluctant to launch heavy attacks against enemy positions without air support.[73] The most notable progress made against the Dunkirk perimeter came when German attacks were made in conjunction with air support.[74] Throughout Dynamo the close air support provided by the Luftwaffe failed to achieve significant results. The effect of close air support for the German Army against Allied troops determined to resist and occupying strong defensive positions on the Dunkirk perimeter was limited because these attacks were not rapidly followed up by ground troops.[75] On days where air support was less forthcoming progress was slower. Orders issued on 30 May specified attacks on enemy transports, warships and embarkations; however, reconnaissance was to be carried out and it was stressed that care was to be taken not to attack nearby German troops.[76] This very clear warning reveals that these attacks were not envisaged as being restricted to anti-surface attacks and air strikes on Allied embarkations. *Luftflotte* 3 had orders to operate against British troops whilst *Fliegerkorps* VIII, as well as attacking Dunkirk, was to support the German Army and by noon was being pressed to carry out attacks against ground targets south of the Somme.[77] The Battle of Abbeville, 27 May–4 June, drew in considerable air resources from the Luftwaffe which might otherwise have been used against Dunkirk. Armed reconnaissance in strength was undertaken frequently in the Abbeville area and dive-bomber attacks south of Abbeville were arranged, despite the urgent need for further operations on the coast.[78] At 21.00 on 30 May AOK 4 were requesting that air attacks previously agreed against targets near Abbeville, which had been postponed from 30 May because of weather conditions, be carried out without fail at 05.00 on 31 May.[79] The Luftwaffe also engaged in operations in the vicinity of Abbeville during the afternoon of 31 May.[80] This experience has been replicated earlier in the evacuation with French resistance at Amiens often holding the Luftwaffe's focus during Dynamo. Repeated requests for dive-bomber support against Allied positions, artillery concentrations and motorized columns had been made on 27 and 28 May by German forces in the area of Amiens.[81] Requests for air support against positions, particularly tank concentrations, near Amiens were again made during 29 May – with AOK 4 crediting these for helping to pacify the situation there – and an Allied counter-attack steadily sucked in air resources that could have been employed against Dynamo.[82] These attacks all diverted air resources which could have been committed against the evacuation. That the Luftwaffe's sole focus was not on bringing about a decisive end to Operation Dynamo needs to be recognized to understand the Luftwaffe's military effectiveness, its operations and its application of air power during Dunkirk.

It is also important, however, not to retrospectively consider this division of focus as being faulty. First, the German Southern Front continued to need air support. Instructions for operations on 31 May stressed that any alteration to ground organization necessary for the continuation of operations must be done in 'such a way that strong forces are always ready for attacks on important objectives on the southern front'.[83] On 31 May Halder recorded in his diary that in the Somme sector 'the enemy tank attacks turn out to have been quite serious'.[84] Furthermore, the Luftwaffe's operational focus on 1 June, when it halted further daylight evacuations, was not dissimilar to those that weather conditions allowed it to commit on 30–31 May.[85] On 1 June, as well as attacking the evacuation at Dunkirk, the Luftwaffe had orders to combat allied attacks on strong points held by AOK 4 near Abbeville and Amiens. Formations of *Fliegerkorps* II were to continue with attacks on Allied columns and railways in the area between Abbeville and Amiens.[86] During the afternoon of 1 June the German Army arranged for the Luftwaffe to undertake attacks that evening along the Dunkirk perimeter focusing on Fort Vallières and Fort Louis as well as the Churches at Teteghem, Uxem and Leffrinckouck. Targets along the railway east of Dunkirk were also identified.[87] Pre-war experience had demonstrated to the Luftwaffe that bombing enemy positions in close proximity to German troops was a most difficult task and it took great care to achieve a high level of accuracy in the ground support it provided around Dunkirk.[88]

During this period the Luftwaffe was also obliged to divert forces to support the German forces fighting the five French divisions surrounded at Lille – it was not until 31 May that the remaining 35,000 soldiers at Lille surrendered.[89] During the course of the evacuation air support was provided to German ground forces in the area between Arras and Lille. On 30 May, for instance, two *Sturzkampfgeschwader* were operating against ground positions in front of the German Army.[90] Support for ground forces, particularly those away from the Dunkirk perimeter, was not, however, the cause of the Luftwaffe's failure to inflict substantial losses on the evacuation fleet before 1 June. Air operations against the evacuation were primarily restricted by the weather conditions – particularly the low cloud base over the French coast – during 30–31 May whilst clearer conditions prevailed inland. The use of Ju 87 formations against targets away from Dunkirk does not mean, therefore, that more successful attacks could have been made against the evacuation. It was understood by both the Luftwaffe and the German Army that the Stukas were urgently needed on the coast against the Allied evacuation.[91] With difficult weather precluding the use of the Stukas against the evacuation, however, they were redirected to alternative targets as the alternative was that they would have remained idle. On both 30 and 31 May the main obstacle preventing the success of the Luftwaffe was the lack of a prolonged period of fine weather in which to utilize dive-bombers over Dunkirk and make concentrated attacks against the evacuation. The success against the evacuation on 1 June demonstrates that it was not the failure to commit the maximum resources at Dunkirk which prevented success earlier in the evacuation.

Analysis of operations on 30–31 May

During 30–31 May over 120,000 troops were lifted from Dunkirk harbour and the beaches.[92] Against this figure only four ships were lost as a definite result of the Luftwaffe's attacks, with a further four Royal Navy ships damaged.[93] It was during these two days that Dynamo became a success story as an evacuation. Up to 30 May 72,783 Allied troops had been evacuated, a number below British hopes at the outset of Dynamo. By the end of 31 May the number of troops evacuated was 194,620.[94] During those final two days of May the Luftwaffe was able to cause only modest losses to the evacuation fleet. The failure to sink a higher number of vessels, or prevent large numbers of troops being evacuated, was primarily because German air operations, particularly those of dive-bombers, were restricted by unfavourable flying condition.

Although attacks on transport vessels and the port of Dunkirk were the intended primary focus of German air operations on both 30 and 31 May, they were largely unfulfilled.[95] Air operations on both days – particularly during the mornings – were restricted by poor flying conditions and ground mist, with only three large air attacks against the evacuation each day.[96] In France and Belgium, German units reported low clouds, ground mist and rainfall, with the sky overcast throughout much of 30 May.[97] The afternoon saw ten-tenths cloud cover at 400 to 900 feet. This cleared in some areas and visibility improved slightly; however, the evacuation remained largely untroubled by the Luftwaffe because poor flying conditions endured on flight routes to the evacuation, over parts of the target area and at German airbases.[98] The situation with regard to air attack was considered by those organizing the evacuation, to be 'better than on any previous day', with Tennant describing the situation as 'rosy' during the morning.[99] On 31 May *Fliegerkorps* I was ready for action from daybreak whilst the aircraft of *Fliegerkorps* II and VIII were ready to start at 07.00 and 09.00, respectively.[100] Large-scale attacks were not possible until the afternoon, however, because of poor weather conditions over German air bases. *Generalmajor* Speidel believed that on these two days 'weather conditions played a decisive role in the inadequate performance of the Luftwaffe ... the weather was as unfavourable as it possibly could have been'.[101] During 30–31 May the weather conditions over the Luftwaffe's air bases were worse than those at the coast, with mist and thick cloud at low altitude during the mornings.[102] In these conditions *Kampfgeschwader* were delayed or restricted in attacking the evacuation and frequently also had to contend with difficult flying conditions on their flight route.[103] Poor visibility and a low cloud base over the evacuation area reduced the accuracy of the attacks which were able to be made.[104] Anti-aircraft fire from batteries at Dunkirk, and from the ships involved in the evacuation, saw a repetition of the failures of high altitude bombing discussed for the period before 29 May.[105] The effect of anti-aircraft fire was such that batteries at Dunkirk were targeted by the Luftwaffe during the afternoon of 31 May.[106] Heavy ground fog across northern France and a low cloud base over the evacuation also shielded the evacuation from dive-bomber attacks. Some units were grounded by the bad weather over their bases; however, Richthofen was unwilling to commit dive-bomber units in conditions where, operating under the low cloud base, they would have been vulnerable to, and incurred heavy casualties from, the anti-aircraft fire at Dunkirk.[107] As discussed in Chapter 1, dive-bomber attacks were far more effective against shipping than those of level-bombers and the absence of the Ju 87 proved a great relief to those at Dunkirk.[108] William Hewitt, at the time a sub-lieutenant aboard the minesweeper *Sutton*, recalled that:

> Bombing was of two kinds, there was high and low level-bombing by normal bombers who just dropped a pattern of bombs and you were very unlucky if they hit you. ... There were several dive-bombing attacks and they were a different matter as there was no way they could miss.[109]

In the absence of the Ju 87 only the Ju 88 could undertake the accurate bombing necessary to imperil the evacuation; attacks were made on the harbour by Ju 88s but not in sufficient numbers, because they too were also limited by the prevailing flying conditions.[110] The low cloud base over Dunkirk also meant that the dive-bomb capability of the Ju 88 was restricted because attacks of this nature in areas with anti-aircraft cover were likely to result in high casualty rates.[111] The restrictions placed on dive-bomber operations by the weather were the primary cause of the Luftwaffe failed to effectively apply air power against the evacuation on either 30 or 31 May. Errors in target selection and a diversion of operational focus meant that on both days the Luftwaffe achieved less than it might have done; however, even if they had applied their full effort, the weather conditions would have prevented them halting the evacuation. The weather conditions also contributed to both target errors – increasing difficulties in bombing aiming and target recognition – and the diversion of air power away from Dunkirk – with the Ju 87s unable to operate over Dunkirk they were used against French forces on other fronts. On only two days, 29 May and 1 June, were Ju 87s able to operate without significant restrictions, and on each day, they imperilled the continuation of Dynamo.[112]

Notes

1 IWM: EDS/AL/1429 – 4. Armee Ia, Kriegstagebuch, 30 May 1940; TNA: HW 5/2 – GC&CS Decrypts, CX/JQ/10.
2 TNA: AIR 22/169 – A.M.W.R. Daily Report for Summary, No. 317, 1 June 1940.
3 TNA: ADM 199/786 – CO *Whitehall* Report; TNA: ADM 199/786 – Commanding Officer of *Winchelsea*, Report of Activities during Operation Dynamo.
4 IWM: EDS/AL/1429 – 4. Armee Ia, Kriegstagebuch, 30 May 1940.
5 TNA: AIR 22/169 – A.M.W.R. Daily Report for Summary, No. 317, 1 June 1940.
6 TNA: ADM 199/786 – CO *Vivacious* Report.
7 TNA: ADM 199/787 – Commanding Officer of *Despatch II*, Report of Activities during Operation Dynamo; TNA: ADM 199/787 – Commanding Officer of *Reiger*, Report of Activities during Operation Dynamo; TNA: ADM 199/787 – Able Seaman Patrick Thomas Sullivan, Survivor of Passenger Launch *Silver Queen*, Statement on Activities during Operation Dynamo.
8 TNA: ADM 199/787 – Officer in Charge of Motor Yacht *Caleta*, Report of Activities during Operation Dynamo.
9 TNA: AIR 24/217 – Bomber Command Intelligence Summary, No. 215, 31 May 1940; TNA: CAB 65/7/43 – War Cabinet, Conclusions of Meeting No. 148, 30 May 1940.
10 TNA: ADM 199/786 – CO *Snaefell* Report; TNA: AIR 35/189 – Wing Commander Spence to Air Marshal Barratt, Notes on the Evacuation of Dunkirk, c. June 1940.
11 TNA: HW 5/2 – GC&CS Decrypts, CX/JQ/8.
12 TNA: ADM 199/786 – Commanding Officer of *Emperor of India*, Report of Activities during Operation Dynamo; TNA: ADM 199/786 – CO *Icarus* Report.
13 TNA: ADM 199/787 – Commanding Officer of *Amazone*, Report of Activities during Operation Dynamo; TNA: ADM 199/787 – Commanding Officer of *Delta*,

Report of Activities during Operation Dynamo; TNA: ADM 199/787 – Officer in Charge Motorboat *Reda* Report.
14 TNA: ADM 199/787 – Commanding Officer of *San Antionio*, Report of Activities during Operation Dynamo; TNA: ADM 199/787 – Resident Naval Officer Poole, Report on the Activities of Skoots during Operation Dynamo.
15 TNA: ADM 199/786 – Commanding Officer of *Codrington*, Report of Activities during Operation Dynamo; TNA: ADM 199/786 – CO *Snaefell* Report.
16 TNA: ADM 199/786 – Commanding Officer of *Anthony*, Report of Activities during Operation Dynamo.
17 TNA: AIR 20/9906 – German Air Force Situation Reports on Western Front, 30 May 1940.
18 IWM: EDS/AL/1428 – *Heeresgruppe* A Ia, War Diary Part II, 31 May 1940; IWM: EDS/AL/1433 – *Heeresgruppe* B Ia, War Diary, 31 May 1940; The National Meteorological Digital Archive (hereafter TNMDA): DWR/1940/05 – Daily Weather Report, 31 May 1940.
19 TNA: HW 5/2 – GC&CS Decrypts, CX/JQ/9.
20 TNA: ADM 199/786 – CO *Express* Report; TNA: ADM 199/786 – CO *Vivacious* Report.
21 TNA: ADM 199/786 – Commanding Officer of *Devonia*, Report of Activities during Operation Dynamo; TNA: AIR 20/9906 – German Air Force Situation Reports on Western Front, 31 May 1940; Gardner, *Evacuation*, p. 83.
22 TNA: ADM 199/786 – CO *Impulsive* Report; TNA: ADM 199/786 – Commanding Officer of *Ivanhoe*, Report of Activities during Operation Dynamo; TNA: ADM 199/787 – Leading Seaman H. Cook, Coxswain of Motorboat *Andorra*, Statement on Activities during Operation Dynamo.
23 TNA: ADM 199/787 – CO *Friso* Report.
24 TNA: ADM 199/788A – Master of *Nephrite*, Report of Activities during Operation Dynamo.
25 TNA: ADM 199/788A – Master of *Levenwood*, Report of Activities during Operation Dynamo.
26 TNA: ADM 199/787 – Officer in Charge of Motorboat *Commodore*, Report of Activities during Operation Dynamo; TNA: ADM 199/787 – Officer in Charge of Motor Yacht *Glala*, Report of Activities during Operation Dynamo; TNA: ADM 199/787 – Master of Motor Yacht *Laroc*, Report of Activities during Operation Dynamo; TNA: ADM 199/787 – Officer in Charge of Motor Yacht *Llanthony*, Report of Activities during Operation Dynamo.
27 TNA: ADM 199/786 – Commanding Officer of *Venomous*, Report of Activities during Operation Dynamo; TNA: ADM 199/786 – CO *Winchelsea* Report; TNA: ADM 199/787 – Officer in Charge Motorboat *Commodore* Report; TNA: ADM 199/787 – CO *Despatch II* Report; TNA: ADM 199/787 – Officer in Charge Motor Yacht *Glala* Report.

28 IWM: EDS/AL/1405 – Ab. Nr. T 645/40g, Telegram Heeresgruppe B to Heeresgruppe A, 1 June 1940; TNA: ADM 199/786 – CO *Shikari* Report; TNA: ADM 199/787 – Coxswain Motorboat *Andorra* Statement; TNA: HW 5/2 – GC&CS Decrypts, CX/JQ/11.
29 TNA: ADM 199/786 – CO *Express* Report; TNA: ADM 199/786 – CO *Whitehall* Report.
30 TNA: ADM 199/786 – CO *Hebe* Report; Gardner, *Evacuation*, p. 83.
31 TNA: ADM 199/788A – Master *St Helier* Report.
32 TNA: ADM 199/786 – CO *Express* Report; TNA: ADM 199/786 – CO *Venomous* Report; TNA: AIR 27/862 – Appendix 184, 110 Squadron Operational Intelligence Debriefing Report, 31 May 1940.
33 TNA: ADM 199/787 – Reports of HM Yachts, HM Motorboats and Small Classification Vessels on Operation Dynamo; Gardner, *Evacuation*, p. 74.
34 Gardner, *Evacuation*, p. 74, Appendix H.26.
35 TNA: ADM 199/786 – CO *Whitehall* Report; TNA: ADM 199/787 – Commanding Officer of *Lord Inchcape*, Report of Activities during Operation Dynamo; TNA: ADM 199/787 – Lieutenant J. E. L. Martin, on board Tug *Sun IV*, Report of Activities during Operation Dynamo; TNA: ADM 199/789 – Report of Lieutenant Commander J. W. McClelland, SNO – La Panne, on Operation Dynamo.
36 TNA: ADM 199/786 – CO *Winchelsea* Report; Gardner, *Evacuation*, p. 74.
37 TNA: ADM 199/786 – CO *Whitehall* Report; TNA: ADM 199/787 – CO *Cariba* Report.
38 TNA: ADM 199/787 – CO *Amazone* Report; TNA: AIR 20/9906 – German Air Force Situation Reports on Western Front, 31 May 1940.
39 IWM: Documents/17217 – Diary of Gunner Sydney Ball, 31 May 1940.
40 IWM: EDS/AL/1433 – *Heeresgruppe* B Ia, War Diary, 31 May 1940.
41 TNA: AIR 20/9906 – German Air Force Situation Reports on Western Front, 31 May 1940.
42 TNA: ADM 199/787 – Master of Motor Yacht *Constant Nymph*, Report of Activities during Operation Dynamo; TNA: ADM 334/83 – Smith, 'Dunkirk Operations'; Gardner, *Evacuation*, p. 84.
43 TNA: ADM 1/12196 – Vice Admiral Commanding, First Cruiser Squadron, to C-in-C Home Fleet, Defence of Ships Against Air Attack, 8 May 1940.
44 TNA: ADM 199/787 – Officer Commanding *Doggersbank*, Report of Activities during Operation Dynamo; TNA: ADM 199/788A – Commanding Officer Motorboat Base, Dover, Report on Motorboats and Motor Anti-Submarine Boats during Operation Dynamo; TNA: ADM 199/788A – Officer in Charge of Motorboat *Fervent*, Report of Activities during Operation Dynamo; TNA: ADM 199/788A – Ramsgate and Margate Dynamo Operations Reports, Appendix 5, Narrative Account of Small Motorboats during Evacuation of Dunkirk.

45 TNA: ADM 199/786 – CO *Jaguar* Report.
46 TNA: ADM 199/788A – Officer in Charge Motorboat *Fervent* Report.
47 TNA: HW 5/2 – GC&CS Decrypts, CX/JQ/14.
48 TNA: ADM 199/792 – CO *Keith* Report.
49 TNA: ADM 199/786 – CO *Express* Report; TNA: ADM 199/786 – CO *Jaguar* Report; TNA: ADM 199/788A – Commanding Officer of *Calcutta*, Report of Activities during Operation Dynamo; TNA: ADM 199/788A – Master *Loch Garry* Report; TNA: ADM 199/788A – Master *Nephrite* Report; TNA: ADM 199/788A – Master *St Helier* Report.
50 TNA: ADM 199/2205 – Naval War Diary Summaries, Operations, Evacuation of BEF from Dunkirk, 29 May 1940.
51 TNA: ADM 199/786 – CO *Sabre* Report.
52 IWM: Documents/11483a (LVM/3, Box No. P65) – Private Papers of Admiral Sir Vaughan Morgan, Letter from Captain Morgan to Captain Tennant, 12 May 1941.
53 IWM: EDS/AL/1433 – Heeresgruppe B Ia, War Diary, 30 May 1940; TNA: HW 5/2 – GC&CS Decrypts, CX/JQ/10.
54 TNA: HW 5/2 – GC&CS Decrypts, CX/JQ/14.
55 TNA: ADM 199/2205 – Naval War Diary Summaries, Operations, Evacuation of BEF from Dunkirk, 29 May 1940; TNA: ADM 199/2205 – Naval War Diary Summaries, Merchant ship Casualties suffered during Evacuation, 31 May 1940.
56 TNA: WO 361/21 – Information Concerning Vessels Involved Operations Dynamo; Gardner, *Evacuation*, p. 41.
57 TNA: AIR 22/169 – A.M.W.R. Daily Report for Summary, No. 318, 2 June 1940.
58 TNA: ADM 199/786 – CO *Saltash* Report.
59 IWM: Audio/6442 – D'Arcy Kenelm McCloughin, Reels 3–4; Collier, *Sands*, p. 214.
60 TNA: ADM 199/787 – CO *Patria* and *Haig* Report.
61 Blond, *L'Epopée Silencieuse*, p. 100; Jackson, *Dunkirk*, p. 122.
62 Jackson, *Dunkirk*, p. 157.
63 TNA: AIR 20/9906 – German Air Force Situation Reports on Western Front, 30–31 May 1940; Harman, *Dunkirk*, p. 166.
64 TNA: ADM 223/28 – War Diary of *Führer der Torpedoboote*; USNWC: Microfilm 354/Part A/Vol. 10 – Oberkommando der Kriegsmarine Kriegstagebuch der Seekriegsleitung, June 1940.
65 TNA: ADM 199/792 – Report of Vice Admiral Ramsay.
66 Churchill, *Finest Hour*, p. 123; Jackson, *Dunkirk*, p. 79.
67 Bernard Gray, *War Reporter* (London: Hale, 1942), p. 125.
68 TNA: AIR 22/168 – A.M.W.R. Daily Report for Summary, No. 315, Part II, 30 May 1940; TNA: HW 5/1 – GC&CS Decrypts, CX/FJ/102.
69 TNA: ADM 199/2205 – Naval War Diary Summaries, Situation Report, Air Ministry 'Air Attacks Expected', 14.30 29 May 1940; ADM 199/2205 – Naval War

Diary Summaries, Situation Report, Air Ministry 'Air Attacks Postponed Owing to Weather', 16.10, 29 May 1940.
70 Eden, *Reckoning*, p. 112.
71 TNA: AIR 16/1070 – Air Ministry to Fighter Command, 29 May 1940; TNA: HW 5/2 – GC&CS Decrypts, CX/JQ/8–9.
72 Galland, *Luftwaffe*, pp. 40–2.
73 BA/MA: N 671/6 – Richthofen, Kriegstagebuch, 24–25, 27 May 1940; Speidel, 'German Air Force', p. 96
74 TNA: CAB 44/62 – Major General H. R. Alexander, Commanding Officer I Corps, Report on BEF Operations in France and Belgium.
75 TsAMO RF: Ф.500 оп.12474 д.168 – Unterlagen der Ia-Abteilung des Generalkommandos des X. Armeekorps: Erfahrungsberichte des Korps zu den Kämpfen in den Niederlanden und bei Dünkirchen, 27 July 1940, pp. 6–7.
76 TNA: HW 5/2 – GC&CS Decrypts, CX/JQ/5.
77 *Ibid.*, CX/JQ/5, CX/JQ/7, CX/JQ/10.
78 IWM: EDS/AL/1429 – 4. Armee Ia, Kriegstagebuch, 24–30 May 1940; TNA: HW 5/2 – GC&CS Decrypts, CX/JQ/4.
79 TNA: HW 5/2 – GC&CS Decrypts, CX/JQ/11.
80 *Ibid.*, CX/JQ/10.
81 IWM: EDS/AL/1429 – 4. Armee Ia, Kriegstagebuch, 27–28 May 1940; TNA: HW 5/1 – GC&CS Decrypts, CX/FJ/110, CX/FJ/114.
82 IWM: EDS/AL/1429 – 4. Armee Ia, Kriegstagebuch, 29 May 1940; TNA: HW 5/2 – GC&CS Decrypts, CX/JQ/4–5.
83 TNA: HW 5/2 – GC&CS Decrypts, CX/JQ/9.
84 Halder, *Kriegstagebuch*, pp. 326–7.
85 TNA: ADM 199/2206 – Naval War Diary Summaries, Situation Report, 1 June 1940; TNA: ADM 223/82 – OIC Daily Report, 1 June 1940; TNA: AIR 22/169 – A.M.W.R. Daily Report for Summary, No. 319, 3 June 1940; TNA: AIR 24/225 – Bomber Command Intelligence Reports, 2–3 June 1940; TNA: HW 5/2 – GC&CS Decrypts, CX/JQ/9; TNA: WO 106/1644 – Military intelligence, Intelligence Summary 273, 2 June 1940; *Der Adler*, 'Hölle Dünkirchen', p. 301.
86 TNA: HW 5/2 – GC&CS Decrypts, CX/JQ/11–12.
87 *Ibid.*, CX/JQ/14.
88 BA/MA: RL 7/160 – Luftwaffe Generalstabsreise 1939, Besprechung der Planübung des 1. Spieltages der Generalstabsreise, 29 June 1939; TNA: AIR 20/9906 – German Air Force Situation Reports on Western Front, 30 May–3 June 1940; TNA: HW 5/1 – GC&CS Decrypts, CX/FJ/114; TNA: HW 5/2 – GC&CS Decrypts, CX/JQ/5.
89 Halder, *Kriegstagebuch*, pp. 326–7; Dominique Lormier, *La Bataille De France Jour Après Jour: Mai-Juin 1940* (Paris: Le Cherche Midi, 2010), p. 373.
90 TNA: AIR 22/169 – A.M.W.R. Daily Report for Summary, No. 317, 1 June 1940.

91 IWM: EDS/AL/1429 – 4. Armee Ia, Kriegstagebuch, 26–31 May 1940.
92 TNA: ADM 199/360 – Dover Command, War Diary, 30–31 May 1940.
93 TNA: ADM 199/793 – HM Ships Lost during the Evacuation of Troops from Dunkirk.
94 Gardner, *Evacuation*, p. 220.
95 IWM: EDS/AL/1428 – *Heeresgruppe* A Ia, War Diary Part II, 30–31 May 1940; TNA: AIR 20/6260 – ORB: Directorate of Operations (Naval Co-Operation), Enemy Air Activity at Sea, 30–1 May 1940; TNA: AIR 22/169 – A.M.W.R. Daily Report for Summary, No. 317, 1 June 1940.
96 BA/MA: RL 8/43 – VIII Fliegerkorps im Frankreich Feldzug Zusammengestellt von Fragmenten des Kriegstagebucher der Fliegerkorps, Richthofen und Deichmann, 31 May 1940; IWM: EDS/AL/1428 – *Heeresgruppe* A Ia, War Diary Part II, 30–31 May 1940; TNA: AIR 20/6260 – ORB: Directorate of Operations (Naval Co-Operation), Enemy Air Activity at Sea, 30–1 May 1940; TNA: AIR 22/169 – A.M.W.R. Daily Report for Summary, No. 317, 1 June 1940; Gardner, *Evacuation*, p. 74.
97 IWM: EDS/AL/1428 – *Heeresgruppe* A Ia, War Diary Part II, 30 May 1940.
98 TNA: ADM 199/115 – Lieutenant Commander Charles Evans, Report on Operations of 806 Squadron While Working in Conjunction with RAF Coastal Command, 27 May–3 June 1940; TNA: AIR 22/169 – A.M.W.R. Daily Report for Summary, No. 317, 1 June 1940; TNA: AIR 27/1941 – ORB: 500 Squadron.
99 TNA: ADM 199/360 – Dover Command, War Diary, 30 May 1940; TNA: ADM 199/2205 – Naval War Diary Summaries, Operations, Evacuation of BEF from Dunkirk, 29 May 1940; TNA: ADM 199/2205 – Naval War Diary Summaries, 'Evacuation Going Well', Captain Tennant to Naval Officer in Charge Dover, 30 May 1940.
100 IWM: EDS/AL/1429 – 4. Armee Ia, Kriegstagebuch, 30 May 1940.
101 Speidel, 'German Air Force', p. 358.
102 TNA: AIR 22/169 – A.M.W.R. Daily Report for Summary, No. 318, 2 June 1940.
103 TNA: AIR 22/58 – Daily Charts of Weather in North-West Europe, 30–31 May 1940; TNMDA: DWR/1940/05 – Daily Weather Report, 30–31 May 1940; Harold A. Winters et al., *Battling the Elements: Weather and Terrain in the Conduct of War* (London: Johns Hopkins University, 1998), p. 22.
104 IWM: EDS/AL/1428 – *Heeresgruppe* A Ia, War Diary Part II, 30–31 May 1940; IWM: EDS/AL/1433 – *Heeresgruppe* B Ia, War Diary, 30–31 May 1940; TNMDA: DWR/1940/05 – Daily Weather Report, 31 May 1940; Winters, *Battling*, p. 22.
105 TNA: ADM 199/786 – CO *Shikari* Report; TNA: ADM 199/787 – CO *Amazone* Report.
106 TNA: AIR 20/9906 – German Air Force Situation Reports on Western Front, 31 May 1940.

107 BA/MA: N 671/6 – Richthofen, Kriegstagebuch, 29–31 May 1940; Speidel, 'German Air Force', p. 359.
108 IWM: Audio/20137 – Leon Wilson, Reel 1; TNA: ADM 199/1189 – Tactical Summary of Bombing Attacks by German Aircraft on HM Ships and Shipping from September 1939 to February 1941.
109 IWM: Audio/13607 – William G. Hewett, Reel 1.
110 TNA: AIR 22/10 – A.M.W.R. Daily Summary, No. 318, Air Intelligence, 2 June 1940.
111 TNA: ADM 199/786 – CO *Shikari* Report; TNA: ADM 199/787 – CO *Amazone* Report.
112 BA/MA: N 671/6 – Richthofen, Kriegstagebuch, 26 May–3 June 1940; TNA: HW 5/1 – GC&CS Decrypts, CX/FJ/111.

6

Results, limitations and potential of Luftwaffe night attacks and mine operations

The previous chapters have considered the effect of the Luftwaffe's attacks on the Dunkirk evacuation up to, and including, 1 June. The Luftwaffe continued to attack Dunkirk after 1 June; however, the evacuation – now only proceeding outside of daylight hours – was little affected. This was in part a combination of unfavourable weather and because, with the majority of Allied troops already embarked and evacuations proceeding only by night meaning there were limited targets of opportunity, the Luftwaffe's focus had shifted to other targets in France.[1] Further daylight attacks on Dunkirk would only have produced valuable results if they had been directed en masse against the Dunkirk Mole to prevent its further use; the difficulty of achieving this has been previously discussed. This chapter does not therefore consider the limited bombing attacks which took place on Dunkirk during daylight hours after 1 June. It instead considers the results, limitations and potential of the Luftwaffe's night attacks and mine operations. It explores whether it was possible for the Luftwaffe to apply air power to terminate Dynamo – or at least prohibit further large-scale embarkations by night – had daylight evacuations been halted before 1 June.

The Luftwaffe's night attacks

Following the Luftwaffe's success on 1 June daylight evacuations were halted, Allied troops, however, continued to be embarked in large numbers during darkness. The Luftwaffe made limited, unsuccessful attempts to halt night embarkations both before daylight evacuations were halted on 1 June and afterwards. Having halted daylight evacuations on 1 June *Fliegerkorps* IV bombed the port installations of Dunkirk harbour, the ships off Dunkirk and along the coast as well as those on passage to and from Dunkirk during the night of 1–2 June.[2] These attacks were not able to prevent large evacuations during the night but the attacks did produce casualties and disruption to the evacuation, restricting the number of troops embarked to a total lower than might otherwise have been the case.[3] Air operations continued against the evacuation on the nights of 2 and 3 June; however, the operational focus of the Luftwaffe had largely shifted to missions against the remaining French forces in the Somme and elsewhere. The large embarkations made on these nights were therefore not meaningfully interrupted by the Luftwaffe.[4] Had daylight evacuations been halted earlier than 1 June – and had the Luftwaffe been confronted with the ongoing evacuation of Allied troops – the Luftwaffe would have required to make large night attacks against Dunkirk. To understand whether the Luftwaffe could have halted evacuations by night it is important to consider the attacks that they did make.

Night attacks against the evacuation were not restricted to the later stages of Dynamo. Air attacks on Dunkirk were ordered for the night of 27–28 May and by 00.45 on 28 May the whole of Dunkirk appeared to be ablaze.[5] The Luftwaffe heavily bombed the harbour and the town of Dunkirk with high-explosive and incendiary bombs whilst the embarkation beaches to the east were also bombed.[6] Between Dunkirk and Gravelines aircraft approached and machine-gunned HMS *Wolsey* and *Wolfhound* registering several hits.[7] At 01.20 *Sabre* was also machine-gunned by an aircraft and at 02.00 *Sandown* experienced heavy bombing and machine-gunning.[8] Ships involved in the evacuation were attacked throughout the night and bombing remained frequent until dawn. *Queen of the Channel* was sunk shortly before dawn after being bombed by a single aircraft whilst *St Seiriol* was unsuccessfully attacked by a single aircraft shortly after.[9] Attacks on the night of 28–29 May once again left the town of Dunkirk 'in flames'.[10] Ships alongside the Mole, however, did not receive any damage and only occasional bombing raids were made against ships at anchor off Dunkirk.[11] As a result the bombing achieved little interference to the embarkation of troops despite three large raids, involving fifty-two aircraft, on Dunkirk shortly before dawn.[12] The night of 29–30 May, following a day of exhaustive effort by the Luftwaffe, saw only restricted bombing. At 00.44 on 30 May Lieutenant-General Haining, Vice-Chief of the Imperial General Staff, reported to Ramsay that there had been no bombing of the beaches since dark with the result that embarkations were 'well organized' and the troops there were 'in good heart'.[13] Isolated bombing did occur after 01.00 on 30 May which occasioned some delays to embarkations from the beaches; however, although some craft suffered slight damage from near-misses, no substantial material damage was sustained.[14]

The pattern of these attacks continued until the end of the evacuation, with individual medium bombers, and occasionally small formations, attacking at low altitude as well as strafing raids also being undertaken during the hours of darkness.[15] Although an obvious point, it should be remembered that the forces available to both sides could not operate continuously. The Luftwaffe was not able to undertake extensive operations over Dunkirk by day and by night. Until 1 June, the majority of troops were being recovered from Dunkirk during daylight hours. Correspondingly the Luftwaffe devoted the majority of its efforts to halting the evacuation during periods of daylight.

The Luftwaffe also faced limitations operating at night, as discussed in Chapter 1. However, many of these limitations were mitigated to a considerable extent because of the illumination cast by the burning oil tanks at Dunkirk. These not only silhouetted certain targets but also provided a beacon and targeting point for the docks. Wing Commander Spence reported that burning oil tanks 'subsequently proved very useful to enemy bombers, who were able to find the port at night without any difficulty'.[16] Indeed Spence believed the bombing of the docks was more accurate by night because the fires provided the bombers the opportunity to locate and attack the target whilst remaining almost immune to Allied retaliation.[17] These night attacks, made shortly before Dynamo commenced, and those made at the beginning of the evacuation, also benefited from the luminosity of the moon.[18] On the night of 26–27 May the Luftwaffe was able to make meaningful attacks on Dunkirk using the light of the moon and the flames from the ammunition dumps, warehouses and oil fuel depots in the port which had already been set alight.[19] The illumination from the moon helped bombers to accurately locate targets and these attacks were effective as a result. These benefits diminished greatly as the moon waned – casting less light and leaving the evacuations from the beaches and outer harbour of Dunkirk cloaked in darkness.

From the night of 29 May onwards the Luftwaffe's attack began to rely more heavily on light sources emanating from Dunkirk.[20] From this point, however, the fires at Dunkirk had subsided to a steady glow providing only a dim light whilst low mists around Dunkirk frequently obscured shipping targets.[21] As targeting points the fires at Dunkirk were also unhelpful by this stage as the docks were already out of action and further bombing of the town was unwarranted. The Luftwaffe was able to augment the light which emanated from Dunkirk by using flares to locate and attack targets.[22] Ships operating off Bray Dunes were illuminated by flares from aircraft spotting for German Artillery batteries near Nieuport.[23] The motor launch *Bonny Heather* was caught in the light of a parachute flare and bombed without result.[24] The Skoot *Friso* was unsuccessfully bombed before dawn on 31 May after being partially illuminated by a flare 400 yards ahead of it.[25] However, the use of flares resulted in few known losses with ships often able to evade the light after a flare was dropped and the aircraft circled round to attack. Had larger formations of bombers been employed to attack the evacuation by night, however, ships could have been continually illuminated by one part of the formation whilst the remainder attacked. The Luftwaffe was capable of skilful bombing during night operations and large formations, employing flares effectively, would have discomforted the ships below.[26] The Luftwaffe was also able to use the phosphorescence of ship's wakes to locate targets underway at sea. The wake of merchant ships produced considerable phosphorescence whilst the Thames Barges which were towed over to Dunkirk produced a notable degree of wake.[27] The use of flares to illuminate individual ships, and the identification of movements at sea through phosphorescence, would not, however, have permitted the Luftwaffe to inflict sufficient losses by night to halt evacuations. The poor visibility conditions which prevailed for much of the evacuation left the individual bombers that were able to attack the evacuation by night unable to inflict notable losses.[28] The problems presented by poor visibility would have been increased if large bomber formations had been employed over Dunkirk at night. Individual aircraft possessed a freedom to manoeuvre and could search for targets in a manner larger formations of bombers would not have been able to safely accomplish. Where targets were identified, however, the concentrated pattern of bombs dropped by a larger formation of bombers would have had the possibility of inflicting damage and disruption which the individual attacks failed to do. If the Luftwaffe had employed medium bombers in large numbers, to undertake formation bombing of the Dunkirk Mole, success may have been possible. The Mole was, however, a difficult target to hit by day; at night the difficulties of accurately hitting either it or the ships alongside it would have been increased. Large formation 'carpet bombing' attacks which saturated the area of the Mole with bombs could have caused damage; however, the Luftwaffe was not in a position to use its entire force in night attacks.[29] Formation bombing on a sufficient scale to saturate the embarkation area and ensure damage to the Mole would have involved the majority of the Luftwaffe's bombers attacking over a short period of time. Outside of these attacks the evacuation would have been largely unhindered. It is therefore more probable that had the Luftwaffe attacked the evacuation by night, with a greater proportion of their forces, they would have replicated the tactics they employed – involving individual aircraft and small formations making targeted attacks – but on a larger scale. It is therefore unlikely that, with the difficulties of accurately bombing during darkness, the Luftwaffe would have been able to imperil the evacuation through bomb damage alone to the extent that further night embarkations would be endangered.

The increased difficulties the Luftwaffe would have encountered operating solely at night would, however, have been shared by the evacuation fleet. With ships operating solely by night the greatest risk they would have faced would not have been from air attacks but collisions, and groundings, in conditions of poor visibility.[30] Navigational lights were frequently used at Dunkirk despite the risk to air attack. During the night of 28–29 May HMS *Grafton* recorded that:

> a considerable amount of shipping was under way proceeding to and from Dunkirk. Navigation lights in all ships were switched on, which apparently attracted the attention of enemy aircraft, as several bombs were heard to fall in the vicinity, and … one bomb appeared to strike a small vessel.[31]

Ramsay issued instructions on the evening of 30 May that 'ships meeting in bad visibility should not hesitate to use sound signals and dimmed navigational lights to avoid collision, any additional risk of contact with the enemy being accepted'.[32] The presence of bombers began, however, to force ships on passage at night to navigate the difficult routes to and from Dunkirk with little use of their lights.[33] The difficult navigation conditions and the presence of the Luftwaffe, limited though it was, resulted in a number of vessels involved in the evacuation suffering damage from collision or misadventure. A number of vessels collided during the night of 30 May with HMS *Leda* and *Sharpshooter* damaged in separate collisions; both had to proceed to Sheerness for repairs.[34] During the night of 31 May German aircraft operated at low-height; these attacks were not limited to bombing. At 23.00 the Skoot *Pacific* was strafed by two fighters soon after it left Dunkirk; the attack on *Pacific* was unsuccessful but the mere presence of these aircraft forced the evacuation fleet to operate without navigation lights.[35] In these conditions HMS *Icarus* and *Scimitar* collided, *Icarus* suffered only slight damage but *Scimitar* was forced to return to Dover with damage which left her seaworthy only in 'very calm weather and at low speed in the gravest emergency'.[36] After daylight evacuations were terminated on 1 June, at least a further sixteen ships as well as numerous small craft were lost or damaged in collisions.[37] It is likely the number of ships lost to such 'misadventure' would have been increased had the Luftwaffe been using a larger number of aircraft to attack the evacuation by night.

The Luftwaffe also promptly bombed all lights shown near Dunkirk causing considerable confusion to night embarkations from the beaches.[38] On the night of 30 May, the motor yacht *Constant Nymph* had been using a fire on the beaches as a navigation point before a Luftwaffe bombing attack caused the fire to be blown out.[39] On 31 May communication with ships offshore became difficult and signal lights were established as a method of identifying from seaward the embarkation beaches where the British rearguard had assembled in order that ships could be evenly distributed and embark as many troops as possible.[40] Bombing by the Luftwaffe ensured, however, that the signal lights on shore could not be maintained to guide vessels to where they were urgently needed off La Panne.[41] In the confusion of the night, and with no signal lights at La Panne, ships started attempting to embark troops from Bray beach or, as in the case of HMS *Duchess of Fife*, proceeded past the embarkation beaches and could find no troops to embark.[42] In these disorganized conditions only 300 troops were being embarked an hour from La Panne.[43] To clear the beach before daylight broke, and German artillery could fire on the troops there, an embarkation rate of 1,000 troops an hour was required. During the darkness of that night, however, with embarkations being disrupted by bombing and artillery fire, some of it directed by German aircraft, this figure fell further to 150 troops an hour.[44] If the Luftwaffe had succeeded in halting daylight evacuations before 1 June they would have been able to badly disrupt the further use of the beaches. Although some two-thirds of the soldiers evacuated from Dunkirk were embarked from Dunkirk harbour the remainder, almost 100,000 troops, were lifted from the beaches.[45] Any large-scale disruption and reduction of the number of men embarked from the beaches, had the evacuation proceed only by night before 1 June, would have seriously reduced the total number of troops evacuated.

Faced with only limited interference from the Luftwaffe on the nights of 2, 3 and 4 June it was possible to evacuate an average of 26,392 men on each night. Had daylight evacuations been halted before 1 June, and had the Luftwaffe dedicated a greater proportion of its forces to attacking embarkations by night, it is reasonable to believe that the number of troops embarked would have been reduced to closer to 20,000. If the suspension of daylight evacuation had occurred on 29 May as opposed to 1 June – and the Luftwaffe had succeeded in reducing the numbers embarked to 20,000 a night – then Dynamo would have been unable to recover half of the Allied troops who reached Dunkirk. Such hypotheticals of course ignore the alternative options the Allies, or indeed the Germans, might have pursued had daylight evacuations been halted before 1 June. Nonetheless, it illustrates that German air power could have effectively restricted the success of Dynamo.

The Luftwaffe's mine operations

Air power can be applied in a maritime environment through the use of aerial mining. Aerial mines were explosive devices delivered by aircraft to inflict damage on enemy vessels, hinder operations and impede the flow of traffic through a given area; they provide aircraft with the ability of exerting a significant and potentially long-lasting effect on the enemy's naval operations.[46] Aerial mines therefore offered the Luftwaffe a method of applying air power against the evacuations from Dunkirk had daylight evacuations been halted before 1 June.

During Dynamo, the Luftwaffe flew 200 mine laying sorties in an attempt to halt the movement of ships along the evacuation routes.[47] The mines employed by the Luftwaffe were the Luftmine A (LMA) and Luftmine B (LMB). Both types were magnetic naval mines dropped by parachute. The LMA was 173cm in length and weighed over 500kg whilst the LMB was 264cm long, 63.5cm in diameter and, when fully filled, weighed slightly less than 1,000kg (of which 700kg was explosive).[48] One of the prohibiting factors for a larger use of mines by the Luftwaffe was that production of both types was limited. Before April

Table 3 Number and location of LMA and LMB mines reported as dropped in May and June 1940 by the Luftwaffe at ports or channels associated with Allied evacuations.[52]

Location	May	June
Dunkirk	110	0
Calais	58	0
Boulogne	75	0
Zeebrugge–Ostend–Nieuport	83	0
Le Havre	58	41
Cherbourg	0	53
Thames Estuary	12	34
The Downs	0	9
Dover	26	16
Folkestone	5	3
Portsmouth–East	34	44
Portsmouth–West	17	51
Poole	0	17
Portland–Weymouth	0	23

Table 4 Luftwaffe minelaying sorties, May–June 1940.[53]

Date	Number of minelaying sorties
26 May	3
27 May	20
28 May	0
29 May	0
30 May	30
31 May	20
1 June	25
2 June	60
3 June	40
4 June	20

1940 there was a monthly supply of 50 LMA and 50 LMB naval mines, which increased in April 1940 to 100 of each type.[49] Despite this increase stocks remained limited and the number dropped was carefully recorded to ensure that they were not wasted.[50] Efforts were made to impede the evacuation from Dunkirk (see Tables 3 and 4) and the threat from magnetic mines forced the British naval authorities in England to undertake the considerable task of degaussing of some 400 ships involved in the evacuation. Degaussing, or 'wiping', was the process by which the residual magnetic field of a ship was decreased by the use of an electric cable, carrying a current of several thousand amperes, being raised along a ship's side.[51]

During the night of 28 May mines were sown along the Dunkirk roads and Route X in an attempt to block the approaches to Dunkirk.[54] At 17.25 on 29 May the drifter HMS *Lord Howard* reported three magnetic mines dropped by aircraft in the vicinity of Kwinte Bank Buoy. During the night of 29 May the minesweepers *Salamander* and *Sutton* as well as ORP *Blyskawica* observed and reported mines near the South Goodwin Light Vessel. The trawlers HMS *Lord Inchcape* and *Corfield*, acting separately, exploded three of the six mines which had been reported.[55] Minelaying along the Dunkirk roads continued during the next two nights and mines were also dropped off La Panne on 30 May.[56] During the course of May 1940 the Luftwaffe dropped at least 110 naval parachute mines in the Dunkirk area, with a further 58 dropped at Calais, 75 at Boulogne and 83 between Zeebrugge, Ostend and Nieuport.[57] On 31 May the Kriegsmarine commented that whilst Allied naval power had allowed for a considerable proportion of troops to be removed to England, the 'extraordinarily great difficulties of this withdrawal' were 'increased by constant aerial minelaying'.[58] The night of 31 May saw the Luftwaffe intensify its mining operations along Route Y, the Dunkirk channels and the focal points of the evacuation.[59] Messages were sent to Dover at 01.00 on 1 June that the 'Dunkirk Roads have been heavily magnetically mined tonight'.[60] Shortly after this the trawler HMS *St Achilleus* was sunk by a mine on Route Y.[61] So too, later on 1 June, were the FAA yacht *Grive* and the cockle fishing boat *Renown*.[62] The mining did not result in large numbers of casualties as the degaussing of ships to remove their magnetic field largely proved effective. Mines did, however, cause the loss of several ships of note in addition to those mentioned above. *Mona's Queen* was lost to magnetic mines on 29 May, as were the French cargo ships SS *St Camille* and *Douaisien* on 26 and 29 May, respectively.[63] HMHS *St David* was also damaged by the explosion of a magnetic mine as it lay at anchor at Dover on the morning of 1 June.[64] FS *Emile Deschamps* was sunk by a mine whilst returning from Dunkirk shortly after Dynamo had terminated.[65] As the Royal Navy attempted to block the Dunkirk harbour channel following the conclusion of the evacuation, Operation C.K., one of the blockships was sunk by a magnetic mine.[66] In addition to these losses British and French Naval authorities were forced to employ minesweepers, which might otherwise have been used to evacuate troops, to ensure the route was clear.[67] The presence of German magnetic mines also forced a number of ships to be withdrawn from Operation Dynamo – sometimes temporarily at other times permanently – because of damage to their on board degaussing equipment.[68] *Vivacious*' final trip to the Dunkirk Mole was the cause of considerable anxiety because an earlier bombing attack by the Luftwaffe had put her degaussing equipment out of action and magnetic mines were known to be present in the area.[69] However, the successful degaussing of the majority of ships involved in Dynamo prevented the Luftwaffe's magnetic mines causing greater losses. It is fair to conclude, as Ramsay later reflected, that if the enemy had had 'the means of laying moored contact mines by aircraft, instead of magnetic mines, the results would have been very different'.[70]

The Luftwaffe also tried to disrupt the disembarkation ports by mining their entrances. In Britain, between the start of May and the end of June, German aircraft dropped 46 naval mines in the Thames Estuary, 9 in the Downs, 42 at Dover, 8 at Folkestone and 146 at Portsmouth.[71] The Luftwaffe succeeded in temporarily closing the entrances to Dover and Portsmouth following heavy mine-laying raids, by thirty-five aircraft, on the night of 25 May.[72] These missions continued throughout Dynamo with another heavy raid on the night of 29 May when *Fliegerdivision 9* – which has been credited with successfully mining both Allied harbours and routes across the Channel during this period – was involved in an attempt to mine Dover and the Downs.[73] The Luftwaffe conducted minelaying operations on a considerable scale during the night of 30 May.[74] The Spithead boom defence vessel *Cambrian* was sunk by a mine and numerous reports of mines were received in an area from Portsmouth, along the south-east coast of England and across the Channel to La Panne.[75] Minelaying along the south-east coast continued on 31 May and 1 June and Harwich was temporarily closed to vessels after being mined.[76] These operations prevented HMS *Whitshed* from proceeding to Dunkirk during the morning of 1 June.[77] On 2 June mines were dropped in Weymouth Bay and round the Isle of Wight with sixty German aircraft reported to have been involved in the operations.[78] Mining also temporarily closed Portsmouth and the Western Entrance of Dover Harbour to shipping and necessitated sweeps to explode the mines which had been dropped.[79] There were further minelaying air raids off the south-east coast ports of England on the night of 3–4 June.[80]

The mining of disembarkation ports and the evacuation routes did cause some interference with Dynamo and these operations indicate the use of some initiative by the units involved. However, the Luftwaffe's mining operations suffered from a division of focus similar to the main air effort against Dynamo. It is indicative of the Luftwaffe's lack of a total effort on Dunkirk that at the same time that daylight evacuation from Dunkirk was halted, and all embarkations were to be completed under the cover of dark, the aircraft of *Fliegerdivision 9* were ordered to lay mines, not at Dunkirk but between Dieppe and Cherbourg.[81] FS *Purfina* was sunk by a mine off Le Havre on 3 June. *Albury* sank a floating mine which had been laid off Cherbourg at 04.22 on 3 June and the Luftwaffe continued to concentrate on Cherbourg laying mines outside the port at 01.00 on 4 June during which time the last evacuations of Dunkirk were being completed.[82] These ports were important to the continuation of French resistance and further British support; however, evacuations were continuing from Dunkirk.[83] The mining of ports on the Normandy coast therefore reveals the extent to which ongoing missions against continuing French resistance diluted operational focus on the Dunkirk evacuations. These operations also show that had demands been made for greater air action against Dunkirk by night, in the event daylight operations had been halted before 1 June, there was the capacity to direct a greater minelaying effort against the evacuations from Dynamo. Aerial minelaying could have increased navigational difficulties to Dunkirk and caused some losses. However, given the degaussing of ships involved in Dynamo the threat from an increased number of magnetic mines would not have prevented further evacuations.

Conclusion

This chapter has explored the effectiveness of German night attacks and mine operations. The proceeding chapters have outlined both the Luftwaffe's successes and it failures. The failures have rightly defined how the Luftwaffe's operations against the evacuations from Dunkirk have been perceived. It is, however, necessary to recognize that German air power played a decisive role in halting daylight evacuations, an achievement hailed as constituting 'a great victory for the Luftwaffe' albeit one that came too late to be of great importance.[84] Had this achievement been made at an earlier date, then the Luftwaffe, with a greater preponderance of its force allocated to night attacks, could have reduced the success that Dynamo achieved. An increased threat of attack by night would have restricted the use of navigation lights and markers which in turn would have impeded the speed with which ships could have taken up position and embarked men. In conditions where a greater number of attacks were being made against the evacuation fleet at night there would inevitably have been an increased number of ships damaged or sunk. These losses would not only have been brought about directly, through bombing, but indirectly, through collisions, ships running aground and other forms of mishap. The Luftwaffe could have added to these difficulties by intensifying its minelaying efforts. The presence of mines added to navigational challenges, which would have impeded the speed of the evacuation, and would have claimed some victims from amongst the evacuation fleet. However, given that the majority of ships engaged in the evacuation had been degaussed the Luftwaffe's magnetic mines would not have been able to halt Dynamo proceeding by night. It is therefore unlikely that had the Luftwaffe directed the majority of its forces against Dunkirk at night it could have caused sufficient losses to halt all further evacuations. The Luftwaffe lacked the means to halt all embarkations by night, and although it could have reduced the number of troops recovered from Dunkirk it possessed only a limited capacity to exert air power against the evacuation outside of daylight hours.

Notes

1. TNA: AIR 22/169 – A.M.W.R. Daily Report for Summary, No. 320, 4 June 1940.
2. IWM: EDS/AL/1433 – *Heeresgruppe* B Ia, War Diary, 1 June 1940; TNA: HW 5/2 – GC&CS Decrypts, CX/JQ/14, CX/JQ/16.
3. TNA: ADM 199/360 – Dover Command, War Diary, 1 June 1940; TNA: ADM 199/786 – Commanding Officer of *Duchess of Fife*, Report of Activities during Operation Dynamo; TNA: ADM 199/786 – CO *Whitshed* Report.
4. TNA: ADM 199/360 – Dover Command, War Diary, 3 June 1940.
5. TNA: HW 5/1 – GC&CS Decrypts, CX/FJ/111.
6. TNA: ADM 199/786 – CO *Wolfhound* Report.
7. *Ibid.*
8. TNA: ADM 199/786 – CO *Sabre* Report; TNA: ADM 199/786 – CO *Sandown* Report.
9. TNA: ADM 199/787 – CO *Oranje* Report; TNA: ADM 199/788A – Master *St Seiriol* Report.
10. TNA: ADM 199/788A – CO *Tilly* Report.
11. TNA: ADM 199/786 – CO *Verity* Report; TNA: ADM 199/788A – Master of *St David*, Report of Activities during Operation Dynamo.
12. TNA: ADM 199/786 – CO *Albury* Report; TNA: AIR 22/168 – A.M.W.R. Daily Report for Summary, No. 313, 28 May 1940.
13. Lieutenant-General Haining to Vice Admiral Ramsay cited in Gardner, *Evacuation*, p. 179.
14. TNA: ADM 199/787 – CO *Locust* Report; TNA: ADM 199/787 – Officer in Charge Motorboat *Reda* Report.
15. TNA: ADM 199/787 – CO *Despatch II* Report; TNA: ADM 199/787 – CO *Locust* Report; TNA: ADM 199/788A – Master *Maid of Orleans* Report; TNA: ADM 199/788A – Master *Prague* Report; TNA: AIR 20/9906 – German Air Force Situation Reports on Western Front, 30 May–3 June 1940; TNA: HW 5/2 – GC&CS Decrypts, CX/JQ/12.
16. TNA: AIR 35/189 – Wing Commander Spence to Air Marshal Barratt, Notes on the Evacuation of Dunkirk, c. June 1940.
17. *Ibid.*
18. TNA: AIR 22/71 – Directorate of Air Intelligence, Air Ministry Weekly Intelligence Summary, No. 39, 30 May 1940.
19. TNA: ADM 199/786 – CO *Vivacious* Report.
20. TNA: ADM 199/787 – Master Motor Yacht *Constant Nymph* Report; TNA: ADM 334/83 – Smith, 'Dunkirk Operations'.
21. TNA: WO 167/474 – 18th Field Regiment Royal Artillery, War Diary, 1 June 1940.
22. TNA: ADM 199/787 – CO *Friso* Report; TNA: ADM 199/787 – Officer in Charge Motor Yacht *Glala* Report; TNA: ADM 199/787 – Commanding Officer

of *Rika*, Report of Activities during Operation Dynamo; TNA: ADM 199/788A – Commanding Officer of *Fair Breeze*, Report of Activities during Operation Dynamo to Naval Officer in Charge, Ramsgate; TNA: ADM 199/788A – Master *St Helier* Report; TNA: ADM 334/83 – Lieutenant C. W. Read, Officer in Charge of Motorboat *Bonny Heather*, Letter to Owner Regarding Activities during Operation Dynamo; Carse, *Dunkirk*, p. 109; Harmann, *Dunkirk*, p. 180.

23 TNA: ADM 199/787 – Master Motor Yacht *Constant Nymph* Report; TNA: ADM 334/83 – Smith, 'Dunkirk Operations'.
24 TNA: ADM 334/83 – Lieutenant Read, Motor Launch *Bonny Heather* during Operation Dynamo.
25 TNA: ADM 199/787 – CO *Friso*, Report.
26 TNA: WO 217/3 – Private Diary of Major A. W. Allen, May 1940.
27 IWM: Audio/9768 – Joscelyne, Reel 2.
28 TNA: AIR 20/9906 – German Air Force Situation Reports on Western Front, 26 May–3 June 1940; Dierich, *Der Verbände der Luftwaffe*, p. 98.
29 Large-scale attacks by night would have prevented the units involved operating on the day proceeding and day following the night attack. This would have been a considerable restriction with consequences for operations against the evacuation, the Dunkirk perimeter and German operations against French forces.
30 TNA: ADM 199/787 – Officer in Charge of Motorboat *Skylark* Report.
31 TNA: ADM 199/786 – Commanding Officer of *Grafton*, Report of Activities during Operation Dynamo.
32 TNA: ADM 199/2205 – Naval War Diary Summaries, Naval Officer in Charge Dover, 30 May 1940.
33 TNA: AIR 199/788A – Master of Steam Hopper Barge *Foremost 102*, Report of Activities during Operation Dynamo.
34 TNA: ADM 199/360 – Dover Command, War Diary, 1 June 1940; TNA: ADM 199/786 – CO *Leda* Report; TNA: ADM 199/786 – Commanding Officer of *Sharpshooter*, Report of Activities during Operation Dynamo.
35 TNA: ADM 199/787 – Commanding Officer of *Pacific*, Report of Activities during Operation Dynamo.
36 TNA: ADM 199/360 – Dover Command, War Diary, 31 May 1940; TNA: ADM 199/2205 – Naval War Diary Summaries, Merchant ship Casualties suffered during Evacuation, 31 May 1940.
37 TNA: ADM 199/786–9 – Operation Dynamo: Evacuation of Troops from Dunkirk; Vol. I–IV.
38 TNA: ADM 199/789 – Report of Lieutenant Commander McClelland.
39 TNA: ADM 199/787 – Master Motor Yacht *Constant Nymph* Report.
40 Gardner, *Evacuation*, p. 59.
41 TNA: ADM 199/789 – Report of Lieutenant Commander McClelland.
42 TNA: ADM 199/786 – CO *Duchess of Fife* Report; Gardner, *Evacuation*, p. 76.

43 Gardner, *Evacuation*, p. 76.
44 TNA: ADM 199/787 – CO *Cariba* Report; TNA: ADM 199/787 – Master Motor Yacht *Constant Nymph* Report; Gardner, *Evacuation*, p. 76.
45 Gardner, *Evacuation*, pp. 214–16.
46 Directorate of Air Staff, *AP3000* [4th Edition], p. 55.
47 TNA: ADM 199/792 – Report of Vice Admiral Ramsay; TNA: AIR 20/6208 – AHB, German Air Force Sorties, 1940.
48 United States Navy Bureau of Ordnance, *Ordnance Pamphlet 1673-A: German Underwater Ordnance Mines* (San Jose, CA: Military Arms Research Service, 1946), pp. 46–51.
49 Gaul, 'German Naval Air Operations', p. 181.
50 TNA: AIR 40/3070 – Information from PoWs, M.I.1.H. Interrogation, S.R.A. 155, 8 July 1940; TNA: CAB 106/1206 – AHB, German Air Force Minelaying Operations, Number of Seamines Dropped by German Aircraft.
51 Charles Frederick Goodeve, 'The Defeat of the Magnetic Mine' *Journal of the Royal Society of Arts*, Vol. 94, No. 4708, (1946), pp. 84–5.
52 TNA: CAB 106/1206 – AHB, Number of Seamines Dropped by German Aircraft.
53 TNA: AIR 20/6208 – AHB, German Air Force Sorties, 1940.
54 TNA: ADM 199/792 – Report of Vice Admiral Ramsay.
55 TNA: ADM 199/360 – Dover Command, War Diary, 29–30 May 1940.
56 TNA: ADM 199/2205 – Naval War Diary Summaries, Aircraft Mining, 30 May 1940; TNA: ADM 223/82 – OIC Daily Report, 31 May 1940.
57 TNA: ADM 199/792 – Report of Vice Admiral Ramsay; TNA: CAB 106/1206 – AHB, Number of Seamines Dropped by German Aircraft.
58 USNWC: Microfilm 354/Part A/Vol. 9 – Oberkommando der Kriegsmarine Kriegstagebuch der Seekriegsleitung, May 1940.
59 TNA: ADM 199/2205 – Naval War Diary Summaries, Situation Report, Mining, 31 May 1940; TNA: ADM 199/2205 – Naval War Diary Summaries, Magnetic Mining Dunkirk, 31 May 1940; TNA: ADM 199/2206 – Naval War Diary Summaries, Situation Report, 1 June 1940; TNA: AIR 20/9906 – German Air Force Situation Reports on Western Front, 31 May–1 June 1940.
60 TNA: ADM 199/2206 – Naval War Diary Summaries, Captain HMS *Malcolm* to Dover Force, 01.00, 1 June 1940.
61 Gardner, *Evacuation*, p. 93.
62 TNA: ADM 199/792 – Sub-Lieutenant J. K. B. Miles, Senior Surviving Officer of HMS *Grive*, Report on Activities during Operation Dynamo; TNA: ADM 199/2206 – Naval War Diary Summaries, U-Boat Campaign and Mining, 1 June 1940.
63 TNA: ADM 199/792 – Report of Vice Admiral Ramsay; TNA: BT 389/43/15 – Allied Merchant Shipping Movement Cards, Ship *St Camille*; Blond, *L'Epopée Silencieuse*, p. 99; Paul Auphan and Jacques Mordal, *The French Navy in World War II* (Annapolis, MD: Naval Institute, 2016), p. 77.

64 TNA: ADM 199/360 – Dover Command, War Diary, 1 June 1940; TNA: ADM 199/789 – Lieutenant C. L. Lambert to Commander Minesweepers, Report on Damage Done to St David by Magnetic Mine, 1 June 1940.
65 TNA: ADM 199/2206 – Naval War Diary Summaries, Situation Report, 4 June 1940; Auphan and Mordal, *French Navy*, p. 80.
66 TNA: ADM 199/2206 – Naval War Diary Summaries, Situation Report, 3 June 1940.
67 TNA: ADM 199/786 – CO *Pangbourne* Report; TNA: ADM 199/789 Captain Auxiliary Patrol, Dover, Report on Operations of Dover Auxiliary Patrol during Operation Dynamo; TNA: ADM 199/789 – Commander Minesweepers, Dover, Report on Operations of Dover Minesweepers during Operation Dynamo; TNA: AIR 35/189 – Wing Commander Spence to Air Marshal Barratt, Notes on the Evacuation of Dunkirk, c. Jun. 1940.
68 TNA: ADM 199/786 – Commanding Officer of *Plinlimmon*, Report of Activities during Operation Dynamo; TNA: ADM 199/786 – CO *Westward-Ho* Report.
69 IWM: Audio/13933 – Gilhespy, Reel 10.
70 TNA: ADM 199/792 – Report of Vice Admiral Ramsay.
71 TNA: CAB 106/1206 – AHB, Number of Seamines Dropped by German Aircraft.
72 TNA: ADM 199/2205 – Naval War Diary Summaries, Ports Closed by Mining, 25 May 1940.
73 TNA: ADM 199/786 – CO *Sutton* Report; TNA: ADM 199/786 – CO *Jaguar* Report; TNA: ADM 199/787 – Commanding Officer of *Vrede*, Report of Activities during Operation Dynamo; TNA: ADM 199/2205 – Naval War Diary Summaries, Aircraft Mining, 30 May 1940; TNA: AIR 22/54 – Air Ministry Weekly Report No. 38, Air Operations and Intelligence for the Week ending 29 May 1940; TNA: HW 5/2 – GC&CS Decrypts, CX/JQ/8; Peter Shenk, *Invasion of England 1940: The Planning of Operation Sealion* (London, Conway Maritime Press, 1990), p. 193.
74 TNA: AIR 22/169 – A.M.W.R. Daily Report for Summary, No. 317, 1 June 1940.
75 TNA: ADM 199/2205 – Naval War Diary Summaries, Situation Report, Mining, 30 May 1940; TNA: ADM 223/864 – Naval Intelligence Division German Naval and Air Activity in Home Water, Weekly Intelligence Summary, No. 38, 1 June 1940. TNA: AIR 22/169 – A.M.W.R. Daily Report for Summary, No. 317, 1 June 1940.
76 TNA: ADM 199/2205 – Naval War Diary Summaries, Situation Report, Mining, 31 May 1940; TNA: ADM 199/2206 – Naval War Diary Summaries, Situation Reports, 1–2 June 1940; TNA: AIR 22/169 – A.M.W.R. Daily Report for Summary, No. 319, 3 June 1940.
77 TNA: ADM 199/786 – CO *Whitshed* Report.
78 TNA: ADM 199/2206 – Naval War Diary Summaries, Situation Report, 3 June 1940.
79 TNA: ADM 199/360 – Dover Command, War Diary, 1–2 June 1940; TNA: ADM 199/787 – CO *Locust* Report; TNA: ADM 199/2205 – Naval War Diary Summaries, Ports Closed, 31 May 1940; TNA: ADM 199/2206 – Naval War Diary

Summaries, Situation Report, 3 June 1940. USNWC: Microfilm 354/Part A/Vol. 9 – Oberkommando der Kriegsmarine Kriegstagebuch der Seekriegsleitung, May 1940.
80 TNA: ADM 199/360 – Dover Command, War Diary, 3 June 1940.
81 TNA: HW 5/2 – GC&CS Decrypts, CX/JQ/16.
82 TNA: ADM 199/2206 – Naval War Diary Summaries, Situation Reports, 3–4 June 1940.
83 TNA: ADM 199/2205 – Naval War Diary Summaries, Situation Report, 31 May 1940.
84 Blaxland, *Destination*, p. 346.

7

RAF and Luftwaffe fighter operations during Dynamo

The proceeding chapters on the Luftwaffe's bombing of Dunkirk have demonstrated that on two days, 29 May and 1 June, the Luftwaffe was able to inflict significant losses on personnel vessels and destroyers and bring daylight evacuations to a halt. This chapter examines how the two sides utilized their fighters and the tactics they employed. It questions whether the success of the Luftwaffe on 29 May and 1 June was enabled by the German fighter force, and conversely whether the Luftwaffe's failure on the other days of Dynamo should be ascribed to the success of Fighter Command.

The objectives assigned to the two fighter forces were dramatically different. The Luftwaffe's fighters sought to attain air superiority over Dunkirk – not as a continual cloak but by saturating the area of operations and engaging enemy fighters – in order that the bomber force could attempt to halt the evacuation.[1] The RAF meanwhile had to prevent the Luftwaffe inflicting enough damage and disruption to the evacuation to prevent the further embarkation of troops. The RAF's task should, therefore, have been to contest air superiority and prevent the Luftwaffe from establishing the operational conditions necessary for the German bomber force to achieve success. As will be discussed, however, in practice the RAF also pursued air superiority. Achieving air superiority was a harder task than contesting air superiority. Air superiority necessitated achieving a degree of dominance in the air battle which permitted the conduct of operations without prohibitive interference from the opposing force.[2] Contesting air superiority, by contrast, involved air denial where an air force achieves a measure of prohibitive interference but does not need to secure a degree of dominance. The purpose of air denial is to reduce, obstruct and ultimately to deny the effectiveness of enemy air power. Therefore, given the different objectives of the air forces at the outset of the evacuation, the results of the contest between the fighter aircraft of the two sides was not based on the number of enemy aircraft destroyed; instead,

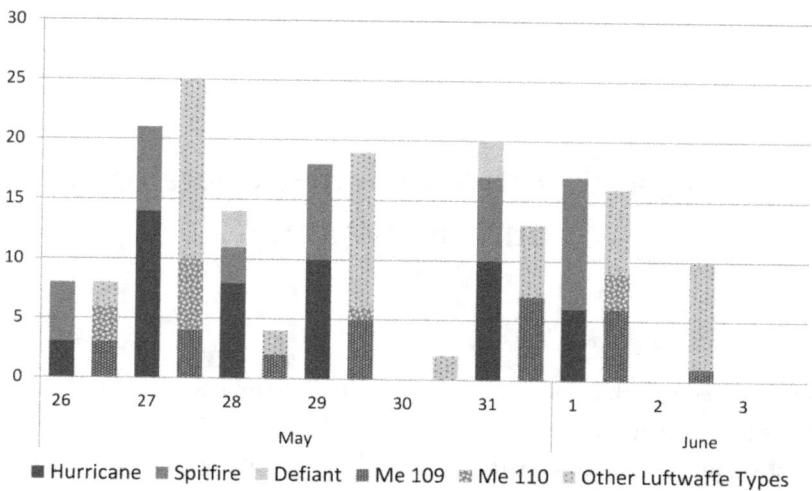

Figure 3 Fighter Command and Luftwaffe aircraft losses over Dunkirk caused by the enemy air force.[4]

success for either side was determined by the freedom of action the Luftwaffe acquired to effectively attack the evacuation. Although the destruction of enemy aircraft should not be conflated with operational success it is useful to consider these figures as part of the discussion. During Operation Dynamo Fighter Command lost eighty-seven airmen and over 100 aircraft to enemy action over Dunkirk whilst the Luftwaffe lost 97 aircraft to the RAF, with others damaged but repairable – these included 28 Me 109s and 13 Me 110s (see Figure 3).[3]

The number of enemy aircraft destroyed by the RAF was achieved despite the Luftwaffe's numerical superiority (as discussed in Chapter 1). For many historians, this has been sufficient to assert that Fighter Command achieved a victory in operations over the Dunkirk evacuation. To a large extent the advocates of Fighter Command's victory present a version of Churchill's claims in the immediate aftermath of Dynamo – that Fighter Command had 'rendered [the] naval work possible', 'decisively defeated the main strength of the German Air force' and achieved a 'glorious victory'.[5] It is important to emphasize again that the success or failure of either side's fighter force at Dunkirk was not tied to their respective losses of men or machines but was instead determined by the Luftwaffe's ability to apply air power against the evacuations from Dunkirk. 'Max' Aitken, of 601 Squadron, recollected that Fighter Command's 'duty, clearly, was to stop the troops on the beach from being bombed or strafed' and that as a result 601 Squadron 'didn't inflict much damage on the enemy because we were trying to protect the troops'.[6] A criticism made of Fighter Command air cover during Dynamo, however, was that it was focused on achieving a 'good bag' rather than protecting the evacuation.[7] In considering the fighter operations of both sides it is necessary to interpret not only the results achieved against one another but the impact of those results on the evacuation.

The previous chapters have demonstrated the importance of the dive-bombers to the Luftwaffe's attempts to halt the evacuation. It is therefore important to consider whether it was the losses inflicted by Fighter Command, and a failure to protect these formations by the Luftwaffe's fighters, which contributed to the Luftwaffe's failure to halt the evacuation. Whether Fighter Command's air cover could have been more effective, and the impact of German fighter operations on this air cover, will also be considered. To judge the Luftwaffe fighters' success or failure it is also necessary to consider the extent to which they prevented Fighter Command from breaking up the formations of German bombers and provided the air superiority necessary for the bombers to attack their targets at Dunkirk.[8] The Luftwaffe's fighters sought to saturate the zone of operations and achieve a degree of air superiority – at the times the bomber force was attacking – that left the RAF incapable of effective interference against their bombers. Conversely, Fighter Command's military effectiveness must be judged by the extent to which they achieved the obstruction of the German bomber effort. Fighter Command's assigned objective was not to achieve air superiority itself but rather to provide air cover to the evacuation by maintaining a degree of prohibitive interference sufficient to restrict German air power – however, the way the RAF conceptualized air superiority was important in how it opted to fight the air battle over Dunkirk. Fighter Command conceived air superiority as 'a state of moral, physical and material superiority which enables its possessor to conduct operations against an enemy, and at the same time deprive the enemy of the ability to interfere effectively by the use of his own air forces'.[9] Using this definition of air superiority, it is possible to see why Fighter Command's air cover was criticized at the time for being too focused on inflicting casualties on the Luftwaffe rather than protecting the evacuation; for Fighter Command the two appeared to be synonymous: inflicting casualties would lead to the RAF securing moral, physical and material superiority and so deprive the enemy of the ability to interfere effectively. The RAF's concept of air defence also played an important part in how Fighter Command fought the battle. For Fighter Command, the principal aim in air defence was 'to stop successful attacks being made on the defended area. If the enemy casualties are sufficiently heavy he will be discouraged from making attacks. The main effort should therefore be directed to the destruction of all enemy aircraft approaching or entering the defended area.'[10] This concept was repeated in the RAF's outline of how air power should be employed to protect ground forces for which it considered 'the main role of fighters is to neutralise the enemy air forces ... the most effective means of neutralising the enemy air forces is to destroy the enemy's aircraft'.[11] Whilst it was accepted in the second edition of the RAF War Manual that 'it may on occasion be necessary to use a part of the fighter force in direct defence of certain vital points' it was felt that 'purely defensive patrols are extravagant in the number of aircraft required to maintain them, and are demoralising and fatiguing to crews, besides depriving our fighters of their initiative'.[12] Acting on the concepts above Fighter Command sought to achieve air superiority over Dunkirk, rather than contest air superiority to deny the Luftwaffe the freedom to operate without interference. Denying the Luftwaffe air superiority and preventing it from establishing the operational conditions in which it could prevent the further embarkation of troops was, however, vital; merely competing for control of the air space over Dunkirk was sufficient to reduce the accuracy of the Luftwaffe's bomber attacks and so prevented German air power being used to its full potential.[13] The RAF's ability to maintain a degree of prohibitive interference, and the Luftwaffe's ability to achieve sufficient air superiority to conduct its operations, need to be examined simultaneously in order to conclude how effective the two sides' fighter forces were during the evacuation.

In considering the above this chapter will explore how the fighter forces engaged each other during Dynamo and the tactics they employed. The extent to which the Luftwaffe's fighters failed to adequately protect bomber formations during Dynamo, and so allowed Fighter Command to prevent these bombers from causing greater losses to the evacuation will be considered. The tactics the Luftwaffe's fighter force employed, to escort the bomber force and to counter the patrols of the RAF, will be examined to explore whether the German fighters successfully opposed the operations of Fighter Command. During Dynamo, the frequency of Fighter Command's patrols was reduced in order to increase the strength of each patrol. The reason for this decision, and effectiveness of these patrols in frustrating the Luftwaffe's attacks, will be discussed. Fighter Command's decision to limit the exposure of its force during Dynamo – and the reasons for this self-imposed limitation – will be examined. This chapter will contend that Fighter Command's air cover was not the decisive reason for the success of Operation Dynamo.

Fighter operations during the period up to 29 May

Before Dynamo commenced on the evening of 26 May, Fighter Command had achieved local air superiority over the Channel ports held by Allied forces. On 24 May General Halder noted that enemy air superiority had been reported over *Panzergruppe* Kleist for the first time since the start of operations.[14] The advantage that Fighter Command held was, however, steadily eroded as the Luftwaffe advanced units closer to the battle. Operating from bases closer to the coast the Luftwaffe was increasingly able to project fighter cover over the battle area for longer periods and in greater numbers. Larger formations of Luftwaffe fighters posed a problem for the squadrons of Fighter Command. Ronald Beamont, of 87 Squadron, recalled that:

> The norm was for up to twelve Hurricanes to be attacking forty or fifty German aeroplanes. Sometimes the odds were greater ... often you'd be fighting as a flight of six aeroplanes and you would still meet 30 or 40 bombers escorted by 30 or 40 or more fighters. So, the numbers were always against us.[15]

The increase in German fighter cover – alongside more active and successful bombing of Dunkirk – resulted in a change to Fighter Command's patrol. As Dynamo commenced Fighter Command had already begun to ensure that at times when strong German air operations were expected two RAF squadrons were on patrol over Dunkirk – although not necessarily operating together.[16] The fighters of both sides engaged one another during 26 May – with the Luftwaffe losing six fighters and Fighter Command eight. More importantly, however, the Luftwaffe was able to bomb Dunkirk and attack shipping off Calais. At the beginning of the evacuation a number of Luftwaffe units had not yet been advanced into range of the coast – as discussed in Chapter 1 – which limited the effort that could be made against Dunkirk. The weather conditions on 26 May also restricted the number of operations the Luftwaffe could conduct over the coast. The conditions in South-East England on 26 May were variable, with a moderate wind blowing from the south, thundery rain – which temporarily improved before resuming heavily – and with fog locally on the coast.[17] Conditions including visibility, cloud density and the height of cloud cover were, however, worse over France – a trend which continued for the next two days.[18]

Early in the morning of 27 May, *Fliegerkorps* I, II and VIII were ordered to gain air superiority over the evacuation area and halt naval movements along the coast.[19] The town and port of Dunkirk were heavily damaged by air attack and, by the end of the day, fewer than 8,000 troops had been evacuated.[20] During the course of 27 May Fighter Command was, however, able to inflict heavy losses on the Luftwaffe.[21] Losses amongst German fighters were limited; losses amongst bomber formations, however, exceeded the total of the previous ten days combined and were close to a tenth of the total bomber force committed against Dunkirk during this day.[22] *Fliegerkorps* II lost twenty-three aircraft and sixty-four personnel over Dunkirk.[23] The Luftwaffe's losses on 27 May were worsened by the weather conditions over the *Zerstörergeschwader* bases which frequently prevented them being despatched to provide planned air cover for bomber formations. Fighter protection was to have been provided to the bombers of *Fliegerkorps* II by Me 110 *Zerstörer*. In the morning of 27 May, however, this was declared impossible on account of the weather conditions.[24] Half the Do 17s of a *Staffel* of III./KG 3 were lost on 27 May when, with no German fighters present, the formation was attacked by a Spitfire squadron shortly after they had bombed Dunkirk.[25] The Luftwaffe was also frustrated in its attempts to provide effective air cover over Dunkirk by bomber formations frequently failing to rendezvous with their fighter escort at the appointed time; this left German fighters often having to withdraw just as bombers arrived over Dunkirk.[26] In these circumstances Fighter Command was able to cause heavy losses to German bombers and achieve a measure of prohibitive interference on the German air operations.

The Luftwaffe would later acknowledge that 'of all the enemy air forces operating in 1940, the British Air Force was the most formidable in battle. Encounters ... with Spitfire and Hurricane formations during the Western campaign, and above all along the Channel at the time of the British retreat to Dunkirk, had been the hardest so far.'[27] General Kesselring, the Commander of *Luftflotte* 2, later argued that 'it was the Spitfire which enabled the British and French to evacuate'.[28] Fighter Command achieved success on 27 May despite limiting the resources they committed over Dunkirk – the fighters of the Luftwaffe completed almost twice as many sorties as Fighter Command on 27 May.[29] Although Fighter Command did contest air superiority on 27 May, and the Luftwaffe was unable to achieve complete operational freedom, the weight of bombing during the evening was such that larger ships were ordered out of the vicinity of Dunkirk as it was considered 'impossible to remain'.[30] Dunkirk harbour had also been heavily bombed and the remaining dock facilities severely damaged.[31] Nonetheless, Fighter Command's patrols reduced both the number of German bombers able to reach Dunkirk and the effectiveness of their bombing.[32]

In addition to the weather conditions at the *Zerstörergeschwader* bases, and co-ordination difficulties with bomber formations, German fighter cover failed to achieve air superiority on 27 May because the RAF was operating in smaller formations against which it was difficult to concentrate. The fighter arm of the Luftwaffe had not specialized on the task of providing close escorts for bomber formations.[33] The German *Begleitschutz*, fighter escorts, attempted to provide 'escorts at distance', operating at least 1,500 metres above the bomber formation, from where they could dive down to engage any British fighters attacking the bomber formation.[34] The German fighters were also employed on *Freie Jagd* (literally 'free-hunting') ranging sweeps over the combat area intended to engage the RAF fighter cover and leave them unable to intercept the bomber formation.[35] Employed in this manner, the fighters of the Luftwaffe found it difficult to both provide close protection to bomber formations and engage the RAF fighter cover who were willing, even in single squadron strength, to separate into sections and engage the German fighters whilst other parts of the squadron attacked the bomber formation. On 27 May, for instance, three Hurricanes were observed attacking a formation of thirty Me 109s inland above the BEF forces retreating into Dunkirk.[36] By contrast the Luftwaffe's fighter units frequently eschewed combat where they did not possess a clear numerical advantage.[37] The larger German fighters demonstrated they could drive off small RAF formations but the frequency of new RAF patrols reaching the combat area meant that German bombers were not assured complete operational freedom. The British fighters were therefore effectively engaging much larger German formations – with effectiveness not necessarily being combat victories but instead a measure of prohibitive interference, the denial of dominance to the Luftwaffe and a reduction in the German bombers operational freedom over the combat area.

Weather conditions would play a significant role during operations on 28 May. During the early morning, there was a thick cloud layer over the coast at some 6,500 feet with intermittent rain showers and local mist in areas.[38] These conditions limited the scale of the German air effort during the morning and, in the absence of heavy air attacks, embarkations from the Dunkirk Mole began. By the late morning the Luftwaffe's bombing of Dunkirk was increasing, with one attack on the Mole driven off only by the anti-aircraft fire of ships at the pier and batteries on shore.[39] The weather deteriorated during the day, however, leading to conditions which curtailed the Luftwaffe's bombing. Ken Anderson, an RAF Meteorologist attached to an artillery regiment, was at Dunkirk on 28 May and recorded that in the face of the Luftwaffe's morning attacks the men on the beach 'fervently prayed for rain and low cloud' and that by the afternoon there was a 'long-running thunderstorm with mountainous cumulonimbus, and heavy rain for hours'.[40] By the evening the cloud had descended to between 500 and

1,000 feet.[41] The low cloud base meant that dive-bomber attacks which had been requested by the German Army could not be carried out. The heavy rain inland over France had also softened the ground at forward airfields, restricting both the Luftwaffe's bombing efforts and its fighters' attempts to intervene in the air battle.[42] Medium bombers continued to attack Dunkirk from height and caused further fires in the town.[43] The Luftwaffe was, however, only able to sink two British vessels of note on 28 May – the personnel vessel *Queen of the Channel* and the Skoot *Alice*. Given the weather conditions on 28 May the fighters of both sides were inhibited in what they could achieve.

At the outset of Dynamo, it was widely believed that the evacuation would be unlikely to last for more than forty-eight hours and that it would not be possible to lift more than 45,000 troops from Dunkirk.[44] The first forty-eight hours of Dynamo elapsed with the evacuation still in progress. Fighter Command, although not able to keep the evacuation unharmed on 27 May and aided by the weather conditions on 28 May, had succeeded in providing sufficient air cover over the evacuation to limit losses to the evacuation fleet. Air cover had also been provided over the Allied Forces retiring towards Dunkirk and the Luftwaffe had been unable to prevent these movements. The Luftwaffe believed that the destruction it had wrought upon the port facilities of Dunkirk had left large embarkations impossible. With the surrender of the Belgian forces the final defeat of the Allies seemed inevitable. In these circumstances Luftwaffe bomber formations were reluctant to press home attacks – and risk losses which appeared unnecessary – choosing instead to attack from higher altitudes where the effect of their bombing was lower but the security of the formation against attacks by fighters was greater.[45] Fighter Command's air cover therefore had an effect beyond the losses inflicted on the Luftwaffe. Fighter Command suffered heavily to achieve this – losing fourteen aircraft to the Luftwaffe's four on 28 May (see Figure 3). In the absence of any opposition, and without the prospect of losses on the scale recorded on 27 May, the Luftwaffe's attacks on 27 and 28 May would have been more effective than they were. Chapter 4 has, however, established that on both days weather conditions and target selection were the principal factors which limited the losses the evacuation suffered.

The operations of the Luftwaffe during 27 and 28 May had limited the number of troops evacuated from Dunkirk and landed in England to less than half the original estimate for the first forty-eight hours. By the end of 28 May fewer than 18,000 troops had been landed in England.[46] The low number of troops evacuated was partially a result of difficulties in embarking troops from the beaches off Dunkirk.[47] There were, however, complaints from the British

Army regarding Fighter Command's air cover; General Dill had to reassure Lord Gort, apologizing for the fact that fighters were not present at the 'right time and right place', assuring him that the 'RAF are all out to give you fullest support', and that the 'whole air effort [was] now directed to support [the] land battle'.[48] The Luftwaffe had already successfully caused such significant damage to the inner harbour facilities at Dunkirk that they were unusable for embarking troops. Beach embarkations on 27 and 28 May were subject to disruption because of the Luftwaffe's bombing; had the Royal Navy not successfully improvised the lifting of hundreds of thousands of troops from the pier at Dunkirk, the Luftwaffe would have successfully prevented the evacuation. Had Fighter Command operated in greater numbers over Dunkirk, it could have reduced the disruption the Luftwaffe was able to achieve but not if the increase in strength came at the expense of the frequency of patrols. An increase in Fighter Command's strength over Dunkirk need to be achieved by a great number of sorties which have required additional squadrons being assigned to the air cover of the evacuation. It is unlikely, however, that an increase in the number of Fighter Command's sorties over Dunkirk would have ensured the security of the inner harbour and allowed these facilities to be used to embark troops.

Although Fighter Command was not the primary cause of the limited results of German bombing on 28 May it did have an effect and was present to contest air superiority in the face of large German air formation.[49] The true test for the two sides' fighter forces would come in the following days as the Luftwaffe sought to halt the ongoing evacuations from Dunkirk, and Fighter Command attempted to provide air cover for the evacuations.

Fighter operations on 29 May

Following operations at the beginning of Dynamo, Fighter Command squadrons complained that their 'losses [were] entirely due to [the] small number of our formations as compared to the enemy and in consequence loss of protection'.[50] Despite Fighter Command's initial apparent success in the air battles over the evacuation the increased activity of German fighters and the large formations the Luftwaffe began to operate over Dunkirk lead to calls from British fighter pilots for the size of their patrols to be increased further.[51] Dowding attributed Fighter Command's proportionally heavier losses on 28 May to the attempt to spread the available force throughout the day without any gaps which he believed had left it without enough strength at any one time to deal effectively with the German forces at Dunkirk.[52] The higher losses were, however, a result of the Luftwaffe's fighters being able to concentrate on engagements with Fighter Command's squadrons. With the weather conditions on 28 May restricting the Luftwaffe's bombing attacks the German fighters which swept the area were largely freed from any responsibility other than engaging the RAF forces; Fighter Command's losses to the Luftwaffe were, as a result, greater than they had been during 27 May.[53] On 29 May 11 Group began to fly patrols of up to four squadrons.[54] The increased strength of Fighter Command's patrols was achieved by a corresponding reduction in the number of patrols flown. A 'principle' was established that when possible 'a minimum of two squadrons should be sent out in company from the same station'.[55] Causing this shift in Fighter Command's tactics was a significant accomplishment for the fighters of the Luftwaffe. To achieve a greater strength for the patrols over Dunkirk, Fighter Command had reduced the number of patrols on 28 May to half the number flown on 27 May (see Table 5); the patrols were, however, spaced to minimize gaps in air cover.

On 29 May the number of patrols was not significantly lower but the patrols were despatched so that the periods of air cover they provided overlapped and there were long periods when there were no Fighter Command patrols over Dunkirk. Dynamo had been proceeding for slightly over forty-eight hours and the German fighter force had already compelled Fighter Command to alter the tactics employed to provide air cover for the evacuation, significantly decreasing

Table 5 Fighter Command sorties, number of patrols and the average strength of patrols during Operation Dynamo.[56]

Date	Hurricane sorties	Spitfire sorties	Defiant sorties	Number of patrols	Average patrol strength
26 May	109	78	24	18	12
27 May	145	113	24	26	11
28 May	150	134	21	13	23
29 May	150	107	24	11	26
30 May	149	113	0	10	26
31 May	122	161	20	10	30
1 June	143	142	0	10	29
2 June	85	107	0	6	32
3 June	57	42	0	7	14
4 June	7	53	0	3	20

the frequency of its air protection to operate larger patrols in the hopes of decreasing its losses.

The adverse weather conditions during the early morning of 29 May, coupled with Fighter Command's patrols – which varied in size with some at a strength of two squadrons and others involving four – limited the operations of the Luftwaffe's bombers and the Royal Navy was satisfied that 'protection has been given to the operation by large numbers of fighter aircraft, and had been effective'.[57] The situation rapidly changed, however, as the weather cleared.[58] In flying conditions which – for the first time since Dynamo had commenced – favoured the attacking bombers of the Luftwaffe, ships embarking troops from the Mole were heavily bombed. The Luftwaffe bombers were able to take advantage of the prolonged gaps in the air cover over Dunkirk to deliver heavy attacks. By the early afternoon Tennant reported that 'bombing of beaches and pier Dunkirk has now commenced without evident opposition from fighters'.[59] Messages from naval officers involved in the evacuation identified the need for British fighter cover and so vociferous were the negative reports emanating from Dunkirk that Churchill directly contacted Air Chief Marshal Newall, Chief of the Air Staff, presumably to ensure that Fighter Command was delivering the maximum effort it had been ordered to provide.[60]

The operations of the fighter forces on 29 May, however, did play a role in shaping the course of events. It was a day where Fighter Command was either present in large numbers and able to record notable casualties to the Luftwaffe or, all too frequently, was entirely absent. Providing fighter escorts for the slow Ju 87 dive-bombers was a particularly difficult task for the Luftwaffe at Dunkirk. Ulrich Steinhilper, of I./JG 52, recalled that when his Me 109 formation, which was engaged on a *Frei Jagd* synchronized with an attacking Ju 87 formations and their escorts, 'first saw the Hurricanes and Spitfires attacking our Stukas it was immediately clear that we were up against very tenacious opposition. Equally clear now was the vulnerability of the Stuka'.[61] The German fighters had to either reduce their speed to maintain contact with the bombers, which left the fighters vulnerable to attack by RAF fighters, or maintain their speed and freedom for manoeuvre but increase their distance from the bombers potentially providing space for the RAF fighters to attack. German fighters were therefore often unable to provide air cover for the Ju 87 unless they had already succeeded in engaging and drawing off the British fighter patrols. For Fighter Command, with fewer patrols over Dunkirk, there were fewer opportunities to impede the bombers who, in the absence of fighter opposition, were able to undertake more effective attacks against ships involved in the evacuation. The limitations of Fighter Command's larger formations are discussed below. It is important to note here, however, that these formations were still outnumbered by the Luftwaffe formations. The German fighters, therefore, continued to engage and disrupt the larger patrols of Fighter Command. Paul Temme recorded that his Me 109 unit was able to provide effective fighter cover to their bomber charges despite the hostile attentions of a Fighter Command squadron.[62] Alan Page, of 56 Squadron, was chased back to England, following an attack on a Ju 87 formation, by a pair of Me 109s from the Ju 87's fighter escort which had been patrolling above them.[63] Other Me 109 formations proved less effective as fighter escorts, because they operated too far from the bomber squadron to provide adequate protection.

Surviving Luftwaffe situation reports record that British fighter formations 'strove to cover the evacuation from the air and fierce air battles developed with German twin engined and single engined fighters which succeeded in maintaining air supremacy'.[64] Despite the efforts of Fighter Command to provide stronger patrols capable of inflicting greater damage against the formations of the Luftwaffe British fighter cover off Dunkirk and over the Channel on 29 May was recorded as 'weak' by some Luftwaffe units.[65] *Kampfgeschwader* 77, for instance, reported that on 29 May they had attacked Dunkirk and encountered no fighter defence.[66] When Fighter Command patrols were present they were able to inflict losses to the German bombers. Werner Baumbach, who flew Ju 88s with KG 30, on the basis of experience over the French coast argued that the question as to 'whether the German fighters could perform the double task of protecting our own bombers and shooting down the enemy fighters had to be answered in the negative'.[67] The escort tactics employed by the fighters of the Luftwaffe on 27 May led the bomber crew to question 'where are our fighters?' and to calls for *Immer Begleitschutz*, or close escorts.[68] It has been suggested by Edward Hooton that the initial losses of the Luftwaffe during Dynamo led to 'tighter fighter escorts and an increased number of sweeps' which 'ensured that the British did not repeat their first-day success'.[69]

The Luftwaffe did not, however, solely resort to close escorts, Me 109s and Me 110s operated in large layered formations and continued to maintain *Freie Jagden*.[70] Indeed, the large bombing attacks of the Luftwaffe on 29 May were designed to arrive after the Luftwaffe's fighters had engaged the British fighter cover.[71] The large layered fighter formations the Luftwaffe operated on 29 May allowed them to maximize the strength of their fighter formations. In particular the larger German fighter formations operating sweeps ahead of the bomber force's arrival allowed the Me 110 to be used more effectively. Wolfgang Falck, commander of I./ZG 1, operated over Dunkirk and recalled that the Me 110 *Zerstörer* did not like engaging either the Hurricane and Spitfire in dogfights because of the Me 110's lack of manoeuvrability and low acceleration speed.[72] These disadvantages were only offset when attacking at speed – typically gained by diving down on an adversary from higher altitude – when the Me 110 could use its heavy forward armament to inflict considerable damage. The *Zerstörer* only sought close engagements in instances where they possessed clear advantages in numbers and height. When Me 110s were used as close escorts for bombers over Dunkirk and were intercepted by RAF fighters they frequently flew in tight circles, which the pilots of Fighter Command assumed were defensive, whilst the bombers often abandoned their attacks, jettisoned their bombs to improve their performance and returned to base.[73] The *Zerstörer* tactic of circling was intended to allow the whole formation to protect each other with intersecting fire zones; it was not, however, wholly defensive. By circling the *Zerstörer* could maintain station over an area, contesting air space and drawing attacks away from bomber formations. In their haste to get at the formations of the Me 110s, Fighter Command's pilots often failed to realize they were conforming to the pattern of attacks their adversary wished them to make. In a subsequent review of the fighting over Dunkirk it was stressed that the aim of attacks was the destruction of bomber formations, and not their escort.[74] The use of these tactics by Me 110s on the morning of 1 June successfully drew 19 Squadron into combat against the twin engine fighters over Dunkirk – during which the squadron suffered losses – at a time when large numbers of medium bombers were present and the evacuation was being heavily bombed.[75]

On 29 May the large fighter formations of the Luftwaffe were not as effective in reducing losses to the attacking bombers as they were on 1 June; they did, however, cause heavy losses to Fighter Command. Furthermore, despite the losses suffered by the bomber formations, the Luftwaffe's fighters, and the gaps in Fighter Command's air cover, ensured only two of the large bombing attacks on Dunkirk were met by British fighters.[76] During these periods of German air superiority the evacuation was disrupted and large losses caused to the ships embarking troops from Dunkirk.

Fighter operations during the period after 29 May

The losses the evacuation fleet suffered to air attack on 29 May were a consequence of the improved flying conditions. Compared to the first days of the evacuation the weather conditions over France and Belgium on 29 May were greatly improved and provided the Luftwaffe with a large window of good visibility with a high cloud base, which enabled them to accurately bomb targets at Dunkirk. On 30 and 31 May, however, the evacuation was relatively untroubled by the Luftwaffe. This was not a consequence of Fighter Command patrols in strength but because the weather once more deteriorated, creating conditions unsuitable for flying. The low cloud base was a particular impediment for the Luftwaffe's dive-bombers and largely prevented their operations.[77] Conditions were also unfavourable at German air bases and along the flight routes over Northern France and Belgium to Dunkirk.[78] The unfavourable conditions on 30 May forced the abandonment of the large attacks planned against the evacuation and only a weak force of bombers was able to bomb the town and installations in the harbour at daybreak.[79] Halder recorded in his diary that with the Luftwaffe grounded by bad weather the German Army had to 'stand by and watch untold thousands of the enemy' escape.[80] An attack on HMS *Anthony* during the evening of 30 May by a single Ju 88 did put the destroyer out of action but the evacuation as a whole was largely untroubled. Air operations during the morning of 31 May were also limited in scale because of unfavourable weather. In the late morning, a formation of He 111s escorted by Me 109s was engaged by a Fighter Command patrol. Later, during the early afternoon, a Fighter Command patrol engaged Me 109s operating over Dunkirk and prevented them from attacking a formation of Bristol Blenheims which were in the area at the same time – with one of Fighter Command's pilots shot down because of the shortcomings of the Command's radio equipment.[81] The afternoon interception, although it provided effective air cover for the Blenheim formation, reflected a number of problems in Fighter Commands patrols. Hurricanes of 17 and 145 Squadron were able to engage the Me 109 formation and attack from higher altitude. However, the Hurricanes of 245 Squadron were not flying in contact with the other squadrons of the patrol and largely failed to observe the German fighters – Pilot Officer McGlashan did observe them but radio interference prevented his alerting the rest of 245 Squadron. A further Fighter Command Squadron – 41 Squadron – was also operating over Dunkirk at this time but was also not in contact with the other squadrons and failed to observe the German formation. The squadrons involved lacked practised methods of operational co-ordination and radio communication was not reliable over Dunkirk. The result was that Fighter Command's decision to reduce the frequency of patrols failed to effectively increase British fighter strength over the battle zone.[82] In a subsequent battle on 31 May a patrol of Hurricanes, Spitfires and Boulton Paul Defiants suffered losses when attempting to break up a He 111 *Gruppe* – escorted by III./JG 26 – because the four squadron patrol failed to operate cohesively due to poor communication and low visibility.[83] Improvements in the weather during the evening of 31 May led to several air battles between large formations. The Luftwaffe made attempts to attack shipping; these were limited in scale but their effect was reduced by the anti-aircraft fire and British fighter cover they encountered over Dunkirk.[84]

The operations of the Luftwaffe on 31 May were, however, once more primarily checked by unfavourable weather conditions. Over Dunkirk the cloud base was near ground level and the operations of *Luftflotte* 2 were hindered by ground mist.[85] With visibility over the coast being reported as being 'near zero' by the RAF and the cloud base over the Luftwaffe's airfields at less than 500 feet sustained air operations against the evacuation were made impossible.[86] Operations by the Me 110 *Zerstörer* were particularly hindered by the unfavourable conditions over their air bases whilst on both 30 and 31 May the Ju 87s were unable to operate.[87] Although weather conditions did improve during 31 May – and formations of up to fifty aircraft were able to attack shipping – low cloud cover persisted over Dunkirk which prevented the use of dive-bombers.[88] In these conditions accurate level-bombing attacks were only possible if bombers descended below the cloud cover. The Luftwaffe's medium bombers were, however, reluctant in instances of even modest anti-aircraft fire to make low level attack and, as a result, bombed from too high an altitude, and were largely unsuccessful.[89] The Luftwaffe was, however, able to undertake bombing in support of the Dunkirk perimeter during 31 May, attacking artillery batteries and observation positions without facing British fighter opposition.[90] German fighters also faced difficulties providing air cover over German Army positions because of the low visibility and cloud cover which prevailed over the perimeter. Bombing attacks by Coastal and Bomber Command met with mixed opposition. Skuas of Coastal Command bombed positions around Nieuport without interference but were intercepted as they re-crossed the coast on their return flight. In the same area, however, a formation of Blenheims successfully bombed German infantry without opposition.[91]

The weather improved on 1 June, permitting the Luftwaffe to inflict sufficient losses on the ships involved in Dynamo to bring further daylight evacuations to a halt.[92] To a large extent the success of the Luftwaffe on this day came when bomber formations were able to exploit gaps in Fighter Command's air cover to attack the evacuation without any meaningful opposition. When Fighter Command was present the Luftwaffe bombers' freedom of action was restricted. This was particularly true for the Ju 87s which struggled to operate in the face of fighter opposition.⁹³ In Fighter Command's absence the Luftwaffe was able to inflict heavy losses. The earliest attacks had begun before dawn and continued throughout the early morning, with a large wave shortly after 05.00. A four squadron patrol of Fighter Command intercepted Luftwaffe formations over Dunkirk during this initial attack. German fighters engaged the patrol of Fighter Command but the RAF's air cover, coupled with naval anti-aircraft fire, limited the effect of the bomber's attacks on the evacuation. A further wave of attacks at 07.00, however, arrived between Fighter Command's patrols over Dunkirk and – with the previous attack having left the evacuation fleet perilously low on, and in some cases without, anti-aircraft ammunition – the attacks were able to inflict heavy losses.⁹⁴ The gaps in Fighter Command's air cover were increased during the late morning and early afternoon by the Luftwaffe's fighters covering the area over Dunkirk, and the Channel, and engaging Fighter Command's patrols.⁹⁵ By operating in this manner the Luftwaffe was frequently able to draw the RAF air cover away from their primary task, which was to protect the evacuation from bombing. The Luftwaffe's subsequent reports indicate that although they encountered strong anti-aircraft fire and RAF fighter opposition at times on 1 June their own fighters secured the air space over evacuation and the approaches to Dunkirk.⁹⁶ In addition to attempting to intercept Fighter Command's patrols and maintaining air superiority, the fighters of the Luftwaffe were operating large numbers of aircraft as escorts for the attacking bombers. Although the first wave of attacks caused only limited losses to ships the bombing had been heavy and caused disruption to the evacuation, despite the presence of a Fighter Command patrol, because the Me 109s and 110s effectively screened the attacking bombers. HMS *Keith* was later sunk during the attack following 07.00 when large numbers of German bombers were observed with considerable fighter cover.⁹⁷

Before 1 June the poor weather conditions had caused the bombers of the Luftwaffe difficulties in rendezvousing with their fighter escorts.⁹⁸ This had resulted in either a reduction of the fighters' and bombers' air time over Dunkirk or forced the bombers to proceed without an escort. With the generally fine conditions during the morning of 1 June the German escorts were more effective, reducing the military effectiveness of Fighter Command's patrols, securing air superiority for long periods and enabling the heavy bombing of the evacuation. As a consequence of the German fighters' ability to engage the patrols of Fighter Command, Luftwaffe bombers were able to attack ships even when large formations of Fighter Command were over Dunkirk.⁹⁹ Even during the period following 09.00, when British fighter cover was present in force, ships at Dunkirk were bombed heavily once again and I./KG 76 was able to attack shipping with considerable success.¹⁰⁰ The third Fighter Command patrol of 1 June, involving thirty-seven Spitfires from four squadrons, was able to intercept an attack during the late morning by an unescorted force of He 111s and Do 17s bombing from cloud level – this patrol recorded a large proportion of all Fighter Command's claims for 1 June. The majority of Fighter Command's patrols during the morning, however, engaged large formations of Me 109s or 110s.¹⁰¹ Despite making representations to the Air Ministry during the morning the Admiralty was unable to secure greater air cover and daylight evacuations were halted shortly after this point.¹⁰² The success of the Luftwaffe fighters against Fighter Command secured air superiority and allowed the Luftwaffe's bombers to halt daylight evacuations whilst suffering lower losses than on either 27 or 29 May (see Figure 3). Fighter Command also suffered heavy losses on 1 June with fighters of *Luftflotte* 2 claiming to have shot down twenty aircraft over the channel by midday (although Fighter Command's entire losses to air attack for 1 June were seventeen aircraft).¹⁰³ The Luftwaffe might have been able to achieve even greater success during the morning of 1 June had attacks by additional bomber formations, and their Me 110 escorts, not been delayed until the afternoon. This delay was caused by poor weather conditions at several of the Luftwaffe's airfields – where low cloud and poor visibility prevailed.¹⁰⁴

Despite the success achieved by the Luftwaffe during the morning of 1 June their attacks on ships and embarkations at Dunkirk throughout Dynamo were limited by Fighter Command's air cover when it was present. Fighter Command had also reduced the opportunity for German fighters to directly attack the evacuation. At time during the morning of 1 June the Luftwaffe's fighters were able to conduct strafing attacks on ships and embarkations at Dunkirk – rather than maintain height to break up enemy fighter patrols – but such attacks were limited.¹⁰⁵ German fighters had also been able to successfully strafe shipping earlier in the evacuation during the absence of RAF patrols. At 08.25, 27 May, *Mona's Isle*, loaded with some 1,400 troops and en route to Dover, was targeted by six Me 109s which carried out four attacks with 'terrific machine-gun fire, a great deal of which missed ahead, but many direct hits with cannon [fire]' which caused casualties to the ship's crew as well as 'the packed troops on the open deck [who] suffered badly. Had the shooting been accurate the losses would have been very much greater.' As it was, *Mona's Isle* returned to Dover with twenty-three men dead and around sixty wounded.¹⁰⁶ During the beginning of Dynamo *Royal Daffodil* was strafed with some thirty casualities including seven men killed in the 'hell' of the attack.¹⁰⁷ Strafing attacks were also made on the troops on the beach by both fighters and bombers.¹⁰⁸ Paul Temme, pilot of a Messerschmitt

109, admitted that he 'hated' Dunkirk. 'It was just unadulterated killing. The beaches were jammed full of soldiers. I went up and down at three hundred feet hose-piping.'[109] Even limited fighter opposition forced the Luftwaffe fighters to maintain height therefore depriving them of the chance to further disrupt the evacuation through strafing. On 1 June the Luftwaffe effectively secured air superiority and during these periods fighters strafed troops on the beaches on the Dunkirk perimeter.[110]

Fighter Command's decision to operate wing patrols

By 1 June the Luftwaffe had halted daylight evacuation and Fighter Command had been found wanting in its attempts to contest air superiority and protect the evacuation. The Luftwaffe's success on 1 June, and the significant damage it inflicted on the evacuation fleet on 29 May, followed Fighter Command's decision to operate four squadron patrols. The decision to reduce the frequency of patrols and to operate over Dunkirk in larger formations resulted in many Luftwaffe bombers being able to take advantage of the lack of fighter opposition to closely press their attack against vessels in the evacuation fleet. This was particularly important as many Luftwaffe pilots lacked experience in attacking naval vessels and were reluctant to press attacks at low heights except in circumstances where there was an almost total absence of effective anti-aircraft fire or fighter cover.[111] Fighter Command's patrols reduced the effectiveness of the Ju 87 attacks against naval targets even when they did not directly attack the formation because the Stuka pilots, aware of their vulnerability as they pulled out of their dive-bomb attacks, lacked the security to make carefully aligned attacks to the low heights necessary to successfully attack ships.[112] In the absence of air cover, and with many of the ships low on anti-aircraft ammunition, the Ju 87s were able to press their attacks to low height achieving considerable success. The presence of even limited numbers of Fighter Command therefore had a notable effect on the security of the evacuation. Captain Clement Moody, Director of the Naval Air Division, would subsequently analyse the air aspect of the operation from the Royal Navy's perspective arguing that:

> The enemy did his upmost with aircraft to stop the evacuation. So long as there was an adequate fighter force in evidence conditions improved, but immediately the fighters disappeared the attacks became intense. It became clear that unless fighter aircraft co-operate in large numbers continuously, any operation of importance would run serious risk of disaster.[113]

As the gaps in Fighter Command's air cover increased the protection the evacuation received was reduced. Fighter Command was ultimately unable to protect the evacuation when Ju 87s were able to operate. This was largely because of the effectiveness of the Luftwaffe's large fighter formations over Dunkirk, which were successful in maintaining air superiority at critical times during the evacuation.

The large fighter formations that the Luftwaffe operated over Dunkirk required Fighter Command to operate patrols involving more than one squadron. The Luftwaffe formations were frequently in layers with fighters flying above the bombers in positions from which they could dive down onto any RAF fighters attempting to reach the bombers. Against these formations the RAF needed to be present in at least enough strength to have a squadron at the same altitude as the German fighters with which to provide top cover to the British fighters attempting to engage the German bombers. Viewing the course of operations, however, the decision to operate patrols involving more than two squadrons was a mistake.[114] Pilots who flew at Dunkirk have argued that the larger formations were difficult to control, particularly amidst cloud where individual sections or squadrons might lose the larger formation.[115] Norman Frank described the difficulties larger formations had in maintaining their cohesion in poor visibility or cloud cover:

> Owing to cloud and smoke, it was impossible for the three squadrons to maintain contact and fight together. By the time Dunkirk was reached the patrol had become separated and was unable to operate as a unified patrol in strength. Instead, part of the patrol operated above cloud layers, while other aircraft of the patrol reduced height and flew beneath the cloud formations, a situation which meant the neither part of the patrol was able to assist the other and a waste of the force structure of the patrol.[116]

The larger patrols also quickly became disorganized in combat, as the squadrons fragmented into sections, largely dissipating the effect of the patrol. Norman Hancock, a Pilot Officer in 1 Squadron, recalled that:

> You went as a squadron towards your target. You were in appropriate formation but once you'd engaged the enemy then by and large people tended to split up … and individually attacked targets. You didn't stay as a solid machine of 12 aeroplanes pointing in the right direction … everybody disappeared. … [After the first attack] there was no cohesion to the squadron.[117]

George Unwin would recount that when operating in a wing, or even a squadron, in combat the formation tended to 'get mixed up and 2 minutes later you're on your own. You can't see an aeroplane anywhere. It's amazing how suddenly the sky seems to clear.'[118] Cyril Bamberger recalled that 'if you had got involved in a combat you were nearly always split up'.[119] Benjamin Bowring argued that 'for big formations it's a holocaust really to lead three squadrons into a mass [dogfight]'.[120] A lack of experience operating as part of large formations undoubtedly worsened the situation.

The larger formations could provide effective protection when they were able to arrive over Dunkirk at the same time as the Luftwaffe. During the afternoon of 1 June, German dive-bombers attacking ships off the coast were engaged by British fighters at the same time as the dive-bombers' fighter escorts, a formation of Me 110s, were intercepted by Spitfires of the patrol. The interceptions achieved by this patrol indicate, however, a further problem with the operation of Fighter Command's squadrons over Dunkirk, with sections of Spitfires seen chasing individual aircraft inland and attacking others along the coast away from the evacuation.[121] Fighter Command's patrols frequently engaged small numbers of bombers, or even individual aircraft, heading away from the combat area. On 26 May, for example, three sections of 54 Squadron were detailed to provide air cover over Dunkirk whilst French ships unloaded ammunition at the port. Spotting two Me 110s, however, 54 Squadron attempted an interception which saw one section chase an Me 110 as far as Lille before breaking-off.[122] In a separate instance the Me 110 of Wolfgang Falck, commander of I./ZG 1, was chased a considerable distance inland by four Spitfires having already been severely damaged during a dogfight over the sea at Dunkirk.[123] This produced larger gaps in the air cover than might otherwise have been the case had the patrol maintained a defensive posture until large numbers of bombers were identified. The Luftwaffe took advantage of this tendency by operating decoy aircraft – either individual bombers or Me 110s – to lure RAF formations into a position from which they could be attacked from above, or to draw them away from the operational area. The individual Luftwaffe aircraft also provided a means to scout the position and height of British patrols and report them to bomber formation.[124]

The tendency of Fighter Command's squadrons to engage in sustained dogfights also led to patrols being broken up leaving the evacuation without air cover. Before Dynamo had begun Park, having had the combat report of Fighter Command's squadrons in France evaluated, wrote to the Commanding Officers of 11 Group's stations to alert them that the 'tendency to dog fight immediately' was 'counterproductive' and that the 'best effective method' was to 'attack in sub formations'.[125] Following the Battle of Britain, Fighter Command prepared a tactical memorandum which identified a number of tactical mistakes made by fighter squadrons many of which also occurred at Dunkirk. The most notable of which were:

> Individual attacks on superior numbers, resulting in a dog-fight, when the Squadron should have, by repeated attacks from above, engaged the enemy fighter screen and so protected other fighter squadrons. ... The whole Squadron divided to attack simultaneously instead of keeping one or more Sections as an above guard. ... When a small number of our fighters, after a general engagement, have found themselves above superior numbers of enemy fighters that have failed to take full advantage of their height, diving down and staying on the same level as the enemy fighters instead of attempting to break up the enemy formation by dive and zoom tactics.[126]

The Luftwaffe rapidly discovered that Fighter Command patrols preferred to engage in dog fights.[127] This was in contrast to the Luftwaffe's preference for 'dive and zoom' attacks to break up enemy formations. The Luftwaffe's tactics allowed their fighters to maintain the advantage of height, make a number of successive attacks, and to maintain their own formation ensuring that they were able to continue to provide air cover after an engagement.[128] A criticism made of Fighter Command by the Royal Navy on 1 June was that 'frightful gaps' in Fighter Command's air cover occurred because they were more concerned with getting a 'good bag' than protecting the evacuation.[129] The diary kept at the headquarters of Fighter Command showed that at least some there saw the purpose of the patrols as 'seeking what they might devour' rather than protecting the forces below them from bombing.[130] Fighter squadrons involved in Dynamo were also informed directly that 'although air superiority [over] Calais and Dunkirk [was the] first requirement good hunting [was] likely to be obtained in [the] area of attack'.[131] Allan Wright, of 92 Squadron, recalled that 'we were just told to go there [Dunkirk], patrol up and down. You'll doubtless see some Me 109s and, when you see them, shoot them down'.[132] On 4 June, the RAF Air Fighting Committee provided a tactical analysis of the combat at Dunkirk and stressed that it must 'be constantly borne in mind that our aim is THE DESTRUCTION OF ENEMY BOMBERS, and that action against fighters is only a means to an end'.[133] This was a point which the British fighter squadrons had neglected during Dynamo to the cost of ships involved in the evacuation.

Despite operating large patrols at less frequent intervals, the pilots of Fighter Command still found themselves outnumbered by larger German formations. Following a patrol of wing strength on 31 May Flight Lieutenant R. D. G. Wight, of 213 Squadron, wrote that 'the whole Luftwaffe seems to leap on us – we were hopelessly outnumbered'.[134] In such conditions the most that the RAF patrols could hope to achieve was for part of the force to make a single attack against the bomber formation before the German fighter escort broke through the cover provided by the other part of the RAF patrol.[135] Frequently outnumbered, and rarely able to maximize the strength they possessed to best effect, wing patrols were less effective in providing air cover to the evacuation than if Fighter Command had operated more numerous patrols at two squadron strength. Later in the evacuation in situations where two squadrons operated together, because a larger patrol had been unable to maintain its cohesion and had broken up, they proved effective in providing air cover. For example, on the evening of 2 June 609 Squadron were able to provide effective top cover against enemy fighters whilst 72 Squadron attacked the Ju 87s these fighters had been escorting.[136] On the morning of 29 May a two squadron patrol, of 17 and 245 Squadrons, was able to break up a large formation of Do 17s before it reached Dunkirk with the German fighter escort unable to intervene.[137]

The limitations of wing patrols, encountered during Dynamo, reoccurred during the Battle of Britain when Air Vice-Marshal Trafford Leigh-Mallory, commanding 12 Group, attempted to intercept German bombers by using his squadrons in wing formations. Theo McEvoy, Leigh-Mallory's assistant, thought that it was during Dynamo that Leigh-Mallory began to believe that larger formations of fighters had to be used to resist German strength.[138] During the first 'big wing' patrol that 12 Group employed in the Battle of Britain the squadrons involved became separated and a general battle ensued in which aircraft fought largely as individual units rather than part of a formation. The patrols also found that they were frequently still outnumbered and that the squadrons involved required considerable experience operating together in larger formations to be effective.[139] Air Vice-Marshal Park, having employed larger formations over Dunkirk, resisted their use during the Battle of Britain. In a memorandum on 1 October Park argued that 'in spite of the favourable conditions during the operations over France for the employment of Wings of three squadrons, the best results during the whole of this operation were obtained by squadrons working in pairs'.[140] James 'Jonnie' Johnson, writing of experiences of larger fighter formations in 1941, also asserted that two squadrons co-operating together was a more effective use of aircraft than three squadrons. Operating in three squadron patrols Johnson found the aircraft 'got in each other's way in a fight and only the leaders were able to bring their guns to bear'.[141] David Cox, a pilot in 19 Squadron during the Battle of Britain, did not consider the wing patrols to be effective arguing that 'while the theory might have been good, in practice it did not work'.[142] Hubert Allen, who flew with 66 Squadron during Dynamo and the Battle of Britain, and later wrote a history of the latter, argued that, in his experience, half of a twelve aircraft patrol would fire their guns but that the proportion of aircraft actively involved in combat in a wing could be less than a third.[143] A further negative consequence of the four squadron patrols was the time, and fuel, required to form-up in the air in order to proceed on patrol to Dunkirk.[144] This had a particularly negative effect at first light because the delay in forming-up meant that the Luftwaffe had a greater window for uncontested action against the evacuation at dawn when the larger, more vulnerable, ships were still withdrawing from Dunkirk.[145] On 1 June urgent representations were made to Fighter Command that the first patrol be despatched as soon as light permitted, because shipping had been attacked continuously by the Luftwaffe since 03.45. Eleven Group agreed to advance the time of the first patrol to 04.45 'if possible' but that forming-up the patrol would be a limiting factor in accomplishing this.[146] Dowding, in his despatch on the Battle of Britain, argued that 'the building up of a four squadron formation ... not only led to delay but resulted in a lack of flexibility in leadership'.[147] Wing patrols produced significant periods where there was no air cover for the evacuation and proved operationally inefficient.

The effectiveness of Wing Patrols in combat was further reduced by the relative inexperience of Fighter Command, particularly the individual squadron, flight and section leaders. Fighter Command's lack of experienced leaders during Dynamo had serious repercussions when the decision to operate larger patrols was made. The Commanding Officer of 605 Squadron delegated the flying leadership of the squadron to Flying Officer Gerald Edge. Operating from Hawkinge during Dynamo, Edge, who as well as being relatively inexperienced, was exhausted at this point and struggled greatly when ordered to lead a mixed wing of Hurricanes and Spitfires over France even briefly mistaking the Spitfires of his own wing for enemy fighters.[148] Where 11 Group failed to provide clear instructions the decision as to what height to patrol at was left to individual squadron leaders. During the first days of Dynamo the Spitfires and Hurricanes approached the combat zone at heights of 10,000 feet or lower. At these heights the fighters of the Luftwaffe, operating at higher altitudes, were able to dive down and attack the British formations with the advantage of surprise and speed.[149] Denys Gillam recalled that 616 Squadron, of which he was a flight commander, were 'invariably at the wrong height' to effectively provide air cover.[150] The inexperience of Fighter Command's combat leaders resulted in poor operational decisions which reduced the effectiveness of the patrols over Dunkirk.[151]

The inexperience in leading larger formations also reduced the military effectiveness of the wings Fighter Command attempted to operate. Reviewing the air fighting at Dunkirk the Air Tactics Branch noted that 'in large scale attacks, bombers are invariably escorted by formations of fighters, whose duty it is to protect them from our fighters'.[152] In these conditions it was emphasized 'it is essential that leaders should weigh up the situation as a whole before delivering attacks. Rushing blindly in to attack an enemy may have disastrous results and will certainly be less effective.'[153] Following the move to larger patrols – and in an attempt to counter Luftwaffe fighter forces flying in layers at varying altitudes – Fighter Command began operating patrols at staggered heights. It was intended that these patrols would be capable of both protecting the evacuation against bomber attacks and guarding against being taken at a disadvantage by German fighters. To be effective, however, the wing patrols, and the squadrons within them, had to be well led if they were to be able to support each other. Often, however, the squadrons operating at higher altitude were unable to effectively support the squadrons operating at lower altitudes when they were attacked. A Fighter Command patrol of 29 May was broken up when operating in this manner as the two Spitfire squadrons flying at 25,000 feet were too far apart to intercept an attack on the Hurricane squadrons of the patrol, flying at 10,000 feet, and were then caught off guard themselves.[154] Fighter Command lost ten aircraft and, with the patrol broken up, Ju 87s were able to attack the evacuation without interference. On the morning of 2 June 611 Squadron patrolled Dunkirk as part of a five squadron patrol, each squadron flying at different altitudes in a layered formation. At 08.05 a formation of enemy bombers was attacked by 92 Squadron, the lowest layer of the patrol at 14,000 feet, while 611 Squadron, the second lowest layer at 17,000 feet, engaged in a twenty-minute dog fight with their escort.[155] With the exception of one aircraft the squadrons above failed to observe the combat and continued onwards becoming involved in a separate combat towards the end of the patrol.[156] These incidents highlight not only the failure of the larger patrols to operate cohesively but also the limitation of Fighter Command's radio equipment, and the failure of squadrons patrolling together to all operate on the same frequency. These factors greatly reduced the efficiency of larger patrols.

Fighter Command's reversion to high frequency radio

Dowding had made a crucial decision, on 26 May, to revert the radio communications of his squadrons to the HF TR9D radio set to preserve supplies of the VHF TR1133. The TR9D was deficient in range and signal clarity as well as being prone to atmospheric and electromagnetic interference.[157] Kenneth McGlashan, of 245 Squadron, likened selecting a frequency on the 'primitive' TR9D to 'finding a modern-day television channel through a sea of white hash and interference. Of course, in the midst of combat, a pilot had limited free hands to attend to such a job.'[158] VHF radio operated on a higher radio frequency and was able to reduce the level of interference experienced whilst increasing the range of effective communication. Following trials at Duxford the TR1133 was considered to be 'infinitely superior to the TR9D from an operational point of view' and the report on the trials stated that 'the introduction of VHF as a medium of communication in Fighter Command will permit of a remarkable advance in the present scope of operational control'.[159]

The RAF was in the process of reequipping with the TR1133 VHF radio when Dynamo commenced. Four squadrons of Spitfires and four Hurricane squadrons had converted to the TR1133.[160] The TR1133 had been designed to be interchangeable with the TR9D and had the same physical dimensions so that it could be installed without the need for modifications to the aircraft. The conversion from HF to VHF, or vice-versa, was designed to be accomplished within two hours. Squadrons which had trialled the TR1133 suggested, however, that experienced personnel could accomplish the conversion in fifteen minutes and considered that 'an average man can effect this change-over in three quarters of an hour'.[161] Fighter Command took the decision, however, to revert the eight TR1133 equipped squadrons back to the TR9D in order to maintain a uniform communication system across the Command – thus simplifying the choice of which squadrons to assign to joint patrols.[162] At times during the air battle over Dunkirk, however, the squadrons of Fighter Command experienced the frustrating effect of being unable to communicate with others on patrol because of the shortcomings of the TR9D. This hindered attempts to provide effective air cover and became a serious problem as Fighter Command began to operate larger patrols. The lack of effective and reliable radio contact made it difficult for the larger formations to function as a single patrol, particularly in poor weather and low visibility.[163] Communication, and therefore military effectiveness, within individual squadrons was also reduced by the TR9D's limitations. Ian Gleed, of 87 Squadron, recalled two incidents in May 1940 when the effectiveness of the squadron in combat was handicapped as a result of radio interference.[164] During the second incident Gleed observed an Me 110 trailing 87 Squadron; using the radio Gleed ordered '"Blue 2 and 3! Break off and fix that plane on our left." I looked behind. Blue section was still weaving as previously. Blast this wireless!

On we flew'.[165] Co-ordinated action between the large patrols, particularly those operating in layered formations where a squadron might be out of visual contact, was often lacking because of the deficient HF radio communication. In the face of the Luftwaffe's fighter tactics of operating above bomber formations, as well as individual reconnaissance or decoy aircraft, or in large layered formations – from where the advantage of height could be used – Fighter Command required good communication in order for its patrols to divide and engage German fighters.[166] Squadrons involved in Dynamo reported that, in a number of cases, radio reception had been 'very poor', and that the leader had 'not been able to understand what message [had] been passed' particularly when enemy aircraft were observed.[167] Difficulties would certainly have existed if Fighter Command had maintained both VHF and HF radio in operation. These would not, however, have been insurmountable. During the process of reequipping Fighter Command with VHD during the Battle of Britain individuals squadrons conducted sorties with a mix of TR9D and TR1133 installed.[168] Although not an ideal situation having some squadrons equipped with VHF would have given a flexibility in communication which lacking when the Fighter Command decided to completely revert to equipment with clear deficiencies. Air Vice-Marshal Park later argued that 'until we have VHF in all squadrons, it is not practicable for three squadrons in a Wing to work on a common R/T frequency; at least that is the considered opinion of the majority of Squadron and Sector Commanders'.[169] The lack of VHF in Fighter Command therefore greatly reduced the military effectiveness and value of the patrols in strength.

Whilst HF was prone to atmospheric interference the most serious problem Fighter Command faced with its communications was that, having decided to remove VHF to ensure a unified communication system, it did not ensure that all its squadrons operating over Dunkirk were communicating on the same radio frequency. Fighter Command did not have a universal radio frequency but rather a range of frequencies, with squadrons from different groups being allotted different frequencies. The TR9D radio set had crystal controlled transmitter channels. With different squadrons being rapidly rotated the correct crystals, to tune the radio-sets to the frequencies of squadrons in 11 Group's area, were not always transferred – when this occurred squadrons were unable to operate on the same radio channel.[170] The problem was exacerbated by the failure of many of Fighter Command's pilots to understand the workings of their radios. The problem continued in Fighter Command during the war with Sholto Douglas, then Commander-in-Chief Fighter Command, complaining in 1941 of the tendency of pilots to consider:

Their R/T [radio] apparatus as something quite beyond their comprehension. They hear a great deal about changing crystals, faulty tuning and noisy generators, but many pilots have no idea the nature of the work performed by signals maintenance personnel, or the procedure for tuning sets, or even where the crystals are fitted.[171]

As a result, squadrons on patrol with one another were frequently left unable to communicate by radio even though they all possessed the TR9D HF radio. On 31 May the Defiants of 264 Squadron were unable to communicate with any of the other squadrons on their patrol as they were working on a different radio frequency.[172] This reduced the military effectiveness of the larger 'wing' formations Fighter Command operated over Dunkirk which suffered losses to German fighters as a direct result of a lack of co-ordination between squadrons patrolling together.[173] The experiences of 264 Squadron led them to conclude at the end of May 1940 that 'when operating with other squadrons all should work on the same frequency, and the squadrons should co-operate more'.[174] Difficulties were also experienced between patrols consisting of Hurricanes and Spitfires; pilots of both types complained of having been attacked by pilots of the other type during larger dogfights. On 31 May Spitfires of 609 Squadron attacked Hurricanes of 111 Squadron, which were operating as top cover to the patrol, believing them to be Me 109s flying above 'on much the same course' and 'marked to look like RAF fighters'.[175]

Maintaining VHF radio communication in those squadrons already equipped would have added complexities to 11 Group's organization of the air battle because it would have had to ensure that these squadrons operated together. These squadrons would, however, have been able to co-operate with each other more effectively, and would possibly have eliminated instances where parts of a patrol engaged an enemy formation whilst the remainder – out of HF radio contact and having failed to observe the enemy aircraft – were unable to attack. When Dowding informed the Under Secretary of State for Air that on 26 May he had taken the decision to revert the squadrons already equipped with the TR1133 to the TR9D, he did not cite the need to maintain complete flexibility within Fighter Command as the main reason for his decision. Instead Dowding argued that the need to indefinitely suspend use of the VHF sets was 'due entirely to inadequacy of supplies and the need for conserving our available reserves so that the equipment shall be on hand for use in its proper sphere'. Dowding took this decision even though he admitted 'the result must be to reduce the operational efficiency of this Command'.[176] Whilst the retreat of the BEF and the evacuations from the Channel coast absorbed the attention of the majority of the military leadership in Britain, Dowding was focused on how he could retain sufficient fighter squadrons, machines, equipment and personnel with which to fight a future Battle of Britain which he saw as inevitable.[177] On 24 May Dowding characterized Fighter Command's general deployment as being arranged 'largely with the view of protecting the aircraft industry' arguing that Fighter Command's commitment over France:

> militates against the maintenance of a force adequate to protect this country in the event of our having to carry on the war single-handed against a power possessed of the resources of Europe. I earnestly beg, therefore, that my commitments may be limited as far as possible unless it is the intention of the Government to surrender the country in the event of a decisive defeat in France.[178]

Speaking with regard for calls for further fighters for France Dowding wrote to Air Marshal Peirse that he wanted 'Fighter Command to pull its full weight in this battle; but I want it to do so by shooting down Germans in this country'.[179] The decision to limit the exposure of important radio equipment 'for use in its proper sphere' was made because Dowding did not perceive Dynamo as a decisive battle.[180] Had the majority of the BEF been captured the consequences for Britain, or the future of the Churchill government, would have been catastrophic. Operation Dynamo, and the German failure to prevent the evacuation of these troops, is frequently perceived as being one of the most consequential moments of the Second World War. It must be noted that at the outset of the evacuation it seemed unlikely that the majority of the BEF could be recovered. Dowding's planning needs to be partly weighted against this possibility. From as early as 19 May, however, Dowding was receiving instructions to prepare for an evacuation of the BEF in which – as long as home defence was not abandoned – the destruction of enemy aircraft over France was to be considered preferable to later engagements over Britain from the 'point of view of future resistance'.[181] Dowding, however, opted not to commit his entire force but to husband it for a future air battle. Dowding's decision to limit the resources committed to the air defence of Dunkirk extended beyond the withdrawal of the TR1133 radio and into the number of squadrons that Fighter Command was to commit to the battle.

The scale of effort made by Fighter Command

Historians and RAF pilots have argued that the maximum air protection possible was afforded to Dynamo and that a failure to provide further air cover was caused by the limited resources of Fighter Command.[182] The number of squadrons involved in Dynamo – almost the entire available single engine fighter force – is often held up as an example of the scale of air cover that Fighter Command provided.[183] A total of thirty Fighter Command squadrons were drawn on to provide daylight air cover for Dunkirk. Only sixteen squadrons, however, were made available to 11 Group for the protection of the evacuation at any one time – although these were supplemented with squadrons from 12 Group on individual days. The decision to limit 11 Group to sixteen squadrons left them unable to ensure both continuity of air cover and operate in sufficient strength to contest air superiority. The Me 109s and Me 110s of the Luftwaffe flew in excess of 2,000 sorties over Dunkirk with a loss of forty-one fighter aircraft.[184] Excluding planned sorties which were cancelled because of weather conditions before the squadrons reached Dunkirk and sorties despatched to intercept radar plots over Britain – none of which met hostile aircraft – Fighter Command can be said to have flown over 2,200 sorties to provide air cover to Dynamo.[185] The number of fighter sorties achieved by the two sides was not, therefore, disproportionately in favour of the Luftwaffe – although Fighter Command was also facing large bomber formations. The fighters of the Luftwaffe did, however, possess the initiative and were able to concentrate their forces and attack when and where they wanted. With the benefit of improved conditions on both 29 May and 1 June the Luftwaffe fighters were able to fly a greater number of sorties over the evacuation, exceeding the number achieved by Fighter Command on both days, and, present in larger numbers, were able to outnumber Fighter Command's patrols and shield the attacking bombers more effectively.[186]

Dowding had been informed that air protection of Dunkirk was considered 'absolutely vital' and the need to 'maintain the greatest possible degree of air superiority' over the evacuation.[187] On 27 May the BEF had requested maximum fighter protection and it was noted at Fighter Command that 'the success of the day is likely to depend chiefly on RAF support'.[188] Having initially been instructed to make an 'exceptional effort' to provide for the air defence of the evacuations from the coast Fighter Command received a direct order at 02.05 on 28 May to adjust their efforts to 'ensure the protection of Dunkirk and beaches (three miles on either side of the town) from first light until darkness by continuous fighter patrols in strength'.[189] Following heavy losses to the evacuation on 29 May the Air Ministry informed Fighter Command that the 'special task' for May 30 was to provide the 'maximum cover' for evacuations from Dunkirk. Fighter Command was given discretion as to how to achieve this air cover but was instructed 'in view of the critical state now reached in the operation' that 'periods without fighter cover should be kept to minimum'.[190]

The objective of continuous air cover in strength was not possible with the squadrons made available to 11 Group; this was not, however, the maximum number possible. Although thirty Fighter Command squadrons were used to provide air cover for the evacuation the air support provided for Dynamo could have been greater. Indeed, the number of Fighter Command aircraft on daylight operations over Dunkirk only exceeded 180 on 2 June (see Table 6).

At the outset of the evacuation Dowding had no reason to expect that evacuations from Dunkirk could be maintained for nine days. As Dynamo commenced it was predicted that evacuations from Dunkirk would only be possible for forty-eight hours.[192] Dowding, aware of the efforts his squadrons had already made over the French coast, may well have envisaged future commitments which might have entailed significant losses and for which he needed to preserve his force. There is no indication, however, that squadrons were withheld from the first days of the operation to maintain a reserve which could be rotated into the battle. The limited strength made available for the air cover of Dunkirk was instead the result of a deliberate decision to minimize the exposure of fighter squadrons to potential losses over Dunkirk. Had Operation Dynamo lasted the forty-eight hours originally predicted only half of the squadrons readily available to Fighter Command would have been involved in providing air cover for the evacuation – although other squadrons had been involved in operations over France in the days leading up to Dynamo.[193] As the importance and potential success of the BEF's evacuation became increasingly clear Dowding still restricted the forces he committed to the battle despite the order he received

Table 6 Number of Fighter Command aircraft made available for daylight air cover of Dunkirk.[191]

Date	Hurricanes	Spitfires	Defiants	Total strength
26 May	76	31	12	119
27 May	77	65	12	154
28 May	78	88	12	178
29 May	87	62	12	161
30 May	84	76	0	160
31 May	69	85	11	165
1 June	74	91	0	165
2 June	85	107	0	192
3 June	56	42	0	98

to provide and maintain 'continuous fighter patrols in strength'.[194] As Dowding looked beyond Operation Dynamo he foresaw that Fighter Command would need to contest air superiority over Britain with a force that had already been depleted during the fighting in France and with replacement machines and pilots in short supply. Dowding evaded the requirement to provide a greater proportion of his Command to the defence of Dunkirk and argued that British 'fighter defences were almost at cracking point' – a view explicitly refuted by the Chief of the Air Staff when it was reported to him.[195]

In considering Dowding's position it should be reflected that – not knowing that Operation Dynamo would evacuate large numbers of troops – he wished to preserve as large a force as possible to operate within Fighter Command's air defence system and safeguard the defence of Britain. Furthermore, Fighter Command's air defence system had yet to be tested in battle and their remained uncertainties regarding its effectiveness in a future Battle of Britain. Nevertheless, the evacuation of Allied forces was a decisive moment in the Second World War – a failure to evacuate the BEF would have jeopardized Britain's ability to continue the war – and Dowding had received orders to provide the maximum degree of air superiority possible over the evacuation.[196]

Fighter Command's air cover of the evacuation might have been even lower if representations from the highest authorities had not compelled it to provide a greater effort. On the morning of 28 May pressure was applied to the Air Ministry for greater air cover over the evacuation by the Deputy Chief of the Naval Staff, the Chief of the Naval Staff and the Prime Minister.[197] By the afternoon of 28 May it was reported to the Naval Air Liaison Officer that the RAF now had 'complete domination in the air over the embarkation. ... What a change!!'[198] Fighter Command deployed more than sixteen squadrons for air cover on only three days: 28 May, when the figure was inflated by three squadrons of 12 Group which flew a composite patrol over the evacuation routes but not the coast or Allied armies; 1 June, when urgent and increasingly desperate calls for air cover were received in the face of mounting naval losses; and 2 June (see Tables 7 and 8). The number of sorties on 2 June was restricted because air cover was concentrated to the periods of dawn and dusk.

Dowding's decision not to commit further forces to the air cover of Dynamo has been explained as being the result of his concern for the air defence of Great Britain.[201] On 2 June, Dowding informed Peirse that Fighter Command was conducting 'an intensive battle over Dunkirk while at the same time maintaining other units in readiness to meet an attack on this country should it be made'.[202] Fighter Command was rightly determined to protect key strategic targets in the

Table 7 Number of Fighter Command squadrons made available for daylight air cover of Dunkirk.[199]

Date	Hurricane squadrons	Spitfire squadrons	Defiant squadrons	Total number of squadrons
26 May	8	4	1	13
27 May	8	7	1	16
28 May	8	9	1	18
29 May	9	6	1	16
30 May	8	7	0	15
31 May	6	8	1	15
1 June	8	9	0	17
2 June	10	11	0	21
3 June	4	4	0	8
4 June	1	5	0	6

Table 8 Number of Fighter Command sorties, total number of hours of air cover and average flight time during Operation Dynamo.[200]

Date	Number of sorties	Hours flown	Average flight time per aircraft (in hours)
26 May	208	356.75	1.7
27 May	287	518.20	1.8
28 May	302	563.90	1.9
29 May	279	533.48	1.9
30 May	262	516.82	2.0
31 May	303	597.00	2.0
1 June	275	515.82	1.9
2 June	192	397.90	2.1
3 June	74	142.00	1.9
4 June	60	143.33	2.4

south of England. Shortly after the outbreak of war Dowding had been instructed to regard protecting the aircraft industry as his most important single task; the directive was still in force when the campaign in the West began.[203] Instructions to provide maximum protection for Operation Dynamo and the critical nature of the evacuation superseded but did not negate the importance of protecting the aircraft industry. The use of a greater number of fighter squadrons in Dynamo would not, however, have prevented Fighter Command from intercepting a large bombing raid. Although squadrons which had been despatched to provide air cover for Dunkirk – or which had returned and were refuelling and rearming – would have been unavailable to respond the remaining squadrons would have been available for the air defence of targets on the coast and Metropolitan England. On 27 May 11 Group provided instructions to this effect to Fighter Stations in its sector stating that 'in the event of a major air attack against South-East England the group controller will have to employ any squadrons earmarked for use on the continent'.[204] Moreover, German attacks away from areas where 11 Group could provide air cover would have been beyond the effective range of the Me 109 and so devoid of fighter support. In these areas, squadrons rotated out of the battle, Spitfire squadrons which had not yet been retrofitted with armour plating, and Blenheim and Gloster Gladiator squadrons, could have provided air defence whilst the evacuation of Dunkirk continued.[205]

Furthermore, the situation of the German bomber force – and the limitations they would have faced attacking against England from the bases they were then operating from – was well understood by Fighter Command. The Luftwaffe lacked the forward airfields to undertake extensive bombing missions of areas other than on the south-east coast of England – where Fighter Command squadrons providing air cover for the evacuation were based and able to attempt to intercept any such bombing raids. Radar tracks of hostile flights off the French and Belgian coast, as well as over the North Sea, were plotted by Fighter Command, with 11 Group despatching aircraft to intercept a number of them.[206] Bombers assembling, joining formation and collecting their escort over Vlissingen provided strong radar plots during Dynamo.[207] Attacks on England by these units would also have generated radar plots and were in range of fighter bases being used for Dynamo.[208]

Fighter Command was also furnished with reports from Air Intelligence on 29 May indicating that preparations for an attack had been received and that it had subsequently been cancelled because of the weather conditions.[209] Meteorological reports for 30 and 31 May demonstrated that the flying conditions for a large attack on Britain by German aircraft would not have been practicable. On 1 June, on the basis of German aircraft tracks generated by Radar – and intelligence provided to Fighter Command providing details of intercepted instructions for the Luftwaffe on 1 June – the conclusion was reached that the Luftwaffe did not have 'any intention to attack our bases'.[210] Subsequent reports by Air Intelligence detailing the Luftwaffe's preparations for large attacks on Paris also removed the probability of an attack on England.[211] With the conclusion of Dynamo, Teleprinter messages passing material of immediate importance from Air Intelligence intercepts to Fighter Command were ceased. Indications of the Luftwaffe's intentions provided through 'special intelligence' (derived from intercepted message sent by Luftwaffe units) and radar tracks had, however, allowed the squadrons responsible for the air defence of southern England to be used economically – reducing the need for standing patrols and allowing a smaller force to provide an effective defence.[212]

With an increased frontline strength Fighter Command could still have maintained a reserve with which to replace losses and pilots who had become exhausted. On average two squadrons who had not flown over Dynamo were rotated into the battle each day after 26 May. Between 28 May and 31 May, a third squadron was rested each day but if 3 June is excluded, when the poor weather resulted in 13 squadrons from the previous day not operating, an average of two squadrons were rotated out of the battle per day. On this basis, one could assume that for every eight squadrons in the frontline a further squadron was required in reserve – a frontline strength of twenty-four squadrons would therefore require three in reserve. Maintaining this strength by rotating squadrons in would, therefore, have been difficult. Of the thirty squadrons which were drawn on during Dynamo, however, only sixteen squadrons were involved in the majority of the days' operations, whilst twelve were only involved on three, or fewer, days. There was, therefore, the capacity in Fighter Command to maintain a higher frontline strength.

Many of the squadrons which Fighter Command rotated out of the battle took no further part in Dynamo. Following their involvement in fighting over France before Dynamo 74, 79 and 605 Squadron were withdrawn from operations on 27 May whilst 65 Squadron was withdrawn on 28 May.[213] Had Fighter Command rotated squadrons in and out of battle it could have sustained a higher frontline strength. Fighter Command typically withheld squadrons because replacements were not sufficiently trained to immediately replace casualties in operational units and remain in operation. Had Fighter Command opted to withdraw more experienced crews from units in the reserve and reinforce squadrons in line with these personnel a greater force could have been maintained. Pilots of 266 Squadron were kept out of the frontline until 2 June when they undertook their first war patrol, and their only sortie of Dynamo.[214] It is difficult to criticize Fighter Command's leadership for not depleting operational squadrons of the majority of their experienced pilots. It is at least debatable, however, whether by maintaining experienced units in line by this expedient, Fighter Command's casualties would have actually been lower. The decision to rotate squadrons, whilst having the benefit of maintaining cohesive units, had unfortunate consequences both for the air cover of the evacuation and for RAF losses. As a squadron was beginning to benefit from combat experience, and starting to operate as a more effective unit by incorporating that experience, they were rotated out of combat and those lessons had to be learnt afresh by others. Inexperienced squadrons in particular made tactical errors on their first patrols over Dunkirk which increased Fighter Command's losses. Reviewing the battle, Park formed the opinion that it would have been more effective to bring squadrons that had suffered losses up to strength rather than rotate them out and bring in fresh squadrons who would then be obliged to relearn the hard-learnt lessons of their predecessors.[215] This approach would have freshened up depleted units whilst minimizing the exposure of, and subsequent losses within, inexperienced squadrons.

Fighter Command's shortage of reserves

Dowding's stated objection to providing greater resources for the air defence of Dunkirk was that British 'fighter defences were almost at cracking point' – a view rejected by the Chief of the Air Staff.[216] Norman Gelb has observed that Dowding was warning that:

> if Fighter Command's effectiveness was sacrificed at Dunkirk, 'the situation would be serious'. He was saying, in effect, that too much rather than too little aerial cover was being provided for Operation Dynamo – not because less would suffice but because the priority requirement remained keeping aerial home defences intact.[217]

Aircraft production had begun to improve by the time of Operation Dynamo and although aircraft reserves were perilously low at the end of the battle this was not solely caused by replacing operational losses.[218] Spitfire losses during Dynamo meant that on 4 June there were only four Spitfires in the Aircraft Storage Unit (ASU) which could be available within twenty-four hours (the demands of non-operational squadrons had also reduced this number).[219] The supply of Spitfire Mark IIs – with the first being completed immediately after the battle – began to ease the aircraft reserve situation.[220] Nor was the situation as severe as the number of aircraft in the ASU on 4 June immediately suggests. In the midst of the battle the number of Spitfires ready for despatch within twenty-four hours stood at twenty-five, on 30 May, and twenty-nine, on 2 June (the two days following the heaviest air combats of Dynamo). The situation for Hurricanes in the ASU was more favourable with forty-five available for despatch within twenty-four hours on 26 May and twenty-three on 4 June. By 7 June 247 Hurricanes and 21 Spitfires were available in various states of readiness in the ASU.[221] Ten days after the end of Dynamo there were 39 Spitfires and 115 Hurricanes ready for despatch in forty-eight hours. By the end of June, and despite the need to re-equip squadrons returning from France, there were 112 Spitfires and 179 Hurricanes ready for despatch in forty-eight hours.[222] In total the ASU held 118 modern fighter aircraft available within forty-eight hours on 2 June. Fighter Command itself possessed a strength of 522 single engine fighters available on 2 June, although a number of the pilots for these aircraft had not been fully converted, meaning this total strength was not yet fully available.[223]

Immediately following Dunkirk Fighter Command's greatest shortage was aircraft, and the need to reinforce squadrons returned from France meaning that operational strength was frequently below establishment. However, pilot shortage was also a weakness for Fighter Command. During the French campaign, the RAF lost 280 fighter pilots killed, missing, or captured and a further 60 wounded.[224] These losses were a high price for Fighter Command and it is not unreasonable that Dowding was concerned and considering the effect this would have on his command in the coming Battle of Britain. Against these losses Fighter Command had started to receive replacements personnel from the RAF Volunteer Reserve and initial training programmes undertaken at the outbreak of war. Fighter Command did face difficulties in replacing personnel and yet this difficulty can be exaggerated beyond proportion. Between June and August, the number of fighter pilots available for operations rose by over a quarter.[225] Without minimizing the shortages that Fighter Command was justly concerned about, they were not serious enough to justify minimizing the air cover Fighter Command provided over Dunkirk if Dowding considered Dynamo to be a decisive moment in the war to which other considerations had to be subordinated.[226]

The strategy that Fighter Command adopted suggests that at no point during Dynamo did it believe it was facing a decisive air battle. Fighter Command's reserve situation would, of course, have concerned Dowding; it was not so critical regarding either men or machines, however, that it justified withholding additional air resources during, what Dowding was aware, was a critical period for the British Army. Fighter Command consistently made decisions which would preserve its men, machines and equipment for a future battle over

England rather than pursue a strategy which would provide the maximum assistance to protect the BEF in and around Dunkirk and the evacuation fleet seeking to rescue it.

Conclusion

The fighter forces of the Luftwaffe and RAF engaged over Dunkirk with differing objectives. The Luftwaffe fighters sought to achieve air superiority and provide the conditions in which the bomber force could bomb Dunkirk so heavily that further evacuation would be prevented. For Fighter Command, the objective was to contest air superiority and ensure the continuation of the evacuations. The success of Dynamo, whilst previously cited as proof of Fighter Command's success, was primarily the result of favourable weather conditions which prevented the Luftwaffe's dive-bombers from being able to attack for all but two days of the evacuation – 29 May and 1 June. As discussed in Chapter 2, on both days the Luftwaffe was able to halt daylight evacuations from the port of Dunkirk. At Dunkirk the periods of heaviest losses also coincided with the periods when naval vessels present had begun to exhaust their anti-aircraft ammunition and – in the absence of RAF fighter cover – German bombers were able to attack from lower heights with less risk. When RAF fighters were present – or in instances of even a moderate amount of anti-aircraft fire – German level-bombers were deterred from pressing home their attacks at lower altitudes, which increased the aiming error of these attacks and reduced the military effectiveness of the Luftwaffe.[227]

The events of 29 May and 1 June do not suggest that the tactics which Fighter Command employed made a substantial difference to the outcome of the success of the Luftwaffe's air attacks. It is almost certain that on 28 May, as well as both 30 and 31 May, some losses to the evacuation fleet were prevented as a result of Fighter Command's air cover; however, this was not decisive in the outcome of the operation. On 27 May weather conditions were more favourable for attacks and Fighter Command's tactics were more effective in countering the air opposition it did face although the rate of casualties per sorties was higher for Fighter Command on this date than on 1 June. As discussed in Chapter 4, however, the Luftwaffe maintained an operational focus on military targets on this date rather than the evacuation itself, and its total commitment against Dynamo was therefore limited. Nonetheless, Fighter Command's success on 27 May represented a failure for the Luftwaffe's fighters who, operating in lower numbers than on 29 May or 1 June, were unable to achieve air superiority. From 27 May, however, Fighter Command shifted away from continuous air cover over the evacuation and increasingly operated patrols in greater strength with longer periods between air cover. This change left the evacuation with less protection; it was made in an attempt to reduce losses and compete with the larger fighter formations of the Luftwaffe. The Luftwaffe's fighters therefore deserve greater credit than they have received. Had Fighter Command maintained more frequent two squadron patrols the impact of the Luftwaffe's bombing might have been lessened. Engagements with Luftwaffe fighters before 29 May had, however, convinced Fighter Command that it needed to operate in larger formations. On 29 May, the losses of the Luftwaffe were greater than those of Fighter Command but the evacuation suffered because the air cover provided by Fighter Command was less effective. It is possible that with a greater number of patrols at two squadron strength the evacuation on 29 May could have been better protected against the Luftwaffe's bombings. The results of 1 June further demonstrate that the larger patrols failed to provide greater protection to the evacuation. The Luftwaffe's fighters also succeeded in drawing the British fighter cover away from the evacuation to a degree which has not previously been recognized. The dogfighting tactics that Fighter Command employed also reduced the military effectiveness of their air cover, and larger formations were frequently caught up in combats which did little to aid the security of the evacuation. The military effectiveness of the Luftwaffe fighters is best judged not on the losses that they sustained, or on the victories they recorded, but rather on the fact that on the two days where weather conditions permitted their bombers to attack without restriction they created the conditions for them to achieve success. Whilst Fighter Command did have an impact on the evacuation, with losses to the evacuation fleet reduced when their patrols were present, it was not a decisive impact. The success of Operation Dynamo rested not on British air power but on favourable weather conditions.

Notes

1   TNA: AIR 16/1172 – Duty Officer, Air Intelligence War Room Watch to Fighter Command, 27 May 1940; Robin Higham 'Introduction', in Higham and Harris, *Why Air Forces Fail*, p. 6.
2   Directorate of Air Staff, *AP3000* [3rd Edition] (London: Ministry of Defence, 1999), 3.13.2.

3   TNA: AIR 16/352 – 11 Group Report, 8 July 1940; TNA: AIR 16/839 – 11 Group, Air Combat Results Chart, May–November 1940; TNA: AIR 27 – ORB: Fighter Command Squadrons, May–June 1940; TNA: CAB 106/1206 – AHB, German Losses based on Returns to Luftwaffe Quarter Master General; TsAMO RF: Ф.500 оп.12452 д.95 – Tägliche Lageberichte West des Führungsstabes der Luftwaffe (1c); Peter D. Cornwell, *The Battle of France: Then and Now* (Old Harlow, Essex: Battle of Britain International, 2007), pp. 370–418; Norman Franks, *Fighter Command Losses of the Second World War, Vol. I Operational Losses – Aircraft and Crews, 1939–1941* (Hersham, Surrey: Midland, 2008), pp. 33–9.

4   *Ibid.* Aircraft lost to anti-aircraft or other causes are not included. A number of Luftwaffe aircraft, at the time considered repairable, were later written off because of battle damage – these are not shown. The figures include aircraft destroyed by Fighter, Bomber, and Coastal Command (and FAA). Where doubt exists as to whether anti-aircraft or air combat was the cause of a loss it has been ascribed to the RAF.

5   Churchill, *Finest Hour*, p. 91.

6   IWM: Audio/2803 – Aitken, Reel 1.

7   TNA: AIR 15/898 – N.L.O. Log, 1–2 June 1940.

8   Buckley, *Air Power*, pp. 10–11, 53, 55–6, 128, 148, 173.

9   Air Ministry, *AP1300: Royal Air Force War Manual, Part I: Operations* (London: Air Ministry, 1928), Chap. VII, Para. 10.

10 *Ibid.*, Chap. VII, Para. 17.

11 Air Ministry, *AP1300: Royal Air Force War Manual, Part I: Operations* [2nd Edition] (London: Air Ministry, 1940), Chap. XI, Para. 52–3.

12 It is noted in AP1300 (1940) that defensive patrols could be appropriate where the area to be defended was small, of outstanding importance and the defence required was for only a limited period. It would not have been lost on readers at the time, however, that the RAF considered that in the first instance fighters should look to achieve air superiority through the destruction of enemy aircraft. Air Ministry, *AP1300* (1940), Chap. XI, Para 56.

13 Buckley, *Air Power*, pp. 10–11, 173.

14 Halder, *Kriegstagebuch*, pp. 326–7.

15 IWM: Audio/10128 – Ronald Prosper 'Bee' Beamont, Reel 1.

16 TNA: AIR 25/193 – ORB: 11 Group, May 1940; TNA: AIR 27 – ORB: Fighter Command Squadrons, May 1940.

17 TNMDA: DWR/1940/05 – Daily Weather Report, 26–28 May 1940.

18 TNA: AIR 14/1019 – Report on Operations Carried out on 27 May 1940; TNMDA: DWR/1940/05 – Daily Weather Report, 26–28 May 1940.

19 TNA: HW 5/1 – GC&CS Decrypts, CX/FJ/107, CX/FJ/110.

20 TNA: CAB 44/60 – War Office Figures for Number of Personnel Evacuated from the Northern French and Belgian Coasts, Operation Dynamo; Gardner, *Evacuation*, p. 18.

21 TNA: AIR 20/9906 – German Air Force Situation Reports on Western Front, 27 May 1940; TNA: CAB 106/1206 – AHB, German Losses based on Returns to Luftwaffe Quarter Master General; Cornwell, *Battle*, pp. 380–3.
22 LHCMA: LIDDELL HART 15/15/22 – Galland, German Day Fighter Arm, 1945; Mombeek, *Jagdwaffe*, pp. 36–7.
23 Mason, *Rise*, p. 354.
24 TNA: HW 5/1 – GC&CS Decrypts, CX/FJ/111.
25 Bekker, *Luftwaffe*, pp. 165–6.
26 LHCMA: LIDDELL HART 15/15/22 – Galland, German Day Fighter Arm, 1945.
27 TNA: AIR 40/2444 – Hauptmann Otto Bechtle, German Air Force Account of The Air War against Great Britain 1940–43: Tactics and Deductions, 2 February 1944.
28 Kesselring, *Memoirs*, p. 59.
29 TNA: AIR 22/107 – Air Ministry Daily Telegraphic Intelligence Summary, 8 June 1940; TNA: AIR 27 – ORB: Fighter Command Squadrons, May–June 1940; Prien, *Jagdfliegerverbände*, p. 66.
30 TNA: ADM 199/788A – Master *St Andrew* Report; TNA: ADM 199/788A – Master *St Julien* Report.
31 TNA: ADM 199/2205 – Naval War Diary Summaries, Dunkerque to Marine National, 27 May 1940.
32 TNA: AIR 22/168 – A.M.W.R. Daily Report for Summary, No. 312, 27 May 1940.
33 Kreipe and Koester, *Technical Training*, p. 182.
34 TNA: AIR 24/520 – Appendices to ORB: Fighter Command Narrative of Events, May–June 1940.
35 LHCMA: LIDDELL HART 15/15/22 – Galland, German Day Fighter Arm, 1945; TNA: AIR 5/1139 – Air Tactics Branch, AFC No. 95, 'French Fighters' Experiences during Period 14–21 May 1940', 4 June 1940.
36 Anderson, 'Weather Service at War', p. 13.
37 Steinhilper, *Spitfire on my Tail*, p. 255.
38 IWM: EDS/AL/1384/1 – 6. Armee Ia, Kriegstagebuch, 28 May 1940; TNA: ADM 199/2205 – Naval War Diary Summaries, Weather, 28 May 1940; TNA: AIR 27/1941 – ORB: 500 Squadron.
39 TNA: ADM 199/786 – CO *Montrose* Report.
40 Anderson, 'Weather Service at War', p. 15.
41 TNA: AIR 27/1941 – ORB: 500 Squadron.
42 IWM: EDS/AL/1429 – 4. Armee Ia, Kriegstagebuch, 28 May 1940.
43 TNA: ADM 199/788A – CO *Tilly* Report; TNA: AIR 22/168 – A.M.W.R. Daily Report for Summary, No. 313, 28 May 1940.
44 LHCMA: ALANBROOKE 5/1/2 – General Alan Brooke's Diary, 26 May 1940; TNA: AIR 15/203 – Wing Commander F. L. Hopps, Deputy Senior Air Staff Officer Coastal Command Headquarters, to Air Chief Marshal Sir Frederick Bowhill,

Report of Activities as Liaison for Coastal Command with Naval Authorities, BEF, and Back Violet during Operation Dynamo, 4 June 1940; Churchill, *Finest Hour*, p. 98; Gardner, *Evacuation*, p. 122.
45 TNA: ADM 199/786 – CO *Icarus* Report; TNA: ADM 199/786 – CO *Shikari* Report; TNA: ADM 199/786 – CO *Wolfhound* Report.
46 TNA: CAB 44/60 – War Office Figures for Personnel Evacuated; Gardner, *Evacuation*, p. 18.
47 Gardner, *Evacuation*, p. 33.
48 LHCMA: BRIDGEMAN 2/4 – Telegram General Sir John Dill to General Lord Gort, 28 May 1940.
49 James, *Growth*, p. 94.
50 TNA: AIR 27/2088 – ORB: 605 Squadron.
51 TNA: AIR 16/281 – Headquarters 11 Group to Headquarters Fighter Command, 26 May 1940.
52 TNA: AIR 14/3555 – Air Marshal Charles Portal to Air Marshal Sir Philip Joubert de la Ferte, 31 May 1940.
53 TNA: CAB 106/1206 – AHB, German Losses based on Returns to Luftwaffe Quarter Master General; Cornwell, *Battle*, pp. 380–3.
54 TNA: AIR 16/1173 – Back Violet to Air Ministry, 'Summary of Air Operations, Period 10.00–13.00', 29 May 1940; TNA: AIR 16/1173 – Violet to Air Ministry, 'Summary of Air Operations Carried Out up to 22.00', 29 May 1940.
55 TNA: AIR 24/520 – Appendices to ORB: Fighter Command, Narrative of Events, May–June 1940.
56 Data drawn from: TNA: AIR 25/193 – ORB: 11 Group; TNA: AIR 25/219 – ORB: 12 Group; TNA: AIR 27 – ORB: Fighter Command Squadrons, May–June 1940.
57 TNA: ADM 199/2205 – Naval War Diary Summaries, Situation Report, 29 May 1940.
58 TNA: AIR 20/9906 – German Air Force Situation Reports on Western Front, 29 May 1940.
59 TNA: ADM 199/2205 – Naval War Diary Summaries, Operations, Evacuation of BEF from Dunkirk, 29 May 1940.
60 TNA: AIR 15/898 – N.L.O. Log, 29 May 1940.
61 Steinhilper, *Spitfire on my Tail*, p. 254.
62 Paul Temme cited in Weal, *Jagdgeschwader 2*, p. 40.
63 IWM: Audio/11103 – Page, Reel 1.
64 TNA: AIR 20/9906 – German Air Force Situation Reports on Western Front, 29 May 1940.
65 TNA: HW 5/2 – GC&CS Decrypts, CX/JQ/8.
66 *Ibid.*, CX/JQ/5.
67 Baumbach, *Life and Death*, p. 79.

68 Edmund Blandford, *Target England: Flying with the Luftwaffe in World War Two* (Shrewsbury: Airlife, 1997), p. 77.
69 Hooton, *Blitzkreig*, p. 73.
70 Prien, *Jagdfliegerverbände*, p. 238.
71 IWM: Audio/10152 – Kingcombe, Reel 1; TNA: AIR 16/234 – Fighter Command Intelligence Summary, No. 210, 29 May 1940; TNA: AIR 16/1173 – Back Violet to Bomber Command, 'Summary of Air Operations for Period 10.00–13.00, 29 May 1940'; TNA: HW 5/2 – GC&CS Decrypts, CX/JQ/11.
72 IWM: Audio/11247 – Falck, Reel 5.
73 IWM: Audio/11086 – Anthony Charles Bartley, Reel 1.
74 TNA: AIR 5/1139 – Air Tactics Branch in Conjunction with Fighter Command, AFC No. 94, 'Tactics for Fighters Versus Escorted Bombers', 4 June 1940. Original Emphasis.
75 TNA: AIR 50/10/30 – Combat Report, Sergeant Potter, 1 June 1940.
76 TNA: AIR 20/9906 – German Air Force Situation Reports on Western Front, 29 May 1940; Evans, *Fall*, p. 109.
77 TNMDA: DWR/1940/05 – Daily Weather Report, 30–31 May 1940.
78 *Ibid.*
79 TNA: AIR 20/9906 – German Air Force Situation Reports on Western Front, 30–31 May 1940; Winters, *Battling*, p. 22.
80 Halder, *Kriegstagebuch*, p. 326.
81 TNA: AIR 20/9906 – German Air Force Situation Reports on Western Front, 30–31 May 1940; TNA: AIR 27/234 – ORB: 17 Squadron; TNA: AIR 27/424 – ORB: 41 Squadron; TNA: AIR 27/984 – ORB: 145 Squadron; TNA: AIR 27/1371 – ORB: 222 Squadron; TNA: AIR 27/2126 – ORB: 616 Squadron; McGlashan, *Down to Earth*, pp. 8–9; Prien, *Jagdfliegerverbände*, p. 205.
82 *Ibid.*
83 TNA: AIR 27/1315 – ORB: 213 Squadron; TNA: AIR 27/1553 – ORB: 264 Squadron; TNA: AIR 27/2102 – ORB: 609 Squadron; Prien, *Jagdfliegerverbände*, p. 228.
84 TNA: ADM 199/788A: – Sub-Lieutenant P.H.E. Bennett, Officer Commanding Motorboat *New Prince of Wales*, Report of Activities during Operation Dynamo; TNA: AIR 199/788A – Master Steam Hopper Barge *Foremost 102* Report; TNA: AIR 15/898 – N.L.O. Log, 31 May 1940; TsAMO RF: Ф.500 оп.12452 д.95 – Tägliche Lageberichte West des Führungsstabes der Luftwaffe (1c), No. 269, Anlage 4, p. 2; James, *Growth*, p. 95.
85 IWM: EDS/AL/1428 – *Heeresgruppe* A Ia, War Diary Part II, 30–31 May 1940; IWM: EDS/AL/1433 – *Heeresgruppe* B Ia, War Diary, 31 May 1940; Speidel, 'German Air Force', p. 358.
86 TNA: AIR 22/168 – A.M.W.R. Daily Report for Summary, No. 316, 31 May 1940; TNA: AIR 22/169 – A.M.W.R. Daily Report for Summary, No. 318, 2 June 1940; TNMDA: DWR/1940/05 – Daily Weather Report, 31 May 1940.

87 Speidel, 'German Air Force', p. 358.
88 TNA: ADM 199/786 – CO *Express* Report; TNA: ADM 199/786 – CO *Venomous* Report; TNA: AIR 27/862 – Appendices to ORB: 110 Squadron, Appendix 184, Wattisham to 2 Group, 'Form "Y"', 31 May 1940.
89 TNA: ADM 199/792 – Report of Vice Admiral Ramsay; Speidel, 'German Air Force', p. 358.
90 IWM: Documents/17217 – Diary of Gunner Sydney Ball, 31 May 1940; TNA: AIR 199/788A – Master Steam Hopper Barge *Foremost 102* Report.
91 TNA: AIR 20/4447 – Letter from Major General Johnson to Lieutenant General Fisher, 8 June 1940; TNA: AIR 22/169 – A.M.W.R. Daily Report for Summary, No. 318, 2 June 1940; TNA: AIR 24/373 – ORB: Coastal Command, Narrative of Events, May–June 1940.
92 TNMDA: DWR/1940/06 – Daily Weather Report, 1 June 1940.
93 T. C. G. James, *The Battle of Britain* (ed.) Sebastian Cox (London: Frank Cass, 2000), p. 401.
94 TNA: ADM 199/792 – Report of Vice Admiral Ramsay; TNA: AIR 22/169 – A.M.W.R. Daily Report for Summary, No. 318, 2 June 1940; TNA: HW 5/2 – GC&CS Decrypts, CX/JQ/11; Gardner, *Evacuation*, p. 18.
95 TNA: AIR 20/9906 – German Air Force Situation Reports on Western Front, 1 June 1940.
96 TsAMO RF: Ф.500 оп.12452 д.95 – Tägliche Lageberichte West des Führungsstabes der Luftwaffe (1c), No. 270, p. 4.
97 TNA: ADM 199/792 – CO *Keith* Report.
98 General Milch cited in James, *Battle*, p. 400.
99 TNA: AIR 22/169 – A.M.W.R. Daily Report for Summary, No. 318, 2 June 1940.
100 TNA: AIR 15/898 – N.L.O. Log, 1 June 1940; TNA: AIR 16/1072 – Fighter Command to 11 and 12 Groups, 1 June 1940; TNA: HW 5/2 – GC&CS Decrypts, CX/JQ/13.
101 TNA: AIR 16/352 – 11 Group Report, 8 July 1940; TNA: AIR 16/839 – 11 Group, Air Combat Results Chart, May–November 1940; TNA: AIR 27 – ORB: Fighter Command Squadrons, May–June 1940.
102 TNA: AIR 15/898 – N.L.O. Log, 2 June 1940.
103 TNA: HW 5/2 – GC&CS Decrypts, CX/JQ/16.
104 *Ibid.*, CX/JQ/13–14.
105 TNA: ADM 199/2206 – Naval War Diary Summaries, Rear Admiral Dover to Vice Admiral Bertram Ramsay, 1 June 1940; TNA: AIR 20/9906 – German Air Force Situation Reports on Western Front, 27 May 1940.
106 TNA: ADM 199/788A – Officer Commanding Mona's Isle, Report of Events Covering Period 26–28 May 1940. TNA: AIR 16/1172 – Coastal Command to Fighter Command, 27 May 1940.
107 IWM: Audio/6823 – Jack Williams, Reel 2.

108 IWM: Audio/9721 – Robert Charles Michael Vaughan Wynn Newborough, Reel 1.
109 Paul Temme cited in Atkin, *Pillar of Fire*, p. 175.
110 TsAMO RF: Ф.500 оп.12452 д.95 – Tägliche Lageberichte West des Führungsstabes der Luftwaffe (1c), No. 270, p. 4.
111 TNA: AIR 35/189 – Wing Commander Spence to Air Marshal Barratt, Notes on the Evacuation of Dunkirk, c. June 1940.
112 TNA: AIR 19/233 – Dive-Bombers and Dive-Bombing, 31 March 1943; Steinhilper, *Spitfire on my Tail*, p. 25.
113 TNA: ADM 199/360 – Captain Clement Moody, Director Naval Air Division, War Diary, General Appreciation for Period 16–31 May 1940.
114 Wood and Dempster, *Narrow Margin*, p. 100.
115 IWM: Audio/12674 – Edge, Reel 2.
116 Franks, *Air Battle*, pp. 66–7.
117 IWM: Audio/10119 – Hancock, Reel 1.
118 IWM: Audio/11544 – George Cecil Unwin, Reel 1.
119 IWM: Audio/27074 – Bamberger, Reel 7.
120 IWM: Audio/12173 – Benjamin Harvey Bowring, Reel 2.
121 TNA: AIR 27/862 – Appendices to ORB: 110 Squadron, Appendix 190, Report to 2 Group on Bombing Attack, 1 June 1940.
122 TNA: AIR 27/511 – ORB: 54 Squadron.
123 IWM: Audio/11247 – Falck, Reel 5.
124 TNA: AIR 16/234 – Fighter Command Intelligence Summaries, German Air Force Tactics, May 1940.
125 TNA: AIR 16/281 – Headquarters 11 Group to Officers Commanding 11 Group Stations, 'Air Fighting between Fighter Formations', 19 May 1940.
126 TNA: AIR 14/176 – Fighter Command Tactical Memorandum No. 9, 'Operation of Fighter Forces by Day', 9 December 1940.
127 TNA: AIR 5/1139 – Air Tactics Branch in Conjunction with Fighter Command, AFC No. 94, 'Tactics for Fighters Versus Escorted Bombers', 4 June 1940; TNA: AIR 22/66 – Air Ministry Weekly Bulletins No. 35–6, 1 June–14 June 1940; TNA: AIR 50/10/19 – Air Combat Report, Flight Lieutenant R. Lane, 26 May 1940; TNA: AIR 50/19/70 – Combat Report, Flying Sergeant Ottewill, 1 June 1940; Air 50/25/18 – Combat Report, Pilot Officer Grant, 26 May 1940; TNA: AIR 50/10/23 – Air Combat Report, Pilot Officer Stevenson, 27 May 1940.
128 TNA: AIR 14/176 – Fighter Command Tactical Memorandum No. 9, 'Operation of Fighter Forces by Day', 9 December 1940.
129 TNA: AIR 15/898 – N.L.O. Log, 1–2 June 1940.
130 TNA: AIR 24/520 – Appendices to ORB: Fighter Command, Narrative of Events, May–June 1940.
131 TNA: AIR 16/1171 – Back Violet to Fighter Command, Air Cover Requirements, 26 May 1940.

132 IWM: Audio/26971 – Allan Wright, Reel 1.
133 TNA: AIR 5/1139 – Air Tactics Branch in Conjunction with Fighter Command, AFC No. 94, 'Tactics for Fighters versus Escorted Bombers', 4 June 1940. Original Emphasis.
134 Richards, *Fight*, p. 142.
135 IWM: Audio/11103 – Page, Reel 1; TNA: AIR 50/10/23 – Air Combat Report, Pilot Officer M. D. Lyne, 26 May 1940; Air 50/26/156 – Combat Report, Squadron Leader Leigh, 2 June 1940; Air 50/33/29 – Combat Report, Flying Sergeant McQueen, 26 May 1940.
136 TNA: AIR 27/624 – ORB: 72 Squadron; TNA: AIR 27/2102 – ORB: 609 Squadron.
137 TNA: AIR 27/234 – ORB: 17 Squadron.
138 Dunn, *Big Wing*, p. 67.
139 Report by Air Vice-Marshal Trafford Leigh-Mallory to Air Chief Marshal Dowding, 17 September 1940, cited in Dunn, *Big Wing*, pp. 70–2.
140 Memorandum by Air Vice-Marshal Keith Park, 1 October 1940, cited in Dunn, *Big Wing*, p. 75.
141 Johnson, *Full Circle*, p. 235.
142 *Daily Telegraph*, 'Obituary: Wing Commander David Cox', 5 February 2004, [http://www.telegraph.co.uk/news/obituaries/1453460/Wing-Commander-David-Cox.html, accessed 25 May 2018].
143 Allen, Who Won, p. 119.
144 IWM: Audio/21291 – James Gilbert Sanders, Reel 1.
145 IWM: Audio/6703 – Anthony Richard Edward Ewart Rhodes, Reel 3; TNA: AIR 16/1072 – Record of Telephone Conversations at Fighter Command Relating to Air Cover for Evacuation of Dunkirk, 1 June 1940; TNA: AIR 27/252 – ORB: 19 Squadron; TNA: AIR 27/424 – ORB: 41 Squadron; TNA: AIR 27/441 – ORB: 43 Squadron; TNA: AIR 27/984 – ORB: 145 Squadron; TNA: AIR 27/1371 – ORB: 222 Squadron; TNA: AIR 27/2126 – ORB: 616 Squadron.
146 TNA: AIR 16/1072 – Record of Telephone Conversations at Fighter Command Relating to Air Cover for Evacuation of Dunkirk, 1 June 1940.
147 TNA: AIR 20/5202 – Air Chief Marshal Dowding, Despatch on the Battle of Britain, para. 198.
148 IWM: Audio/12674 – Edge, Reel 2.
149 Gelb, *Dunkirk*, p. 107.
150 IWM: Audio/10049 – Denys Edgar Gillam, Reel 1.
151 IWM: Audio/10159 – Dundas, Reel 1; IWM: Audio/11510 – Cox, Reel 1; IWM: Audio/14368 – Bidsee, Reel 1; Dundas, *Flying*, pp. 28–9.
152 TNA: AIR 5/1139 – Air Tactics Branch in Conjunction with Fighter Command, AFC No. 94, 'Tactics for Fighters versus Escorted Bombers', 4 June 1940.
153 *Ibid*.

154 TNA: AIR 27/589 – ORB: 64 Squadron; TNA: AIR 27/1418 – ORB: 229 Squadron; TNA: AIR 27/1471 – ORB: 242 Squadron; TNA: AIR 27/2106 – ORB: 610 Squadron; Donald Caldwell, *JG 26 Luftwaffe Fighter Wing War Diary, Vol. I, 1939–42* (London: Grub Street, 1996), p. 32.
155 TNA: AIR 27/2109 – ORB: 611 Squadron.
156 TNA: AIR 27/2109 – ORB: 611 Squadron; TNA: AIR 50/26/133 – Air Combat Report, Campbell-Colquhoun, 2 June 1940.
157 Zimmerman, *Britain's Shield*, p. 187.
158 McGlashan, *Down to Earth*, pp. 7–8.
159 TNA: AIR 2/2946 – Air Officer Signals 1 (a), Notes on VHF Trials at Duxford, 31 October 1939; TNA: AIR 16/185 – Air Officer, Ops. 1, Report of VHF R/T Trial at Duxford 30 October 1939, 31 October 1939.
160 TNA: AIR 2/2946 – Air Officer Signals 1 (a) to Group Captain Lywood, Principal Deputy Director of Signals, 4 June 1940.
161 TNA: AIR 16/185 – Air Officer, Ops. 1, to Air Officer, D/C.S.O., 20 December 1939.
162 Zimmerman, *Britain's Shield*, p. 187.
163 Franks, *Air Battle*, pp. 66–7.
164 Gleed, *Arise*, p. 43.
165 *Ibid.*, p. 76.
166 TNA: AIR 5/1139 – Air Tactics Branch in Conjunction with Fighter Command, AFC No. 94, 'Tactics for Fighters versus Escorted Bombers', 4 June 1940.
167 TNA: AIR 16/281 – Officer Commanding 74 Squadron to 13 Group, 5 June 1940.
168 TNA: AIR 27/252/24 – ORB: 19 Squadron.
169 Memorandum by Air Vice-Marshal Keith Park, 1 October 1940, cited in Dunn, *Big Wing*, p. 75.
170 TNA: AIR 16/352 – 11 Group Report, 8 July 1940.
171 TNA: AIR 16/185 – Air Marshal S. Douglas, AOC-in-C Fighter Command, to Fighter Command Groups, 14 July 1941.
172 TNA: AIR 16/281 – Wing Commander E. S. Burns, Assistant Director of War Training and Tactics, Report of Visit to RAF Duxford, 31 May 1940.
173 *Ibid.*
174 TNA: AIR 27/1553 – ORB: 264 Squadron.
175 TNA: AIR 27/866 – ORB: 111 Squadron; TNA: AIR 27/2104 – Appendices to ORB: 609 Squadron, App. E 'Composite Combat Report of 609 Squadron for 31 May 1940', 1 June 1940.
176 TNA: AIR 2/2946 – Air Chief Marshal Dowding to Under-Secretary of State for Air, 'Withdrawal of VHF Radio Equipment from Operational Fighter Squadrons', 1 June 1940.
177 General Frederick Pile, Officer Commanding Anti-Aircraft Command, cited in Robert Wright, *Dowding and the Battle of Britain* (London: MacDonald, 1969), p. 109.

178 TNA: AIR 2/7068 – Air Chief Marshal Dowding to Under-Secretary of State for Air, 'Retention of the Minimum Fighter Strength Necessary for the Defence of this Country', 24 May 1940.
179 TNA: AIR 14/449 – Air Chief Marshal Dowding to Air Marshal Richard Peirse, 14 May 1940.
180 TNA: AIR 2/2946 – Air Chief Marshal Dowding to Under-Secretary of State for Air, 'Withdrawal of VHF Radio Equipment from Operational Fighter Squadrons', 1 June 1940.
181 TNA: AIR 2/7068 – Winston Churchill to General Ismay, 'Notes on W.P. 40', 19 May 1940.
182 IWM: Audio/10093 – Harold Arthur Cooper Bird-Wilson, Reel 1; IWM: Audio/10128 – Beamont, Reel 1; Franks, *Air Battle*, 160–1; Havercroft, *Dunkirk*, p. 120; Ray, *Battle*, p. 29; Smith, 'The RAF', p. 34.
183 TNA: 16/963 – Fighter Command Order of Battle, 22 May, 29 May, 2 June, 10 June 1940; Gray, 'Dowding', p. 271; Isby, *Decisive*, p. 109; Orange, *Park*, p. 86.
184 Hooton, *Phoenix Triumphant*, p. 260; Claude Huan and Alain Marchand, 'La Bataille aéronavale de Dunkerque (18 Mai–3 Juin 1940)', *Revue Historique Des Armées*, No. 172 (1988), p. 39; Marchand and Huan, 'Dunkerque', p. 47.
185 TNA: AIR 27 – ORB: Fighter Command Squadrons, May–June 1940.
186 TNA: AIR 27 – ORB: Fighter Command Squadrons, May–June 1940; Hooton, *Phoenix Triumphant*, p. 260; Huan and Marchand, 'La Bataille', p. 39.
187 TNA: AIR 16/1170 – Officers at Dunkirk, via Admiralty, to Fighter Command, Fighter Support, 25 May 1940; TNA: AIR 16/1172 – Headquarters RAF component to Fighter Command, Fighter Support of BEF Withdrawal, 27 May 1940.
188 TNA AIR 24/507 – ORB: Fighter Command, May 1940.
189 TNA: AIR 20/2061 – Air Ministry Signal to Fighter Command, 28 May 1940.
190 TNA: AIR 16/1070 – Air Ministry to Fighter Command, Forwarded to 11 Group, Operational Instructions, 29 May 1940.
191 Data drawn from: TNA: AIR 25/193 – ORB: 11 Group; TNA: AIR 25/219 – ORB: 12 Group; TNA: AIR 27 – ORB: Fighter Command Squadrons, May–Jun. 1940.
192 Churchill, *Finest Hour*, p. 88; Gardner, *Evacuation*, p. 122; First Sea Lord Sir Dudley Pound to Vice Admiral Ramsay, 26 May 1940, cited in Ramsay, 'Despatch', p. 3229, col. 2.
193 TNA: AIR 27 – ORB: Fighter Command Squadrons, May 1940.
194 TNA: AIR 20/2061 – Air Ministry Signal to Fighter Command, 28 May 1940.
195 TNA: CAB 65/7/39 – War Cabinet, Conclusions of Meeting No. 144, 28 May 1940.
196 TNA: AIR 16/1170 – Officers at Dunkirk, via Admiralty, to Fighter Command, Fighter Support, 25 May 1940; TNA: AIR 16/1070 – Air Ministry to Fighter Command, Forwarded to 11 Group, Operational Instructions, 29 May 1940; TNA: AIR 16/1172 – Headquarters RAF component to Fighter Command, Fighter

Support of BEF Withdrawal, 27 May 1940; TNA AIR 24/507 – ORB: Fighter Command, May 1940.
197 TNA: AIR 15/897 – N.L.O. Log, 28 May 1940.
198 *Ibid.*, 28 May 1940.
199 Data drawn from: TNA: AIR 25/193 – ORB: 11 Group; TNA: AIR 25/219 – ORB: 12 Group; TNA: AIR 27 – ORB: Fighter Command Squadrons, May–June 1940.
200 Ibid.
201 Atkin, *Pillar of Fire*, p. 205; Johnson, *Full Circle*, p. 121; Lord, *Miracle*, pp. 221–2; Smith, *Stuka*, p. 45.
202 TNA: AIR 20/2778 – Air Chief Marshal Dowding to Air Marshal Peirse, 2 June 1940
203 James, *Battle*, pp. 12, 267.
204 TNA: AIR 16/1172 – Headquarters 11 Group to 11 Group Fighter Stations, 27 May 1940.
205 Allen, *Who Won*, pp. 132–3.
206 TNA: AIR 22/168 – A.M.W.R. Daily Report for Summary, No. 314, 29 May 1940; TNA: AIR 24/507 – ORB: Fighter Command, May 1940; TNA: AIR 25/193 – ORB: 11 Group, May 1940.
207 TNA: AIR 16/1070 – Air Ministry to Fighter Command, 29 May 1940; TNA: HW 5/2 – GC&CS Decrypts, CX/JQ/9.
208 TNA: AIR 25/193 – ORB: 11 Group, May–June 1940.
209 TNA: ADM 199/2205 – Naval War Diary Summaries, Situation Report, Air Ministry 'Air Attacks Expected', 14.30 29 May 1940, Air Ministry 'Air Attacks Postponed Owing to Weather', 16.10 29 May 1940; TNA: AIR 15/898 – N.L.O. Log, 29 May 1940; TNA: AIR 24/217 – Bomber Command Intelligence Report No. 618, 29 May 1940.
210 TNA: AIR 16/1072 – Duty Officer, Air Intelligence War Room Watch to Fighter Command, 1 June 1940; TNA: AIR 20/2063 – Analysis of Luftwaffe Raids, 28 May–2 June 1940.
211 TNA: ADM 199/2206 – Naval War Diary Summaries, Situation Report, 1 June 1940; TNA: ADM 223/82 – OIC Daily Report, 1 June 1940; TNA: AIR 16/1072 – Air Ministry to Fighter Command 'Telegraphic Intelligence Summary', 1 June 1940; TNA: HW 5/2 – GC&CS Decrypts, CX/JQ/9–14.
212 TNA: AIR 16/1072 – Air Intelligence to Fighter Command, 21.29, 1 June 1940; TNA: AIR 25/193 – ORB: 11 Group, May–Jun. 1940; TNA: AIR 25/219 – ORB: 12 Group, May–Jun. 1940; Asher Lee, 'Trends in Aerial Defense', *World Politics*, Vol. 7, No. 2 (1955), p. 238; Ferris, 'Fighter Defence', p. 872.
213 TNA: AIR 27/592 – ORB: 65 Squadron; TNA: AIR 27/640 – ORB: 74 Squadron; TNA: AIR 27/664 – ORB: 79 Squadron; AIR 27/2088 – ORB: 605 Squadron.
214 Franks, *Air Battle*, p. 140.

215 TNA: AIR 16/352 – 11 Group Report, 8 July 1940.
216 TNA: CAB 65/7/39 – War Cabinet, Conclusions of Meeting No. 144, 28 May 1940.
217 Gelb, *Dunkirk*, p. 132.
218 TNA: CAB 65/7/54 – War Cabinet, Conclusions of Meeting No. 159, 'Aircraft Production', 9 June 1940; Telford Taylor, *The Breaking Wave: The German Defeat in the Summer of 1940* (London: Weidenfeld and Nicolson, 1967), p. 20.
219 TNA: AIR 22/362 – State of Aircraft in Aircraft Servicing Units, 1940.
220 Wood and Dempster, *Narrow Margin*, p. 203.
221 TNA: AIR 16/359 – Air Vice-Marshal Sholto Douglas, Deputy Chief of the Air Staff, Notes on the Despatch of Fighter Squadrons to France, 11 June 1940.
222 TNA: AIR 22/362 – State of Aircraft in Aircraft Servicing Units, 1940.
223 TNA: AIR 8/287 – Confidential Annex to War Cabinet Conclusions, WM 153 (40), 3 June 1940.
224 James, *Growth*, p. 99.
225 TNA: AIR 22/296 – Cabinet Statistical Branch, Statistics Relating to RAF Personnel, June–August 1940.
226 TNA: AIR 6/60 – Preliminary Statement to the Air Council by the Air Member for Training on Training Arrangements Generally, 23 July 1940; Wood and Dempster, *Narrow Margin*, p. 235.
227 TNA: AIR 35/189 – Wing Commander Spence to Air Marshal Barratt, Notes on the Evacuation of Dunkirk, *c.* June 1940.

8

The operations of Coastal Command

During Operation Dynamo, Coastal Command squadrons undertook a wide spectrum of air power operations which included combat air patrols, surveillance and reconnaissance, close air support, anti-shipping and anti-submarine sorties. Squadrons of the Fleet Air Arm (FAA), the air arm of the Royal Navy, also made an important contribution whilst temporarily under the direction of Coastal Command. Air patrols over the evacuation took several forms with some more consciously designed to provide air cover than others, where the main objective was surveillance and reconnaissance. Squadrons from both Coastal Command and the FAA maintained fighter patrols over the evacuation fleet's sea route to and from Dunkirk; this role left Fighter Command free to concentrate their efforts in an attempt to provide a fighter screen above the embarkation beaches and the port and town of Dunkirk. Aircraft from Coastal Command were also used over Dunkirk itself where – operating in very low strength with the intention to 'show the flag' to Allied troops there – they provided air cover at times when Fighter Command was not present.[1] Coastal Command did not undertake as many sorties as Fighter Command but these missions did contribute to the air cover the RAF provided for the evacuation. Both the FAA and Coastal Command undertook bombing missions in direct support of Allied troops fighting on the defensive perimeter around Dunkirk. Bombing missions were also flown against other targets of importance during Dynamo. Such missions were amongst the first of the RAF's 'great help' to be celebrated, although the attack in question was conducted by units of the FAA.[2] The work of Coastal Command also extended to protection of Dynamo against enemy naval interference, in particular against E-Boats and U-Boats.[3] Charles Lamb, of 815 (FAA) Squadron, would later recall the difficulties of operations under Coastal Command during the evacuation of Dunkirk as 'flying was intense throughout those nine days and nights, because we had to continue to chase the E-Boats at night as well as by day'.[4] Despite these difficulties, Coastal Command and the FAA made a direct contribution to the evacuation of Dunkirk.

Air cover over the evacuation

The Sands patrol, flown by sections of Coastal Command and FAA squadrons over the area of North Foreland-Calais-Dunkirk-Ostend, provided low altitude air cover to the evacuation fleet. These patrols – also referred to as Goodwin patrols and 'battle flights' – offered a means of protecting shipping in the English Channel and off the French Coast from low level attacks and dive-bombing. This allowed Fighter Command's patrols to range inland and operate at higher altitudes as they attempted to intercept the Luftwaffe's larger formations.[5] The patrols also provided important information as to the state of the evacuation, reporting on the movement of vessels and the situation over the coast as it appeared from the air. Blenheim aircraft of 254 Squadron patrolling in the late morning of 30 May recorded a number of naval vessels wrecked between Calais, Dunkirk and Nieuport as well as the progress of troop convoys and heavy German anti-aircraft fire from Calais, Ostend and Zeebrugge. A later Blenheim patrol was also able to provide details of the number and disposition of troops still awaiting embarkation on the beaches at Dunkirk.[6] These missions were conducted throughout Dynamo and frequently engaged German bombers. During the evening of 27 May three He 111s heading towards Dunkirk were attacked and badly damaged by two Blenheims of 235 Squadron.[7] During the heavy Luftwaffe attacks on 29 May these patrols were conducted throughout the day, in the face of strong German fighter cover, providing cover to the evacuation fleet. Several interceptions of note were recorded by aircraft of Coastal Command and the FAA on 29 May. Three Blenheims of 235 Squadron undertook a patrol in the morning and drove a single Ju 88, probably engaged in armed reconnaissance, away from the evacuation.[8] Hudsons and Skuas operating over the sea routes to Dunkirk engaged enemy bombers in the vicinity of the evacuation fleet as well as those which were actively bombing it. At 17.15 three Hudsons of 220 Squadron attacked two He 111s off Ostend forcing them to dive to low altitude and escape away from the evacuation.[9] At the same time five Ju 88s, at a height of 1,000 feet, which were bombing a convoy of ships on Route Y, were intercepted by Skuas and a Blackburn Roc of 806 (FAA) Squadron. The leading Ju 88 was attacked in the middle of its dive with the Roc getting in a long burst of fire which left the Ju 88 looking as though 'it had been carved by a chainsaw' before it crashed into the sea.[10] The attack damaged a second Ju 88 and the remainder were driven off.[11]

These patrols were designed to interfere with German bomber attacks and not to intercept German fighters, which comprehensively outclassed the aircraft of Coastal Command and the FAA.[12] In providing air cover over Dunkirk, however, the patrols did encounter German fighters. On both 29 May and 1 June Blenheim fighters of Coastal Command were lost to Me 109s as they attempted to provide air cover to the evacuation during gaps in Fighter Command's air cover.[13] Despite their limited strength, however, the presence of Coastal Command and FAA patrols was often sufficient to deter individual German aircraft and, on occasion larger bomber formations, from pressing attacks against the evacuation. On 30 May aircraft of the Sands patrols prevented several attacks on ships, by individual bombers from low-height. A Hudson section attacked a single He 111 north of Ostend; machine-gun fire hit the Heinkel before it dived to sea level, jettisoned eight bombs and escaped inland.[14] A Skua section intercepted a single He 111 off Dunkirk as it was making a low altitude attack on a large merchant vessel; the Heinkel jettisoned four bombs before retreating from the area through cloud cover.[15] At 04.50 on 31 May two Blenheims of 235 Squadron attempted to intercept a Ju 88 north of Calais, at 5,000 feet, forcing it to take evasive action into cloud cover. Shortly before midday three aircraft of 806 (FAA) Squadron reported medium bombers flying in line astern, north of Calais, in sub-flights of three aircraft which took avoiding action on sighting the patrol of 806 (FAA) Squadron and evaded interception.[16]

The air cover provided by Coastal Command and the FAA on 1 June was of considerable importance. Nine Coastal Command patrols were made directly over the evacuation between Gravelines and Ostend. The patrols complemented the air cover of Fighter Command and provided the only deterrent to the Luftwaffe during gaps in Fighter Command's air cover. Blenheim, Hudson and Skua aircraft were all called upon and – amid ongoing attacks by the Luftwaffe on 1 June – protected a number of ships from attacks from both dive-bombers and medium bombers.[17] A patrol by three Blenheims of 254 Squadron chased a Ju 88 away from Dunkirk at 05.45, with the aircraft jettisoning its bombs as it escaped into the clouds, before at 07.45 a Ju 87 was attacked. The Blenheims of 254 Squadron, one of which had returned to base after its guns had jammed, were at this time the only air cover over the evacuation. Continuing their patrol amid the ongoing heavy Luftwaffe attacks the Blenheims attempted to provide further protection to the evacuation; however, shortly after their attack on the Ju 87 the remaining two Blenheims were shot down by 11 Me 109s.[18] At 10.15 two Blenheims of 235 Squadron sighted one He 111 as it prepared to bomb two naval units 25km east of Dover; the two Blenheims attacked and chased the He 111 towards France before losing contact with the bomber within cloud cover.[19] Six He 111s bombing a merchant vessel off Dover at 9,000 feet were engaged by Blenheims and driven off, with one He 111 claimed to have been destroyed.[20] At 16.45 Hudsons of 220 Squadron observed a formation of forty dive-bombers at 1,500 feet attacking a small motor launch 5km from Dunkirk. Attacking individually the Hudsons engaged the Luftwaffe formation. The Hudsons claimed to have destroyed three Ju 87 and two Ju 88s – the rear gunner from one of these being seen to fall into the sea – and badly damaged two more Ju 87s firing at close-range. The pilot of the third Hudson attacked three Ju 87s, which avoided the attack, before the remainder of the Luftwaffe formation was broken up by the arrival of three Spitfires.[21] At 18.30 Hudsons were engaged directing tugs north of Gravelines towards two broken down lifeboats full of soldiers when six medium bombers and two Me 109s were observed at 4,000 feet; the Hudsons successfully dispersed and drove away these aircraft.[22] At 19.50 three Blenheims sighted two He 111s at 3,000 feet which retreated away from Dunkirk towards the Belgian coast on sighting the British aircraft.[23] In total, the patrols of Coastal Command over the evacuation fleet on 1 June involved thirty-four sorties, 12 per cent of the effort of Fighter Command, and provided a small measure of direct relief to the evacuation fleet. Smaller formations of German bombers were repelled by these patrols – frequently without even being engaged – which also broke up attacks on ships during 1 June. By operating in this manner Coastal Command guarded the ships concerned and prevented patrols of Spitfires and Hurricanes having to be maintained over the channel. The flight routes of Fighter Command patrols to Dunkirk did give some cover to the evacuation routes but they did not have to provide sustained air cover at low level in this area. Instead Fighter Command was able to contest air superiority with the Luftwaffe over Dunkirk.

Between 08.30 and 11.30 on 2 June Coastal Command provided air cover for shipping returning from Dunkirk. Fighter Command aircraft did not patrol during this period having provided air cover from dawn as troops were still being embarked from Dunkirk and whilst the ships involved were closer to the French coast. The 'essential object' of these patrols was 'to prevent enemy aircraft from attacking shipping' and to achieve this Hudsons and Blenheims flew high level fighter cover whilst Skuas and Rocs of the FAA operated at low altitude.[24] Thirty-nine sorties were despatched during this period to provide air cover and a reserve of Blenheims and Hudsons was maintained at operational readiness in the event of large attacks on the ships during their return from Dunkirk. For the most part air attacks on the evacuation fleet were limited during this period, the only incident of note coming at 10.35 when 806 (FAA) Squadron observed a Ju 88 commence a dive-bombing attack on the anti-aircraft cruiser HMS *Calcutta* – which had already been attacked by two Ju 88s during this period. The lead Skua of 806 (FAA) Squadron attacked the Ju 88 which disappeared into the clouds in a slow spiral towards the water. Shortly after this 806 (FAA) Squadron attacked another Ju 88 which dived away into the clouds and was later observed endeavouring to reach the French coast with its port engine on fire.[25] Coastal Command's operations on 2 June were important; not only did these patrols provide air cover against the Luftwaffe's attacks but they permitted Fighter Command's squadrons to be used over a concentrated region and during a short time window. The RAF was therefore able to ensure the most effective fighter cover was available to the evacuation fleet whilst it was at its most vulnerable.

Reconnaissance over the evacuation

Missions were also flown over the evacuation by Avro Anson squadrons of Coastal Command during Dynamo which were primarily designed to provide reconnaissance reports. The collection of information regarding enemy activity, the location of shipping and the progress of embarkations was an important air power contribution during the evacuation. Reports from the Ansons provided up-to-date intelligence on the progress of Dynamo as well as the situation on the evacuation routes, along the coast and at Dunkirk. On 28 May Ansons of 500 Squadron – supplemented by Ansons from 48 Squadron – flew two reconnaissance missions along the coast between Calais and the Hook of Holland before dawn and was scheduled to conduct four patrols over the evacuation route during the day. An Anson section of 500 Squadron on patrol during 28 May observed the transport *Queen of the Channel* aground and abandoned. The patrol encountered German aircraft bombing British destroyers on Route Y and also reported by wireless that they had observed forty German aircraft attacking between Dunkirk and Ostend, with incendiary and high explosive bombs.[26] On 29 May Ansons of 48 and 500 Squadron undertook fifteen air reconnaissance sorties over the evacuation fleet between Dunkirk and Ostend.[27] These patrols, which could remain airborne over the area of operations for three hours, continued throughout Dynamo and came to play an important role in monitoring the situation on the evacuation routes, particularly Route Y. Ansons made thirty-nine sorties over Route Y in total between 31 May and 2 June.[28] Information from these patrols provided situational awareness and helped naval planners to manage the flow of shipping on the evacuation routes; this both regulated the arrival of large ships – so that embarkations from Dunkirk could be made at a continuous rate – and ensured that there weren't too many personnel vessels exposed on the journey to Dunkirk.

Anson patrols also reported the presence and location of mines they observed along the evacuation routes. At 06.35, 1 June, an Anson patrol reported three floating mines 65km north of Ostend and provided further details regarding an absence of vessels along the Dutch coast. During the afternoon an Anson patrol over Route Y observed and reported five floating mines 30km to the north-east of Ostend.[29] This information was important to the naval planners of the evacuation who were concerned regarding the German minelaying efforts and its potential to disrupt shipping to Dunkirk.[30]

As well as providing real-time reports from over the evacuation routes the Ansons also gave a measure of air cover and provided a deterrent against a number of individual German bombers pressing closer to the evacuation. On 30 May, for instance, Anson aircraft of 500 Squadron patrolled over Dunkirk and sighted a Ju 88 flying north-west of Ostend at 800 feet.[31] The Ansons, which were at a height of some 500 feet, challenged the enemy aircraft which jettisoned its bombs and made off to the north-east.[32] The extent of this air cover was more illusionary than real, however, as the Ansons were restricted in their ability to catch or shoot-down the Luftwaffe types they encountered. The importance of the patrols was that they delivered a core component of air power: intelligence surveillance and reconnaissance.[33]

Operations against E-Boats

Coastal Command and the FAA also provided patrols against E-Boats during Operation Dynamo. E-Boats posed a considerable threat to the evacuation as in addition to their torpedo armament they were capable of high speeds – in excess of 30 knots – and were relatively stable gun platforms.[34] They were also comparatively heavily armed. The Class A and Class B types both possessed one 2cm gun and one machine-gun; however, the Class B was also armed with two 3.7cm guns.[35] As Dynamo began Coastal Command received calls for assistance to help counter the threat of E-Boats to ships involved in the evacuation, particularly during the night.[36] The Royal Navy was aware of the threat E-Boats posed to ships involved in the evacuation but limited in what it could do to counter it. On 29 May Admiral Plunkett messaged the Admiralty that he was 'much concerned at [the] difficulty of countering German E-Boats' because British destroyers had proved 'too big and are not effective' whilst British motor torpedo boats were 'small and too few'.[37] Types smaller than destroyers were also limited in their effectiveness, the Kingfisher class of sloop's 4-inch gun proved too unwieldy to track the fast-moving E-Boats and its muzzle flash was blinding on the gunners which further inhibited their ability to bring their weapon to bear.[38] With the Royal Navy limited in the protection it could provide, air cover was identified as being needed to counter the E-Boat threat.[39]

The tactics employed by the German E-Boats involved quietly moving into position – by cruising at moderate speed with auxiliary engines – along a well-travelled channel and waiting for a suitable target of opportunity. This method was facilitated by the heavy traffic along clearly defined routes to and from Dunkirk.[40] During this period E-Boats were forearmed with radio messages intercepted from Dover Command which provided times and details of the evacuation of the rearguard, as well as the route the evacuation fleet would take, which the E-Boats attempted to make use of.[41] Individual German aircraft also appear to have co-operated with E-Boats during night attacks. On 31 May FS *Sirocco* was sunk on Route Y in an attack by E-Boats positioned off the main route which were stationary and had remained unseen in the dark.[42] Those on *Sirocco* firmly believed that the E-Boat they spotted had been waiting for Allied ships at a route marker and that it was probable that it had been in communication with an aircraft which had not attacked the *Sirocco* 'but had been shadowing us for some time'.[43] The presence of low-flying aircraft was commented on by the Admiralty who felt that the purpose of the aircraft was 'either to locate the vessel to attack or to distract its attention and conceal the noise of the attacking boats engines'.[44]

The speed, manoeuvrability and small size of E-Boats made them difficult targets for Coastal Command's aircraft to attack and sink outright, when they were at sea and underway.[45] A meeting was held on 29 May to discuss E-Boats and the measures that might be taken against them; it was considered that 'with the freedom to take avoiding action [E-Boats] are a difficult bombing target'.[46] When operating as part of a well-organized formation E-Boats could also put up sufficient anti-aircraft fire to make them a threat to attacking aircraft. Three Ansons of 48 Squadron were involved in the first recorded instance of the RAF attacking E-Boats on 20 May near Texel, off the coast of Holland; one Anson was shot down and another damaged during dive-bombing and strafing attacks on the E-Boats. However, this attack was not only made in bad weather conditions but was also made against a flotilla of nine E-Boats; the E-Boats hunting at Dunkirk did so in groups of smaller numbers. On 25 May, an Anson was hit in the port engine as a result of the anti-aircraft barrage put up by two E-Boats and was forced to ditch in the sea.⁴⁷ Despite isolated successes, such as that achieved on 25 May, the anti-aircraft armament of individual and small groups of E-Boats, moving at speed to evade bombing, was unlikely to bring down an aircraft. Attacks on E-Boats made in favourable conditions detail the anti-aircraft fire received as 'ineffective' and the E-Boats' main threat to aircraft came when a larger formation of E-Boats was able to put up a barrage of anti-aircraft fire.⁴⁸ The meeting to discuss the E-Boat menace on 29 May noted that during attacks machine-gun fire from the front guns of aircraft appeared to have had 'little apparent effect'.⁴⁹ Nevertheless an appreciation made regarding the E-Boats considered machine-gun fire from aircraft, particularly from rear gunners, to be probably the greatest threat to E-Boats underway at sea.⁵⁰ Concerns regarding the E-Boat menace, and the lack of a suitable counter to their threat, were such that Admiral Sir Charles Forbes, C-in-C Home Fleet, messaged the Admiralty on 1 June regarding the possibility of Fairey Swordfish aircraft being fitted with cannon for use in a fleet protection role.⁵¹ The conclusion reached at the meeting on 29 May was that the most effective form of attack was to locate their bases and to bomb the boats in harbour.⁵² At a further meeting to discuss measures against E-Boats on 30 May Group Captain Lloyd, a member of Coastal Command's planning staff, was strongly of the opinion that 250lb Anti-Submarine bombs set to burst with minimum delay were the best weapon available and that:

> A motor torpedo boat at sea is best attacked by a pair of aircraft. One should try to fix the boat by circling it and engaging it with machine-gun fire from rear turret guns, while the other carries out a bombing attack, preferably down sun.⁵³

The E-Boats were a difficult target for air attack, however, with Royal Navy limited in its ability to counter the E-Boat threat – and already heavily drawn upon evacuating troops from Dunkirk – the squadrons of Coastal Command and the FAA were asked to protect the evacuation against the E-Boat attacks.

Before considering the Coastal Command and FAAs patrols and bombing missions conducted against E-Boats it is important to understand the threat the E-Boats posed to the evacuation. On 25 May five boats of the 2nd E-Boat Flotilla and two boats of the 1st E-Boat Flotilla arrived at Den Helder. They were reinforced on 26 May by the arrival of the senior officer of 1st E-Boat Flotilla with a further two E-Boats.⁵⁴ On 25 May E-Boats operated off Nieuport and Ostend in two groups both of which fired torpedoes against destroyers without result. From 26 May to the morning of 1 June the E-Boats claimed to have sunk four destroyers, and two large transports. On 31 May, E-Boats were advanced to the Hook of Holland to bring them closer to the evacuation. An E-Boat sortie during the night of 2 June, which was originally to have extended as far as North Goodwin, had to be broken off north-west of Dunkirk because of severe loss of time caused by Coastal Command's air cover and the patrol was therefore a 'blank'.[55] On this day *Kapitän zur See* Hans Büttow, *Führer der Torpedoboote*, observed that boats could not leave the Hook of Holland by daylight without fighter cover and it was considered that operations of the type of 2 June were now 'only practicable with fighter cover'.[56] E-Boat patrols by the 1st E-Boat Flotilla on 3 June and the 2nd E-Boat Flotilla on 4 June, both in the North Goodwins and Dunkirk area, were uneventful.[57] The operations division of the German naval staff were, however, satisfied that the appearance of German torpedo boats 'night after night' had increased the already great difficulties the Allies faced in withdrawing troops from Dunkirk.[58]

The E-Boats did disrupt the evacuation but as the events of 2 June demonstrate their operations were limited by Coastal Command's air cover. To counter the E-Boat threat the various aircraft of Coastal Command and the FAA were employed in a number of roles. To best understand the effect these had it is useful to consider the operations of each type separately. Both the Ansons and Hudsons of Coastal Command conducted missions with the object of giving early warning of the approach of E-Boats; these missions were, however, bounded by different areas.

The role of Anson Squadrons

Reconnaissance of the Dutch coast was an important aspect of Coastal Command's missions against E-Boats. Patrols towards the Frisian Islands were flown along the French and Belgian coast by sections of Ansons which reported on shipping and maintained a watch for enemy naval interference.[59] Patrols were conducted throughout the days but with a specific focus on the periods of dawn and dusk. A patrol along the Dutch coast during the evening of 26 May by three Anson of 500 Squadron observed three E-Boats 10km south-west of Texel. No bombing attack was possible as clouds were too low but the activity of the E-Boats was reported by wireless transmission.[60] On 27 May dawn patrols against E-Boats were flown by Ansons along the French and Belgian coast to Holland and were repeated between 17.33 and 21.35 during which – at 19.00 – four E-Boats 20km south-west of Texel were unsuccessfully bombed. During the late morning and early afternoon of 27 May Ansons had undertaken three reconnaissance patrols of the Belgian and Dutch coast up to

Texel Island. One of these patrols observed E-Boats off the Hook of Holland which broke off their movements down the coast and escaped into Rotterdam while the Ansons were climbing to bombing height.[61] During the morning of 28 May a section of Ansons flew a parallel track search beginning 30km west of Ijmuiden and continued down the coast to 30km north of Calais where the Ansons circled back along the coast to Holland before returning to base.[62] This track search was repeated during the evening and at 19.40 the Ansons observed five E-Boats which put up a heavy anti-aircraft barrage; thunderstorm and low clouds prevented the Ansons from bombing the E-Boats.[63] Night operations by Ansons had begun on 26 May – with coastal patrols from Calais to the West Frisian Islands and track searches over the North Sea for E-Boats operating from Holland – but in the darkness frequently produced no results.[64] At 02.10 on 29 May, however, an Anson bombed two E-Boats 25km south-west of Maas Light. The bombing was unsuccessful but attacks on E-Boats during the night did delay and hinder their operations. Ansons patrols continued to operate dawn and dusk patrols against E-Boats on 30 May and Ansons also patrolled to Texel and then down the coast to Dunkirk between 11.15 and 13.41.[65] During the course of 31 May and 1 June a section of Ansons patrolled against E-Boats at dawn and dusk 20km off the Belgian and Dutch coasts between Dunkirk and Ijmuiden. Individual Ansons also flew along the English coast from Detling on 1 June – patrolling from Newhaven to Cromer and Bircham Newton – tasked with detecting German naval activity in the area and reporting on any mines observed. One reconnaissance sortie was also despatched over the North Sea to the Scheldt Estuary and two Ansons were also involved in a search for E-Boats in an area off the coast of North France from Boulogne to Le Havre. Patrol along the Belgian and Dutch coast was also made by Anson sections from dawn on 2 and 3 June. During the nights of 2 and 3 June three reconnaissance sorties were made by Ansons over the North Sea and a further patrol against E-Boats was flown by two Anson on 3 June.[66]

The role of Hudson Squadrons

In addition to providing air cover directly over the evacuation routes, which have been discussed above, Hudsons of Coastal Command undertook patrols to provide early warning of the approach of E-Boats and prevent their operations during daylight hours. On 27 May eleven Hudson sorties were made over the North Sea to the Dutch coast. At 13.00 a Hudson of 220 Squadron observed an E-Boat 20km south-west of Willemsoord which escaped into cover inland after the Hudson dropped a stick of four 250lb bombs in an unsuccessful dive-bombing attack.[67] On 28 May ten patrols, each involving one Hudson, were flown over the North Sea to Holland. At 16.35 a Hudson reported motorboats off Ameland heading west and at 16.40 six E-Boats were seen moving 50km north of Terschelling with a further four stationary. The Hudson made two attacks against one of the stationary E-Boats without causing any visible damage. At 17.20 a Hudson reported three E-Boats 50km east of Den Helder heading west at 20 knots.[68] On 29 May nine reconnaissance sorties against E-Boats were made by Hudson aircraft with one Hudson of 220 Squadron reporting on the movements of three E-Boats south-west of Texel Island. Hudson patrols also reported on the situation at Ijmuiden Harbour, where what was believed to be a destroyer was observed, and on the presence of mines off both the English and Dutch coast.[69] Weather hindered operations on 30 May but six reconnaissance sorties against E-Boats were made with a further eight patrols on 31 May.[70] At 18.25 on 31 May a Hudson attacked two E-Boats, underway at 15 knots, 20km west of Terschelling, from a height of 2,000 feet without achieving any visible results. The E-Boats were reported zig-zagging on a south-westerly heading and were later spotted at Texel Island where they were later attacked by a Hudson, with a near-miss causing one E-Boat to violently swerve.[71] The attacks on 31 May if not damaging the E-Boats certainly delayed them from taking up position to attack the evacuation. Hudson patrols against E-Boat movements along the Dutch coast continued on 1 June. At 05.00 a patrol was made over an area 65km west and south of Den Helder until 09.00 and was then repeated between 09.00–13.10 and 15.00–19.10. Six Hudson patrols also maintained continuous reconnaissance over an area west of Texel Island from 03.50 to 23.10 on 1 June.[72] Similar patrols were maintained on 2 June during the course of which one E-Boat was unsuccessfully bombed off Texel Island at 21.30.[73] The morning of 2 June also saw two Hudsons fly a reconnaissance patrol over the North Sea to Terschelling and along the Friesian Islands to protect the flank of the evacuation fleet from approaching E-Boats. A patrol by three Hudsons was also made during the afternoon along the coast between Ijmuiden and the Hook of Holland.[74] During the evening of 2 June seven Hudsons – which had been standing by in the event that ships on the evacuation routes from Dunkirk required further air cover – conducted two patrols on a parallel track about 20km from the Belgian and Dutch coasts between Dunkirk and Ijmuiden. Four Hudsons bombed and strafed three E-Boats 35km north of Ostend at 21.20 recording several near-misses. No E-Boats were lost to these attacks; however, the attacks did delay the

E-Boats – with the E-Boats forced to alter course away from the evacuation to evade further bombing – which ultimately resulted in the abandonment of the E-Boat's planned attacks for that night.[75] Patrols to Den Helder and Texel Island to report on E-Boats movements were maintained throughout 3 June with eight sorties conducted from 03.00 to 21.50. On the night of 3 June six Hudsons flew a patrol along the Belgian and Dutch coasts in an attempt to obstruct further E-Boat operations and a further reconnaissance patrol to the Hook of Holland and Vlissingen was made by a single Hudson.[76]

As well as providing advanced warning of E-Boat movements the operations by both Ansons and Hudsons of Coastal Command made the movement of E-Boats on the Dutch Coast difficult during daylight. These operations delayed the E-Boats' attempts to reach advance position – from which they could then proceed closer to the evacuation during the night – and were a source of inconvenience for the E-Boat flotillas; however, they did not prevent their operations. Coastal Command operations on the night of 2 June did, however, cause the E-Boats to abandon their attacks against the evacuation.[77] The reconnaissance provided by the patrols of Coastal Command was also used to despatch offensive patrols against reported E-Boats. Coastal Command's sorties detected, located, identified, tracked and attacked E-Boats. The E-Boat flotillas were unable to operate from the Hook of Holland by daylight because of Coastal Command's missions – which prevented them from reaching the large movements of ships involved in the evacuation – and greatly reduced their threat for the remainder of Dynamo.[78]

The role of Swordfish, Albacore, Beaufort Squadrons

Swordfish and Albacores of the FAA as well as Beauforts of Coastal Command were also employed against E-Boats. On 28 May seventeen Swordfish sorties were despatched against E-Boats following reports made at 16.30 by a Hudson of 206 Squadron. Eight Swordfish undertook an offensive sortie to attack six E-Boats reported at Ameland whilst a strike force of nine Swordfish were given the target of three E-Boats which had been observed off Den Helder heading towards Ostend.[79] Following reports of E-Boats in Ijmuiden Harbour five Beauforts were despatched to bomb shipping, no E-Boats were observed in the harbour, however, and attacks were made against alternative targets in the vicinity.[80] On the evening of 31 May nine Albacores, despatched to bomb E-Boats working from the Scheldt estuary, unsuccessfully attacked E-Boats off

Zeebrugge.[81] During the evening of 1 June a patrol was made over the North Sea by five Swordfish to ensure that E-Boats were not moving into position to attack ships on Route Y. The use of Swordfish despatched at hourly intervals on 1 June for night patrols against E-Boats was abandoned, after two aircraft had been despatched, because of low visibility.[82] On the morning of 2 June seven Beauforts flew an offensive sortie to attack German naval movements an aircraft of Bomber Command had observed 15km west of Terschelling.[83] The Beauforts were unable to observe their primary target; however, at 09.15 one Beaufort sighted two navy-grey ships and seven E-Boats in 30km north of Borkum. The Beaufort attacked the E-Boats from 1,500 feet dropping six 250lb bombs with the first two hitting the water a few feet ahead of the target whilst the others were unobserved as an intense anti-aircraft barrage from the E-Boats forced the Beaufort into cloud cover.[84] The patrols of Coastal Command and the FAA created considerable difficulty for the E-Boats. The report of the 1st E-Boat flotilla observed that 'strong enemy air patrols … created considerable difficulties' during the Dunkirk evacuation and hindered attempts to 'penetrate to the actual operational areas and to the operational targets'.[85]

Missions were also made to bomb and mine ports suspected of harbouring E-Boats or depot ships capable of supplying these vessels. The repeated observation of E-Boats in the area of the Frisian Islands, and their tendency to seek shelter in the channels between the islands when observed by aircraft, had convinced Coastal Command that the area was being used as a base for E-Boats and their supply vessels.[86] During the course of Dynamo Swordfish aircraft of the FAA flew bombing missions against vessels and facilities at the ports of Willemsoord, Den Helder and Texel Harbour whilst the Marsdiep Channel, between Den Helder and Texel, was also mined by Swordfish with 'B' Bombs.[87] The 'B' bomb was designed to be dropped in the water, sink and then re-float under the hull of a ship and explode; a small modification could be made, however, to make them float just awash where they would be difficult to detect or sweep, for a period of twelve hours, and remain effective for a period of forty-eight hours.[88] A number of mine-laying raids in coastal waters were made by Beauforts.[89] On 26 May, mines were sown by Beauforts in the Weser river, Rotersand Light (Weser estuary) Elbe Channel, Terschelling, Heligoland.[90] Swordfish aircraft were also despatched on patrol across the North Sea to sow mines at points along the Frisian Islands during Dynamo with the area between Vlieland and Terschelling focused on between 1 and 3 June.[91] Ijmuiden was also reconnoitred for E-Boat activity by Beauforts during Dynamo and several bombs were dropped on targets in the harbour.[92] The effect of the British minelaying appears to have been negligible. Both the mines and 'B' bombs were capable of destroying E-Boats; however, the E-Boats small profile meant that there was only a low probability of achieving a hit unless the waters could be mined on a scale beyond the limited resources available.[93]

The conclusion of Dynamo would only offer a short respite from bombing missions against German E-Boats. On 12 June five Skuas of 801 (FAA) Squadron carried out dive-bombing of E-Boats in Boulogne harbour, an operation which was repeated later that day.[94] These raids resulted in damage to a number of E-Boats, as well as several crewmen being killed and injured.[95] The FAA's success against E-Boats at Boulogne indicates that the bombing of such ships in harbour could be effective; a lack of similar success during Dynamo was partly because the E-Boats were dispersed to minimize their vulnerability to bombing. The bombing of harbours during Dynamo did, however, delay the advance of E-Boats to more advanced bases during Dynamo which prevented the E-Boat's approach routes to Dunkirk being shortened and therefore reduced the E-Boats' ability to inflict losses on the evacuation fleet.

The operations of Albacores, Beauforts and Swordfish against the E-Boats operating against the evacuation were limited but they played a part in reducing what was a serious threat to the evacuation. These types – along with aircraft from Number 2 Anti-Aircraft Co-Operation Unit – were also involved in patrolling the flanks of the evacuation at night using flares to identify and attack E-Boats which were approaching the evacuation routes.[96] Patrols involving either two or three aircraft were operated clear of the evacuation routes at times when E-Boats were likely to be approaching. One of the aircraft on the patrol was equipped with a long cable, several hundred metres long, capable of igniting powerful flares and towing them behind the aircraft. The concept being that the flares (which each burnt for a period of approximately four minutes) would illuminate an E-Boat and the escorting aircraft, flying above the aircraft towing the flare, would descend and attack.[97] The employment of towed flares was in addition to the use of parachute flares dropped over areas E-Boats were suspected of operating but not where Allied ships would be silhouetted by the flare's illumination.[98] Excluding the night patrols flown against E-Boats along the Dutch coast a total of eleven flare patrols, involving twenty-five aircraft, were made during Dynamo beginning on the night of 31 May.[99] The need for patrols of this nature was only realized after the destroyers HMS *Grafton* and *Wakeful* were lost to torpedo attacks during the night of 29 May, *Grafton* to a U-Boat and *Wakeful* to an E-Boat.[100] The number of these patrols was also limited because the equipment needed to tow the flares was not immediately available and the evacuation finished before a great many of these operations could be flown.[101] The first patrol, undertaken by a flare towing Skua and an Albacore, sighted three E-Boats at 23.46 on 31 May 25km north-east of Ostend, proceeding on a westerly course at a speed of 25 knots, and attacked the last of these with a 250lb general-purpose bomb, achieving what it believed to be a direct hit.[102] After the attack the aircraft identified two stationary E-Boats with no sign of a third.[103] Although the number of flare patrols was limited those that did occur were made during the period when daylights evacuations from Dunkirk had been suspended and the greatest amount of shipping traffic was underway on the evacuation routes. In these circumstances, the flare patrols provided a further impediment to the operations of E-Boats during a period when, despite the availability of targets, the success of their operations was restricted. The importance of flare patrols was, however, limited with several unable to report observations of any significance and with the attack aircraft frequently unable to keep pace with the slower towing aircraft without overheating. Pilots from 763 (FAA) and 815 (FAA) Squadrons also considered that the success of the flare operations was limited and believed that more effective illumination and observation would have been achieved by using parachute flares.[104]

Operations against U-Boats

Coastal Command's patrols were not confined to targeting German E-Boats. The flare patrols were also intended as a means of observing submarines silhouetted by the illumination of the towed flares.[105] Patrols undertaken along the Belgian and Dutch coast also provided the means to observe and target U-Boats. The threat U-Boats posed to the evacuation was realized from the outset of Dynamo and starkly demonstrated by the sinking of *Grafton* by the submarine *U-62*.[106] Coastal Command aircraft reported on U-Boats observed off the Dutch coast from 25 May and numerous antisubmarine sweeps were conducted during Dynamo.[107] The threat from U-Boat was not restricted to torpedoing; U-Boats were able to lay moored-mines and the personnel vessel SS *Thuringia* was sunk by one such mine. U-Boats were operating off the coast of the Low Countries in the North Sea as well as off the west coast of France. They were, however, largely prevented from operating against the evacuation.[108] As well as missions flown along the Belgian and Dutch coast Coastal Command also made anti-submarine patrols over the North Sea and in areas where shipping was concentrated along the British coast.[109] Hudsons, Blenheims and Ansons of Coastal Command as well as Swordfish of the FAA were all involved in these missions and a number of patrols made direct contact with U-Boats.[110] On 26 May a Hudson of 220 Squadron forced a submarine in the North Sea to dive and evade it.[111] On 28 May three Blenheim aircraft of 235 Squadron carried out a square search for an enemy submarine 16 miles north of Dunkirk between 13.37 and 15.50 throughout the course of which a very extensive patch of oil in the search area was observed.[112] The air cover over the Channel and the North Sea, from both anti-submarine patrols and aircraft returning from other missions in support of Dynamo, left little opportunity for U-Boats to operate on the surface and instead forced them to submerge earlier than they would have wished.[113] Operating below the surface reduced the opportunity for U-Boats to cause notable losses against the evacuation fleet.

Coastal Command and the FAA's bombing missions

Aircraft of both Coastal Command and the FAA also undertook a number of bombing missions in support of Dynamo. Coastal Command Hudsons were also called upon to bomb Rotterdam, where E-Boats were based, with a desire to deprive German forces of the large supplies of oil stored in the port. Repeated missions were despatched to attack targets at Rotterdam both immediately before and during Dynamo.[114] Numerous fires were caused at Rotterdam as a result of the bombing and the plants and stores were considered to have been destroyed with reports of this nature being detailed in the *Daily Telegraph* under the headline 'RAF Defence of Dunkirk'.[115] Oil tanks at Ghent were also targeted by Beauforts of Coastal Command towards the latter part of Dynamo.[116] The impact Coastal Command's bombing of oil targets had directly on operations at Dunkirk was negligible. These attacks did, however, permit the squadrons of Bomber Command to be used against tactical targets to a greater extent than might otherwise have been possible and, therefore, contributed to the evacuation indirectly.

The main bombing contribution of the aircraft under Coastal Command's control came, however, against German positions in close proximity to the Dunkirk perimeter as well as at Calais whilst British forces were believed to be offering resistance there. As the Allied forces retreated towards Dunkirk aircraft of the FAA were despatched to bomb and delay pursuing German mechanized forces.[117] German artillery batteries which were covering the entrance of Calais were also heavily attacked in the period immediately before the start of Dynamo. Swordfish of 825 (FAA) Squadron dropped 6,000lb of explosives in one such bombing sortie.[118] As Dynamo commenced the units of the FAA played an important role in bombing German land positions near the coast which allowed Bomber Command to attack targets inland. At the time, these operations were reported as having been very successful and having made a positive contribution to the forces around Dunkirk. *The Times* reported on the 'series of heavy and effective attacks' undertaken by the FAA on 27 May against enemy positions on the French and Belgian coasts in which 'batteries and transports were destroyed by bombs and troops scattered by machine-gun fire'.[119] Batteries near Calais which had closed Route Z to shipping during daylight were successfully bombed and strafed. A concentration of German infantry was also bombed despite low cloud hampering visibility over the area.[120] This mission formed part of Operation Black Velvet; the Swordfish of the FAA, working in co-operation with Hawker Hectors of BAFF, were intended to distract any Luftwaffe fighters away from a supply drop at Calais by Westland Lysanders of 613 Squadron.[121] German troops at Calais complained that they had suffered heavy losses to air attacks on 27 May, which they believed were by their own ground-support aircraft but coincided with attacks of the Swordfish and Hectors.[122] The attacks of Coastal Command were part of the bombing effort that led Hermann Balck, in command of a mechanized regiment of 1. *Panzer-Division*, to recall that during the period of Dynamo they were bombed 'without interruption' and that as a result his 'command post building shook constantly'.[123] Air attacks were also recorded by 10. *Panzer-Division* who noted that, with their heavier Flak batteries on the coast at Calais, they lacked adequate anti-aircraft defences as they had only 2cm Flak batteries, which had not proved sufficient to prevent attacks.[124] Swordfish of 812 (FAA) Squadron also stood by for operations bombed up with 250lb bombs on both 26 May and 27 May but were ultimately not called on for operations on either occasion.[125] An offensive sortie by six Swordfish of 825 (FAA) Squadron was despatched to attack batteries near Dunkirk which had been reported as firing on shipping. Air Marshal Joubert – previously Commander-in-Chief Coastal Command (a post he returned to in 1941) and temporarily in control of the Air Component – BEF Rear-Headquarters (Back Violet) which directed air operations in support of the BEF until it was disbanded on 4 June – organized this attack direct with 16 Group without first consulting Coastal Command's staff.[126] The position identified was at Mardyck. The consequence of circumventing the staff at Coastal Command was that an attack was immediately made on a position, on the edge of the French perimeter, which would have represented an incredibly exposed position for a German battery. It seems probable that the target was not a German artillery battery but a French anti-aircraft position. At 17.30 it was learnt at Coastal Command that this was a 'French battery and they have NOT been firing at shipping' and frantic, but unsuccessful, efforts were made to recall the attack.[127] The six Swordfish arrived at their objective at 17.45 – encountering heavy and accurate anti-aircraft fire – and delivered a series of successful attack dropping 9,960lb of high explosives which destroyed the first battery, as well as some covered lorries nearby, and achieved similar success against a second battery.[128] In considering the attack Commander Robert Bower, Naval Liaison Officer to the AOC-in-C Coastal Command, grimly recorded that 'the worst seems highly probable'.[129] On 29 May an attack by ten Swordfish of 825 (FAA) Squadron did hit German positions to the south-east of Dunkirk but it was not very successful. The main target, a German artillery battery, was not located and attacks were instead made on a farmhouse in the vicinity – from which light anti-aircraft fire was observed – and an armoured vehicle was destroyed. The squadron lost five aircraft.[130] Other FAA missions undertaken against German positions around the Dunkirk perimeter did, however, have a positive impact. Nine Skuas of 801 (FAA) Squadron took off from RAF Hawkinge at 19.20 on 31 May to bomb suspected pontoon bridges over the Nieuport canal.[131] At 20.00, unable to observe any pontoons in the vicinity of the canal and with no troop movements or anti-aircraft fire seen, six of the Skuas dive-bombed a reinforced pier, on a small island on the canal near Nieuport, simultaneously the remaining three Skuas attacked two piers on the Nieuport foreshore. The attack on the small island resulted in a number of direct hits along the pier as well as on forty catamarans which were nearby.[132] Ronald Hay, who flew with 801 (FAA) Squadron on 31 May, later recalled the attack in rather less positive terms:

> There was a pontoon bridge over the canal at Nieuport ... and [the RAF] insisted that that was a suitable target for the Navy to deal with rather than dive-bombing a tank division in the field. ... We got to Nieuport ... there was the canal ... I suppose there was a bit of permanent roadway over it so we all had a go at that. Heaven knows whether we hit it or not.[133]

Two Skuas of 801 (FAA) Squadron were shot down by Me 109 on the return flight and a further Skua was disabled on landing.[134] The cost of 801 (FAA) Squadron's attack on 31 May was neither as high as those of 825 (FAA) Squadron's attack on 29 May nor as unproductive – the catamarans they bombed almost certainly being part of the German bridging effort at Nieuport. British positions on the east of the Dunkirk perimeter were under considerable pressure on 31 May and delays to German movements were important in this position being stabilized. Ten Skuas of 806 (FAA) Squadron were also despatched on 31 May to bomb road junctions at Westende in order to prevent forces being brought up to engage the British flank which ran through the sand dunes to the east of La Panne. The Skuas attacked from 2,000 feet and delivered a heavy bombload on the target; cars and troops near road junctions leading to Nieuport were hit as was a German staff car attended by two motorcycles. The Skuas also achieved a direct hit on two lorries 100 yards east of the road junction at Westende-Bain where a large red building was also demolished at the road junction. A further direct hit was registered on a large house and two more were scored on the coast road at the south-west end of the village of Middelkerke.[135] As the Skuas were leaving the target a 'particularly fierce explosion' was seen at Westende road junction on which there had been one direct hit with a further five bombs exploding in close proximity.[136] In addition to this attack on 31 May Albacores of 826 (FAA) Squadron attacked vehicle and troop concentrations – which were observed to be attempting to cut off Allied troops from Dunkirk – on crossroads to the East of Nieuport.[137] These attacks followed a bombing sortie in the same area by Blenheims of Bomber Command and helped to stabilize the British position on the Dunkirk perimeter on 31 May. Along with earlier strikes against artillery positions near Calais this was an important, if limited, contribution to the success of Dynamo.

Conclusion

Coastal Command's operations during Dynamo did contribute to the overall success of the evacuation of Allied forces from Dunkirk and the surrounding beaches. Coastal Command's air cover provided protection against low level attacks and in areas directly above the evacuation fleet. The squadrons of Coastal Command and the FAA intercepted and drove off a number of bombing attacks on the evacuation fleet during the course of Dynamo. The air cover provided by Coastal Command and the FAA ensured that Fighter Command was not required to maintain standing patrols at low-height over the evacuation. With Coastal Command and FAA squadrons providing low level cover Fighter Command was able to concentrate their fighter cover at higher altitudes. This reduced the opportunity for German fighters to gain the advantage of height over Fighter Command's patrol and improved their ability to intercept German bomber formations.

The bombing and minelaying missions conducted were less important to the success of Dynamo. Coastal Command's bombing of oil targets at Rotterdam and Ghent prevented squadrons of Bomber Command which were involved in tactical bombing being diverted to these tasks – this was, however, only a tangential impact on the success of the Dunkirk evacuation. The bombing of targets in the West Frisian Islands, and the mine-laying which occurred in the channels around them, achieved relatively little and flare reconnaissance operations also had only a limited impact to the outcome of Dynamo. Bombing missions in support of the perimeter achieved some success; however, these attacks were limited in the effect they had on the success of Dynamo.

The work of Coastal Command and the FAA in patrolling against the E-Boat threat was, however, of considerable importance to the success of Dynamo. Although the aircraft did not sink large numbers of E-Boats they consistently hampered their movements and prevented their operations. This was of considerable importance during the latter nights of Dynamo when evacuations were no longer being made during daylight. Had the E-Boats achieved any significant disruption or losses to the evacuations at night during this period the continuation of further embarkations might have been permanently suspended. The aircraft of Coastal Command made a definite contribution preventing E-Boats reaching their attack points and forcing them to suspend daylight operations. The German E-Boat commanders themselves acknowledged that on at least one occasion they had had to curtail their night mission due to the delays incurred as a result of British air operations designed to forestall their work and that further operations were dependant on the E-Boats being provided with sufficient air cover.[138] Coastal Command's operations against E-Boats represented an effective use and contribution of air power in a maritime environment; by delaying and at times denying E-Boats access to the approaches to Dunkirk Coastal Command reduced the vulnerability and enhanced the capabilities of Allied surface vessels involved in the evacuation.[139]

That Coastal Command and the FAA managed to execute the range of the tasks they accomplished, at the intensity they were required to operate at, was a valuable addition to the air defence of Operation Dynamo. Without their patrols against E-Boats the evacuation fleet would have had to provide greater naval forces to this responsibility, reducing the numbers available to embark troops, and would almost certainly have incurred greater losses.

Notes

1. IWM: Audio/31394 – Hoskin, Reel 1.
2. *The Times*, 'RAF's Great Help', 29 May 1940, p. 6.
3. TNA: AIR 15/898 – N.L.O. Log, 3 June 1940.
4. Lamb, *War*, p. 65.
5. TNA: ADM 199/115 – Lieutenant Commander Evans, Report on Operations of 806 Squadron, 27 May–3 June 1940; TNA: AIR 27/1222 – ORB: 206 Squadron; TNA: AIR 27/1365 – ORB: 220 Squadron.
6. TNA: AIR 22/168 – A.M.W.R. Daily Report for Summary, No. 316, 31 May 1940.
7. TNA: AIR 20/6260 – ORB: Directorate of Operations (Naval Co-Operation), May 1940; TNA: AIR 22/168 – A.M.W.R. Daily Report for Summary, No. 313, 28 May 1940.
8. TNA: AIR 22/168 – A.M.W.R. Daily Report for Summary, No. 315, 30 May 1940.
9. TNA: AIR 27/1365 – ORB: 220 Squadron.
10. IWM: Audio/11534 – Vincent-Jones, Reel 1; TNA: AIR 20/6260 – ORB: Directorate of Operations (Naval Co-Operation), May 1940; TNA: AIR 22/168 – A.M.W.R. Daily Report for Summary, No. 315, 30 May 1940.
11. TNA: ADM 199/115 – Lieutenant Commander Evans, Report on Operations of 806 Squadron, 27 May–3 June 1940.
12. TNA: AIR 22/168 – A.M.W.R. Daily Report for Summary, No. 316, 31 May 1940.
13. TNA: AIR 22/168 – A.M.W.R. Daily Report for Summary, No. 315, 30 May 1940; TNA: AIR 22/169 – A.M.W.R. Daily Report for Summary, No. 317, 1 June 1940; TNA: AIR 20/6260 – ORB: Directorate of Operations (Naval Co-Operation), May 1940; TNA: AIR 24/373 – ORB: Coastal Command, Narrative of Events, May–June 1940.
14. TNA: AIR 22/168 – A.M.W.R. Daily Report for Summary, No. 316, 31 May 1940; TNA: AIR 27/1365 – ORB: 220 Squadron.
15. TNA: ADM 199/115 – Lieutenant Commander Evans, Report on Operations of 806 Squadron, 27 May–3 June 1940; TNA: AIR 22/168 – A.M.W.R. Daily Report for Summary, No. 316, 31 May 1940.
16. TNA: AIR 22/169 – A.M.W.R. Daily Report for Summary, No. 317, 1 June 1940.
17. TNA: AIR 22/169 – A.M.W.R. Daily Report for Summary, No. 317–18, 1–2 June 1940.
18. TNA: AIR 27/1514 – ORB: 254 Squadron.
19. TNA: AIR 22/169 – A.M.W.R. Daily Report for Summary, No. 318, 2 June 1940; TNA: AIR 24/373 – ORB: Coastal Command, Narrative of Events, June 1940.
20. TNA: AIR 20/6260 – ORB: Directorate of Operations (Naval Co-Operation), June 1940; TNA: AIR 22/169 – A.M.W.R. Daily Report for Summary, No. 318, 2 June 1940; TNA: AIR 24/373 – ORB: Coastal Command, Narrative of Events, June 1940; TNA: AIR 27/1514 – ORB: 254 Squadron.

21 TNA: AIR 22/169 – A.M.W.R. Daily Report for Summary, No. 319, 3 June 1940; TNA: AIR 24/373 – ORB: Coastal Command, Narrative of Events, June 1940; TNA: AIR 27/1365 – ORB: 220 Squadron.
22 TNA: AIR 15/758 – Air Marshal Bowhill, Review of Operational Work in Coastal Command, June 1940; TNA: AIR 22/169 – A.M.W.R. Daily Report for Summary, No. 319, 3 June 1940.
23 TNA: AIR 22/169 – A.M.W.R. Daily Report for Summary, No. 319, 3 June 1940; TNA: AIR 24/373 – ORB: Coastal Command, Narrative of Events, June 1940.
24 TNA: AIR 25/314 – Appendices to ORB: 16 Group, Narrative for 2 June 1940; TNA: AIR 25/314 – Appendices to ORB: 16 Group, CH/G3/2/6, 16 Group Order for Air Protection to Squadrons at Bircham Newton and Detling, 2 June 1940.
25 TNA: ADM 199/115 – Lieutenant Commander Evans, Report on Operations of 806 Squadron, 27 May–3 June 1940; TNA: ADM 199/790 – Commanding Officer HMS Calcutta, Report on Operations Connected to the Evacuation of the BEF from the Dunkirk Area; TNA: AIR 20/6260 – ORB: Directorate of Operations (Naval Co-Operation), June 1940; TNA: AIR 22/169 – A.M.W.R. Daily Report for Summary, No. 319, 3 June 1940; TNA: AIR 25/314 – Appendices to ORB: 16 Group, Narrative for 2 June 1940.
26 TNA: AIR 22/168 – A.M.W.R. Daily Report for Summary, No. 314, 29 May 1940; TNA: AIR 27/1941 – ORB: 500 Squadron.
27 TNA: AIR 22/168 – A.M.W.R. Daily Report for Summary, No. 315, 30 May 1940; TNA: AIR 27/1941 – ORB: 500 Squadron.
28 TNA: AIR 22/169 – A.M.W.R. Daily Report for Summary, No. 317, 1 June 1940 TNA: AIR 27/1941 – ORB: 500 Squadron.
29 TNA: AIR 22/169 – A.M.W.R. Daily Report for Summary, No. 318, 2 June 1940.
30 TNA: ADM 199/792 – Report of Vice Admiral Ramsay; TNA: ADM 199/2206 – Naval War Diary Summaries, 1 June 1940; Goodeve, 'The Defeat of the Magnetic Mine'.
31 TNA: AIR 22/168 – A.M.W.R. Daily Report for Summary, No. 316, 31 May 1940.
32 TNA: AIR 22/169 – A.M.W.R. Daily Report for Summary, No. 317, 1 June 1940.
33 Development, Concept and Doctrine Centre, *Joint Defence Publication 0-30*, p. 4.
34 TNA: ADM 223/29 – Naval Staff Director of Training and Staff Duties Division, Minutes of Meeting Considering Measures Against MTBs, 31 May 1940; TNA: ADM 223/29 – Lürssen Shipyard, 'General Remarks about Lürssen Motor Torpedo Boats: Motor Torpedo Boat 40', 30 May–1 June 1940.
35 TNA: ADM 223/621 – GC&CS German Naval Section, Z-No. 151, Intelligence Report on German Schnellboote, 7 July 1940.
36 TNA: ADM 199/2205 – Naval War Diary Summaries, Enemy MTBS: Message to Coastal Command Headquarters Requesting 806 Squadron Provide Striking Force Against E-Boats, 27 May 1940; TNA: AIR 15/897 – N.L.O. Log, 27 May 1940.

37 TNA: ADM 199/2205 – Naval War Diary Summaries, Continuing German MTB Attacks: Message from C-in-C The Nore Regarding Counter-Measures, 29 May 1940.
38 TNA: ADM 223/29 – Report of HMS Shearwater Night of 26 May 1940.
39 TNA: ADM 199/2205 – Naval War Diary Summaries, Continuing German MTB Attacks: Message from C-in-C The Nore Regarding Counter-Measures, 29 May 1940; TNA: ADM 223/29 – Naval Staff Director of Training and Staff Duties Division, Minutes of Meeting Considering Measures against MTBs, 31 May 1940.
40 TNA: ADM 199/360 – Dover Command: War Diaries, General Appreciation for Period 16–31 May 1940.
41 USNWC: Microfilm 354/Part A/Vol. 9 – Kriegstagebuch der Seekriegsleitung, 28 May 1940.
42 TNA: ADM 199/788A – Lieutenant Commander de Toulouse-Lautier, Commanding Officer Sirocco, Report on the Sinking of FS Sirocco, 31 May 1940; USNWC: Microfilm 354/Part A/Vol. 10 – Kriegstagebuch der Seekriegsleitung, 1 June1940.
43 TNA: ADM 199/788A – Lieutenant Commander de Toulouse-Lautier, Commanding Officer Sirocco, Report on the Sinking of FS Sirocco, 31 May 1940.
44 TNA: ADM 199/360 – Dover Command: War Diaries, General Appreciation for Period 16–31 May 1940; TNA: ADM 199/2205 – Naval War Diary Summaries, Enemy Air Activity Work with MTBs: Message from C-in-C The Nore Regarding E-Boat Co-operation with Low Flying Aircraft, 31 May 1940.
45 TNA: ADM 199/2205 – Naval War Diary Summaries, Continuing German MTB Attacks, Message from C-in-C The Nore Regarding Counter-Measures, 29 May 1940; TNA: ADM 223/29 – Naval Staff Director of Training and Staff Duties Division, Minutes of Meeting Considering Measures against MTBs, 31 May 1940; Hendrie, *Cinderella Service*, p. 174.
46 TNA: ADM 223/29 – Naval Staff Director of Training and Staff Duties Division, Minutes of Meeting Considering Measures Against MTBs, 31 May 1940.
47 TNA: AIR 27/1941 – ORB: 500 Squadron; Hendrie, *Cinderella Service*, p. 174.
48 TNA: ADM 223/29 – Naval Intelligence Division and OIC, Short Appreciation of German S-Boats, c. May 1940; TNA: AIR 22/169 – A.M.W.R. Daily Report for Summary, No. 320, 4 June 1940.
49 TNA: ADM 223/29 – Naval Staff Director of Training and Staff Duties Division, Minutes of Meeting Considering Measures Against MTBs, 31 May 1940.
50 *Ibid.*
51 TNA: ADM 199/2206 – C-in-C Home Fleet to Admiralty, 1 June 1940.
52 TNA: ADM 223/29 – Naval Staff Director of Training and Staff Duties Division, Minutes of Meeting Considering Measures Against MTBs, 31 May 1940; TNA: ADM 199/2205 – Naval War Diary Summaries, Continuing German MTB Attacks: Message from C-in-C The Nore Regarding Counter-Measures, 29 May 1940.

53 TNA: ADM 223/29 – Naval Staff Director of Training and Staff Duties Division, Minutes of Meeting Considering Measures Against MTBs, 31 May 1940.
54 TNA: ADM 223/28 – War Diary of *Führer der Torpedoboote*; USNWC: Microfilm 354/Part A/Vol. 10 – Kriegstagebuch der Seekriegsleitung, June 1940.
55 *Ibid.*
56 TNA: ADM 223/28 – War Diary of *Führer der Torpedoboote*.
57 *Ibid.*
58 USNWC: Microfilm 354/Part A/Vol. 9 – Kriegstagebuch der Seekriegsleitung, May 1940.
59 TNA: AIR 27/1941 – ORB: 500 Squadron.
60 TNA: AIR 22/168 – A.M.W.R. Daily Report for Summary, No. 312, 27 May 1940; TNA: AIR 27/1941 – ORB: 500 Squadron.
61 TNA: AIR 20/6260 – ORB: Directorate of Operations (Naval Co-Operation), May 1940; TNA: AIR 22/168 – A.M.W.R. Daily Report for Summary, No. 313, 28 May 1940; TNA: AIR 27/1941 – ORB: 500 Squadron.
62 TNA: AIR 22/168 – A.M.W.R. Daily Report for Summary, No. 314, 29 May 1940; TNA: AIR 27/1941 – ORB: 500 Squadron.
63 *Ibid.*
64 TNA: AIR 22/168 – A.M.W.R. Daily Reports for Summary Nos. 312–13, 27–28 May 1940; TNA: AIR 27/1941 – ORB: 500 Squadron.
65 TNA: AIR 20/6260 – ORB: Directorate of Operations (Naval Co-Operation), May 1940; TNA: AIR 22/168 – A.M.W.R. Daily Reports for Summary Nos. 312, 315, 27 May, 30 May 1940; TNA: AIR 27/1941 – ORB: 500 Squadron.
66 TNA: AIR 22/169 – A.M.W.R. Daily Reports for Summary Nos. 317–19, 1–3 June 1940; TNA: AIR 27/1941 – ORB: 500 Squadron.
67 TNA: AIR 20/6260 – ORB: Directorate of Operations (Naval Co-Operation), May 1940; TNA: AIR 22/168 – A.M.W.R. Daily Report for Summary, No. 313, 28 May 1940; TNA: AIR 27/1365 – ORB: 220 Squadron.
68 TNA: AIR 22/168 – A.M.W.R. Daily Report for Summary, No. 314, 29 May 1940; TNA: AIR 27/1365 – ORB: 220 Squadron.
69 TNA: AIR 22/168 – A.M.W.R. Daily Report for Summary, No. 315, 30 May 1940; TNA: AIR 27/1365 – ORB: 220 Squadron.
70 AIR 27/1222 – ORB: 206 Squadron; TNA: AIR 27/1365 – ORB: 220 Squadron.
71 TNA: AIR 20/6260 – ORB: Directorate of Operations (Naval Co-Operation), May 1940; TNA: AIR 22/169 – A.M.W.R. Daily Report for Summary, No. 318, 2 June 1940; TNA: AIR 27/1365 – ORB: 220 Squadron.
72 TNA: AIR 22/169 – A.M.W.R. Daily Report for Summary, No. 318, 2 June 1940.
73 TNA: AIR 20/6260 – ORB: Directorate of Operations (Naval Co-Operation), June 1940; TNA: AIR 22/169 – A.M.W.R. Daily Report for Summary, No. 319, 3 June 1940; AIR 27/1430 – ORB: 233 Squadron.

74 TNA: AIR 22/169 – A.M.W.R. Daily Report for Summary, No. 319, 3 June 1940.
75 TNA: AIR 20/6260 – ORB: Directorate of Operations (Naval Co-Operation), June 1940; TNA: AIR 22/169 – A.M.W.R. Daily Report for Summary, No. 320, 4 June 1940; TNA: AIR 27/1365 – ORB: 220 Squadron.
76 TNA: AIR 22/169 – A.M.W.R. Daily Report for Summary, No. 320, 4 June 1940.
77 TNA: ADM 223/28 – War Diary of *Führer der Torpedoboote*; USNWC: Microfilm 354/Part A/Vol. 10 – Kriegstagebuch der Seekriegsleitung, June 1940.
78 TNA: ADM 223/28 – War Diary of *Führer der Torpedoboote*.
79 TNA: ADM 199/115 – Commanding Officer 815 Squadron, Monthly Progress Report, 5 June 1940; TNA: ADM 199/115 – Temporary Commanding Officer 825 Squadron, Report on Operations Whilst Attached to Coastal Command, 11 June 1940; TNA: AIR 22/168 – A.M.W.R. Daily Report for Summary, No. 314, 29 May 1940.
80 TNA: AIR 22/168 – A.M.W.R. Daily Report for Summary, No. 315, 30 May 1940; TNA: AIR 27/278 – ORB: 22 Squadron.
81 TNA: ADM 207/22 – FAA 826 Squadron Diary; TNA: ADM 207/23 – FAA 826 Squadron Diary (Operational History).
82 TNA: ADM 207/13 – FAA 815 Squadron Diary; TNA: AIR 22/169 – A.M.W.R. Daily Report for Summary, No. 318, 2 June 1940.
83 TNA: AIR 20/6260 – ORB: Directorate of Operations (Naval Co-Operation), June 1940; TNA: AIR 22/169 – A.M.W.R. Daily Report for Summary, No. 319, 3 June 1940.
84 TNA: AIR 20/6260 – ORB: Directorate of Operations (Naval Co-Operation), June 1940; TNA: AIR 22/169 – A.M.W.R. Daily Report for Summary, No. 319, 3 June 1940; TNA: AIR 27/278 – ORB: 22 Squadron.
85 USNWC: Microfilm 354/Part A/Vol. 10 – Kriegstagebuch der Seekriegsleitung, June 1940.
86 TNA: AIR 15/897 – N.L.O. Log, 27 May 1940.
87 TNA: ADM 199/115 – Commanding Officer 815 Squadron, Monthly Progress Report, 5 June 1940; TNA: ADM 207/13 – FAA 815 Squadron Diary; TNA: AIR 20/6260 – ORB: Directorate of Operations (Naval Co-Operation), May–June 1940; TNA: AIR 22/168 – A.M.W.R. Daily Report for Summary, No. 315, 30 May 1940; TNA: AIR 22/169 – A.M.W.R. Daily Reports for Summary, No. 317–18, 1–2 June 1940; TNA: AIR 24/373 – ORB: Coastal Command, Narrative of Events, June 1940.
88 TNA: ADM 223/29 – Naval Staff Director of Training and Staff Duties Division, Minutes of Meeting Considering Measures Against MTBs, 31 May 1940; TNA: AIR 20/6260 – ORB: Directorate of Operations (Naval Co-Operation), June 1940; Colin Sinot, *The RAF and Aircraft Design: Air Staff Operational Requirements, 1923–1939* (London: Routledge, 2013), p. 171.

89 TNA: AIR 20/6260 – ORB: Directorate of Operations (Naval Co-Operation), May 1940.
90 TNA: AIR 22/168 – A.M.W.R. Daily Report for Summary, No. 311, 26 May 1940; TNA: AIR 27/278 – ORB: 22 Squadron.
91 TNA: ADM 199/115 – Commanding Officer 812 Squadron, Summary of Operations Carried out by 812 Squadron, 11 June 1940; TNA: AIR 22/169 – A.M.W.R. Daily Reports for Summary Nos. 317–20, 1–4 June 1940.
92 TNA: AIR 20/6260 – ORB: Directorate of Operations (Naval Co-Operation), May 1940.
93 TNA: ADM 223/29 – Naval Staff Director of Training and Staff Duties Division, Minutes of Meeting Considering Measures Against MTBs, 31 May 1940.
94 TNA: ADM 199/115 – Commanding Officer 801 Squadron, Monthly Letter of Proceedings, 13 June 1940.
95 TNA: ADM 223/28 – War Diary of *Führer der Torpedoboote*; TNA: ADM 223/29 – Photograph Taken during Bombing of Boulogne Harbour, 12 June 1940.
96 TNA: AIR 15/203 – Headquarters 17 Group, Report on Towing of Flare Targets during Period 30 May–3 June 1940, 11 June 1940.
97 IWM: Audio/28766 – Tuke, Reel 2; TNA: ADM 223/29 – Naval Staff Director of Training and Staff Duties Division, Minutes of Meeting Considering Measures Against MTBs, 31 May 1940; TNA: AIR 22/169 – A.M.W.R. Daily Report for Summary, No. 320, 4 June 1940.
98 TNA: ADM 223/29 – Naval Staff Director of Training and Staff Duties Division, Minutes of Meeting Considering Measures Against MTBs, 31 May 1940.
99 TNA: AIR 22/169 – A.M.W.R. Daily Reports for Summary Nos. 317–20, 1–4 June 1940; TNA: AIR 24/373 – ORB: Coastal Command, Narrative of Events, June 1940.
100 TNA: ADM 223/28 – War Diary of *Führer der Torpedoboote*; TNA: AIR 15/203 – Report on Towing of Flare Targets, 11 June 1940; USNWC: Microfilm 354/Part A/ Vol. 9 – Kriegstagebuch der Seekriegsleitung, May 1940.
101 IWM: Audio/28766 – Tuke, Reel 2; TNA: ADM 223/29 – Naval Staff Director of Training and Staff Duties Division, Minutes of Meeting Considering Measures Against MTBs, 31 May 1940; TNA: AIR 22/169 – A.M.W.R. Daily Report for Summary, No. 320, 4 June 1940.
102 TNA: AIR 20/6260 – ORB: Directorate of Operations (Naval Co-Operation), June 1940; TNA: AIR 22/169 – A.M.W.R. Daily Report for Summary, No. 318, 2 June 1940.
103 TNA: ADM 199/115 – Commanding Officer 826 Squadron, Report of Proceedings 7 May to 7 June, 10 June 1940; TNA: AIR 22/169 – A.M.W.R. Daily Report for Summary, No. 318, 2 June 1940.
104 TNA: AIR 22/169 – A.M.W.R. Daily Report for Summary, No. 319–20, 3–4 June 1940.
105 *Ibid.*

106 Axel Niestlé, *German U-Boat Losses during World War II: Details of Destruction* (London: Frontline, 2014), p. 34.
107 TNA: AIR 15/897 – N.L.O. Log, 26 May 1940; TNA: AIR 25/314 – Appendices to ORB: 16 Group, Narrative for 25 May 1940.
108 USNWC: Microfilm 354/Part A/Vol. 9 – Kriegstagebuch der Seekriegsleitung, May 1940; USNWC: Microfilm 354/Part A/Vol. 10 – Kriegstagebuch der Seekriegsleitung, June 1940.
109 TNA: AIR 22/168 – A.M.W.R. Daily Report for Summary Nos. 311–16, 26–31 May 1940.
110 TNA: AIR 22/168 – A.M.W.R. Daily Report for Summary Nos. 311–16, 26–31 May 1940; TNA: AIR 22/169 – A.M.W.R. Daily Reports for Summary Nos. 317–20, 1–4 June 1940.
111 TNA: AIR 22/168 – A.M.W.R. Daily Report for Summary, No. 313, 28 May 1940.
112 *Ibid.*, No. 314, 29 May 1940.
113 TNA: AIR 20/6260 – ORB: Directorate of Operations (Naval Co-Operation), May–June 1940; TNA: AIR 24/373 – ORB: Coastal Command, Narrative of Events, May–June 1940; TNA: AIR 25/313 – Appendices to ORB: 16 Group, Narrative for May 1940; TNA: AIR 25/314 – Appendices to ORB: 16 Group, Narrative for June 1940.
114 TNA: AIR 15/758 – Air Marshal Bowhill, Review of Operational Work in Coastal Command, May–June 1940; TNA: AIR 20/6260 – ORB: Directorate of Operations (Naval Co-Operation), May–June 1940; TNA: AIR 22/168 – A.M.W.R. Daily Reports for Summary Nos. 311–12, 26–27 May 1940; TNA: AIR 22/169 – A.M.W.R. Daily Reports for Summary Nos. 318, 320, 2 June, 4 June 1940; TNA: AIR 24/373 – ORB: Coastal Command, Narrative of Events, June 1940; TNA: AIR 27/1365 – ORB: 220 Squadron.
115 *Daily Telegraph*, 'RAF Defence of Dunkirk', 3 June 1940, p. 3; TNA: AIR 20/6260 – ORB: Directorate of Operations (Naval Co-Operation), June 1940.
116 TNA: AIR 20/6260 – ORB: Directorate of Operations (Naval Co-Operation), June 1940; TNA: AIR 22/169 – A.M.W.R. Daily Reports for Summary Nos. 318–20, 2–4 June 1940.
117 TNA: ADM 199/115 – Commanding Officer 812 Squadron, Summary of Operations.
118 TNA: AIR 22/168 – A.M.W.R. Daily Reports for Summary Nos. 310–11, 25–6 May 1940.
119 *The Times*, 'RAF's Great Help', 29 May 1940, p. 6.
120 TNA: AIR 15/897 – N.L.O. Log, 27 May 1940. TNA: AIR 20/6260 – ORB: Directorate of Operations (Naval Co-Operation), May 1940; TNA: AIR 22/168 – A.M.W.R. Daily Report for Summary, No. 313, 28 May 1940.
121 TNA: AIR 27/2117 – ORB: 613 Squadron.

122 TNA: HW 5/2 – GC&CS Decrypts, CX/JQ/2.
123 Hermann Balck, *The Memoirs of General of Panzer Troops Hermann Balck: Order in Chaos* (Lawrence, KS: University Press of Kentucky, 2015), p. 182.
124 IWM: EDS/AL/1399 – 10. *Panzer-Division*, Extract from War Diary, 27 May 1940.
125 TNA: ADM 199/115 – Commanding Officer 812 Squadron, Summary of Operations.
126 TNA: AIR 15/897 – N.L.O. Log, 27 May 1940; TNA: AIR 35/308 – Back Violet: Operational Diary, 26–27 May.
127 TNA: AIR 15/897 – N.L.O. Log, 27 May 1940.
128 TNA: AIR 20/6260 – ORB: Directorate of Operations (Naval Co-Operation), May 1940; TNA: AIR 22/168 – A.M.W.R. Daily Report for Summary, No. 313, 28 May 1940.
129 TNA: AIR 15/897 – N.L.O. Log, 27 May 1940.
130 TNA: ADM 199/115 – Temporary Commanding Officer 825 Squadron, Report on Operations Whilst Attached to Coastal Command, 11 June 1940; TNA: AIR 20/6260 – ORB: Directorate of Operations (Naval Co-Operation), May 1940; TNA: AIR 22/168 – A.M.W.R. Daily Report for Summary, No. 315–17, 30 May–1 June 1940.
131 TNA: AIR 22/169 – A.M.W.R. Daily Report for Summary, No. 317–18, 1–2 June 1940; TNA: ADM 199/115 – Commanding Officer 801 Squadron, Monthly Letter of Proceedings, 13 June 1940.
132 TNA: AIR 22/169 – A.M.W.R. Daily Report for Summary, No. 318, 2 June 1940.
133 IWM: Audio/13856 – Ronald Cuthbert Hay, Reels 1–2.
134 TNA: ADM 199/115 – Commanding Officer 801 Squadron, Monthly Letter of Proceedings, 13 June 1940; TNA: AIR 22/169 – A.M.W.R. Daily Report for Summary, No. 318, 2 June 1940; TNA: AIR 24/373 – ORB: Coastal Command, Narrative of Events, June 1940.
135 TNA: AIR 22/169 – A.M.W.R. Daily Report for Summary, No. 317, 1 June 1940.
136 TNA: AIR 20/6260 – ORB: Directorate of Operations (Naval Co-Operation), May 1940; TNA: AIR 22/169 – A.M.W.R. Daily Report for Summary, No. 317, 1 Jun. 1940.
137 IWM: Audio/28766 – Tuke, Reel 2; TNA: ADM 207/22 – FAA 826 Squadron Diary; TNA: ADM 207/23 – FAA 826 Squadron Diary (Operational History); TNA: AIR 22/169 – A.M.W.R. Daily Report for Summary, No. 317, 1 Jun. 1940.
138 TNA: ADM 223/28 – War Diary of *Führer der Torpedoboote*; USNWC: Microfilm 354/Part A/Vol. 10 – Kriegstagebuch der Seekriegsleitung, Jun. 1940.
139 Development, Concept and Doctrine Centre, *Joint Defence Publication 0-30*, pp. 34, 51–3.

9

The operations of Bomber Command

Operation Dynamo represented a period of intense activity for Bomber Command which conducted 1,015 bombing sorties between 26 May and 3 June.[1] In addition to the direct support that Bomber Command provided to the Allied Armies, the other objects of Bomber Command's air strikes included the dislocation of the transport system in Western Germany, the disruption of vital German war industries and the destruction of German oil targets.[2] The total tons of bombs dropped by Bomber Command during Dynamo accounted for 23 per cent of the total dropped from 10 May, the start of the German invasion, to 14 June, when Paris was captured and Bomber Command's operations virtually stopped for two days – considering only daylight missions during this same period the percentage of tons dropped during Dynamo increases to 33 per cent.[3] Indeed, the figure for the number of tons dropped during Dynamo would have been higher if the prevailing weather conditions had permitted the unrestricted use of the night bomber force.[4] This chapter explores the results that Bomber Command claimed to have achieved, the extent to which their attacks delayed German forces and the effect on the evacuation – particularly on the Allied withdrawal to, and subsequent defence of, the Dunkirk perimeter.

The majority of Bomber Command's missions during Dynamo were directed against targets they believed could influence the land battle through either close air support or air interdiction; daylight attacks, by Blenheims of 2 Group, were an important part of this effort (see Figure 4). Despite this, the interdiction and close-support missions undertaken by Bomber Command during Dynamo have been considered to have had a relatively limited effect.[5] Critics of the results achieved by tactical bombing during this period included those involved in the attacks. Air Commodore James Robb, AOC 2 Group, was largely critical of the attempts to delay enemy movements, arguing that:

> It is doubtful whether this group is getting adequate return for its effort. On several occasions I have felt sure that whilst we may have destroyed a few lorries or a few tanks, the actual results in holding up the enemy has been negligible.[6]

Wing Commander Basil Embry, who escaped from German captivity and witnessed the effect of British bombing on German positions, believed that whilst columns were 'sometimes delayed and no doubt extensive damage was done, the effect of the bombing was usually very local'.[7] The damage to roads that Embry witnessed was frequently of a superficial nature requiring little work, material or time to effect repairs.[8] Bomber crews involved in the attacks complained during Dynamo that orders to attack a named crossroad if road movements could not be seen were 'a waste of time and effort' for 'had the bombs hit the crossroads no damage could have resulted'.[9] These targets were not as vulnerable as might be considered, partly because the bombs dropped were frequently not big enough to create craters of sufficient size to make the road impassable.[10] Embry also noted that as the bombing took place on open roads the movement of German vehicles, whether combat or supply transports, was often only temporarily delayed with the damaged portion of the road or wrecked vehicles merely requiring small detours before regular progress could be resumed.[11]

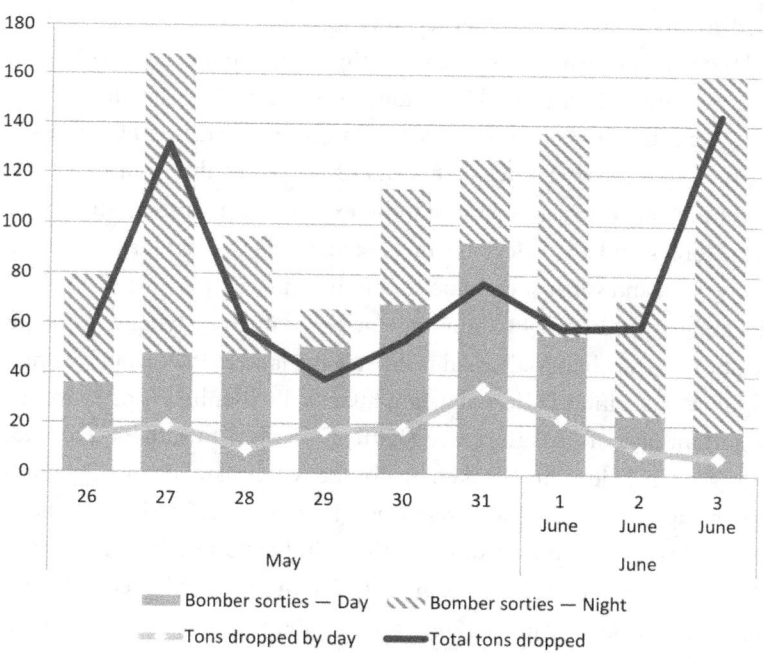

Figure 4 Bomber sorties despatched [Left Axis] and bomb tons dropped [Right Axis].[12]

Nevertheless, it will be shown that Bomber Command's attacks were important in the context of Operation Dynamo. The situation at Dunkirk was exceptional in that small delays, both to supplies and the movement of troops, could have a pronounced effect. Despite the consolidation of their supply position the German forces were still not well insulated from attacks which caused delays to their logistics system. Preparations for further offensive action against French forces on the Somme, as part of *Fall Rot*, increasingly occupied the German rear services.[13] Maintaining the supply position of the forces which had encircled the Allies on the coast, already at the end of a long supply line, as well as the German forces at Lille and those on the Somme was complicated.[14] Leonard Fearnley, of 107 Squadron, recalled the object of these attacks 'was to delay the enemy advance … and stop the supplies getting through, like the petrol, and the tanks and the howitzers'.[15] The destruction of many of the bridges leading up to the advanced German positions, the congested roads immediately behind them and the damaged railways were severely retarding the German supply situation.[16] Furthermore, at the outset of Operation Dynamo, German forces were still in close contact with Allied troops withdrawing into the Dunkirk perimeter. These conditions meant that temporary delays and respites produced by Bomber Command interdicting both supplies and German forces were of greater importance in maintaining the Dunkirk perimeter, and allowing further troops to withdraw into it, than might otherwise have been the case. It is in this context that Bomber Command's missions in direct support of Dynamo must be considered.

Having examined the attacks made by 2 Group this chapter will consider the effort made by the Wellingtons, Armstrong Whitworth Whitleys and Handley Page Hampdens – of 3, 4 and 5 Groups – to disrupt the German military lines of communication and their attacks against other tactical targets.[17] Night bombing in tactical support of the Allied Armies was in part directed against objectives in the enemy forward area and part against German communications farther back in France, Belgium and the Rhineland.[18] Attacks on marshalling yards in North-West Germany were principally intended to interfere with German communication systems and disrupt the movement of supplies and reinforcements towards the frontline. These air interdict missions are considered alongside Bomber Command's tactical bombing because they were ultimately intended to have an effect on the battlefield.

The missions against German movements and supplies in France and Belgium became the subject of considerable criticism from figures within Bomber Command itself. Air Marshal Charles Portal, AOC Bomber Command, considered the use of Bomber Command's resources as a misemployment of the strategic striking force and saw the use of night bombers in the direct support role 'as none other than a prostitution of its true function'.[19] Air Vice-Marshall Arthur Harris, AOC 5 Group, reported to Portal that his Group's aircraft were employed in a role 'for which they are fundamentally unsuitable', that involved 'considerable loss of effort' and that 'even unlimited experience in night operations is unlikely to increase the proportion of successful attacks against targets such as roads, railway bridges, road crossings and the like'.[20] Harris would repeat this criticism after the war arguing that the bombers were 'misdirected to the task of blocking enemy communications' which for his Hampden crews typically involved 'attempting to push down houses ... [and] to block important crossroads'.[21] Harris considered this task 'impracticable' given the Hampden's bomb load and lack of navigation aids and he criticized the 'considerable waste of effort' stating that 'although the damage was higher than anticipated, operations of this nature are a misemployment of heavy bomber aircraft'.[22] Air Commodore Arthur Conigham, AOC 4 Group, reported that in close support of land forces 'it is inevitable that targets will be extremely difficult to find and will generally be relatively unprofitable as targets for our type of aircraft'.[23] Portal himself recounts in his despatch on the operations in France that the switch to strategic targets 'was welcomed by all as it was felt that at long last our bomber force was fulfilling its true role'.[24] The subsequent decision, in the face of further collapse by the Allied land forces, to provide yet more tactical air support led, in Portal's opinion, to 'the necessity of misemploying our strategical striking force by attempting to attack by night targets that were difficult to identify and, which if destroyed, probably had little effect on the general campaign'.[25]

Such criticism of tactical bombing by Bomber Command's senior officers suggests the attacks were considered of little value. It is necessary to note, however, that much of this criticism was made because the targets were tactical and not strategic. The criticism was, at least in part, a means of ensuring the future strategic use of the force and not its further 'prostitution' fulfilling the role of 'field artillery'.[26] Portal's despatch was, in essence, the foundation of future arguments against the dilution of the strategic force and for refuting the value of an enlarged army co-operation force created at its expense. In it he argued that to sufficiently bomb targets in direct support of the army would require a bomber specifically designed for such work 'in numbers that would take up the greater part of the aircraft industry in their production'.[27] Even then, however, Portal argued that, unless these units were immediately available in positions in direct contact with frontline units, little value would be gained from their attacks. The need to provide support for Allied land forces in France frustrated the constant wish of the Air Staff that Bomber Command should be allowed to concentrate against strategic industrial targets in Germany, in particular the bombing of German oil targets.[28] Arguments that tactical missions had been of less value than if the effort had been expended elsewhere also allowed Bomber Command to argue that, had they been permitted to pursue the 'true role' of strategic bombing, they could have achieved substantial results.[29]

This chapter will conclude by assessing what contribution strategic bombing made, if any, to the evacuation of Dunkirk given that figures both within Bomber Command and across the RAF felt that the bombing effort should be directed against strategic targets. In part it was believed Bomber Command should be used in a strategic role because, in the words of Group Captain John Baker – Deputy Director of Plans – this met the RAF's 'primary aim' of destroying Germany's vital industrial objectives.[30] Baker also argued in favour of strategic bombing, however, because the 'most critical feature of the present operations in France is their domination by the German Air Force' and that strategic bombing might divert the Luftwaffe to attack on targets in England 'thus relieving the pressure on the Allied armies'.[31] Arguments against the deployment of the Command's efforts against the forces of the German Army, logistical targets and interdiction objectives likely to slow the German advance were not just made by figures within Bomber Command. On 14 May Dowding had called for 'an immediate assumption of the air offensive against Germany, and particularly her oil supplies' which he felt as well as having an influence on German land forces 'might serve to slow up the intensity of the enemy's air operations'.[32] Ten days later Dowding renewed his calls for strategic air attacks on Germany:

> I would ask that the efforts of the bomber force may be expended mainly or exclusively on objectives which will slow up the impetus of the German air attack. Damage done to crossroads or railway siding is very quickly repaired, but damage done to enemy aerodromes and aircraft on the ground will have an immediate effect, while the destruction of industrial plant and oil stocks will have an effect which, though slower, may prove to be decisive.[33]

On 17 May Portal argued that 'apart from the material and morale damage inflicted' the 'bombing of vital military objectives in the Ruhr' would force the 'withdrawal of enemy fighters for the protection of the back areas in Germany, making it easier for our fighters to deal with enemy bombers on the battle front'.[34] Portal also believed that it would force the withdrawal of anti-aircraft units from positions near the frontline for the protection of targets in Germany.

Portal noted that anti-aircraft had been 'very effective by day and night at the front but has proved practically useless in protecting objectives in the back area, which can be bombed from medium height'.[35] It is therefore important to consider whether Bomber Command's strategic mission achieved an operational effect during Dunkirk either by diverting a proportion of the Luftwaffe's bomber forces against Britain or by forcing German fighters to be recalled to provide for the defence of the areas attacked – thereby reducing German air superiority over France.[36]

Tactical bombing during daylight

Blenheims of 2 Group, bombing by day, were an important part of Bomber Command's attempts to support the evacuation. On 25 May, 2 Group issued instructions to its Squadrons as to the nature of the situation they faced:

> Examination of photographs shows very important targets and of such a size, which if attacked effectively could not fail to materially assist the situation on the ground. … the critical situation of the BEF in Northern France and Belgium [means] it is essential that all our attacks are pressed home with vigour.[37]

The primary objective of daylight operations varied at different points of the Dunkirk evacuation; however, the attacks aimed to disorganize, and cause the maximum interference to, the enemy's lines of communication and logistics network and were maintained throughout Dynamo.[38] The number of operations 2 Group was able to make was in part limited by a shortage of information and intelligence upon which to act. Robb reported that:

> The difficulty in keeping up a continuous attack was the absence of information until middle morning consequently the turn around to make two sorties each day by each squadron would have involved a rush for rearming. If therefore squadrons may be called upon to make such an effort in the future it is essential that squadrons begin operating early and continue throughout the day.[39]

One of the criticisms made by Bomber Command's crews during Dynamo was that they were often stood by awaiting orders for further sorties against targets which were known and could be attacked profitably but that they were not promptly despatched.[40] As a result, the number of sorties they were able to undertake was restricted, despite the short distances to the targets being attacked meaning crews could have maintained an effort of two sorties a day. In the case of 2 Group the number of sorties made only exceeded the number of aircraft operationally available on one day between 26 May and 3 June (see Table 9). This was on 31 May when 2 Group carried out more sorties than on any other previous day in the war and did so without loss.[41] Nonetheless, attacks by 2 Group in support of Dynamo did contribute to the success of the Allied withdrawal to, and evacuation from, Dunkirk.

On 26 and 27 May Blenheims of 2 Group made significant attacks on the German advance to provide relief to the Allied withdrawal. The German advance from Courtrai was considered to be one of the main threats to the withdrawal of the BEF.[43] During the morning of 26 May German troops and transports crossing the River Lys were targeted by eighteen Blenheims with the bombing intended to coincide with a heavy German attack. A number of bridges over the Lys had been demolished during the Allied withdrawal and attacks against those which remained, and pontoon bridges which had been erected, had the opportunity to delay the German advance.[44] The Blenheims claimed direct hits on pontoon bridges north-east of Menin and between Harlebeke and Courtrai, where roads and a stationary column were also attacked. Between Harlebeke and Courtrai one bridge was straddled by bombs and at three more bridges bombs were observed to hit surrounding buildings, roads and railway lines. Direct hits were claimed on the main Courtrai-Harlebeke road, on a road and railway bridge to the east of Harlebeke, and on a junction between these – with hits also claimed on Harlebeke.[45] Photographs from the attacks confirmed bomb bursts on Harlebeke; they also identified motor transports on the road whose

Table 9 Aircraft available for operations and number of sorties made by 2 Group during Operation Dynamo.[42]

Date	Aircraft available for operations	Number of sorties
26 May	64	36
27 May	63	48
28 May	63	48
29 May	79	51
30 May	74	68
31 May	87	93
1 June	87	56
2 June	83	24
3 June	86	18

further progress was likely delayed as a result of the attacks. In the morning of 27 May, twelve Blenheims were despatched to attack troops and transports leaving Courtrai with the road exits from the town also given as targets.[46] The Blenheims attacked crossroads, bridges and railway junctions west of Courtrai. The Courtrai-Heule road was hit in these attacks and large columns of smoke were seen to rise from the railway junction at the western exit of Courtrai following its bombing. One direct hit was also observed on the railway bridge over the Lys and two hits on the railway bridge which crossed the south-western road were suspected, with burst observed 'on or close to the target'.[47] The bombing undertaken in support of the Allied ground forces during 26 and 27 May did not produce a dramatic halt to the German advance and reports of direct hits often proved wishful rather than realistic. However, air interdiction did produce short delays which were aided the withdrawal of Allied troops towards the coast. The German advance was slowed on at least one occasion by these attacks and AOK 6 noted that Allied air support had become involved in the ground battle in West Belgium for the first time.[48]

The withdrawal of the BEF was also threatened by the German advance on Wormhoudt from the St Omer area and on 27 May this thrust was considered to be the more threatening.[49] During the afternoon of 27 May therefore, attacks were made on mechanized units in the St. Omer region and the squadrons involved were informed of the 'paramount importance' of pressing home their attacks to delay the German advance.[50] In the area of St. Omer a number of bridges had been destroyed – although the railway bridge near Arques had been captured intact providing an important crossing point for heavy transports – and the Germans had erected a military bridge at Wardrecques.[51] Tanks and transports moving on the road to Forêt de Clairmarais were attacked as were transports on the road at Blendecques – where a warehouse was also knocked down and appeared to block the road. Hits were also observed on the road south-east of Arques.[52] Attacks on armoured fighting vehicles (AFVs) and columns passing through St. Omer were continued by twenty-four Blenheims during the evening. Motor transports and AFVs between Rubrouck and Arneke were bombed – with bursts seen near tanks and on the crossroads – and bombs were dropped on what appeared to be a stationary troop train. Direct hits were obtained on the train which was 'completely demolished'.[53] The road and junction south of St. Omer were bombed as were anti-aircraft batteries at Forêt de Clairmarais. Bombs were observed to straddle these batteries, with fire from one battery being noticeably decreased following the bombing and ceasing altogether at another.[54] Following these attacks, I./*Flak-Regiment* 38 reported heavy losses in this area, although they believed they had been attacked by their own aircraft.[55] Bomber Command's attacks on 27 May also caused AOK 4 to seek fighter protection over the area to guard against further bombing.[56] Six Blenheims also undertook a low level attack on the village of Belle-et-Houllefort during 27 May and 'completely demolished' a suspected German headquarters there.[57] Earlier, on 26 May, eighteen Blenheims, originally despatched to interfere with the unloading of petrol at St. Pol, attacked enemy concentrations and mechanized units in the Forêt d'Hesdin. Over forty direct hits, as well as other very near-misses, were seen amongst the German columns – the longest of which was formed of some fifty vehicles – and on the road.[58]

As Allied troops continued to withdraw into the Dunkirk perimeter on 28 May, Bomber Command made further attacks on the German advance. At first light six Blenheims carried out a reconnaissance in force against enemy concentrations advancing from St. Omer. Fifty large motor transports were seen to the south and fifty AFVs were observed in Forêt d'Eperlecques. Attacks were made, and hits scored, on the centre of St. Omer, as well as on roads in Forêt d'Eperlecques at points where obstructions could be caused. The morning also saw nine Blenheims ordered to delay an artillery and motor transports column observed at Courtrai, on the Menin-Ypres road. Crossroads, roads and railway lines in the area were bombed and a junction on the Courtrai-Menin road, just east of Menin, was reported as 'definitely hit'.[59] Crossroads in these areas were important to the German advance because they offered positions where columns, both motorized and infantry, could easily cross one another.[60] Damage to crossroads could therefore slow the supply of troops and material. Despite claims of success around Menin, photographs from these attacks showed that one of these aircraft had actually dropped bombs 15km south of Menin near an aerodrome on the outskirts of Lille.[61] The effect of Bomber Command's efforts was reduced by such examples of navigational failures. The failure to effectively identify targets when weather conditions were less than ideal also reduced Bomber Command's influence on the ground battle. A Blenheim of 21 Squadron was unable to attack during 28 May after becoming lost in cloud. The squadron's eight remaining Blenheims attacked lorries in Forêt de Clairmarais; amidst heavy cloud cover, however, only the lead section could confirm a successful attack has been made.[62] During the afternoon and evening of 28 May, twenty-seven Blenheims were despatched with orders to attack 'enemy columns debouching from St. Omer'.[63] Several motor transports columns and a concentration of tanks were bombed – with direct hits reported on the latter – and a column in the area was also strafed. The road east of St. Momelin was bombed, and hit, and buildings adjacent to the road bridge at Watten were destroyed during these attacks.[64] Once more, however, Bomber Command's limitations in adverse weather conditions reduced the effect of these attacks. In conditions where the results of bombing could not be observed the probability of accurate strikes must be considered low. Four of the twenty-seven Blenheims despatched were unable to bomb at all because of the weather conditions; one lost the target in clouds and three were unable to bomb after encountering ice in clouds at 10,000 feet which frosted the windows of the aircraft and persisted even at low levels.[65]

Despite such reductions to Bomber Command's effort the attacks on 28 May were effective. Churchill would later describe 28 May as 'a day of tension, which gradually eased as the position on land was stabilised with the powerful help of the Royal Air Force'.[66] The weight of Bomber Command's attacks was made in those areas that the German Army was advancing through with tank concentrations and the march route of forward units bombed.[67] The German advance, particularly in the area of West Belgium, was slowed by the conditions of the roads as well as the large numbers of refugees and prisoners on the restricted number of roads which were available.[68] The problem of prisoners on the German march routes was such that, after the Belgian surrender, motorized Belgian units were temporarily allowed to retain their vehicles in order to expedite their withdrawal from the area.[69] The only factor which prohibited the rapid advance of 29. *Infanterie-Division* (mot) when it faced little resistance in the St. Omer area was that their vehicles could not keep up with the troops because of the condition of roads, tracks, highways and byways; many of these routes were completely clogged with abandoned Allied material, and could be approached only by foot.[70] Bomber Command's attacks therefore fell in areas where even small successes could cause important delays.

Attempts by Bomber Command to delay the advance of German forces continued on 29 May. In the morning, eighteen Blenheims undertook a reconnaissance in force to ascertain whether there were any road movements north of St. Omer and in the area Ostend-Thourout-Dixmude-Nieuport. Direct hits were recorded on a convoy north-west of St. Omer, along the Hazebrouck-Dunkirk railway and on a bridge, and adjacent housing on the approaches, to the north at St. Momelin. Direct hits were also achieved on a concentration of lorries on the road at Koekelare, south-east of Nieuport. Several of the aircraft involved were, however, unable to identify their position because of the bad weather and therefore did not drop their bombs.[71] During the afternoon eighteen Blenheims were despatched to attack AFVs and transports on the Dixmude-Furnes road. Bombs were dropped on a short motor transport column and two groups of thirty lorries in the area of Pervyse, with the results unobserved, whilst twenty AFVs south of Pervyse and two large groups of motor transports near Ichtegem were unsuccessfully bombed. Ichtegem itself, which was observed to be full of vehicles, was heavily attacked with explosion seen in the village. Direct hits were reported on a column of covered lorries on the Pervyse-Nieuport road and very near-misses were achieved against a column, including two tanks, south-east of Nieuport and a column south-east of Dixmude, which was believed to have been damaged.[72] Further attacks during the afternoon were made by six Blenheims with targets in Forêt d'Eperlecques bombed.[73] The evening of 29 May saw nine Blenheims return to the Dixmude-Nieuport area. A crossroad in use by large numbers of German transports – where many cars were observed overturned and destroyed from what appeared to have been an earlier attack – was bombed. Direct hits were achieved on the road itself and a number of adjacent houses were collapsed and observed to fall right across the road, blocking it. A stationary column east of Nieuport and vehicles south of Ostend were also attacked, with near-misses reported in both instances. The crossroads at Ichtegem were also bombed, with several burning vehicles observed there, as were a number of transport columns, troop transports and crossroads east and north-east of Dixmude.[74]

The attacks around Nieuport came at an important time. The British defence in this area was, until the evening of 29 May, a scratch force composed of several hundred men – mainly drawn from the 53rd (London) Medium Regiment, Royal Artillery, bolstered by other stray rear-echelon personnel, commanded by Brigadier Clifton. On 28 May, advanced troops from 206. and 256. *Infanterie-Divisionen* reached the perimeter; the destruction of bridges in the area, however, delayed the advance of the main component and Bomber Command's attacks further disrupted the German advance, which was also under artillery fire, as it pressed forward during 29 May.[75]

Weather conditions hampered Bomber Command's attempts to provide further support on 30 May. Missions against roads leading towards Nieuport had to be abandoned during the morning because of poor visibility. No attacks were made, therefore, until the afternoon during which twenty-seven Blenheims were despatched to attack transports on the Dixmude-Thourout and Dixmude-Roulers roads as well as columns, AFVs, roads and bridges, south and east of Furnes. Attacks were made on the road junction and bridges at Roulers as well as on motor transports and AFVs north of the town. Air strikes on crossroads and motor transports in several villages west of Dixmude effected the supply of *Infanterie-Regiment* 56.[76] Eight of the twenty-seven Blenheims despatched failed to bomb because of weather conditions and many more failed to observe the results of bombing because of the poor visibility over the area.[77] During the evening twenty-four Blenheims were despatched to bomb the road adjacent to the Plassendale Canal, 5km north-east of Nieuport, and roads, junctions and columns in villages on the approach to Dunkirk from the south. Conditions prevented many of the results being observed; however, bomb bursts were seen along the Plassendale Canal road after transports there were attacked. A further six Blenheims were despatched to attack transports on the Furnes-Ghistelles road along which led to XVI A.K.'s advanced positions at Nieuport. Only two Blenheims were able to bomb in conditions of low cloud; nevertheless, transports south of Ostend were bombed and an effective attack was made on a motorized column moving west from Ghistelles which left three vehicles overturned.[78] German attacks during the night of 30 May failed to overcome Allied resistance and discussing the failure *Heeresgruppe* B noted that the troops had been left disturbed by British bombing.[79]

Bomber Command's attacks on 31 May were directed against German movements leading to positions on the perimeter whose defence was vital for the continuation of the evacuation. Shortly after dawn, in conditions 'perfect for bombing', eight Blenheims successfully attacked transports on the road in three areas – Nieuport-Ghistelle, Furnes-Pervyse-Dixmude and Furnes-Oostvleteren-Ypres.[80] Bombs were dropped on lorries in the centre of Furnes, where houses in the main street were seen to collapse on the transports and hits were achieved on thirty stationary lorries at the crossroads north of Pervyse. The Westvleteren road was bombed and strafed, near-misses likely to have caused damage were recorded on closely packed motor transports moving slowly on the Furnes-Oostvleteren road and, in a separate attack, a column of tanks and lorries on the same road was bombed – with explosions seen amidst the centre of the column. Observations of important German movements in this area by the crews involved in the attack led to a further twelve Blenheims being ordered to target columns on the Furnes-Oostvleteren-Ypres road.[81] Three motor transport columns were attacked along this road; two were unsuccessfully bombed; however, the third, of fifty motor transports and AFVs, was hit which left four vehicles left on fire after bombs exploded along the road. Direct hits were also made on troops and horse-drawn heavy artillery north of Elverdinghe – with troops there also strafed by the Blenheims – and on the centre of a column of fifty motor transports on the Loo-Forthem road. Fifteen motor transports were attacked on the Lizerne-Noordschoote road and smoke was afterwards seen rising following hits which were 'thought to be certain'. Bombs were also dropped on crossroads at Loo, motor transports on the road at Linde – where houses adjacent to the road were hit – and on the Furnes-Oostvleteren road near Sint-Rijkers.[82] Further attacks on these targets were made by twelve Blenheims during the afternoon. A motor transport column protected by anti-aircraft was bombed in Oostvleteren with bursts observed close to the road and a column of smoke subsequently seen rising from Oostvleteren.[83] Nine Blenheims were also despatched during the afternoon – to attack AFVs, troops and transports proceeding towards Bergues – and attacked three columns of motor transports, with bombs observed to explode amongst transports in the first and third columns.[84] Flooding in the areas between Bergues and Furnes meant that these two points were vital to the defence of the perimeter and reduced the number of routes which the Germans could use to advance further supplies and forces to the frontline.[85] The Furnes-Oostvleteren-Ypres road was one of the more important routes which remained open and relatively unobstructed for German forward supplies whilst Bergues was an important junction for several roads intersecting immediately in front of the Dunkirk perimeter.[86] The attacks made on movements in both areas were therefore important in delaying further German forces and supplies reaching, and increasing pressure on, the Dunkirk perimeter.

The focus of Bomber Command's operations changed, however, in the late afternoon of 31 May. All available sections from RAF Watton and Wattisham were ordered to attack bridges around Nieuport, with road bridges to the north and east designated as most important – those to the west having been previously destroyed.[87] Eighteen Blenheims attacked the canal bridges east of Nieuport 'without much success'.[88] Two direct hits were achieved on bridges – one was believed to have destroyed a bridge tower and the other hit the St. George–Nieuport road bridge – with other bridges straddled by bomb salvoes and several near-misses reported. Although it was considered probable that the road approaches to the bridge had 'been blocked in several instances', the general results were considered unsatisfactory and 'every bridge seemed to be intact' after the attacks.[89] Attacks on pontoon bridges over the canal at Nieuport were also made by eight Blenheims.[90] At the eastern edge of Nieuport pontoon bridges being constructed were identified and attacked by two of these Blenheims – with one direct hit reported – the remainder, however, unsuccessfully attacked bridges to the north and east of Nieuport and only succeeded in hitting the roads and houses leading to the bridges.[91] At 19.10 twenty-four Blenheims attacked these targets with bridges to the north-east of Nieuport and the bridge over the canal at Wulpen, 5km south-west of Nieuport, heavily bombed. The results were almost entirely obscured by the dust and smoke produced by the explosions; hits were observed, however, on the southernmost bridge at Nieuport as well as on the lock bridge over the canal.[92]

Effective attacks against the bridges at Nieuport were made more difficult by the limitations of the bombs dropped. Perhaps the most significant flaw of the bombs used was the number which simply failed to explode. At the start of the war the 250lb General Purpose bomb, the main bomb used by Bomber Command during Dynamo, had a failure rate of 10 to 15 per cent.[93] The bombs were also of questionable value against the objectives of close support missions.[94] The General Purpose bombs suffered from the weight of the metal casing to explosive filling ratio – British bombs had a charge-to-weight-ratio of roughly 25 per cent, half that of the comparable German bombs – and left them lacking in explosive power.[95] The report of 2 Group noted that before the attacks on Nieuport 'the sections set off at short notice ... with 250 and 40 [lb] General Purpose bombs. Before and after the attacks the crews stated that little or nothing could be accomplished with such bombs.'[96] The bombs were also not particularly aerodynamic; even accurate aiming therefore produced a greater number of misses than would otherwise have been the case. This was a serious limitation in tactical operations which typically required a considerable degree of accuracy to hit the target and produce the delays or destruction necessary to affect ground operations.[97]

Nevertheless, the attacks at Nieuport, where a number of bridges were known to already have been destroyed, achieved some success.[98] The previous destruction of bridges over the canals, and the congestion and blockage of roadways, meant that German troop movements and formations became increasingly concentrated. Bomber Command's attacks also made a direct contribution to the defence of the Dunkirk perimeter. The Commander of the British 12th Infantry Brigade, which held the perimeter from opposite Nieuport to the sea, recorded that during the afternoon of 31 May:

> a determined attack was launched upon our front – the third within a period of 12 hours. The leading German waves were stopped by our light machine-gun force and mortar fire, but strong enemy reserves were observed moving through Nieuport and on the roads to the canal north-west of Nieuport. At this moment some RAF bombers arrived and bombed Nieuport and the roads north-west of it. The effect was instantaneous and decisive – all movement of enemy reserves stopped: many of the forward German troops turned and fled, suffering severely from the fire of our machine-guns.[99]

Lance-Corporal Alf Hewitt – 1st Battalion, South Lancashire Regiment – recalled the attack occurring as the Germans massed for an attempt to cross the

Yser canal behind an artillery barrage. On hearing aircraft approaching Hewitt recalled that:

> we were fed up with being attacked from the air so we got really panicky as they flew low over our heads. But they were RAF planes and right before our eyes they gave Jerry a real pasting. That was the only time I saw the RAF in action, but it really worked. The Germans broke and ran.[100]

David Tyacke – 2nd Battalion, Duke of Cornwall's Light Infantry – also witnessed the attack and recalled that:

> there was a roar of engines from behind us ... and suddenly in swept the most marvellous sight ... nine Blenheims very close in three vics of three. ... They went straight over us and dropped their bombs obviously on the Germans. We could see the bomb splashes going up.[101]

These attacks, the effectiveness of which was recognized by those on the perimeter, helped stabilize the eastern side of the perimeter at a critical moment of Operation Dynamo.[102] The British official history would describe this bombing as 'one of the really successful examples of close co-operation' during the Battle of France delivered 'as the enemy were moving up additional troops and the threat of a real break-through was serious'.[103] Following the bombing no further attacks were made before 4th Division, holding these positions, retired to the beaches.[104]

At 06.00, on 1 June twelve Blenheims were despatched to attack road movements in the Bergues and Furnes area, directly to the rear of the German forward units. The crews involved were informed by 2 Group prior to attacking that the 'importance of our task necessitates attacks in the absence of fighter support or cloud cover'.[105] Direct hits were claimed on eighteen heavy transports in the area as well as on motor transports and troops at Socx. A column on the Bergues-Wormhout road was also bombed, with some of the lorries reported to have been set on fire, as were transports on an adjoining road. The Bergues-Wormhout road and the Furnes-Hoogstade road were hit at several points. Houses adjacent to the Bergues-Wormhout road were destroyed at La Belle Vue, the canal bridge at Draaiburg was bombed and hits were observed on transports crossing the canal bridge near the village of Steenkirke. With no large concentrations observed, the majority of the targets attacked were tactical points where bombing could create road blocks.[106] This was more effective in the areas Bomber Command was now targeting. The roads leading towards the Dunkirk perimeter were elevated by several metres above the fields with irrigation ditches on either side and many were either blocked or impeded, depending on their proximity to Dunkirk, by abandoned motor transports; both factors meant that it was more difficult to circumvent blockages where they were successfully created.[107]

As German pressure increased, during 1 June twelve Blenheims were despatched to attack AFVs, motor transports and troops on the road to Furnes, with the secondary task of creating road blocks. Direct hits were recorded on the Hondschoote-Furnes road and attacks were also made on the Bergues-Hondschoote road, the centre of Furnes and the Nieuport-Furnes road, with hits observed on the junction of the railway and canal on the eastern outskirts of Furnes.[108] In the afternoon twelve Blenheims were despatched against enemy movements on roads to the south and east of Dunkirk. The first two sections attacked eighty motor transports in Hondschoote, with bursts seen on the crossroads and houses at the south-west entrance to the town accompanied by large sheets of flame from exploding ammunition or petrol. The remaining Blenheims bombed motor transports and troops in Wormhout, with bursts observed on houses adjacent to the southern road exit which blocked the road with falling masonry.[109] During the evening, eighteen Blenheims were ordered to destroy Hondschoote, where German troops and material were concentrated. Successful medium level, low level and shallow dive-bombing attacks achieved direct hits across the village including on houses adjacent to road exits – as well as on the roads themselves – and on transports in the village square. Motor transports on the road to Hondschoote were bombed, with hits on the tail of the column and on the crossroads south of Hondschoote, and attacks were made on the Hondschoote-Furnes road. The Furnes-La Panne road was also bombed and reported successfully blocked. Two Blenheims were unable to bomb, however, because they failed to locate the target in thick clouds.[110]

Following 1 June, the Blenheims of 2 Group were despatched against artillery positions on the coast with the object of neutralizing their fire and assisting the final phase of the BEF withdrawal from Dunkirk.[111] This tactical role was different to bombing the approaches to the Dunkirk perimeter. The missions were, however, considered essential to allow the evacuation to be completed.[112] On 2 June twenty-four Blenheims, of 107 and 110 Squadrons, were ordered to maintain a sustained attack on an artillery battery on the coast 11km west of Dunkirk, as soon as possible after first light.[113] Although vertical visibility for the attack was good, which allowed the majority of the aircraft involved to successfully identify and engage battery positions on the coast, conditions were hazy which left the crews largely unable to observe the results of bombing.[114] Assessing the results of these attacks is therefore difficult. Between 05.40 and

06.22 four sections of 107 Squadron attacked positions along the coast. The first three sections attacked positions from medium altitude with a 'symmetrical shape in the sand dunes', believed to be a battery, attacked. Bombs were then dropped on 'four rectangles', identified as probable battery positions, with hits across the target area, and 'a row of emplacements' in the area was bombed with bursts observed to 'cover the target'. The final section of 107 Squadron attacked an anti-aircraft battery in the area from 700 feet.[115] Leonard Fearnley, an observer in 107 Squadron, recalled the heavy anti-aircraft fire with the whole squadron being 'shot up badly that day but we all got back to our utter amazement'.[116] Three Blenheims of 107 Squadron did, however, crash on landing at RAF Wattisham as a result of damage from the 'very intense' anti-aircraft fire experienced 'all over the area'.[117] Blenheims of 110 Squadron also experienced intense anti-aircraft fire over the area and the first section also bombed anti-aircraft batteries firing from positions, near the coast, close to a small copse. The second and third section of 110 Squadron received wireless instructions to bomb between this copse and the village of Le Clipon, where the battery position attacked by 107 Squadron had been identified. Between 07.00 and 07.20 the sections bombed the positions from medium altitude with bursts observed in the village and to the north of it. The final section attacked the road leading west from Le Clipon at 07.45 from low altitude, and bursts were observed on the southern road junction to the village. Photographs taken during the strikes showed that both squadrons seemed to have located and bombed positions 4km south-west of Le Clipon in an area of scrub forest and sand dunes with a wood running up its eastern boundary, which appeared 'a likely location for batteries', north-east of Gravelines and some 15km west of Dunkirk.[118] Fearnley remembered that:

> We bombed enemy shore batteries which were dug into the sand dunes at Gravelines hindering the BEF evacuation. ... We went over the channel in line abreast so that we'd cover a wider scope of target ... and we had to fire where we saw the burst from the guns. This we did with the pilot shooting up as we approached them with his front guns and then the air gunner taking a wide sweep being careful not to hit our comrades in one aircraft each side of us.[119]

The strikes on artillery positions were repeated on the morning of 3 June with six sections ordered to maintain a continuous offensive patrol for ninety minutes from 04.30 hours. Each section was to harass the enemy artillery as much as possible with the object of neutralizing their fire. The smoke columns from the burning fuel tanks at Dunkirk left the crews involved in the attacks on the battery positions largely unable to observe the results of their bombing. Bomb bursts were, however, observed around the targeted location although the crews did not observe artillery fire or anti-aircraft fire in the target area.[120]

Portal considered that 'very limited results were achieved' in connection to the operations against German artillery 'owing to [the] great resources of the enemy'.[121] By 2 June, however, German artillery batteries were being withdrawn for *Fall Rot*.[122] The effect of these operations was, therefore, greater than Portal realized at the time because at this point of the evacuation the Germans lacked the preponderance of artillery they had enjoyed before. The importance of these operations was also not limited to the physical destruction of the batteries but the suppression of fire from these positions on the evacuation fleet as the last ships left Dunkirk. The likelihood is that the attacks caused little loss amongst the German batteries; however, the evacuation fleet encountered little fire from these positions during the morning of either 2 or 3 June.

Tactical bombing by night

During Operation Dynamo, Bomber Command's night air strikes in support of Allied ground forces were primarily planned to interdict the transportation of troop movements and supplies by roads and railways. They were also intended to cause confusion, prevent rest and stop work in the German rear areas.[123] To achieve these aims Wellingtons of 3 Group were directed to carry out 'sustained attack on columns and concentrations of troops, transports and A.F.V.s and on trains' in Belgium during the night of 26 May.[124] Eleven Wellingtons claimed a number of hits on road targets, most notably on a convoy near Grammont, and on railway lines, in West Belgium.[125] Twelve Wellingtons were also despatched to attack airfields in Belgium in order 'to disorganise and interfere with enemy air activity'.[126] Five of the Wellingtons were unable to bomb their target; the other crews, however, reported positive results. At Jumet Aerodrome, north of Charleroi, thirty-three 250lb bombs were dropped with twenty-one hits reported on the aerodrome, and further hits on the railway running due north, whilst Brussels-Evere aerodrome was hit by twenty-six 250lb bombs and 120 incendiaries.[127] Antwerp-Deurne aerodrome was also bombed and a petrol dump there was believed to have been hit.[128] Despite the claims of success the bombing of airfields by small numbers of bombers was unlikely to have caused significant disruption to German air operations. Shortly before Dynamo commenced Richthofen recalled a night attack on a German airfield which, having used flares to illuminate the target, 'rather pointlessly scattered explosive bombs around'.[129] To achieve more than short-term disruption to these airfields Bomber Command needed to have made a greater effort against them as part of a sustained counter force strategy. Further attacks to dislocate the German supply organization were made during the night of 26 May by 5 Group. Nine Hampdens were despatched to attack bridges, road and rail junctions in areas of close communication with German land forces. A further twelve Hampdens were despatched to attack trains in motion and railway communications in Belgium and North-West Germany with the intention of interdicting the movement of supplies for forward units.[130]

The efforts to delay the German advance by disrupting the movement of supplies continued during the nights of 27 and 28 May with troop concentrations and rear areas behind German lines targeted. On 27 May, thirty-six Wellingtons and twenty-six Hampdens attacked tactical targets with the objective of disrupting enemy road and rail movements and preventing general activity and rest.[131] Attacks were carried out throughout the night, at irregular intervals, in order to create the maximum possible disturbance.[132] Wellingtons bombed St. Omer and Aire, and the bridges at these points, with the objective of creating road blocks; heavy explosions were reported amongst two columns of vehicles and two large fires were caused at Aire.[133] Attacks on Courtrai, and the road junction there, set oil refineries alight and Wellington crews also reported hits on roads and railways across Flanders.[134] Hampdens attacked ammunition dumps, road and railway targets during the night of 27 May, with one train believed to have been derailed near Liege.[135] During the night of 27 May thirty-six Whitleys were despatched to attack marshalling yards in North-West Germany. The main station at Düsseldorf was damaged, the express track was hit, trains received light damage and a train shed was destroyed. At Cologne, the line was blocked for three hours and a driver killed. The bombs dropped on Hamm did less damage but elsewhere the Dortmund-Mengede main line was temporarily closed by two bomb strikes. On the night of 28 May Wellingtons and Whitleys made attacks intended to interfere with the German advance. It was hoped the bombing of roads as they passed through town would create obstructions, both from bomb craters and falling masonry from adjacent building, which would prevent German movements as well as disturbing units resting in the towns targeted.[136] Eighteen Wellingtons made attacks on Roulers, Menin, Aire and St. Omer; hits observed across the centre of the Roulers and buildings were also seen to already be ablaze at St. Omer and Aire.[137] Whitley squadrons of 4 Group attacked road junctions and roads leading out of Givet and Guise – both of which were important centres through which supplies for the German

Army and the Luftwaffe had to pass.[138] Hirson was also attacked; a direct hit was claimed on the railway station and bombs were seen to straddle the road and rail crossing south of the town.[139] The attacks of both the Wellingtons and Whitleys were directed to areas where disruption to supplies and rear-echelon units could cause important delays to the German advance.[140] The attacks by 4 Group fell in areas the Luftwaffe had secured advanced air bases and supplies were needed. Bombing attacks made on Givet did achieve results, causing 173 German casualties and necessitating an increase in the anti-aircraft requirement that was believed necessary at captured airfields.[141] Poor weather conditions, however, resulted in thirteen Wellingtons failing to locate targets in Belgium and France and prevented any operations by the Hampdens of 5 Group.[142] Difficult weather conditions also meant that the attacks which were made against road targets were largely ineffectual.[143]

Poor weather conditions continued during the night of 29 May and largely prevented any Bomber Command missions. Tactical operations to attack rail and road junctions at Guise, St Quintin, and in the Ruhr involving 36 Hampden were scheduled but were all cancelled because of unsuitable weather conditions. In response to urgent requests from the BEF for further bombing of German position, however, fifteen Wellingtons made attacks on St. Omer, Aire, Roulers and Thourout. Direct hits were reported on a convoy near Thourout, the town itself, and the roads around it, whilst nineteen hits were recorded on Roulers, where a large explosion occurred. During attacks on Aire a large factory was hit which immediately burst into flames. Attacks on the railway junction and marshalling yards to the east of St. Omer, at Hazebrouck, had caused a large explosion, whilst forty-eight hits were recorded on St. Omer itself.[144] The results of these attacks were considered 'fairly successful' given the difficulties locating targets.[145] The attacks on Roulers and Thourout may have caused some delays to the German Army advancing towards Dunkirk from the east, falling as they did in areas where roads were already congested, but those to the south were probably limited in the disruption they achieved.

The passing of the moon phase on 30 May led Air Chief Marshal Newall to adjudge that Bomber Command now lacked the necessary illumination to 'operate with sufficient accuracy against road objectives and defiles in the forward area, to make an effective contribution to the land situation'.[146] Bomber Command was therefore directed to employ its Whitleys and Hampdens against railway objectives during clear nights as the Air Staff believed that operations against these targets now formed the 'most important contribution' that the heavy bombers would be able to 'make against the enemy's lines of communications'.[147]

As a result of this directive the Whitley and Hampdens were not deployed on tactical operations on the night of 30 May. Twenty-eight Wellingtons were, however, despatched to attack enemy road movements at Cassel, Roulers, Thourout Ypres, Hazebrouck and Dixmude.[148] A number of aircraft failed to locate their targets but fires were started at Dixmude and 'weighty attacks' were delivered at Ypres, Roulers and Hazebrouck and a motor transport column travelling in close company was hit on the Menin-Ypres road.[149] Disruption to German road movements at night had the opportunity to cause considerable delays because of the lack of route discipline within the German rear-services. German motor transports travelling in column failed to leave sufficient distance between each vehicle as they feared vehicles from other units would enter and disrupt their column.[150] The close distance between the vehicles meant that direct hits and near-misses could cause greater damage than would otherwise have been the case. Delays as a result of attacks, even where no direct destruction was caused amidst the column, were also increased as a result because it became harder to clear obstructions on the road and restore order to the column.[151] As British night bombing increased *Heeresgruppe* B criticized the lack of anti-aircraft and fighter protection which had caused troops in the area, who not previously experienced heavy bombing, to be disturbed by the attacks.[152]

On the nights of both 31 May and 1 June Bomber Command undertook attacks in direct support of Allied troops at Dunkirk. On 31 May, thirty-three Wellingtons were despatched to attack objectives in front of the BEF on the Dunkirk perimeter.[153] One Wellington failed to attack these targets, having bombed the dock area of Ostend instead, and four Wellingtons returned with their bomb load after unsuccessfully attempting to locate their target.[154] The remaining Wellingtons, however, delivered heavy attack on the targets. Many hits were observed on buildings and roads in and around Nieuport, where fires were reported, and an ammunition dump in the south part of town was hit. Hits were obtained on villages along the roads to Bergues by Wellingtons using parachute flares to locate their targets.[155] Bursts were also observed from bombs dropped on a motor transport column on the road to Furnes. These attacks were made ahead of areas which, as discussed above, were vital points to the defence of the Dunkirk at a time when BEF troops were beginning to withdraw from the perimeter. By harassing the larger centres and road junctions in the German rear areas the Wellingtons were able to impede German offensive operations on the night of 31 May – and preparations for attacks on the morning of 1 June. Air strikes in support of the perimeter were also made on the night of 1 June with sixteen Wellingtons despatched to interdict road movements and railway lines in the area between Nieuport and Socx.[156] Attacks were made, with some success, on German movements, rear areas and railway lines at Rexpoede, Socx and Furnes.[157] *Heeresgruppe B* recorded that German positions were heavily bombed during this night, with the area occupied by X. *Armeekorps* around Bergues being particularly heavily hit.[158] These air strikes disrupted further German attacks in an area where 18. and 254. *Infanterie-Divisionen* had gained narrow bridgeheads over the canal.[159] Although these attacks did not achieve notable success in terms of material damage or destruction they interfered with German operations against the perimeter. Against these air strikes German troops on the Dunkirk perimeter could only adopt passive defence measures – preventing any use of illumination, avoiding areas which were targeted such as crossroads and bridges, and halting all movements.[160] Bomber Command's use of air power in tactical support of the Dunkirk perimeter at night was therefore effective in delaying and disrupting German operations.

Road and rail targets as well as Marshalling yards in Western Germany were also attacked on the night of 1 June by twenty-six Whitleys, of 4 Group, and twelve Hampdens, of 5 Group.[161] The attacks on marshalling yards by 5 Group were largely unsuccessful because of weather conditions in the region. The Whitleys of 4 Group attacked rail targets at Hamburg, Osnabrück, Hamm and Düsseldorf, with bursts observed on marshalling yards at Osnabrück and Hamm. A column of forty vehicles was also attacked on a bridge east of Rheine, with hits observed on the column and vehicles seen to explode. Sixteen of the Whitleys returned with their bombload, however, having failed to locate targets because of the weather conditions over the area.[162] Although 4 Group recorded these missions as tactical the majority appeared to have had objectives which would impact heavily on German industry. Indeed, these attacks saw bursts observed on two blast furnaces in North-West Germany.[163] At a time when the last British troops were being embarked from Dunkirk, and French troops continued to hold the perimeter whilst awaiting evacuation, the bombing of targets in Germany was of little consequence to the success of Dynamo.

The lack of suitable targets, combined with the reservations regarding using the night bomber force against tactical targets in the absence of sufficient illumination, resulted in no night operations in direct support of Dynamo being planned for the night of 2 June. Instead forty Wellingtons of 3 Group were standing by for operations against the high-grade lubricant oil refineries at Bremen and Hamburg. At 20.42, on 2 June, however, these attacks were cancelled and Bomber Command issued instructions to 3 Group for operations to 'interfere with enemy movements' and to 'aid the evacuation from Dunkirk'.[164]

In response to these instructions sixteen Wellingtons were despatched to attack German forces in the area around the Dunkirk perimeter at Socx, Rexpoede, Houthem and Hondschoote. The Wellingtons were able to deliver heavy attacks on these targets with some success. At Socx, hits were observed on crossroads and buildings to the east of the village, and bursts straddled the southern road. The fork road to the west of Rexpoede was straddled and hits were observed on railway lines, the adjacent road and the northern exit of the village. Hits were recorded on the southern outskirts of Houthem whilst at Hondschoote hits were observed on the crossroads and in the village.[165] These attacks were delivered on points behind the German lines which formed staging points for troops and supplies intended to support the more advanced elements of 14. and 61. *Infanterie-Divisionen* as they attempted to overcome the remaining forces on the Dunkirk perimeter.[166]

Marshalling yards in the Ruhr, and targets east of Antwerp, were attacked during the night of 2 June, however, by Hampdens and Whitleys.[167] Only six Hampdens were able to bomb railway targets; however, sixteen Whitleys were able to bomb Osnabrück, Soest, Hamm and Gelsenkirchen. At Osnabrück bombs were observed to hit the Osnabrück-Rheine and Osnabrück-Bremen railway lines as well as road and rail junctions. Hits were also observed on railway tracks, and a bridge, west of Hamm, as well as on the centre of marshalling yards at Duisburg and Soest – where the bombing was reported as very effective with a moving train believed to have suffered a direct hit and a group of closely spaced waggons set on fire. Three Whitleys, having failed to locate their primary targets, attacked aerodromes. Hits were observed on airfields at Deventer, Rotterdam and Wesel and large explosions at the latter also set ablaze to a hangar there.[168] The scale of effort was, however, too low to cause significant disruption. This was true for many of Bomber Command's attacks during Dynamo with too many targets attacked by small formations of bombers which meant that even when accurate strikes were delivered they failed to cause significant destruction.

Bomber Command's night attacks, particularly on roads and rear areas, have attracted criticism by those who believed that these missions were an ineffective use of the limited resources available. Before the evacuation of Allied troops from Dunkirk had commenced, Portal, who wished Bomber Command to be used against strategic targets, argued that:

> Bombing the enemy's lines of movement and supply by night is unlikely to have much effect. Bridges and road defiles are ... very heavily defended and many direct hits are not to be expected. Near-misses are quite useless and ... even if a

road is hit, it is almost always possible to make a short detour round the crater, and the collapse of village houses and [other obstacles] … across the roads is unlikely to delay a determined enemy for very long.[169]

Robb, reviewing the tactical day bombing of 2 Group during the Battle of France, asserted that:

> The attack of vehicles forward of the enemy railheads is, in my opinion, hardly worth the effort involved, as once supplies and ammunition are loaded on to the maintenance vehicle they cease to become a profitable objective.[170]

Given the difficulties Bomber Command's crews faced in locating targets by night, particularly those further inland, and accurately bombing objectives, the critical view of Bomber Command's efforts by night is largely justified. Nevertheless, difficulties in the German supply system at this point in the campaign meant that efforts against the German Army rear-areas and logistics did have an impact. Although the shortages of ammunition and fuel for frontline units had largely been solved by the time of Dynamo, there remained difficulties in advancing sufficient supplies, with many of the crossing points over the canals in Belgium and Holland having been destroyed.[171] Many of the tactical night missions targeted the railway system to impede the flow of supplies to the German forces in France and Belgium. Numerous trains were destroyed and derailed and Portal would later report that 'undoubtedly the railway system on the German border must have been considerably disorganised as a result.'[172] German forward units at Dunkirk were said to have experienced food shortages during the fighting on the perimeter. On 3 June, *The Times* military correspondent, reporting on the continuation of the evacuation, stated that it was 'definitely known' that such a shortage existed and ascribed the cause of it to British bombers 'constant harrying of the enemy's communications [which] has undoubtedly hindered the forward flow of supplies to a very great extent'.[173] A shortage of food for captured Allied troops was certainly experienced on 30 May at the temporary prisoner of war camps in and around Courtrai. This area was directly influenced by Bomber Command's attacks. Although a very large number of prisoners had been captured the extent of the supply shortage at Courtrai suggests the German experienced difficulties transporting sufficient resources into their rear areas.[174]

The attacks made by Bomber Command's night force against the railheads supplying the German advance produced delays both to supplies being brought forward by rail and to the supply system for forward units. These delays were rarely extensive but, nonetheless, they achieved a measure of disruption and, in at least one instance, required German forward units to divert transports to the rear areas to maintain the flow of supplies.[175] The Advanced Air Striking Force (AASF) supplemented Bomber Command's attacks against the German logistics base. During the period of Dynamo, the AASF made over 125 sorties at night against German road movements and railway targets, including 'revictualling yards and ammunition dumps' at the latter.[176] Fairey Battles of the AASF caused considerable damage and disorganization to the railway infrastructure at Charleville and around Libramont. Extensive fires were started on hangars and buildings at St. Hubert and Ochamps, supplies and stores at the railhead at Libramont were set on fire and a train was hit at Charleville.[177] Attacks in these areas caused disruption to the German supply system, tracks were damaged and rail traffic temporarily suspended.[178] On 26 May, Von Rundstedt had complained of the confusion in the rear services, which continued all the way to Libramont, stressing that order in this area had to be created and that this was almost more important than forward operations.[179] Successful attacks on the German railheads by the AASF and Bomber Command – and the need from 26 May onwards to rapidly restore the supply connections to Libramont – forced *Panzergruppe* Kleist to divert one-and-a-half of its *Kraftwagen-Transport-Abteilungen* (motorized transport battalion) to help move supplies, slowing the German advance.[180] Attacks on the rail system were all the more effective in disrupting the German rear organization because, although repairs were often rapidly made, the German *Eisenbahntruppe* were too few in number to work the rail system efficiently.[181] Attacks on towns, stations and railheads also caused disruption to the German use of the French and Belgian railway systems to supply advancing forces. This came at a time when many of the road bridges capable of taking heavy vehicles had been destroyed, leaving few alternatives to rapidly bring up supplies other than the captured railway lines.[182] Bomber Command's attacks on the German rear services, despite isolated instances of disruption to the supply of forward units, failed to achieve the level of interdiction necessary to meaningfully impede German operations.

Strategic bombing

In addition to the tactical missions undertaken in support of the Dunkirk evacuation Bomber Command also despatched 231 strategic sorties during Operation Dynamo. As well as the destruction of German industry it was hoped these missions would divert units of the Luftwaffe and anti-aircraft batteries.

On the night of 27 May, twenty-four Hampdens were despatched to bomb oil refineries in North-West Germany.[183] During this period thirty-six Whitleys were also despatched to bomb marshalling yards in the Ruhr. These attacks were intended to interdict supplies to the German armed forces and have been considered in the tactical section; however, their alternative targets – attacked by thirteen of the Whitleys – were any self-illuminating targets in the Ruhr area.[184] This led to a number of scattered attacks on factories in the target area. These air strikes – described by Joseph Goebbels, the German Minister for Propaganda and Culture, in his diary as merely being 'senseless attacks' in revenge for the situation the British forces found themselves in at Dunkirk – had little to no effect on the fighting in France and Belgium.[185] Nonetheless, despite search light activity and thunderstorms over the area, these attacks did cause some damage to industry and rail targets. At Hamburg, a cooking oil plant was hit with five tanks and a storage shed struck. Other bombs fell near ship-building plants and in residential areas but damage was minimal. Hits were recorded on other small factories in the Düsseldorf region with small fires started in places but in general other damage, where it occurred, was only light.[186] The effect of Bomber Command's attacks was reduced because the Command's deficiencies in night navigation skills prevented an effective concentration of air strikes. As a result, attacks were scattered and capable of producing only small, localized, delays and disruptions. To exert an operational effect on the Luftwaffe these attacks would have had to have caused extensive and concentrated damage on industrial targets. Bomber Command's navigational short-comings were well-illustrated on the night of 27 May when a Whitley bombed RAF Bassingbourn in error, believing it was Flushing, Belgium.[187]

The night of 30 May saw eighteen Hampdens despatched to attack and destroy oil refineries near Hamburg but unfavourable weather conditions over the target meant only a few aircraft were able to locate and attack the primary target.[188] The limited success attained on the night of 30 May, as a result of the difficult weather conditions over Germany, suggests that the Hampdens of 5 Group should once again have been directed to support land operation in France, where the weather conditions were far more favourable for successful night operations.[189] On the night of 1 June, twenty-four Hampdens were despatched, to attack oil plants near Hamburg – 4 Group was assigned missions with dual tactical and strategic aims which have been discussed previously – however, almost all of the aircraft assigned industrial targets in North-West Germany were unable to locate their targets because of weather conditions.[190] This night, in particular, exposed the limitations of Bomber Command's crews to effectively navigate and identify targets in unfamiliar areas in difficult conditions. The operations on the night of 1 June were a further example of Bomber Command's effort being diluted against strategic targets which were harder to navigate to than tactical targets in France and Belgium. Unsuitable weather conditions also limited the operations of 4 Group – with only twelve Whitleys despatched to bomb synthetic oil plants at Hamburg – and led to the cancellation of an attack, by twenty-four Hampdens of 5 Group against an oil plant on the Kiel canal.[191]

The failure to navigate to, and bomb, strategic targets reduced the effect of Bomber Command's attacks and its potential to force the Luftwaffe to redistribute its force. The limited results of Bomber Command's attacks produced little need for the Luftwaffe to provide air defence for industrial targets or divert even a proportion of its bomber force to engage in retaliatory attacks against targets in England.[192] Despite this, in the midst of Dynamo some Luftwaffe units were withdrawn from the frontline in order to provide protection of targets in Germany. JG 52 was withdrawn from operations against the evacuation to protect the chemical-industrial works and the Junkers factory in Merseburg and Dessau, respectively.[193] I./JG 77 was withdrawn from the Western front to Döberitz to protect Berlin.[194] That the Luftwaffe attempted to provide air defence for industrial targets is also indicated by the encounters of Bomber Command's aircraft with German night fighters. On the night of 26 May Hampdens encountered accurate fire, at Jülich, from German aircraft and on the night of 27 May night fighters attacked both Hampdens and Whitleys over Germany.[195] German aircraft were also reported to be shadowing British bombers on several occasions, with suggestions that they were relaying details of the bomber's flight to ground defences.[196] The Luftwaffe resources committed to the air defence of Germany against Bomber Command's attacks were, however, limited and – in the case of JG 52 – at least partly, a response to the unit's large loss of aircraft in bad weather rather than a need to provide greater fighter cover at night.[197]

Importantly strategic bombing does not appear to have influenced the operation of the German bombing force. That strategic bombing could bring about a realignment of the German bombing effort and cause them to attack Britain, so relieving some of the pressure from bombing on the Allied land forces, had been one of the central claims of advocates for strategic bombing. The bombing of German industries in the Ruhr failed, however, to cause the Germans to launch counter-strikes against either airfields or industries in Britain. Instead German efforts to counter Bomber Command attacks were directed towards the use of passive defences, which did not represent a diversion of German resources from the main battle. On the night of 1 June an aircraft of 5 Group saw a series of lights in lines and rectangles which gave the appearance of a marshalling yard or factory; however, on dropping a reconnaissance flare the lights were seen to be placed in empty fields.[198] An objective of the attacks against strategic targets was also to force the withdrawal of German anti-aircraft batteries from positions close to the front for the purpose of defending industrial targets in Germany.[199] Although anti-aircraft batteries were withdrawn from positions around Dunkirk during Dynamo these movements were not a response to strategic bombing. They were instead reallocated to German forces in preparation for *Fall Rot* and to defend vulnerable tactical objectives, with no obvious increase in the anti-aircraft defence of Western Germany. The redistribution of anti-aircraft batteries to captured airfields, as opposed to positions around strategic targets in West Germany, occurred during the evacuation of Dunkirk and continued in the immediate aftermath of Dynamo.[200] This was despite heavy attacks against German industries during the night of 3 June which saw 130 aircraft despatched to targets in West Germany. Despite heavy attacks this night, which saw a bomb weight of over 140 tons delivered against strategic targets, little of consequence was achieved.[201]

Ultimately Bomber Command' strategic effort was largely wasteful at a time when a greater tactical effort could have made a meaningful contribution. Sir John Slessor would later argue, after he had retired from the RAF as Chief of the Air Staff, that Bomber Command's strategic effort failed in the face of dispersal of effort caused by French pressure for aid on the battlefield:

> When the time came we drifted inevitably into the cardinal error, failure to concentrate the maximum force on a few carefully selected objectives of decisive importance. ... The smaller your force the more essential it is to use it concentrated against the minimum number of those objectives on which attack is most likely to be decisive at the time.[202]

The strategic effort failed, however, because Bomber Command was incapable of accurate air strikes of sufficient scale to destroy industrial targets at night.[203] The RAF's belief that offensive operations provided the most effective use of air power explains Bomber Command's strategic bombing during this period.[204] Slessor's criticism regarding the failure to concentrate on 'the number of those objectives on which attack is most likely to be decisive at the time' is the correct way of viewing the effort by Bomber Command during Dynamo. This point should, however, largely refute the validity of having heavy bombers attack industrial targets at a moment when the evacuation of the Allied forces at Dunkirk was the pre-eminent necessity of all military operations. Strategic bombing could bring no immediate relief in this area, to which all other operations should have been subsumed.

Before the evacuation of Allied troops had commenced, Group Captain John Baker, Deputy Director of Plans, argued in favour of strategic operations, rather than tactical. Baker advocated this view – which met with a receptive audience in Bomber Command – on the grounds that 'even were the whole of the heavy bomber force diverted to this role of close support, it could not have more than a limited, local and very temporary effect on the land operations'.[205] An intensification of Bomber Command's effort to achieve what Baker considered as limited, local and very temporary would, however, have been a valuable contribution in support of the Allied withdrawal to, and evacuation from, Dunkirk. Having been instructed to provide close support for the Allied forces at Dunkirk it is questionable whether the limited effort they were able to provide against strategic objectives was ever likely to have had an impact commensurate to that achieved had targets of a tactical nature been attacked instead. For strategic bombing to have been an effective application of air power during Dynamo, Bomber Command would have had to have damaged and destroyed German industrial targets rapidly – to an extent that the effects could not be offset by temporary substitution, conservation or repair – and which German political or popular will could not withstand. Even if such targets existed and could be destroyed within the nine days of the evacuation Bomber Command did not have the capability to do so. The offensive use of air power against industrial targets of a strategic nature had no impact on the evacuation of Dunkirk.[206]

Conclusion

Bomber Command's operations during the Dunkirk evacuation have largely been viewed as having had little impact on German forces and have received little attention as a result. This chapter has demonstrated that Bomber Command's missions achieved more than has previously been recognized. The success that Bomber Command achieved was not, however, rooted in the destruction that their attacks caused. Rather it was the delays and disorganizations created in a strained German logistics system that produced the greatest effects.

With the exception of isolated successes 2 Group's day attacks on German formations moving along roads and in close proximity to the battle zone were limited in the destruction they caused. This, in part, led to much of the criticism of Bomber Command's tactical strikes on road positions. As has been noted, however, the bombing of roads undertaken during Dynamo does appear to have caused delays to the advance of German forces. During the initial period, the roads leading towards Dunkirk were heavily congested with refugees, prisoners of war and abandoned Allied equipment and vehicles. The heavy traffic the roads had experienced had also left them in a deteriorated condition with German vehicles struggling to keep up with the advance of troops on foot a result.[207] German road organization and control was also not always effective increasing the effects of delays.[208] Lorries were also in short supply in the German Army and slow heavily loaded horse-drawn transports clogged the roads, creating delays and bottle necks.[209]

Bomber Command was, however, unable to disrupt the advance of many German Army units. Despite the tightly massed advance of numerous divisions and the inevitable road jams which occurred, both of which provided ideal target for bombing, XIV. *Armeekorps* reported that the forward movement of its units was not subject to air strikes.[210] Other attacks, on Courtrai and St. Omer, did cause delays to German forces. These occurred as Allied forces continued to retreat towards the coast. In this situation even minor delays may have been significant – preventing the Germans maintaining a stronger and closer pursuing force which might have jeopardized the Allied withdrawal. Night attacks were also made in these areas. Several valuable attacks against road movements were made by Bomber Command's night forces against roads and columns but overall the attacks caused little disruption to the German Army. Attacks against German railhead supplying forward positions were important, however, and caused motor transports from combat units to be withdrawn. This caused considerable frustration for these units and slowed their advance.[211]

Attacks on the rear areas immediately behind the German forces on the Dunkirk perimeter were also beneficial during the latter period of Dynamo. The bombing of targets around Furnes, particularly the roads leading towards it, and troop concentrations on the approach to the perimeter caused significant disturbances and prevented the Germans exploiting the retraction of the perimeter as the British rearguard were gradually evacuated. It should not be forgotten how few Allied troops, capable of effectively resisting the German forces on the perimeter at Dunkirk, were available to form the rearguard screening the evacuation. The delays and disruption produced by bombing – which were almost certainly heightened by the high percentage of officer casualties suffered by the

German forces on the Dunkirk perimeter – were important in allowing Allied forces first to establish and occupy a defensive cordon around Dunkirk and then to hold it.[212] Accounts from German forces on the perimeter demonstrate that night bombing also caused considerable 'inconvenience'.[213] Attacks on Nieuport on 31 May, intended to destroy any remaining or newly constructed crossing points, scattered German troops forming up for an attack on the perimeter and stabilized the situation there. Bomber Command also made attacks on the artillery positions said to be firing on the evacuation fleet and imperilling daylight movements along the coast. Again, the destruction caused in these areas was of less consequence than the disruption and suppression of fire from these positions. The Blenheims of 2 Group which attacked these batteries encountered heavy anti-aircraft fire from the targeted positions before their bombing attacks; however, Allied ships which left Dunkirk during and after this period did not take fire from the positions which had been attacked.

The strategic effort Bomber Command made throughout Dynamo was largely ineffective. Targets were attacked by aircraft in too few numbers to cause important damage to industrial objectives. Even had German industry suffered any meaningful dislocation or reduction in its output as a result of these attacks this would not have influenced the battle at Dunkirk. This was the decisive point of operations and Bomber Command could have achieved greater results against the German Army's logistics system had the whole of the medium bomber force been directed against forward railheads. Another stated aim of strategic bombing was to cause the redistribution of the Luftwaffe and German anti-aircraft defences. In this it almost wholly failed. The German bomber effort was not redirected against Britain in revenge attacks for what was perceived in Germany as the senseless bombing of the Ruhr. Several German fighter units did operate against the British night force, with more withdrawn to this role during Dynamo. There is no sense, however, that the Luftwaffe withdrew fighter units at the expense of the forces they could operate over Dunkirk; instead fighter units needing to reequip were withdrawn from the frontline. Strategic bombing also failed to significantly influence the German anti-aircraft distribution facing the Allied forces. German anti-aircraft batteries were withdrawn to vulnerable areas behind the German frontlines to increase the defence against the bombing of tactical targets.

Whilst the tactical strikes in support of the Dunkirk evacuation have been criticized, they did play a limited role in delaying the German advance and provided meaningful support to the defence of the Dunkirk perimeter.

Notes

1. TNA: AIR 24/217-8 – Bomber Command Intelligence Reports and Summaries, May–June 1940; TNA: AIR 27 – ORB and Appendices: Bomber Command Squadrons, May–June 1940; Martin Middlebrook and Chris Everitt, The Bomber Command War Diaries: An Operational Reference Book, 1939–1945 (New York: Viking, 1985), pp. 46–9.
2. TNA: AIR 14/676 – Air Marshal Portal, Dispatch on Operations, 9 May–16 June 1940.
3. TNA: AIR 14/927 – Bomber Command Daily Operational Summaries of Aircraft Despatched, Effective Raids and Tons of Bombs Dropped, May–June 1940; TNA: AIR 14/933 – Bomber Command Daily Operational Summaries of Sorties and Casualties, May–June 1940; TNA: AIR 24/218 – Bomber Command Intelligence Reports and Summaries, June 1940.
4. TNA: AIR 14/673 – Bomber Operations, Reports for the Period 5–16 June 1940; TNA: AIR 14/676 – Bomber Operations, Reports for the Period 9 May–16 June 1940.
5. Jackson, Air War, p. 109; Slessor, Central Blue, pp. 296–7.
6. TNA: AIR 14/676 – 2 Group Report, 10 May–3 June 1940.
7. TNA: AIR 20/2760 – Report of Wing Commander Embry, August 1940.
8. Ibid.
9. TNA: AIR 14/676 – 2 Group Report, 10 May–3 June 1940.
10. Ibid.
11. TNA: AIR 20/2760 – Report of Wing Commander Embry, August 1940.
12. TNA: AIR 14/927 – Operational Summaries, Aircraft–Raids–Bombs, May–June 1940; TNA: AIR 14/933 – Operational Summaries, Sorties–Casualties, May–June 1940; TNA: AIR 24/217-8 – Bomber Command Intelligence Reports and Summaries, May–June 1940; TNA: AIR 27 – ORB and Appendices: Bomber Command Squadrons, May–June 1940.
13. IWM: EDS/AL/1371 – Heeresgruppe A Ia Diary, Ab. Nr. 1123/40g.kdos, HeeresgruppenBefhel Nr. 6, 25 May 1940; IWM: EDS/AL/1371 – Heeresgruppe A Ia Diary, Ab. Nr. 1140/40g.kdos, HeeresgruppenBefhel Nr. 8, 30 May 1940. IWM: EDS/AL/1372 – Heeresgruppe B Ia Diary, Ab. Nr. 350/40gk, Erläuterungen zur Anlage 2 – Verteilung der Heerestruppen, 31 May 1940.
14. IWM: EDS/AL/1371 – Heeresgruppe A Ia Diary, Anlage 42, Notizen uber ein gesprach zwischen Generalleutnant v.Sodenstern und Chef des Generalstabes des Heeres, 26 May 1940.
15. IWM: Audio/12303 – Leonard Stanley Fearnley, Reel 3.
16. IWM: EDS/AL/1429 – 4. Armee Ia, Kriegstagebuch, 26 May 1940; TNA: HW 5/1 – GC&CS Decrypts, CX/FJ/107.

17 Webster and Frankland, *Preparations*, p. 215.
18 TNA: AIR 22/54 – Air Ministry Weekly Report No. 38, Air Operations and Intelligence for the Week Ending 29 May 1940.
19 TNA: AIR 14/676 – Portal, Dispatch.
20 TNA: AIR 14/676 – 5 Group Report, 9 May–4 June 1940.
21 Harris, *Bomber Offensive*, p. 40.
22 TNA: AIR 14/673 – 5 Group 3 Group Report on Operations during the Period 5–16 June 1940; Harris, *Bomber Offensive*, p. 40.
23 TNA: AIR 14/673 – 4 Group 3 Group Report on Operations during the Period 5–16 June 1940.
24 TNA: AIR 14/676 – Portal, Dispatch.
25 *Ibid.*
26 *Ibid.*
27 *Ibid.*
28 Webster and Frankland, *Preparations*, p. 145.
29 TNA: AIR 14/676 – Portal, Dispatch.
30 TNA: AIR 20/2768 – Group Captain Baker, 'Our Air Policy during the Present Phase', 18 May 1940.
31 *Ibid.*
32 TNA: AIR 14/449 – Air Chief Marshal Dowding to Air Marshal Peirse, 14 May 1940.
33 TNA: AIR 2/7068 – Telegram Air Chief Marshal Dowding to H. Balfour, Under-Secretary of State for Air, 24 May 1940.
34 TNA: AIR 20/2780 – Memorandum by Air Marshal Portal, 17 May 1940.
35 *Ibid.*
36 TNA: AIR 20/2768 – Group Captain Baker, 'Our Air Policy during the Present Phase', 18 May 1940.
37 TNA: AIR 25/29 – Appendices to ORB: 2 Group, Operational Instructions (Ops. 113.), 25 May 1940.
38 TNA: AIR 14/676 – 3 Group Report, 9 May–4 June 1940.
39 TNA: AIR 14/676 – 2 Group Report, 10 May–3 June 1940.
40 *Ibid.*
41 TNA: AIR 14/1019 – Reports on Bombing Operations Carried Out on 31 May 1940.
42 TNA: AIR 14/676 – 2 Group Report, 10 May–3 June 1940.
43 TNA: AIR 16/1172 – Operations of Fighter Squadrons in Support of BEF Withdrawal, 27 May 1940.
44 TNA: AIR 14/213 – Reports on Bombing Operations Carried Out on 26 May 1940; TNA: AIR 22/168 – A.M.W.R. Daily Report for Summary, No. 312, 27 May 1940; TNA: AIR 25/29 – Appendices to ORB: 2 Group Report on Operations Carried out on 26 May 1940.

45 TNA: AIR 14/1019 – Reports on Bombing Operations Carried Out on 26 May 1940; TNA: AIR 27/263 – ORB: 21 Squadron.
46 TNA: AIR 14/1019 – Reports on Bombing Operations Carried Out on 26–27 May 1940; TNA: AIR 25/22 – ORB: 2 Group.
47 TNA: AIR 14/1019 – Reports on Bombing Operations Carried Out on 27 May 1940; TNA: AIR 24/217 – Bomber Command Intelligence Reports and Summaries, May 1940; TNA: AIR 25/22 – ORB: 2 Group; TNA: AIR 27/412 – ORB: 40 Squadron.
48 NARA: T315, R1689, Frame 380 – AOK 6, Armee-Befehl Nr. 14, 27 May 1940; IWM: EDS/AL/1429 – 4. Armee Ia, Kriegstagebuch, 27 May 1940; TNA: AIR 14/1019 – Reports on Bombing Operations Carried Out on 26 May 1940.
49 TNA: AIR 16/1172 – Operations of Fighter Squadrons in Support of BEF Withdrawal, 27 May 1940.
50 TNA: AIR 20/2760 – Report of Wing Commander Embry, August 1940; TNA: AIR 25/29 – Appendices to ORB: 2 Group, Operational Instructions (Ops. 144), 27 May 1940.
51 IWM: EDS/AL/1374 – XXXXI. A.K. Ia, War Diary, 24 May 1940.
52 TNA: AIR 14/1019 – Reports on Bombing Operations Carried Out on 27 May 1940.
53 TNA: AIR 14/1019 – Reports on Bombing Operations Carried Out on 27 May 1940; TNA: AIR 22/51 – Resume of Air Operations for the Period up to 06.00, 28 May 1940; TNA: AIR 27/412 – ORB: 40 Squadron.
54 TNA: AIR 14/1019 – Reports on Bombing Operations Carried Out on 27 May 1940.
55 TNA: HW 5/2 – GC&CS Decrypts, CX/JQ/2.
56 IWM: EDS/AL/1429 – 4. Armee Ia, Kriegstagebuch, 27 May 1940.
57 TNA: AIR 14/1019 – Reports on Bombing Operations Carried Out on 27 May 1940.
58 TNA: AIR 14/1019 – Reports on Bombing Operations Carried Out on 27 May 1940; TNA: AIR 22/168 – A.M.W.R. Daily Report for Summary, No. 312, 27 May 1940; TNA: AIR 25/22 – ORB: 2 Group; TNA: AIR 25/29 – Appendices to ORB: 2 Group, Operational Instructions (Ops. 128), 26 May 1940; TNA: AIR 27/841 – ORB: 107 Squadron.
59 TNA: AIR 14/1019 – Reports on Bombing Operations Carried Out on 28 May 1940.
60 TsAMO RF: Ф.500 оп.12454 д.54 – Erfahrungsbericht des Generalkommando XIV. A.K. und Stellungnahme zu den Erfahrungsberichten der 9. und 10. *Panzer-Division* über die Kämpfe im Westen, 28 July 1940, p. 4.
61 TNA: AIR 14/1019 – Reports on Bombing Operations Carried Out on 28 May 1940.

62 TNA: AIR 14/1019 – Reports on Bombing Operations Carried Out on 28 May 1940; TNA: AIR 27/263 – ORB: 21 Squadron.
63 TNA: AIR 14/1019 – Reports on Bombing Operations Carried Out on 28 May 1940.
64 Ibid.
65 Ibid.
66 Churchill, *Finest Hour,* p. 94.
67 TNA: AIR 24/217 – Bomber Command Intelligence Report No. 616, 26 May 1940.
68 IWM: EDS/AL/1372 – *Heeresgruppe* B Ia Diary, Anruf General Mieth, *c.* 26 May 1940; TNA: AIR 14/676 – Portal, Dispatch; NARA: T315, R1689, Frame 307 – Anruf Generalmajor Schlieper von AOK 18 O.Qu., 2 June 1940; TNA: CAB 146/452 – EDS Report on Daily Movements of German Divisions, 28 May 1940.
69 NARA: T315, R1689, Frame 314 – Instructions of 223. Infanterie-Division to Infanterie-Regiment 344., 1 June 1940.
70 IWM: EDS/AL/1374 – XXXXI. A.K. Ia, War Diary, 29 May 1940.
71 TNA: AIR 14/1019 – Reports on Bombing Operations Carried Out on 29 May 1940; TNA: AIR 24/217 – Bomber Command Intelligence Reports and Summaries, May 1940.
72 TNA: AIR 14/1019 – Reports on Bombing Operations Carried Out on 29 May 1940; TNA: AIR 27/841 – ORB: 107 Squadron.
73 TNA: AIR 14/1019 – Reports on Bombing Operations Carried Out on 29 May 1940; TNA: AIR 27/857 – ORB: 110 Squadron.
74 TNA: AIR 14/1019 – Reports on Bombing Operations Carried Out on 29 May 1940.
75 Ellis, *War in France,* p. 211; Lord, *Miracle,* p. 105; Sebag-Montefiore, *Dunkirk,* p. cccxxvi.
76 TNA: AIR 14/1019 – Reports on Bombing Operations Carried Out on 30 May 1940; TNA: AIR 22/9 – A.M.W.R. Daily Summary of Air Operations for 30 May, No. 316, 31 May 1940.
77 Ibid.
78 Ibid.
79 IWM: EDS/AL/1405 – Ab. Nr. T 641/40g, Telegram Heeresgruppe B to Heeresgruppe A, 31 May 1940.
80 TNA: AIR 14/1019 – Reports on Bombing Operations Carried Out on 31 May 1940.
81 TNA: AIR 14/1019 – Reports on Bombing Operations Carried Out on 31 May 1940; TNA: AIR 27/681 – ORB: 82 Squadron.
82 TNA: AIR 14/1019 – Reports on Bombing Operations Carried Out on 31 May 1940; TNA: AIR 25/29 – Appendices to ORB: 2 Group, Report on Operations Carried out on 31 May 1940.

83 TNA: AIR 14/1019 – Reports on Bombing Operations Carried Out on 31 May 1940; TNA: AIR 24/217 – Bomber Command Intelligence Reports and Summaries, May 1940; TNA: AIR 27/841 – ORB: 107 Squadron.

84 TNA: AIR 14/1019 – Reports on Bombing Operations Carried Out on 31 May 1940; TNA: AIR 24/217 – Bomber Command Intelligence Reports and Summaries, May 1940; TNA: AIR 27/857 – ORB: 110 Squadron; TNA: AIR 27/862 – Appendices to ORB: 110 Squadron, Appendix 179, Operational Instructions from 2 Group, 12.15, 31 May 1940.

85 TNA: AIR 16/1173 – Back Violet to Bomber Command, 'Summary of Air Operations for Period 10.00–13.00, 29 May 1940'; TNA: CAB 44/62 – BEF Operations, I Corps: Part II.

86 TNA: WO 167/700 – 1 Grenadier Guards War Diary.

87 TNA: AIR 14/1019 – Reports on Bombing Operations Carried Out on 31 May 1940; TNA: AIR 27/847 – Appendices to ORB: 107 Squadron, 31 May 1940; TNA: AIR 27/862 – Appendices to ORB: 110 Squadron, Appendix 183–5, Operational Instruction from 2 Group, 31 May 1940; TNA: WO 167/134 – I Corps Assistant Director Survey.

88 TNA: AIR 14/1019 – Reports on Bombing Operations Carried Out on 31 May 1940; TNA: AIR 27/681 – ORB: 82 Squadron.

89 Ibid.

90 TNA: AIR 14/1019 – Reports on Bombing Operations Carried Out on 31 May 1940.

91 TNA: AIR 14/1019 – Reports on Bombing Operations Carried Out on 31 May 1940; TNA: AIR 24/217 – Bomber Command Intelligence Reports and Summaries, May 1940; TNA: AIR 27/412 – ORB: 40 Squadron.

92 TNA: AIR 14/1019 – Reports on Bombing Operations Carried Out on 31 May 1940; TNA: AIR 24/217 – Bomber Command Intelligence Reports and Summaries, May 1940; TNA: AIR 27/857 – ORB: 110 Squadron.

93 Nina Burls, 'RAF Bombs and Bombing: 1939–1945', *Royal Air Force Historical Society*, Vol. 45 (2009), p. 31.

94 TNA: AIR 20/2760 – Report of Wing Commander Embry, August 1940.

95 TNA: AVIA 46/163 – Bombs, Development and Production; TNA: AVIA 46/285 – Bombs, Development; Burls, 'RAF Bombs', p. 31.

96 TNA: AIR 14/676 – 2 Group Report, 10 May–3 June 1940.

97 IWM: Audio/3189 – Robert Victor Goddard, Reel 8–9.

98 TNA: AIR 24/218 – Bomber Command Intelligence Reports and Summaries, June 1940; TNA: WO 167/134 – I Corps Assistant Director Survey; Churchill, *Finest Hour*, p. 103; Goebbels, *Tagebücher: Band 8*, p. 147; Jacobsen, *Dünkirchen*, p. 147.

99 TNA: AIR 20/4447 – Letter from Major General Johnson to Lieutenant General Fisher, 8 June 1940.

100 Hewitt cited in Atkin, *Pillar of Fire*, p. 184.
101 IWM: Audio/16053 – David Noel Hugh Tyacke, Reel 14.
102 TNA: AIR 20/4447 – Letter from Major General Johnson to Lieutenant General Fisher, 8 June 1940.
103 Ellis, *War in France*, p. 235.
104 *Ibid.*
105 TNA: AIR 25/29 – Appendices to ORB: 2 Group, Operational Instructions (Ops. 202), 1 June 1940.
106 TNA: AIR 14/213 – Reports on Bombing Operations Carried Out on 1 June 1940; TNA: AIR 27/263 – ORB: 21 Squadron.
107 IWM: Audio/11247 – Falck, Reel 5; TNA: AIR 24/218 – Bomber Command Intelligence Summary, No. 217, 1 June 1940; Jacobsen Dünkirchen p. 146.
108 TNA: AIR 14/213 – Reports on Bombing Operations Carried Out on 1 June 1940; TNA: AIR 25/29 – Appendices to ORB: 2 Group, Operational Instructions (Ops. 214), 1 June 1940; TNA: AIR 27/202 – ORB: 15 Squadron.
109 TNA: AIR 14/213 – Reports on Bombing Operations Carried Out on 1 June 1940; TNA: AIR 22/169 – A.M.W.R. Daily Report for Summary, No. 318, 2 June 1940; TNA: AIR 24/218 – Bomber Command Intelligence Reports and Summaries, June 1940.
110 TNA: AIR 14/213 – Reports on Bombing Operations Carried Out on 1 June 1940.
111 *Ibid.*
112 IWM: Audio/12303 – Fearnley, Reel 3; TNA: AIR 14/213 – Reports on Bombing Operations Carried Out on 2 June 1940.
113 TNA: AIR 25/29 – Appendices to ORB: 2 Group, Operational Instructions (Ops. 552), 2 June 1940.
114 TNA: AIR 27/862 – Appendices to ORB: 110 Squadron, Appendix 192, Report to 2 Group on Bombing Attack, 2 June 1940.
115 TNA: AIR 14/213 – Reports on Bombing Operations Carried Out on 2 June 1940.
116 IWM: Audio/12303 – Fearnley, Reel 3.
117 TNA: AIR 14/213 – Reports on Bombing Operations Carried Out on 2 June 1940; TNA: AIR 27/841 – ORB: 107 Squadron; TNA: AIR 27/848 – Appendices to ORB: 107 Squadron, Appendix 50C, Report to 2 Group on Bombing Attack, 2 June 1940.
118 TNA: AIR 14/213 – Reports on Bombing Operations Carried Out on 2 June 1940.
119 IWM: Audio/12303 – Fearnley, Reel 3.
120 TNA: AIR 14/213 – Reports on Bombing Operations Carried Out on 3 June 1940; TNA: AIR 25/58 – Appendices to ORB: 3 Group, Results of Operations for Night of 3 June 1940; TNA: AIR 27/263 – ORB: 21 Squadron.
121 TNA: AIR 14/676 – Portal, Dispatch.
122 IWM: EDS/AL/1372 – *Heeresgruppe* B Ia Diary, Ab. Nr. 350/40g.Kdos.v., Forces Available for Fall Rot, 31 May 1940.

123 TNA: AIR 14/676 – 3 Group Report, 9 May–4 June 1940.
124 TNA: AIR 27/894 – Appendices to ORB: 115 Squadron, Appendix C.41, Operational instruction from 3 Group for night of 26 May 1940.
125 TNA: AIR 25/51 – ORB: 3 Group.
126 TNA: AIR 27/894 – Appendices to ORB: 115 Squadron, Appendix C.41, Operational Instruction from 3 Group for Night of 26 May 1940.
127 TNA: AIR 24/217 – Bomber Command Intelligence Summary, No. 206, 27 May 1940; TNA: AIR 25/51 – ORB: 3 Group; TNA: AIR 27/125 – ORB: 9 Squadron.
128 TNA: AIR 24/217 – Bomber Command Intelligence Summary, No. 206, 27 May 1940; TNA: AIR 27/887 – ORB: 115 Squadron; TNA: AIR 27/894 – Appendices to ORB: 115 Squadron, Appendix D.45, Report on Operations for Night of 26 May 1940.
129 BA/MA: N 671/6 – Richthofen, Kriegstagebuch, 24 May 1940.
130 TNA: AIR 25/109A – ORB: 5 Group.
131 TNA: AIR 20/4447 – Air support of the BEF in France, May–June 1940; TNA: AIR 22/168 – A.M.W.R. Daily Report for Summary, No. 314, 29 May 1940; TNA: AIR 25/109A – ORB: 5 Group; TNA: AIR 27/894 – Appendices to ORB: 115 Squadron, Appendix C.42, Operational Instruction from 3 Group for Night of 27 May 1940.
132 TNA: AIR 27/125 – ORB: 9 Squadron.
133 TNA: AIR 22/51 – Resume of Air Operations for the Period up to 06.00, 28 May 1940; TNA: AIR 25/51 – ORB: 3 Group; TNA: AIR 27/397 – ORB: 38 Squadron; TNA: AIR 27/404 – Appendices to ORB: 38 Squadron; TNA: AIR 27/894 – Appendices to ORB: 115 Squadron, Appendix D.46, Report on Operations for Night of 27 May 1940.
134 TNA: AIR 27/125 – ORB: 9 Squadron; TNA: AIR 27/887 – ORB: 115 Squadron.
135 TNA: AIR 22/168 – A.M.W.R. Daily Report for Summary, No. 314, 29 May 1940; TNA: AIR 25/109A – ORB: 5 Group.
136 TNA: AIR 24/217 – Bomber Command Intelligence Reports and Summaries, May 1940; TNA: AIR 25/51 – ORB: 3 Group; TNA: AIR 25/97 – Appendices to ORB: No. 4 Group, May 1940; AIR 27/894 – Appendices to ORB: 115 Squadron, Appendix C.43, Operational Instruction from 3 Group for Night of 27 May 1940.
137 TNA: AIR 27/388 – ORB: 37 Squadron; TNA: AIR 27/397 – ORB: 38 Squadron; TNA: AIR 27/645 – ORB: 75 Squadron; AIR 27/649 – Appendices to ORB: 75 Squadron; TNA: AIR 27/887 – ORB: 115 Squadron.
138 TNA: AIR 25/93 – ORB: 4 Group; TNA: AIR 27/655 – ORB: 77 Squadron.
139 TNA: AIR 24/217 – Bomber Command Intelligence Reports and Summaries, May 1940.
140 Air Vice-Marshal Douglas to Air Marshal Portal 'Directives to the Air Officer Commanding-in-Chief, Bomber Command', 4 June 1940, reproduced in Charles Webster and Noble Frankland, *The Strategic Air Offensive against Germany, 1939–1945, Vol. IV, Annexes and Appendices* (London: HMSO, 1961), p. 115.

141 TNA: HW 5/2 – GC&CS Decrypts, CX/JQ/32.
142 TNA: AIR 25/109A – ORB: 5 Group.
143 TNA: AIR 16/1071 – Air Ministry Air Intelligence, AI1W, to Back Violet, Bomber Command and Fighter Command, 31 May 1940; TNA: AIR 22/168 – A.M.W.R. Daily Report for Summary, No. 314, 29 May 1940; TNA: AIR 27/655 – ORB: 77 Squadron; TNA: AIR 27/807 – ORB: 102 Squadron.
144 TNA: AIR 15/898 – N.L.O. Log; TNA: AIR 25/51 – ORB: 3 Group.
145 TNA: AIR 25/51 – ORB: 3 Group; Major F. A. de V. Robertson, 'At a Wellington Station', *Flight*, XXXVIII, No. 1669, (19 December 1940), p. C.
146 TNA: AIR 20/6107 – Air Vice-Marshal Douglas, Message Regarding the Decision on Employment of the Bomber Force made by the Chief of the Air Staff, 30 May 1940.
147 *Ibid.*
148 TNA: AIR 27/887 – ORB: 115 Squadron.
149 TNA: AIR 22/51 – Air Ministry Daily Resume of Air Operations for the Period up to 06.00, 31 May 1940; TNA: AIR 25/51 – ORB: 3 Group.
150 TsAMO RF: Ф.500 оп.12454 д.54 – Erfahrungsbericht des Generalkommando XIV. A.K. und Stellungnahme zu den Erfahrungsberichten der 9. und 10. *Panzer-Division* über die Kämpfe im Westen, 28 July 1940, p. 5.
151 *Ibid.*, pp. 4–5.
152 IWM: EDS/AL/1405 – Ab. Nr. T 641/40g, Telegram Heeresgruppe B to Heeresgruppe A, 31 May 1940.
153 TNA: AIR 25/51 – ORB: 3 Group.
154 TNA: AIR 24/217 – Bomber Command Intelligence Reports and Summaries, May 1940; TNA: AIR 24/218 – Bomber Command Intelligence Reports and Summaries, June 1940.
155 TNA: AIR 25/51 – ORB: 3 Group; TNA: AIR 27/125 – ORB: 9 Squadron.
156 TNA: AIR 27/894 – Appendices to ORB: 115 Squadron, Appendix C.45, Operational Instruction from 3 Group for Night of 1 June 1940.
157 TNA: AIR 22/51 – Resume of Air Operations for the Period up to 06.00, 3 June 1940; TNA: AIR 27/887 – ORB: 115 Squadron.
158 IWM: EDS/AL/1405 – Ab. Nr. T654/40g, Telegram Heeresgruppe B to Heeresgruppen A and C, 2 June 1940.
159 IWM: EDS/AL/1405 – Ab. Nr. T650/40g, Telegram Heeresgruppe B to Heeresgruppen A, 1 June 1940.
160 TsAMO RF: Ф.500 оп.12474 д.168 – Unterlagen der Ia-Abteilung des Generalkommandos des X. Armeekorps: Erfahrungsberichte des Korps zu den Kämpfen in den Niederlanden und bei Dünkirchen, 27 July 1940, pp. 6–7.
161 TNA: AIR 25/109A – ORB: 5 Group.
162 TNA: AIR 24/218 – Bomber Command Intelligence Reports and Summaries, June 1940; TNA: AIR 25/93 – ORB: 4 Group.

163 TNA: AIR 24/218 – Bomber Command Intelligence Reports and Summaries, June 1940.
164 TNA: AIR 25/51 – ORB: 3 Group.
165 TNA: AIR 24/218 – Bomber Command Intelligence Reports and Summaries, June 1940; TNA: AIR 25/51 – ORB: 3 Group; TNA: AIR 27/1000 – ORB: 149 Squadron.
166 IWM: EDS/AL/1405 – Heeresgruppe B Headquarters, Tagesendmeldung, 3 June 1940.
167 TNA: AIR 24/218 – Bomber Command Intelligence Reports and Summaries, June 1940; TNA: AIR 25/93 – ORB: 4 Group; TNA: AIR 25/109A – ORB: 5 Group.
168 TNA: AIR 24/218 – Bomber Command Intelligence Reports and Summaries, June 1940; TNA: AIR 25/93 – ORB: 4 Group; TNA: AIR 27/543 – ORB: 58 Squadron; TNA: AIR 27/543 – ORB: 58 Squadron.
169 TNA: AIR 20/2780 – Memorandum by Air Marshal Portal, 17 May 1940.
170 TNA: AIR 14/676 – 2 Group, 10 May–3 June 1940.
171 NARA: T315, R1761, Frame 726 – Aerial Photo of Ypres with Demolished Bridges Marked, c.29 May 1940; Frame 728-254. Divisionsbefehl für den Angriff über den Ypern-Kanal, 29 May 1940; TNA: AIR 24/218 – Bomber Command Intelligence Reports and Summaries, June 1940.
172 TNA: AIR 14/676 – Portal, Dispatch.
173 *The Times*, 'Men's Gratitude to the Navy: Narrowing Defence Zone', 3 June 1940, p. 6.
174 NARA: T315, R1689, Frame 337 – Kommando 223. Infanterie-Division, Versorgung der Gerfangenen, 30 May 1940.
175 TsAMO RF: Ф.500 оп.12454 д.54 – Erfahrungsberichte über die Versorgung der Gruppe von Kleist im Feldzug gegen Frankreich, 27 July 1940, p. 12.
176 TNA: AIR 20/4447 – Air support of the BEF in France, May–June 1940; TNA: AIR 22/51 – Resume of Air Operations for the Period up to 06.00, 28 May 1940.
177 TNA: AIR 22/51 – Resume of Air Operations for the Period up to 06.00, 30 May.
178 TsAMO RF: Ф.500 оп.12452 д.95 – Tägliche Lageberichte West des Führungsstabes der Luftwaffe (1c), No. 267, Anlage 2, 30 May 1940.
179 IWM: EDS/AL/1429 – 4. Armee Ia, Kriegstagebuch, 26 May 1940.
180 TsAMO RF: Ф.500 оп.12454 д.54 – Erfahrungsberichte über die Versorgung der Gruppe von Kleist im Feldzug gegen Frankreich, 27 July 1940, p. 12.
181 Martin Van Creveld, *Supplying War: Logistics from Wallenstein to Patton* (Cambridge: Cambridge University Press, 2004), p. 147.
182 TNA: AIR 24/218 – Bomber Command Intelligence Reports and Summaries, June 1940.
183 TNA: AIR 24/217 – Bomber Command Intelligence Summary, No. 209, 28 May 1940; TNA: AIR 25/109A – ORB: 5 Group.
184 In addition to this alternative target, 4 Group squadrons were given the aerodrome at Flushing as a target of last resort should the Ruhr area be unapproachable owing to thunderstorms.

185 Goebbels, *Tagebücher*: Band 8, p. 141.
186 TsAMO RF: Ф.500 оп.12452 д.95 – Tägliche Lageberichte West des Führungsstabes der Luftwaffe (1c), No. 265, Anlage 2, 28 May 1940.
187 TNA: AIR 14/676 – 4 Group Report, 10 May–4 June 1940; TNA: AIR 14/773 – Air Bombardment to Delay Invasion Holland and Belgium; TNA: AIR 25/93 – ORB: 4 Group.
188 TNA: AIR 25/109A – ORB: 5 Group.
189 TNA: AIR 22/51 – Resume of Air Operations for the Period up to 06.00, 31 May 1940.TNA: AIR 24/217 – Bomber Command Intelligence Reports and Summaries, May 1940.
190 TNA: AIR 24/218 – Bomber Command Intelligence Reports and Summaries, June 1940; TNA: AIR 25/109A – ORB: 5 Group.
191 TNA: AIR 24/218 – Bomber Command Intelligence Reports and Summaries, June 1940; TNA: AIR 25/93 – ORB: 4 Group; TNA: AIR 25/109A – ORB: 5 Group.
192 TNA: AIR 20/2768 – Group Captain Baker, 'Our Air Policy during the Present Phase', 18 May 1940; Webster and Frankland, *Preparations*, p. 213.
193 Steinhilper, *Spitfire on my Tail*, pp. 259–61.
194 Gebhard Aders and Werner Held, *Chronik Jagdgeschwader 51 'Mölders'* (Stuttgart: Motorbuch, 2009), p. 53.
195 TNA: AIR 24/217 – Bomber Command Intelligence Summary, No. 206, 27 May 1940; TNA: AIR 14/676 – 5 Group Report, 9 May–4 June 1940; TNA: AIR 25/109A – ORB: 5 Group.
196 TNA: AIR 14/676 – 3 Group, 9 May–4 June 1940.
197 Steinhilper, *Spitfire on my Tail*, pp. 259–61.
198 TNA: AIR 24/218 – Bomber Command Intelligence Summary, No. 218, 2 June 1940.
199 TNA: AIR 20/2768 – Group Captain Baker, 'Our Air Policy during the Present Phase', 18 May 1940.
200 TNA: HW 5/2 – GC&CS Decrypts, CX/JQ/47, 64.
201 TNA: AIR 14/927 – Operational Summaries, Aircraft–Raids–Bombs, May–June 1940.
202 Slessor, *Central Blue*, pp. 296–7.
203 Richard Overy, *The Bombers and the Bombed: Allied Air War Over Europe, 1940–1945* (New York: Penguin, 2014), pp. 37–8, 49–51.
204 TNA: AIR 41/40 – RAF Narrative, Restricted Bombing, 1939 to 1941, p. 82.
205 TNA: AIR 20/2768 – Group Captain Baker, 'Our Air Policy during the Present Phase', 18 May 1940.
206 Koch, 'Strategic Air Offensive', p. 131.
207 IWM: EDS/AL/1374 – XXXXI. A.K. Ia, War Diary, 29 May 1940.
208 TsAMO RF: Ф.500 оп.12454 д.54 – Erfahrungsbericht des Generalkommando XIV. A.K. und Stellungnahme zu den Erfahrungsberichten der 9. und 10. *Panzer-Division* über die Kämpfe im Westen, 28 July 1940, p. 5.

209 TsAMO RF: Ф.500 оп.12454 д.58 – *Heeresgruppe* B, Erfahrungsbericht der Heeresgruppe B an das OKH über die Kämpfe im Westen: Anlage C – Bewaffnung und Ausrüstung, 24 September 1940, p. 2.
210 TsAMO RF: Ф.500 оп.12454 д.54 – Erfahrungsbericht des Generalkommando XIV. A.K. und Stellungnahme zu den Erfahrungsberichten der 9. und 10. *Panzer-Division* über die Kämpfe im Westen, 28 July 1940, p. 3.
211 TsAMO RF: Ф.500 оп.12454 д.54 – Erfahrungsberichte über die Versorgung der Gruppe von Kleist im Feldzug gegen Frankreich, 27. July 1940, p. 12.
212 Goebbels, *Tagebücher*: Band 8, p. 147.
213 IWM: EDS/AL/1405 – Ab. Nr. T 641/40g, Telegram Heeresgruppe B to Heeresgruppe A, 31 May 1940.

Conclusion

This book has explored the role of air power, the air operations of the RAF and the Luftwaffe, and the effectiveness of the air forces during the evacuation of Dunkirk. Reviewing the historical literature regarding Operation Dynamo and wider studies of the air forces during the Second World War revealed a consistent lack of detailed analysis regarding the use of air power or military effectiveness of the RAF and Luftwaffe during the evacuation. A significant study of the locations, condition and capabilities of the two air forces to achieve the operations they were assigned during the evacuation was also lacking. This work has established that German air power alone halted further daylight evacuations from Dunkirk on 1 June. Having established that the Luftwaffe was capable of halting daylight evacuations, this work has then explored the air operations throughout the evacuation to consider why similar success was not achieved before 1 June. In doing so, it has demonstrated the RAF's contribution to the evacuation, in particular, that the operations of Coastal Command and Bomber Command had greater value during Dynamo than previously appreciated. At times, Fighter Command successfully contested German air superiority over Dunkirk; however, this work has shown that British air power did not enable the success of the evacuation.

In considering the above it has been possible to contribute to the wider understanding of Operation Dynamo, the role that air power played in the evacuation, and the military effectiveness of the air forces in 1940. The successes and failures of both forces have been considered; by ascertaining the context in which the air forces engaged in operations during the evacuation of Dunkirk and the nature of their air operations, it has been possible to determine the extent to which the role of air power can be considered as having been effective during the evacuation. This concluding chapter brings together the key findings which relate to the issues above and re-evaluates the extent to which both sides achieved their objectives during Operation Dynamo. It concludes with a section which explores the implications of the research findings, both for understanding Dynamo and for considering the air forces in the context of the wider war.

The frequent criticism of the RAF voiced by the troops on the beach has led scholars to ask and answer the question 'where was the RAF?' Operating frequent sorties, the RAF were engaged in providing air cover of the evacuation. This work, however, questions how effective the RAF was in protecting the Dunkirk evacuation. By extension, the answer to this question required a thoughtful consideration of the Luftwaffe's operations. This has revealed that although the Luftwaffe failed to halt the Dunkirk evacuation they were able, when given suitable conditions, to inflict significant losses on the evacuation fleet. On 1 June, and temporarily on 29 May, the Luftwaffe successfully employed air power to deny Allied naval forces control of the sea in the vicinity of Dunkirk. On both days, the Luftwaffe influenced Allied maritime operations and the course of events. This work has demonstrated that unfavourable weather conditions were the primary cause for the Luftwaffe's failure and that Fighter Command was a secondary factor. The Luftwaffe's military effectiveness, its ability to produce a favourable outcome by applying air power through counter-sea operations, was restricted by the need for favourable flying conditions. Successful anti-surface vessel operations at Dunkirk also took place in conditions where ships had limited channels of navigation and restricted room for evasive action. Furthermore, the Luftwaffe's limitation in attacking targets with effective anti-aircraft defence during Dynamo is particularly noteworthy. The Royal Navy's anti-aircraft provision is frequently referenced as inadequate for deterring air attacks. During the evacuation of Dunkirk, however, Luftwaffe bomber crews frequently avoided ship-based anti-aircraft fire, opting instead to attack smaller, less important, targets which lacked such defences. These factors are all relevant when one considers whether the Luftwaffe could have successfully defended an attempted German invasion of Britain in 1940, had they proved capable of defeating the RAF in the Battle of Britain. It should not be assumed, however, that the Luftwaffe could not have translated at least part of the success it achieved on 1 June into operations to support an invasion. The extent to which the Luftwaffe could have prevented the Royal Navy from defeating an invasion attempt is impossible to state – there are too many unknowns as to the operating conditions either side would have sought to impose on the other before an invasion commenced – what Dynamo does indicate is that the Luftwaffe possessed the military effectiveness to have inflicted heavy losses to the Royal Navy if it was able to apply the full range of its air power.

In studying the operations of the RAF and the Luftwaffe during Dynamo it is notable that at various instances they both reduced their effort over Dunkirk in order to afford greater resources for alternative missions. In the case of the Luftwaffe, the need to support German Army forces and planning for future offensive action against the French reduced the resources available to attack evacuations from Dunkirk. Agility is a key characteristic of air power which can provide the flexibility to quickly and decisively shift the scale and scope of air operations needed to secure an objective. To do so, it is crucial to determine which objective is decisive – and requires the greatest weight of effort – and then to apply the necessary resources to achieve that objective. The Luftwaffe failed to achieve this; however, it is worth noting that weather prevented the use of certain forces over Dunkirk when the Luftwaffe would otherwise have chosen to employ them. Furthermore, the Luftwaffe did apply sufficient force to prevent large-scale embarkations using the facilities of Dunkirk harbour. Only the Royal Navy's extemporized use of the Dunkirk Mole allowed for the majority of the BEF to be recovered. Fighter Command also minimized its operational commitment, ostensibly for the immediate protection of British industries, but in reality to preserve its forces for the future air defence of Great Britain. Dunkirk was a decisive point in the Second World War and Fighter Command could have committed greater resources to contest air superiority over Dunkirk. Coastal Command and the FAA provided a level of operational commitment beyond what might reasonably have been expected. However, Bomber Command maintained strategic operations at a time when tactical necessities were of decisive importance to Britain's ability to continue the war. The lack of operational focus contributed to the lack of success which both sides experienced during the evacuation. The RAF and the Luftwaffe, therefore, both demonstrated shortcomings in their attempts to apply air power during Dynamo.

This study has revealed that neither side held an advantage in the distance that their forward air bases were located from the operations at Dunkirk. It does, however, note that the limitations of the Me 109's range left it at a disadvantage compared to the RAF's Spitfires and Hurricanes. The Luftwaffe's fighters were restricted in their loiter time over the evacuation area to a greater extent than has previously been considered. The lack of advanced air bases for the Luftwaffe's fighter units also reduced the time they were able to escort bomber formations over Dunkirk. Chapter 1 demonstrates that both sides had produced pilots sufficiently trained in general flying skills, but that training in navigation and night-flying was a limitation of both sides' pre-war training. This was, however, a greater impediment to the Luftwaffe's operations than it was to those of the RAF. The German fighter force was handicapped by weather conditions because in the absence of clear skies fighters struggled to make timely rendezvous with bomber formations. Unfavourable conditions therefore reduced the length of time German fighters could escort the bomber formations which increased the opportunities for Fighter Command's patrols to disrupt German attacks and reduce their military effectiveness. Fighter Command's larger patrols also struggled to operate effectively on days of low visibility. This was a consequence of not only the RAF fighter pilot's truncated training in low-visibility flying but also their lack of experience. RAF squadrons which operated over Dunkirk using Fighter Command's outdated tactics had only a small number of aircraft which were actively observing the air patrol areas for enemy aircraft, with the majority concentrating on maintaining station in close formation. The Luftwaffe's fighters, operating in looser formations, therefore found themselves at an advantage at times over Dunkirk when visibility was low.

The training of the bomber forces was also a factor in the evacuation of Dunkirk. It has previously been argued that 'the Luftwaffe became better trained in the fundamental navigation and flying skills required for strategic bombing' and was the only force in Europe that 'was even moderately competent at night flying and bad weather navigation' at the start of the Second World War.[1] Assessing the Luftwaffe's training, however, demonstrates that many of its crews were not sufficiently trained in the skills and techniques necessary to meet the challenges they faced during Operation Dynamo. This influenced the tasks to which they were assigned. Attacks on the disembarkation ports in England were planned but cancelled because of unfavourable weather. Night bombing of Dunkirk was also restricted, with bomber formations not being used en masse in this role to prevent troops being embarked during darkness. This was in part a consequence of the Luftwaffe's limited training in this area. In both cases the Luftwaffe opted to use their forces to attack the targets they were best trained to deal with rather than to carry out the attacks which might have caused the most disruption to the evacuation. Chapter 4 indicates that the Luftwaffe's operational focus was not solely on Dunkirk; this reduced the motivation to use their forces in this manner. Furthermore, with difficult conditions restricting daylight operations on a number of days, the Luftwaffe was unwilling to trust its crews' night-flying skills to attack the evacuation. The Luftwaffe's training syllabus aimed for a high standard in the skills required for night-flying; however, these were not always realized. The Luftwaffe did possess some crews well trained in navigation; however, this was by no means universal and many crews were lacking in the necessary navigation skills required during Dynamo. This limitation directly affected operations against the evacuation.

Bomber Command was also handicapped by the limitations of its pilot's navigational abilities. The weather conditions posed some difficulty for 2 Group's daylight operations. However, whilst the Luftwaffe's bombers operating against the evacuation were required to make attacks in a confined area, where weather conditions could prevent accurate bombing, the Blenheims of Bomber Command attacked a larger area of operations with numerous targets of opportunity. As a result, they were frequently able to find areas of sufficiently clear visibility and make attacks that the crews reported in positive terms – although the damage caused was limited. Bomber Command's training limitations were of most consequence in their night strikes against both tactical and strategic targets. Operations closer to the coast were least affected because there was less time and less opportunity for error in the bomber crew's navigation and reckoning from confirmed landmarks and radio bearings. Chapter 9 demonstrates, however, that the bombing itself was often not accurate. Lacking in accuracy, these attacks required enough bombs to be dropped to saturate the target area, negating bomb aiming errors and ensuring the target was hit. This was infrequent. The analysis of the training in Chapter 1, considered alongside the result of operations in Chapter 9, indicates that attacks on strategic targets were handicapped by navigation errors, greatly reducing the effect of Bomber Command's attacks.

Assessing the figure for the tonnage dropped in strategic missions demonstrated the extent to which Bomber Command's effort in support of Operation Dynamo was diluted in this regard. Considering Bomber Command's missions during Dunkirk it is impossible not to agree with Portal that the 'cardinal error' of diluting effort away from the decisive point was made. Unlike proponents of Bomber Command, this work concludes that the decisive point was tactical and operational support for the evacuation of the Allied armies, and that long-term strategic aims should have been temporarily subsumed. For British strategic bombing to have been an effective application of air power during Dynamo it would have had to have achieved a coercive effect on the Luftwaffe, forcing the reallocation of their air assets and compelling a change in their use of air power. To accomplish this Bomber Command would have had to have rapidly destroyed industrial targets in Germany which were directly linked to, and whose destruction would have had an immediate effect on, the German ability or will to continue prosecuting the war. Bomber Command did not have the capability to destroy such targets in 1940 and it certainly did not possess the means to do so with sufficient speed to influence the evacuation.

The RAF's use of air power against industrial targets of a strategic nature had no impact on the evacuation of Dunkirk. Bomber Command's tactical missions were of value, albeit limited, but they were smaller than the effort that might have been achieved had it been considered desirable to provide full support for Dynamo. That Bomber Command did not do so reveals two important aspects. The first was its commitment to the strategic effect of bombing, where attacks against industries of decisive importance were conceived as having the ability to bring a hostile power to its knees. The second was the Bomber Command did not undertake further effort from the tactical perspective because Bomber Command believed its ability to effectively attack them was limited. Bomber Command doubted the ability of its crews to find the precise targets necessary to interdict German troop and supply movements through Belgium and France. More than this, however, it also did not believe its attacks were capable of accurately hitting and destroying targets which could affect a meaningful disruption of either German forward movements or their logistics in the rear areas. Further efforts were rejected by Bomber Command, not because the importance of Dunkirk was not realized, but because it was believed that such efforts would not achieve meaningful results.

The decision to suspend daylight evacuations on 1 June was a consequence of naval losses to German air attacks and was not caused by artillery fire on Route X. The interpretation that artillery was not a primary cause of the suspension of daylight evacuation is significant in the historical literature of Operation Dynamo as it resolves a subject long lacking a clear consensus. This conclusion is also of considerable consequence to the study of the air forces during Dynamo as it determines that the Luftwaffe achieved a measure of success and that it possessed the capabilities to halt evacuations. Chapter 4 draws on the conclusion that daylight evacuations were halted by the Luftwaffe alone and establishes why the Luftwaffe was able to achieve success on this day. Chapter 4 then considers the cause of the Luftwaffe's failure to halt the evacuation before it was accomplished on 1 June. The assessment of the Luftwaffe's operations demonstrated that Fighter Command was not the primary cause for the Luftwaffe's failure to halt Operation Dynamo. Unfavourable weather conditions are instead established as the primary cause for the Luftwaffe's failure. The limitations of the Luftwaffe's crews in attacking targets in the face of anti-aircraft fire are demonstrated, as is the extent to which the Luftwaffe's night operations were limited.

The analysis of the Luftwaffe's operations demonstrates that having successfully damaged the inner harbour on 27 May the Luftwaffe struggled to operate in difficult weather conditions against targets which required precise bombing. Dive-bombing in particular was restricted by the low cloud base prevalent over Dunkirk for much of the evacuation. Furthermore, the failure of German medium bombers to achieve greater results was also influenced by unfavourable weather conditions. The Luftwaffe's medium bomber crews were not proficient in delivering individual anti-shipping air strikes with sufficient accuracy to halt the evacuation. Medium bombers were able to cause significant damage to the town and inner harbour of Dunkirk but the Dunkirk Mole remained a viable jetty for the embarkation of large numbers of troops throughout Dynamo. Successful attacks by the German medium bombers on the Mole, and other vulnerable embarkation targets, were handicapped by the low visibility over Dunkirk. As significant, however, were the weather conditions over the Luftwaffe's bomber airfields, which prevented operations, and on the approach routes to Dunkirk, which delayed attacks and prohibited the effective rendezvous of formations. This restricted the number of aircraft which could simultaneously arrive over Dunkirk to intensively bomb vulnerable embarkation targets and ships in the area. The scale of the effect that poor weather conditions had was magnified by the limitations of the Luftwaffe's training discussed in Chapter 1. In considering the Luftwaffe's operations it is reasonable to reflect on their lack of sufficient all-weather capabilities to safeguard mission assuredness when undertaking large-scale counter-sea operations – a short-coming which would have been shared by almost every air force in existence in 1940. It is also necessary, however, to conclude that no reasonable projection of the Dunkirk evacuation would have predicted that large embarkations would have been possible after the destruction of the inner harbour facilities. Criticism of the Luftwaffe at Dynamo should be tempered by the Royal Navy's feats of organization and endurance but most notably by their extraordinarily successful use of the Dunkirk Mole during the evacuation.

Chapter 6 provides an assessment of the effect and potential of German air attacks against the evacuation by night. It has been argued that night evacuations were vulnerable to disruption. However, the notion that the Luftwaffe could prohibit all evacuations during darkness is difficult to reconcile with their failure to meaningfully interfere with embarkations during days of poor visibility and difficult weather conditions. This was a consequence of limitations in the Luftwaffe's training. The Luftwaffe was always limited in the extent to which it could have prevented Operation Dynamo being at least a partial success.

Accounts by Luftwaffe senior figures which credited Fighter Command with ultimate responsibility for the Luftwaffe's failure have helped conceal the fact that it was the Luftwaffe's own limitations which prevented success.

The operations of the fighter forces over Dunkirk demonstrate that Fighter Command was a secondary factor in the Luftwaffe's failure to halt the evacuation. Fighter Command did undertake a considerable number of sorties in support of Operation Dynamo and, at times, was successful in breaking up German bomber formations. These successes came, however, on days of unfavourable weather conditions when the German fighter escorts were frequently delayed from rendezvousing with bomber formations. After 27 May, when Fighter Command had been able to inflict sizable losses on the German bombers, the fighter escorts of the Luftwaffe were largely able to protect its bomber formations. Even on 27 May, however, Fighter Command was unable to protect the evacuation. The inner harbour was rendered unusable following attacks on this day. That the evacuation continued was a consequence of the extemporized use of the Dunkirk Mole. On 29 May the Luftwaffe's fighters were largely successful in protecting the attacking bombers and permitting them the opportunity to attack the evacuation. Weather conditions on 30 May largely curtailed German air operations. On 31 May difficult conditions continued. Although Fighter Command impeded the bombing operations that occurred as conditions improved on 31 May the Luftwaffe's lack of significant success lay in the poor weather conditions and no Ju 87 operations were possible on this day. Furthermore, German fighter escorts were delayed, or unable, to achieve a timely rendezvous with bomber formations. This restricted the opposition that Fighter Command faced. Me 110 formations were handicapped by difficult weather conditions at their air bases, and along their flight routes to Dunkirk. Low visibility over Dunkirk also meant that the German fighter escorts had to come into closer contact with bomber formations to provide protection and from this position Fighter Command was able to achieve greater success against them. The losses of the evacuation fleet on 1 June demonstrated the limitations of Fighter Command's air cover of the evacuation.

The switch to larger patrols at less frequent intervals produced gaps in the air cover in which large losses to the evacuation fleet were caused on both 29 May and 1 June. Fighter Command's decision to operate larger four squadron patrols was a consequence of the success of the Luftwaffe's fighters. This work has argued that Fighter Command's change to four squadron patrols was a mistake because the larger patrols were unable to operate effectively over Dunkirk, with squadrons frequently being out of communication with each other and therefore failing to provide mutual support. Furthermore, the fighters patrolling Dunkirk frequently sought to achieve combat victories at the expense of maximizing the air cover of the evacuation. This had a more pronounced effect in larger patrols with an increased number of British aircraft engaging individual German aircraft, or chasing bombers far beyond the area of operations. The tactic of large wing patrols therefore not only opened up larger periods of time where Dunkirk lacked air defence but also reduced the combat potential of the forces involved.

That 11 Group chose to operate larger patrols, which were less effective in providing air cover for Dunkirk, was a consequence of the Luftwaffe's fighter operations. With large numbers of German fighters in both the *Frei Jagd* and escort role, Fighter Command opted not to contest air superiority throughout the day but to make a definite attempt to achieve air superiority at critical times. As has been discussed, the Luftwaffe's bombers, when permitted by good weather, were able to exploit the increased gaps in the air defence of Dunkirk. The events of 1 June illustrate that when clear weather allowed the Luftwaffe's fighters and bombers to co-operate effectively, Fighter Command's patrols were not able to protect the evacuation. Fighter Command succeeded in temporarily contesting air superiority but could not prevent the Luftwaffe achieving long periods in which they controlled the skies and the only restraint to bombing was the anti-aircraft provision of ships involved in the evacuation.

The analysis of fighter operations in Chapter 7 suggests that, in favourable weather conditions, German fighters proved capable of providing adequate air escorts and intercepting Fighter Command's larger formations. The German escort tactic was not to provide close escorts, where the manoeuvrability of the fighter was restricted by the need to keep station with the bomber formation, but instead to undertake free-ranging escorts. These proved effective against the standing patrols of the RAF. This contrasts to the close escorts German fighters were called on to provide during the Battle of Britain. Despite a high intensity of operations on 29 May and 1 June the German bombers did not suffer losses on the scale of 27 May.

Chapter 7 determined that the success that the Luftwaffe was able to achieve was not inevitable. Instead, Fighter Command failed to protect the evacuation because of the patrol tactics it operated and the military effectiveness of the German fighters. In addition, Dowding's decision to limit the number of squadrons available was an important factor in Fighter Command's failure to effectively protect the evacuation. The chapter argued that Dowding fought the battle with the aim of reducing the exposure of both the men and material under his command at the expense of providing the maximum air cover for Dunkirk. It refuted suggestions that the total number of Fighter Command squadrons which came to be used in Dynamo demonstrates the Command's support for the operation. It is shown that, with the expectation that Dynamo would last only forty-eight hours, the forces committed were below what Fighter Command might have made available to meet the demands for 'maximum' air support.[2] This conclusion has been reached after assessing whether Fighter Command's engagement at Dunkirk was reasonably limited by the simultaneous need to ensure the air defence of Britain. Fighter Command had reason to be concerned for the security of vulnerable targets in Britain; however, Fighter Command was provided with intelligence regarding Luftwaffe operations which should have allowed for a greater distribution of their forces over Dunkirk than was the case. Radar ensured that standing patrols for the air defence of the south of England were not required. As a result, a small reserve capable of intercepting bombing attacks could have been maintained whilst simultaneously increasing the air defence of Dunkirk. Contrary to claims that it was the air defence of Britain which reduced the force Fighter Command used, this work has demonstrated that Dowding consciously restricted the forces and equipment available for the air defence of Dunkirk in order to preserve Fighter Command for 'use in its proper sphere' – a future Battle of Britain.[3]

This study has also considered the operations of Coastal Command and the FAA, arguing that they were of greater significance to Dynamo than has previously been acknowledged. Low level patrols over the Channel and above the evacuation fleet were important in allowing Fighter Command to concentrate its squadrons at higher altitudes. Operating at height, Fighter Command was able to make more effective attacks to break up approaching bomber formations, whilst guarding against attacks from Luftwaffe fighter escorts. The patrols of Coastal Command also supplied valuable reconnaissance information to the organizers of the evacuation which was used to regulate the flow of shipping across the Channel and to ensure embarkations were maintained at a regular pace. The patrols guarding the flank of the evacuation from E-Boat and U-Boat attacks were a critical contribution to the success of night operations. Although the number of E-Boats was limited, they were capable of inflicting significant losses. The U-Boat menace caused a diversion of ships which might otherwise have been used for evacuation, to conduct sweeps to prevent their intrusion. These must have been increased further without Coastal Command's support and would have required further reinforcement if E-Boat operations were not delayed and disrupted by air patrols over the approach routes to the evacuation route. On the night of 2 June Coastal Command aircraft prevented E-Boats from closing on the evacuation routes; had E-Boats successfully added to the shipping casualties incurred on 1 June it is possible that the Royal Navy would have deemed evacuations were no longer viable from Dunkirk. Other attacks during this period caused disruption to the E-Boats' preparations. Coastal Command was therefore important in preventing the E-Boats from achieving greater successes against shipping engaged in Operation Dynamo.

This study of the air forces at Dunkirk has demonstrated both the utility and limitations of air power during the evacuation. The RAF and the Luftwaffe both achieved some limited successes during Dynamo. Ultimately, however, both air forces failed in their wider objectives; for both the RAF and Luftwaffe, Dunkirk represented an aerial defeat. Unfavourable weather conditions were the primary cause of the Luftwaffe's failure to prevent the evacuation of the Allied forces from Dunkirk. The docks were severely damaged on 27 May, important shipping losses were caused on 29 May, and further losses to air attack caused the suspension of daylight evacuations on 1 June. These successes must be seen, however, in the context of the wider failure to prevent the embarkation of the BEF and of substantial numbers of French troops. The Luftwaffe was slow to understand the improvised nature of embarkations from Dunkirk and, on days when weather conditions restricted the use of dive-bombers, the Luftwaffe's medium bombers made ineffectual attacks on shipping. The Luftwaffe's almost total failure to interfere with operations at night contributed to the evacuation's successful outcome. For the RAF Dynamo was in part a story of marginal contributions by Bomber Command as well as successful low level air defence, reconnaissance and anti-naval patrols by Coastal Command. The main operations of the RAF, undertaken by Fighter Command, represented, however, a significant defeat. During Operation Dynamo Fighter Command failed to effectively contest air superiority over the evacuation and protect the embarkation and shipping at Dunkirk.

Notes

1 Corum, *Luftwaffe*, p. 223.
2 TNA: AIR 16/1070 – Air Ministry to Fighter Command, Forwarded to 11 Group, 29 May 1940; Gardner, *Evacuation*, p. 122.
3 TNA: AIR 2/2946 – Air Chief Marshal Dowding to Under-Secretary of State for Air, 'Withdrawal of VHF Radio Equipment from Operational Fighter Squadrons', 1 June 1940.

Appendices

Appendix I Map of the Routes to Dunkirk and the Beaches

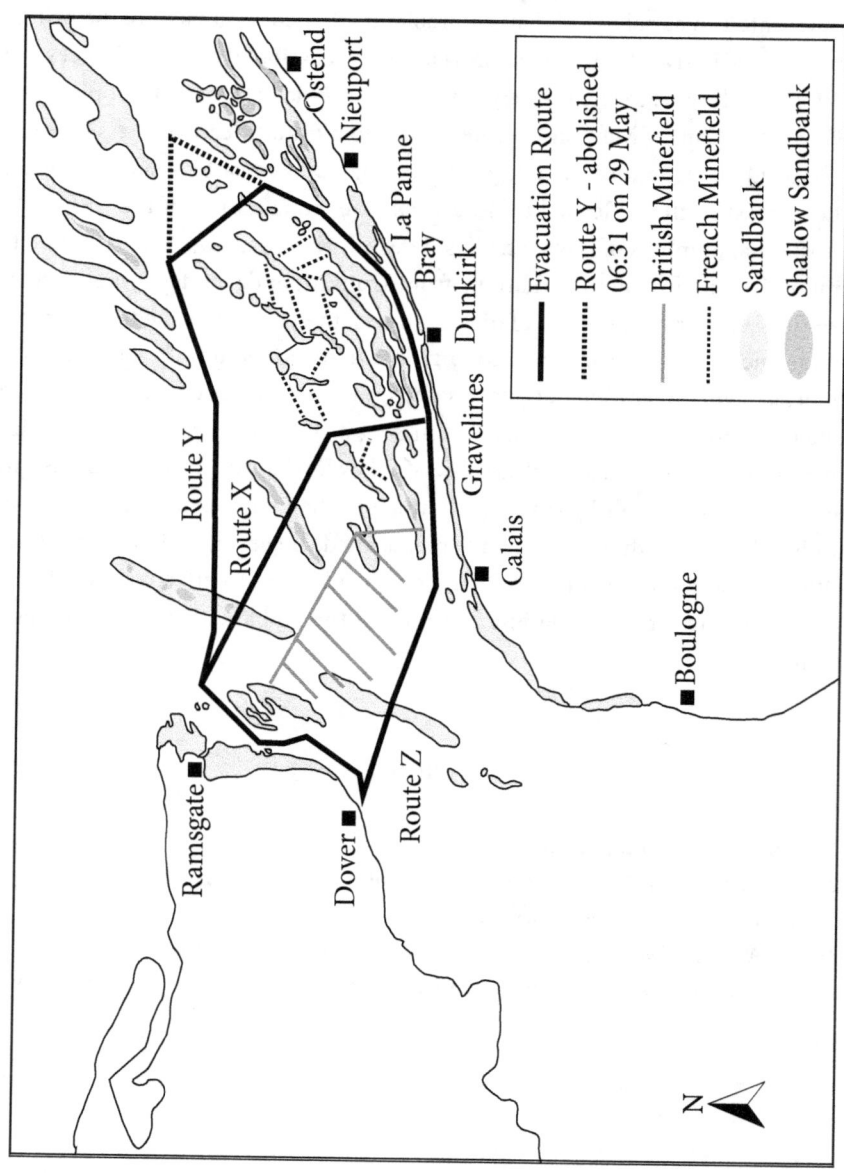

Appendix II List of Ships Mentioned

Name:	Type:
Abel Tasman	Skoot
SS *Aden*	Cargo Ship
HMS *Albury*	Minesweeper
Alice	Skoot
Amazone	Skoot
HMS *Amethyst*	Anti-Submarine Trawler
Andorra	Motorboat
HMS *Anthony*	Destroyer
HMS *Argyllshire*	Anti-Submarine Trawler
HMS *Basilisk*	Destroyer
SS *Ben-My-Chree*	Personnel Vessel
HMS *Bideford*	Sloop
ORP *Blyskawica*	Destroyer
Bonny Heather	Motorboat
FS *Bourrasque*	Destroyer
Brandaris	Skoot
HMS *Brighton Belle*	Paddle Minesweeper
HMS *Brighton Queen*	Paddle Minesweeper
HMS *Calcutta*	Anti-Aircraft Cruiser
HMS *Calvi*	Minesweeper Trawler
Caleta	Motor Yacht
Cambrian	Boom Defence Vessel
SS Canterbury	Personnel Vessel
Cariba	Skoot
SS *Ceres*	Cargo Ship
FS *Chacal*	Destroyer
SS *Clan Macalister*	Cargo Ship
HMS *Clythness*	Minesweeper Trawler
HMS *Codrington*	Destroyer
Commodore	Motorboat
Constant Nymph	Motor Yacht
HMS *Corfield*	Mine Destructor Trawler
SS *Côte d'Azur*	Personnel Vessel
HMS *Crested Eagle*	Paddle Minesweeper

Contest	*Tug*
Delta	Skoot
FS *Denis Papin*	Minesweeper Trawler
Despatch II	Skoot
HMS *Devonia*	Minesweeper
Doggersbank	Skoot
SS *Douaisien*	Cargo Ship
HMS *Duchess of Fife*	Paddle Minesweeper
Elizabeth Green	Motor Yacht
FS *Emile Deschamps*	Minesweeper
HMS *Emperor of India*	Paddle Minesweeper
HMS *Express*	Destroyer
HMS *Fair Breeze*	Drifter
SS *Fenella*	Personnel Vessel
Fervent	Motorboat
HMS *Fitzroy*	Minesweeper
Foremost 102	Steam Hopper Barge
FS *Foudroyant*	Destroyer
Fredanja	Skoot
Friso	Skoot
HMS *Gallant*	Destroyer
Glala	Motor Yacht
HMS *Glen Gower*	Paddle Minesweeper
HMS *Gracie Fields*	Paddle Minesweeper
HMS *Grafton*	Destroyer
HMS *Grenade*	Destroyer
HMS *Greyhound*	Destroyer
HMS *Grive* (also given as *Grieve*)	FAA yacht
Haig	War Ministry Fast Motorboat
HMS *Halcyon*	Minesweeper
HMS *Harvester*	Destroyer
HMS *Havant*	Destroyer
HMS *Hebe*	Minesweeper
Hilda	Skoot
Hondsrug	Skoot
HMS *Icarus*	Destroyer

HMS *Impulsive*	Destroyer
HMS *Intrepid*	Destroyer
HMS *Ivanhoe*	Destroyer
HMHS *Isle of Guernsey*	Hospital Ship
HMS *Jaguar*	Destroyer
HMS *Javelin*	Destroyer
FS *Joseph Marie*	Minesweeper
Jutland	Skoot
Kaap Falga	Skoot
HMS *Keith*	Destroyer
HMS *Kellett*	Minesweeper
SS *Killarney*	Personnel Vessel
HMS *Kindred Star*	Minesweeper Trawler
SS *King George V*	Personnel Vessel
SS *King Orry*	Armed Boarding Vessel
HMS *Kingfisher*	Corvette
HMS *Kingston Peridot*	Anti-Submarine Trawler
FS *L'Adroit*	Destroyer
Lady Brassey	Tug
Laroc	Motor Yacht
HMS *Leda*	Minesweeper
SS *Levenwood*	Personnel Vessel
Llanthony	Motor Yacht
SS *Loch Garry*	Personnel Vessel
HMS *Locust*	Gunboat
HMS *Lord Cavan*	Minesweeper Trawler
HMS *Lord Grey*	Minesweeper Trawler
HMS *Lord Howard*	Drifter
HMS *Lord Inchcape*	Minesweeper Trawler
SS *Lorina*	Personnel Vessel
HMS *Mackay*	Destroyer
SS *Maid of Orleans*	Personnel Vessel
HMS Malcolm	Destroyer
SS *Malines*	Personnel Vessel
SS Manxman	Personnel Vessel
SS *Manx-Maid*	Personnel Vessel

HMS *Marmion*	Paddle Minesweeper
SS *Mona's Isle*	Armed Boarding Vessel
SS *Mona's Queen*	Personnel Vessel
SS *Monique Schiaffino*	Cargo Ship
HMS *Montrose*	Destroyer
HMS *Mosquito*	Gunboat
FS *Moussaillon*	Minesweeper Trawler
HMS Nautilus	Danlayer Trawler
SS *Nephrite*	Coaster
New Prince of Wales	Motorboat
MV *Ngaroma*	Personnel Vessel
SS *Normannia*	Personnel Vessel
Oranje	Skoot
SS *Orford*	Personnel Vessel
HMS *Oriole*	Minesweeper
Pacific	Skoot
HMS *Pangbourne*	Minesweeper
HMHS *Paris*	Hospital Ship
Patria	Skoot
Persia	Tug
HMS *Plinlimmon*	Paddle Minesweeper
HMS *Polly Johnson*	Minesweeper Trawler
SS *Prague*	Personnel Vessel
HMS *Princess Elizabeth*	Paddle Minesweeper
FS *Purfina*	Patrol Boat
SS *Queen of the Channel*	Personnel Vessel
Reda	Motorboat
Reiger	Skoot
Renown	Bawley Cutter – Cockle Fishing Boat
Rika	Skoot
HMS *Ross*	Minesweeper
MV *Royal Daffodil*	Personnel Vessel
MV *Royal Sovereign*	Personnel Vessel
HMS *Sabre*	Destroyer
HMS *Saladin*	Destroyer
HMS *Salamander*	Minesweeper

HMS *Saltash*	Minesweeper
San Antonio	Skoot
HMS *Sandown*	Paddle Minesweeper
HMS *Scimitar*	Destroyer
SS *Scotia*	Personnel Vessel
MV *Sequacity*	Cargo Ship
HMS *Sharpshooter*	Minesweeper
HMS *Shikari*	Destroyer
Silver Queen	Passenger Launch
FS *Sirocco*	Destroyer
HMS *Skipjack*	Minesweeper
Skylark	Motorboat
HMS *Snaefell*	Paddle Minesweeper
HMS *Spurs*	Anti-Submarine Trawler
HMS *St Abbs*	Tug
HMS *St Achilleus*	Minesweeper Trawler
HMHS *St Andrew*	Hospital Ship
SS *St Camille*	Cargo ship
HMHS *St David*	Hospital Ship
HMS *St Fagan*	Tug
SS *St Helier*	Personnel Vessel
SS *St Seiriol*	Personnel Vessel
HMHS *St Julien*	Hospital Ship
HMS *Stella Dorado*	Anti-Submarine Trawler
Sun IV	Tug
HMS *Sutton*	Minesweeper
HMS *Thrifty*	Minesweeper Trawler
SS *Thuringia*	Personnel Vessel
Tilly	Skoot
Tiny	Skoot
Twente	Skoot
SS *Tynwald*	Personnel Vessel
HMS *Venomous*	Destroyer
FS *Vénus*	Minesweeper Trawler
HMS *Verity*	Destroyer
HMS *Vimy*	Destroyer

HMS *Vivacious*	Destroyer
Vrede	Skoot
Walton and Frinton RNLB	Lifeboat
HMS *Wakeful*	Destroyer
HMS *Waverley*	Paddle Minesweeper
HMS *Westward-Ho*	Paddle Minesweeper
HMS *Whitshed*	Destroyer
HMS *Whitehall*	Destroyer
HMS *Wild Swan*	Destroyer
HMS *Winchelsea*	Destroyer
HMS *Windsor*	Destroyer
HMS *Wolfhound*	Destroyer
HMS *Wolsey*	Destroyer
HMS *Worcester*	Destroyer
HMHS *Worthing*	Hospital Ship
Zeus	Skoot

Appendix III Glossary

Armeekorps	German Army Corps
Armee Ober Kommando	German Army Command
Back Violet	Air Component, BEF Rear-Headquarters
Begleitschutz	Fighter escorts
Blindflugschulen	Luftwaffe all-weather blind-flying training schools
E-Boat	British term for a German Motor Torpedo Boat (Schnellboot)
Erster Generalstabsoffizier	First General Staff Officer, Operations Officer
Fall Rot	Case Red. The Second Stage of the German Invasion of France
Fliegerkorps	Luftwaffe Corps
Fliegerdivision	Luftwaffe Division
Freie Jagd	Counter-force fighter sweeps over the combat area
Führer der Torpedoboote	Senior officer of torpedo boats
Geschwader	Luftwaffe Wing

Gruppe	Luftwaffe Group, comprising of three *Staffeln*, Commanding thirty to forty aircraft
Heeresgruppe	German Army Group
Immer Begleitschutz	Close fighter escorts
Jafü/Jagdführer	Officer commanding the fighters of a *Luftflotte*
Jagdgeschwader	Fighter Wing
Jagdstaffel	Squadron size unit of Luftwaffe fighter aircraft
Kampfgeschwader	Bomber Wing
Kette	Air formation comprising three aircraft
Lehrgeschwader	Multi-purpose Wing, could contain a range of units including fighter, reconnaissance, bomber and dive-bomber G*ruppen*
Luftflotte	Air Fleet
Lufttorpedo	Air launched torpedo
Oberkommando des Heeres	German Army High Command Headquarters
Oberkommando der Kriegsmarine	German Navy High Command Headquarters
Oberkommando der Luftwaffe	German Air Force High Command Headquarters
Okret Rzeczypospolitej Polskiej	Ship of the Republic of Poland
Operation Black Velvet	Air drop of supplies at Calais
Operation Corona	The broadcast of false and misleading information to German night-fighters by German-speaking Allied controllers
Operation Dynamo	The evacuation of Dunkirk and adjacent beaches
Rot/te	Fighter section/s comprising two aircraft
Schwarm	Fighter *Schwarm* comprised two *Rot*. Bomber *Schwarm* comprised two Ketten
Skoot	Dutch flat-bottomed motor Coasters (*Schuits*), designed to take the ground at low-water
Staffel	Typically between nine and twelve aircraft
Sturzkampfgeschwader	Dive-bomber Wing
Zerstörer	A Luftwaffe heavy 'Destroyer' twin engine fighter
Zerstörergeschwader	Luftwaffe heavy fighter Wing

Bibliography

Primary Unpublished

Bundesarchiv-Militärarchiv, Freiburg

N 671 – Nachlaß Richthofen [Richthofen Papers].
RL 2-II – Generalstab der Luftwaffe [Luftwaffe General Staff], Luftwaffenführungsstab.
RL 4 – Ausbildungsdienstellen im Reichsluftministerium [Training Offices in the Reich Aviation Ministry].
RL 7 – Oberste Truppenkommandobehörden der Luftwaffe [Luftwaffe Supreme Troop Command Authorities].
RL 8 – Kommandobehörden und Kommandostellen der Fliegertruppe [Headquarters and Command Posts, Flying Branch].
RL 10 – Fliegende Verbände [Flying Units].
RM 7 – Seekriegsleitung [Naval War Staff].

Central Archive of the Ministry of Defence of the Russian Federation (TsAMO RF)

Ф.500 оп.12451 д.50 – Documents from the Plans for 'Fall Rot', the Continuation of Operations to Occupy Northern France after the end of the Fighting in Artois and Flanders [http://wwii.germandocsinrussia.org/ru/nodes/872, accessed 20 June 2018].
Ф.500 оп.12452 д.95 – Daily Situation Reports of Air Force Command, West (1c) [https://wwii.germandocsinrussia.org/de/nodes/2447, accessed 31 July 2020].
Ф.500 оп.12454 д.50 – Reports on the Campaign in the West (1940) by Army Group Leader, the General of the Pioneers and Pioneer Battalion 51, the Commander of Artillery, and the Koluft with Heeresgruppe B [http://wwii.germandocsinrussia.org/de/nodes/52, accessed 20 June 2018].
Ф.500 оп.12454 д.54 – Reports on the Campaign in the West (1940) by *Panzergruppe* Kleist, XXII. *Armeekorps*, and 7., 9. and 10. *Panzer-Divisions* [http://wwii.germandocsinrussia.org/de/nodes/56, accessed 20 June 2018].
Ф.500 оп.12454 д.58 – Report on the Campaign in the West (1940) by Heeresgruppe B to OKH [http://wwii.germandocsinrussia.org/de/nodes/60, accessed 20 June 2018].
Ф.500 оп.12474 д.168 – Report on the Fighting in the Netherlands and Near Dunkirk, X. *Armeekorps* Ia, pp. 6–7 [http://wwii.germandocsinrussia.org/de/nodes/3206, accessed 20 July 2020].

Churchill Archives Centre, Cambridge (CAC)

CHAR 9 – Winston S. Churchill Speeches, Speech Notes and Other Material.
RMSY 8 – Papers of Admiral Sir Bertram Home Ramsay, Dover Command.

Imperial War Museum, London (IWM)

Audio Interviews

Audio/1062 – Royal Navy, Electrical Artificer, F. C. Turner.
Audio/2803 – RAF, Group Captain, John William Maxwell 'Max' Aitken.
Audio/3189 – RAF, Air Marshal, Robert Victor Goddard.
Audio/6365 – British Army, Colonel, Colin Merriam Glover.
Audio/6442 – British Army, Major, D'Arcy Keneln McCloughin.
Audio/6462 – British Army, Private, Leslie John Kearnes.
Audio/6703 – British Army, Captain, Anthony Richard Edward Ewart Rhodes.
Audio/6818 – British Army, General, James Louis Moulton.
Audio/6823 – British Army NCO, Jack Williams.
Audio/7186 – Royal Navy, Able Seaman, Ian Alan Nethercott.
Audio/7336 – RAF, Aircraftsman, Arthur Taylor.
Audio/7462 – RAF, Group Captain, Frederick William Winterbotham.
Audio/9721 – British Civilian, Small Boat Commander, Robert Charles Michael Vaughan Wynn Newborough.
Audio/9768 – British Civilian, aboard Thames Barge, Arthur William Joscelyne.
Audio/10049 – RAF, Group Captain, Denys Edgar Gillam.
Audio/10086 – British Civilian Sea Scout, aboard Motor Yacht Sundowner, Gerald Edward Ashcroft.
Audio/10093 – RAF, Air Vice-Marshal, Harold Arthur Cooper Bird-Wilson.
Audio/10119 – RAF, Wing Commander, Norman Patrick Watkins Hancock.
Audio/10128 – RAF, Wing Commander, Ronald Prosper 'Bee' Beamont.
Audio/10152 – RAF, Group Captain, Charles Brian Fabris Kingcombe.
Audio/10159 – RAF, Wing Commander, Hugh Spencer Lisle Dundas.
Audio/10478 – RAF, Air Commodore, Alan Christopher Deere.
Audio/11036 – RAF, Flight Lieutenant, Eric Francis Chandler.
Audio/11086 – RAF, Squadron Leader, Anthony Charles Bartley.
Audio/11103 – RAF, Wing Commander, Alan Geoffrey Page.
Audio/11247 – Luftwaffe, Colonel, Wolfgang Julius Feodor Falck.
Audio/11388 – Luftwaffe, General Walter Krupinski.
Audio/11449 – RAF, Squadron Leader, Peter Derrick Macleod Down.
Audio/11510 – RAF, Wing Commander, David George Samuel Richardson Cox.
Audio/11534 – FAA, Captain, Desmond Vincent-Jones.
Audio/11544 – RAF, Wing Commander, George Cecil Unwin.

Audio/11616 – RAF, Group Captain, George Binmore Johns.
Audio/12173 – RAF, Squadron Leader, Benjamin Harvey Bowring.
Audio/12217 – RAF, Flight Lieutenant, Maurice Equity Leng.
Audio/12303 – RAF, Flight Lieutenant, Leonard Stanley Fearnley.
Audio/12405 – RAF, Squadron Leader, John Beville Howard Nicholas.
Audio/12611 – RAF, Flying Officer, Norman Percy Gerald Barron.
Audio/12674 – RAF, Group Captain, Gerald Richmond Edge.
Audio/12780 – Royal Navy, Seaman, Victor Leslie Thomas Ayles.
Audio/13152 – RAF, Wing Commander, Peter Lawrence Parrott.
Audio/13607 – Royal Navy Volunteer Reserve, Sub-Lieutenant, William G. Hewett.
Audio/13663 – Royal Navy, Seaman, Robert William Eunson.
Audio/13856 – FAA, Commander, Ronald Cuthbert Hay.
Audio/13933 – Royal Navy, Lieutenant Commander, John Teague Gilhespy.
Audio/14368 – RAF, Group Captain, John Bidsee.
Audio/15985 – RAF, NCO, John Thompson.
Audio/16053 – British Army, Major General, David Noel Hugh Tyacke.
Audio/16056 – Major, Eldred Porter Banfield.
Audio/20137 – French Army, Gunner, Leon Wilson.
Audio/21291 – RAF, Wing Commander, James Gilbert Sanders.
Audio/22132 – Royal Navy, Seaman, William George Ridgewell.
Audio/26971 – RAF, Group Captain, Allan Wright.
Audio/27074 – Squadron Leader, Cyril Bamberger.
Audio/28766 – FAA, Lieutenant Commander, Anthony Montague 'Steady' Tuke.
Audio/30001 – RAF, Wing Commander, Peter Ayerst.
Audio/31394 – RAF, Wing Commander, Jack Hubert Hoskin.

Documents

Documents/11483a [LVM/3] – Private Papers of Admiral Sir Vaughan Morgan.
Documents/17217 – Private Papers of Sydney Ball.

Documents (Captured Enemy Documents Section)

EDS/AL/1371 – *Heeresgruppe* A Ia, War Diary, Appendices (February–May 1940).
EDS/AL/1372 – *Heeresgruppe* B Ia, War Diary, Appendices (May–June 1940).
EDS/AL/1374 – XXXXI. *Armeekorps* Ia, War Diary (February–July 1940).
EDS/AL/1384 – 6. Armee Ia, War Diary (May 1940).
EDS/AL/1399 – 10. Panzer-Division Ia, Extract from War Diary (May 1940).
EDS/AL/1405 – *Heeresgruppe* B Ia, Situation Reports (May–June 1940).
EDS/AL/1407 – XVI. *Armeekorps* Ia, War Diary (May 1940).
EDS/AL/1428 – *Heeresgruppe* A Ia, War Diary (February–May 1940) (trans.), War Office Translation Station, Captain Hilton, in 1948.
EDS/AL/1429 – 4. Armee Ia, War Diary (April–May 1940).

EDS/AL/1433 – *Heeresgruppe* B Ia, War Diary (May–June 1940) (trans.), War Office Translation Station, Captain Hilton, in 1948.

Film

Film/ADM/5059 – Royal Navy Instructional Film, *Smoke Screens at Sea* (1944).

Liddell Hart Centre for Military Archives, King's College, London (LHCMA)

ALANBROOKE 5 – General Brooke's [Later Field Marshal Alanbrooke] Diaries (1939–46).
BRIDGEMAN 2 – Major Robert Bridgeman's File on the BEF and the Flanders Campaign (1940), Including Lessons Learnt and Recommendations for Improvements (1940–43).
LIDDELL HART 15/15 – Papers of Reginald William Winchester ('Chester') Wilmot.
LINDSELL 1 – Papers relating to Lieutenant General Lindsell's service as Quartermaster General of the BEF in France and Belgium during World War Two (1939–42).

National Archives and Records Administration, Washington, DC (NARA)

T78, R269 – Records of OKH, Reports of General Stabes des Heeres, General der Artillerie (1941–45)
T315, R1689 – Records of German Field Commands, 223. Infanterie-Division.
T315, R1761 – Records of German Field Commands, 254. Infanterie-Division.
T321, R68 – Records of OKL, Files Produced by the Office of the Reichsminister der Luftfahrt und Oberbefehlshaber der Luftwaffe and the Luftwaffenführungsstab.
T321, R90 – Records of OKL, Files Produced by the Luftwaffenführungsstab.
T1022, R3979 – Records of the Befehlshabers der U-Boote.

The National Archives, Kew (TNA)

ADM 1 – Navy Department: Correspondence and Papers
ADM 199 – War History Cases and Papers, Second World War.
ADM 207 – Diaries and Standing Orders of Fleet Air Arm Squadrons.
ADM 223 – Intelligence Reports and Papers of the Naval Intelligence Division and Operational Intelligence Centre.
ADM 334 – Papers of Commander W. B. Luard.
ADM 358 – Admiralty Casualty Branch: Enquiries into Missing Personnel, 1939–45 War.
AIR 2 – Registered Files of the Air Ministry and Ministry of Defence.
AIR 5 – British Air Historical Branch Papers (Series II).

AIR 6 – Minutes, Meetings and Memoranda of the Air Board and Air Council.
AIR 8 – Registered Files of the Department of the Chief of the Air Staff.
AIR 10 – Air Publications and Reports
AIR 14 – Registered Files and Reports of Bomber Command.
AIR 15 – Registered Files and Reports of Coastal Command.
AIR 16 – Registered Files and Reports of Fighter Command.
AIR 19 – Private Office Papers of the Air Department.
AIR 20 – Papers Accumulated by the British Air Historical Branch.
AIR 22 – Periodical Returns, Intelligence Summaries and Bulletins.
AIR 24 – Operations Record Books: Commands.
AIR 25 – Operations Record Books: Groups.
AIR 26 – Operations Record Books: Wings.
AIR 27 – Operations Record Books: Squadrons.
AIR 32 – Registered Files and Reports of Flying Training Command and Technical Training Command.
AIR 35 – Registered Files of the British Air Forces in France
AIR 40 – Intelligence Reports and Papers of the Directorate of Intelligence and Related Bodies.
AIR 41 – Narratives and Monographs of the British Air Historical Branch.
AIR 50 – Combat Reports of the Second World War.
AVIA 13 – Registered Files of the Royal Aircraft Establishment.
AVIA 46 – Registered Files (Series 1) of the Ministry of Supply Establishment.
BT 389 – Merchant Shipping Movement Cards, Registry of Shipping and Seaman during the Second World War.
CAB 44 – Draft Chapters and Military Narratives for the War Histories of the Committee of Imperial Defence Historical Branch and Cabinet Office Historical Section.
CAB 65 – Minutes of the Cabinet and War Cabinet.
CAB 79 – Minutes of the Chiefs of Staff Committee.
CAB 106 – Archivist and Librarian Files (AL Series) of the Cabinet Office Historical Section.
CAB 146 – Files and Papers of the Enemy Documents Section (Cabinet Office Historical Section).
HW 5 – German Section: Reports of German Army and Air Force High Grade Machine Decrypts (CX/FJ, CX/JQ and CX/MSS Reports).
WO 106 – Correspondence and Papers of the Directorate of Military Operations and Military Intelligence, and Predecessors.
WO 167 – War Diaries of the British Expeditionary Force to France (1940).
WO 190 – German and Adjacent Countries Military Situation Reports of the Directorate of Military Operations and Intelligence.
WO 195 – Reports and Papers of the Advisory Council of Scientific Research and Technical Development, and the Later Scientific Advisory Council.

WO 208 – Directorate of Military Operations and Intelligence, and Directorate of Military Intelligence: Defence Intelligence Staff, Files.
WO 217 – Private War Diaries of Various Army Personnel, Second World War.
WO 219 – Military Headquarters Papers of the Supreme Headquarters Allied Expeditionary Force (1944–45).
WO 232 – Papers of the Directorate of Tactical Investigation.
WO 361 – Casualties (L) Branch (Department of the Permanent Under Secretary of State of the War Office) Enquiries into Missing Personnel (1939-45).

The National Meteorological Digital Archive (TNMDA)

DWR/1940 – Daily Weather Reports (1940).

USA Naval War College (USNWC)

Microfilm 354 – Oberkommando der Kriegsmarine Kriegstagebuch der Seekriegsleitung [War Diary of the German Naval Staff Operations Division] (trans.) U.S. Office of Naval Intelligence, 1948.

Primary Published

Books

Air Ministry, *AP1300: Royal Air Force War Manual, Part I: Operations* (London: Air Ministry, 1928).

Air Ministry, *AP1300: Royal Air Force War Manual, Part I: Operations* [2nd Edition] (London: Air Ministry, 1940).

Balck, Hermann, *The Memoirs of General of Panzer Troops Hermann Balck: Order in Chaos* (Lawrence, KS: University Press of Kentucky, 2015).

Barlone, D., *A French Officer's Diary: 23 August 1939 to 1 October 1940* (trans.) L. V. Cass (New York: Macmillan, 1943).

Bartlett, Captain Basil, *My First War: An Army Officer's Journal for May 1940, through Belgium to Dunkirk* (London: Chatto & Windus, 1940).

Baumbach, Werner, *The Life and Death of the Luftwaffe* (Costa Mesa, CA: Noontide, 1991).

Bouchier, Cecil 'Boy', *Spitfires in Japan: From Farnborough to the Far East – A Memoir* (Folkestone: Global Oriental, 2005).

Churchill, Winston S., *The Second World War, Vol. II: Their Finest Hour* (London: Cassell, 1949).

Cook, Denys, *Missing in Action: Or My War as a Prisoner of War* (n.p.: Trafford Publishing, 2013).

Development, Concept and Doctrine Centre, *Joint Defence Publication 0-30: UK Air and Space Power* [2nd Edition] (Shrivenham: Ministry of Defence, 2017).

Directorate of Air Staff, *AP3000* [3rd Edition] (London: Ministry of Defence, 1999).

Directorate of Air Staff, *AP3000* [4th Edition] (London: Ministry of Defence, 2009).

Douglas, Sholto, *Years of Command* (London: Collins, 1963).

Dundas, Hugh, *Flying Start: A Fighter Pilot's War Years* (Barnsley: Pen & Sword, 2011).

Eden, Anthony, *The Reckoning* (London: Cassell, 1965).

Ellis, L. F., *The War in France and Flanders, 1939–40* (London: Her Majesty's Stationary Office, 1953).

Galland, Adolf, Ries, K., and Ahnert, R., *The Luftwaffe at War, 1939–1945* (ed.) David Mondey (London: Ian Allan, 1972).

Gleed, Ian, *Arise to Conquer* (London: Grub Street, 2010).

Gray, Bernard, *War Reporter* (London: Hale, 1942).

Goebbels, Joseph, *Die Tagebücher von Joseph Goebbels: Teil I, Aufziechnungen 1923–1941; Band 8, April–November 1940* (ed.) Jana Richter (München: K.G. Saur, 1998).

Halder, Generaloberst Franz, *Kriegstagebuch: Tägliche Aufzeichnungen des Chefs des Generalstabes des Heeres, 1939–1942*, Vol. I (ed.) Hans-Adolf Jacobsen (Stuttgart: W.Kohlhammer, 1962).

Harris, Arthur, *Bomber Offensive* (Barnsley: Pen & Sword, 2005).

Hillary, Richard, *The Last Enemy* (London: Vintage, 2010).

Ironside, Field Marshal Sir Edmund, *The Ironside Diaries: 1937–1940* (eds.) Roderick Macleod and Denis Kelly (London, Constable, 1962).

Ismay, General Hastings Lionel, *The Memoirs of Lord Ismay* (London: Heinemann, 1960).

Joubert de la Ferte, Air Chief Marshal Sir Philip, *Birds and Fishes: The Story of Coastal Command* (London: Hutchinson, 1960).

Kesselring, Albert, *The Memoirs of Field Marshal Kesselring* (London: Greenhill, 2007).

Lamb, Charles, *War in a Stringbag* (London: Cassell, 2001).

McGlashan, Squadron Leader Kenneth Butterworth, and Zupp, Owen, *Down to Earth: A Fighter Pilot's Experience of Surviving Dunkirk, the Battle of Britain, Dieppe and D-Day* (London: Grub Street, 2007).

Montgomery, Field Marshal Bernard Law, *The Memoirs of Field Marshal Montgomery* (Barnsley: Pen & Sword, 2010).

Richardson, Group Captain Frederick, *Man Is Not Lost: The Log of a Pioneer RAF Pilot/Navigator, 1933–1946* (Shrewsbury: Airlife, 1997).

Ries, Karl, *Luftwaffen-Story: 1935–39* (Mainz: Dieter Hoffman, 1974).

Slessor, John, *The Central Blue: Recollections and Reflections* (London: Cassell, 1956).

Spears, Major-General Sir Edward, *Assignment to Catastrophe, Vol. I: Prelude to Dunkirk, July 1939–May 1940* (London: William Heinemann, 1954).

Steinhilper, Ulrich, and Osborne, Peter, *Spitfire on My Tail: A View from the Other Side* (Bromley: Independent Books, 2009).

Weygand, General Maxime, *Mémoires: Rappelé au Service* (Paris: Flammarion, 1950).
Witzel, Rudolf, *Mit Mörsern, Haubitzen und Kanonen: Aks Artillerieoffizier im Freiden und Krieg 1936–1945* (Würzburg: Flechsig, 2008).

Articles

Churchill, Winston S., 'This Was Their Finest Hour', *The Listener*, Issue 597, 20 June 1940 (London: British Broadcasting Corporation).
Daily Telegraph, 'RAF Defence of Dunkirk', 3 June 1940.
Der Adler, 'Hölle Dünkirchen' Heft 13, 25 June 1940.
Douglas, Air Marshal Sholto, 'Fighter Command', *Flying and Popular Aviation*, Vol. 31, No. 3 (1942).
Eden, Anthony, 'The Spirit of the BEF', *The Listener*, Issue 595, 6 June 1940 (London: British Broadcasting Corporation).
Goodeve, Charles Frederick, 'The Defeat of the Magnetic Mine', *Journal of the Royal Society of Arts*: Vol. 94, No. 4708 (1946).
Joubert de la Ferte, Air Marshal Sir Philip, 23 May 1940, 'Broadcast "War in the Air: Air War in Brief"', *Flight*, 30 May 1940.
Manchester Guardian, 'Bombers' Efforts in Support of Troops', 31 May 1940.
Military Intelligence Division (USA War Department), 'Tactical Employment of Flak in the Field', *Intelligence Bulletin*, Vol. II, No. 3 (1943).
New York Times, 'Dunkerque', 1 June 1940.
Pattinson, Air Vice-Marshal L. A., 'The Training of a Royal Air Force Pilot', *Journal of the Royal United Service Institute*, Vol. 83, No. 529 (1938).
Robertson, Major F. A. de V., 'At a Wellington Station', *Flight*, Vol. XXXVIII, No. 1669, 19 December 1940.
Ramsay, Vice Admiral B. H., 'The Evacuation of the Allied Armies from Dunkirk and Neighbouring Beaches', *London Gazette*, 17 July 1947.
The Times, 'RAF's Great Help', 29 May 1940.
The Times, 'Men's Gratitude to the Navy: Narrowing Defence Zone', 3 June 1940.

Published Handbooks and Technical Documents

Aufklärungsfliegerschule (F) 3, Abt. I Technik, 'Merkblatt Ju88 A' [https://web.archive.org/web/20180620110914/http://www.germanluftwaffe.com/archiv/Dokumente/ABC/j/Junkers/Ju%2088/Ju_88__Aufklarungsfliegerschule.pdf].
Dornier-Werke, *Ersatzteil-Liste Do 17 E und F* (Friedrichshafen: Dornier, 1937).
Messerschmitt A. G., *L.Dv.556/3 (Entwurf) Bf 109 E Flugzeughandbuch* (Berlin: Reichsminister der Luftwaffe, 1939).

Messerschmitt A.G., *Betriebs und Rüstanleitung Me 109 mit Motor DB 601* (Berlin: Reichsminister der Luftwaffe, 1941).

Messerschmitt A.G., *BF 109 E: Lehrbildreihe Nr.42, Zelldias* (Berlin: Mathiesen, n.d.).

Published Interviews, Accounts and Documents

Anderson, K. D., 'Weather Service at War', *Royal Meteorological Society Occasional Papers on Meteorological History*, No. 7 (2009), p. 15.

Bob, Hans-Ekkehard, 'Memories of a German Veteran', in Paul Addison and Jeremy A. Crang (eds.), *The Burning Blue: A New History of the Battle of Britain* (London: Pimlico, 2000).

Churchill, Winston S., Prime Minister, House of Commons Debate (Series 5) Vol. 361, Col. 790, 4 June 1940.

Curtiss-Wright Corporation, Propeller Division, *Propeller Theory* (Caldwell, NJ: Curtiss-Wright Corporation, 1944).

Galland, Adolf, 'Defeat of the Luftwaffe', in Eugene M. Emme (ed.), *The Impact of Air Power* (Princeton, NJ: D. Van Nostrand, 1959).

Gaul, Walter, 'Navy-Air Force Planning and Build-up of the Naval Air Forces; Their Disbandment, and the Transfer of Naval Air Commitments to the Operational Air Force', in *Essays by German Officers and Officials on World War II, Part II* (Wilmington, DE: Scholarly Resources, 1991).

Gaul, Oberst (i.G.) Walter, 'German Naval Air Operations in the First Six Months of the War', in David C. Isby (ed.), *The Luftwaffe and the War at Sea 1939–45* (London: Chatham, 2005).

Heaton, Colin D., 'Interview with Luftwaffe Ace Walter Krupinski', *Military History Magazine*: Vol. 15, No. 2 (1998).

Martin, *Unteroffizier*, 'Tank Destroyers in the Dunkirk Blocking Force', in Alan Bance (ed., trans.), *Blitzkrieg in Their Own Words: First-Hand Accounts from German Soldiers, 1939–1940* (Barnsley: Pen & Sword, 2005).

Nettle, Commander S. A. (ed.), *Dunkirk: Old Men Remember* (Frome, Somerset; March Press, 1988).

OKL, 8. Abteilung, January 1944, 'The Operational Use of the Luftwaffe in the War at Sea, 1939–43', in David C. Isby (ed.), *The Luftwaffe and the War at Sea 1939–45* (London: Chatham, 2005).

Steinhoff, Johannes, 'The German Fighter Battle against the American Bombers', in Lieutenant Colonel William Geffen (ed., trans.), *Command & Commanders in Modern Military History: Proceedings of the USAF Academy Second Military History Symposium, US Air Force Academy 2–3 May 1968* [2nd Edition] (Washington, DC: Office of Air Force History – Headquarters USAF, 1971).

Official Histories, Studies, and Published Narratives

Air Ministry, *Bomber Command: The Air Ministry Account of Bomber Command's Offensive against the Axis, September, 1939–July, 1941* (London: HMSO, 1941).
Ellis, L. F., *The War in France and Flanders* (London: Her Majesty's Stationary Office, 1953).
Gardner, W. J. R., *The Evacuation from Dunkirk: Operation Dynamo, 26 May–4 June 1940* (London: Routledge, 2000).
James, T. C. G., *The Battle of Britain* (ed.) Sebastian Cox (London: Frank Cass, 2000).
James, T. C. G., *The Growth of Fighter Command, 1936–1940* (ed.) Sebastian Cox (London: Frank Cass, 2002).
Kreipe, Werner, and Koester, Rudolf, 'Technical Training Within the German Luftwaffe', USAF Historical Study No. 169 (1955).
Probert, Henry, *The Rise and Fall of the German Air Force* (Poole: Arms & Armour Press, 1983).
Richards, Denis, *The Royal Air Force 1939–1945, Vol. I: The Fight at Odds* (London: HMSO, 1953).
Roskill, Captain S. W., *The War at Sea, 1939–1945, Vol. I: The Defensive* (London: HMSO, 1954).
Speidel, Wilhelm, 'The German Air Force in France and the Low Countries 1939–1940', USAF Historical Study No. 152 (1958).
Suchenwirth, Richard, 'The Development of the German Air Force, 1919–1939', USAF Historical Studies No. 160 (1968).
United States Navy Bureau of Ordnance, *Ordnance Pamphlet 1673-A: German Underwater Ordnance Mines* (San Jose, CA: Military Arms Research Service, 1946).
Webster, Charles, and Frankland, Noble, *The Strategic Air Offensive against Germany, 1939–1945: Vol. I, Preparations* (London: HMSO, 1961).
Webster, Charles, and Frankland, Noble, *The Strategic Air Offensive against Germany, 1939–1945: Vol. IV, Annexes and Appendices* (London: HMSO, 1961).

Secondary Literature

Books

Abrams, Lynn, *Oral History Theory* (Abingdon: Routledge, 2010).
Aders, Gebhard, and Held, Werner, *Chronik Jagdgeschwader 51 'Mölders'* (Stuttgart: Motorbuch, 2009).
Allen, H. R., *Who Won the Battle of Britain* (London: Arthur Baker, 1974).
Andrews, Allen, *The Air Marshals: The Air War in Western Europe* (New York: William Morrow, 1970).

Atkin, Ronald, *Pillar of Fire: Dunkirk 1940* (Edinburgh: Birlinn, 2000).
Auphan, Paul, and Mordal, Jacques, *The French Navy in World War II* (Annapolis, MD: Naval Institute, 2016).
Barker, A. J., *Dunkirk: The Great Escape* (London: Dent, 1973).
Beaux, Jean, *Dunkerque: 1940* (Paris: Presses Pocket, 1969).
Bekker, Cajus, *The Luftwaffe War Diaries: The German Air Force in World War II* (London: Corgi, 1969).
Bergström, Christer, *The Battle of Britain: An Epic Conflict Revisited* (Oxford: Casemate, 2015).
Bird, Andrew, *Coastal Dawn: Blenheims in Action from the Phoney War through the Battle of Britain* (London: Grub Street, 2012).
Bishop, Patrick, *Battle of Britain: A Day-to-Day Chronicle, 10 July 1940–31 October 1940* (London: Quercus, 2010).
Blandford, Edmund, *Target England: Flying with the Luftwaffe in World War Two* (Shrewsbury: Airlife, 1997).
Blaxland, Gregory, *Destination Dunkirk: The Story of Gort's Army* (London: William Kimber, 1973).
Blond, Georges, *L'Epopée Silencieuse: Service à la Mer, 1939–1940* (Paris: Le Livre de Poche, 1970).
Bond, Brian, *France and Belgium, 1939–1940* (London: Davis Poynter, 1975).
Buckley, John, *Air Power in the Age of Total War* (London: University College London Press, 1999).
Bungay, Stephen, *The Most Dangerous Enemy: A History of the Battle of Britain* (London: Auram, 2000).
Butler, Lieutenant-Colonel Ewan, and Bradford, Major J. S., *The Story of Dunkirk* (London: Arrow, 1955).
Caldwell, Donald, *JG 26 Luftwaffe Fighter Wing War Diary, Vol. I, 1939–42* (London: Grub Street, 1996).
Carse, Robert, *Dunkirk: 1940* (New Jersey: Prentice-Hall, 1970).
Chalmers, W. S., *Full Cycle: The Biography of Admiral Sir Bertram Home Ramsay* (London: Hodder and Stoughton, 1959).
Chatterton, E. Keeble, *The Epic of Dunkirk* (London: Hurst & Blackett, 1940).
Colledge, J. J., and Warlow, Ben, *Ships of the Royal Navy: The Complete Record of All Fighting Ships of the Royal Navy* (Newbury: Casemate, 2010).
Collier, Basil, *A History of Air Power* (London: Weidenfeld and Nicolson, 1974).
Collier, Richard, *The Sands of Dunkirk* (Glasgow: Fontana, 1974).
Cooper, Mathew, *The German Air Force, 1933–1945: An Anatomy of Failure* (London: Jane's, 1981).
Connelly, Mark, *We Can Take It: Britain and the Memory of the Second World War* (London: Routledge, 2014).
Cornwell, Peter D., *The Battle of France: Then and Now* (Old Harlow, Essex: Battle of Britain International, 2007).

Corum, James S., *The Luftwaffe: Creating the Operational Air War, 1918–1940* (Lawrence, KS: University Press of Kansas, 1997).

Cummings, Anthony J., *The Royal Navy and the Battle of Britain* (Annapolis, MD: Naval Institute Press, 2010).

Deighton, Len, *Fighter: The True Story of the Battle of Britain* (New York: Alfred A. Knopf, 1978).

Deighton, Len, *Blitzkrieg: From the Rise of Hitler to the Fall of Dunkirk* (London: Jonathan Cape, 1979).

Dierich, Wolfgang, *Die Verbände der Luftwaffe 1935–1945: Gliederungen und Kurzchroniken, eine Dokumentation* (Stuttgart: Motorbuch, 1995).

Dierich, Wolfgang, *Kampfgeschwader 51 'Edelweiss': The Complete History of KG 51 in World War II* (Atglen, PA: Schiffer, 2014).

Dildy, Douglas C., *Dunkirk 1940: Operation Dynamo* (London: Osprey, 2010).

Divine, David, *The Nine Days of Dunkirk* (London: Pan, 1964).

Dunn, Bill Newton, *Big Wing: The Biography of Air Chief Marshal Sir Trafford Leigh-Mallory* (Shrewsbury: Airlife, 1992).

Engelmann, Joachim, and Scheibert, Horst, *Deutsche Artillerie, 1934–1945: Eine Dokumentation in Text, Skizzen und Bildern* (Limburg an der Lahn, Hesse: C.A. Starke, 1974).

Evans, Martin Marix, *The Fall of France: Act with Daring* (Oxford: Osprey, 2000).

Falconer, Jonathon, *RAF Fighter Airfields of World War 2* (Shepperton, Surrey: Ian Allan, 1993).

Fleischer, Wolfgang, *German Motorized Artillery and Panzer Artillery in World War II* (Atglen, PA: Schiffer, 2004).

Franks, Norman, *Air Battle for Dunkirk: 26 May–3 June 1940* (London: Grub Street, 2006).

Franks, Norman, *Fighter Command Losses of the Second World War, Vol. I, Operational Losses – Aircraft and Crews, 1939-1941* (Hersham, Surrey: Midland, 2008).

Frieser, Karl-Heinz, *Blitzkrieg Legend: The 1940 Campaign in the West* (Annapolis, MA: Naval Institute, 2012).

Gates, Eleanor M., *End of the Affair: The Collapse of the Anglo-French Alliance, 1939–40* (Berkeley, CA: University of California Press, 1981).

Gelb, Norman, *Dunkirk: The Incredible Escape* (London: Michael Joseph, 1990).

Glancey, Jonathon, *Spitfire: The Biography* (London: Atlantic, 2006).

Goss, Chris, *Sea Eagles*, Vol I., *Luftwaffe Anti-Shipping Units, 1939–41* (Hersham, Surrey: Classic, 2005).

Gray, Peter, *Air Warfare: History, Theory and Practice* (London: Bloomsbury, 2016).

Green, William, *Warplanes of the Third Reich* (London: Macdonald and Jane's, 1979).

Haar, Geirr, *The Battle for Norway: April–June 1940* (Barnsley: Pen & Sword, 2010).

Harman, Nicholas, *Dunkirk: The Necessary Myth* (London: Hodder & Stoughton, 1980).

Harr, Geirr H., *The Gathering Storm: The Naval War in Northern Europe, September 1939–April 1940* (Barnsley: Seaforth, 2013).

Harris, John, *Dunkirk: The Storms of War* (Newton Abbot: David & Charles, 1988).
Hastings, Max, *Bomber Command* (London: Pan, 1999).
Hendrie, Andrew, *Seek and Strike: The Lockheed Hudson in World War II* (London: William Kimber, 1983).
Hendrie, Andrew, *The Cinderella Service: Coastal Command, 1939–1945* (Barnsley: Pen & Sword, 2007).
Hermann, Hauptmann, *The Rise and Fall of the Luftwaffe* (Stroud: Fonthill, 2012).
Hogg, Ian V., *German Artillery of World War Two* (London: Frontline Books, 2013).
Holland, James, *The Battle of Britain: Five Months That Changed History, May–October, 1940* (London: Corgi, 2011).
Hooton, E. R., *Phoenix Triumphant: The Rise and Rise of the Luftwaffe* (London: Brockhampton, 1999).
Hooton, E. R., *Luftwaffe at War, Vol. II: Blitzkreig in the West, 1939–1940* (Hersham, Surrey: Ian Allan, 2007).
Hooton, E. R., *The Luftwaffe: A Study in Air Power, 1933–1945* (London: Classic, 2010).
Horsley, Terence, *Find, Fix and Strike: The Work of the Fleet Air Arm* (London: Eyre and Spottiswoode, 1943).
Hyde, H. Montgomery, *British Air Policy between the Wars: 1918–1939* (London: Heinemann, 1976).
Isby, David, *The Decisive Duel: Spitfire vs 109* (London: Little, Brown, 2012).
Jackson, Julian, *The Fall of France: The Nazi Invasion of 1940* (Oxford: Oxford University Press, 2003).
Jackson, Robert, *Before the Storm: The Story of Royal Air Force Bomber Command, 1939–42* (London: Arthur Baker, 1972).
Jackson, Robert, *Air War over France: 1939–40* (London: Ian Allan, 1974).
Jackson, Robert, *Dunkirk: The British Evacuation, 1940* (London: Cassell, 2002).
Jacobsen, Hans-Adolf, *Dünkirchen* (Neckargemünd: Kurt Vowinckel, 1958).
Jefford, J., *Observers and Navigators: And Other Non-Pilot Aircrew in the RFC, RNAS and RAF* [2nd Edition] (London: Grub Street, 2014).
Johnson, J. E., *Full Circle: The Story of Air Fighting* (London: Cassell, 2001).
Jourdan, John, and Moulin, Jean, *French Destroyers: Torpilleurs d'Escadre and Contre-Torpilleurs, 1922–1956* (Barnsley: Seaforth, 2015).
Ketley, Barry, and Rolfe, Mark, *Luftwaffe Fledglings: 1935–1945: Luftwaffe Training Units and Their Aircraft* (Aldershot: Hikoki, 1996).
Killen, John, *The Luftwaffe: A History* (Barnsley: Pen & Sword, 2013).
Koch, Adalbert, *Die Geschichte der Deutschen Flakartillerie: 1935–1945* (Friedberg: Podzun-Pallas, 1982).
Lauck, Friedrich, *Der Lufttorpedo: Entwicklung und Technik in Deutschland 1915–1945* (Munich: Bernard & Graefe, 1987).
Lee, Asher, *Goering: Air Leader* (London: Duckworth, 1972).
Lord, Walter, *The Miracle of Dunkirk* (Ware, Hertfordshire: Wordsworth, 1998).

Lormier, Dominique, *La Bataille De France Jour Après Jour: Mai-Juin 1940* (Paris: Le Cherche Midi, 2010).
Lormier, Dominique, *La Bataille de Dunkerque, 26 Mai–4 Juin 1940: Comment l'Armée Française a Sauvé l'Angleterre* (Paris: Tallandier, 2011).
Lyet, Commandant Pierre-Jean, *La Bataille de France Mai–Juin 1940* (Paris: Payot, 1947).
Mason, Herbert, *Rise of the Luftwaffe: Forging the Secret German Air Weapon* (New York: Dial, 1973).
Masters, David, *So Few: The Immortal Record of the R.A.F.* (London: Eyre & Spottiswoode, 1941).
McKinstry, Leo, *Spitfire: Portrait of a Legend* (London: John Murray, 2008).
McMurtie, Francis E. (ed.), *Jane's Fighting Ships: 1939* (Newton Abbot: David and Charles, 1971).
Middlebrook, Martin, and Everitt, Chris, *The Bomber Command War Diaries: An Operational Reference Book, 1939–1945* (New York: Viking, 1985).
Miles, M. B., and Hubermann, A. M., *Qualitative Data Analysis: An Expanded Sourcebook* [2nd Edition] (London: Sage, 1994).
Mombeek, Eric, *Jagdwaffe*, Vol I, Part 4, *Attack in the West, May 1940* (Crowborough, East Sussex: Classic, 2002).
Morgan, Eric B., and Shacklady, Edward, *Spitfire: The History* (London: Guild, 1989).
Murray, Williamson, *Strategy for Defeat: The Luftwaffe 1933–1945* (Royston: Eagle, 2000).
Niestlé, Axel, *German U-Boat Losses during World War II: Details of Destruction* (London: Frontline, 2014).
Noakes, Lucy, and Pattinson, Juliette (eds.), *British Cultural Memory and the Second World War* (London: Bloomsbury, 2014).
Oddone, Patrick, *Dunkirk 1940: French Ashes, British Deliverance, The Story of Operation Dynamo* (trans.) Malcolm Hall (Stroud, Gloucestershire: Tempus, 2000).
Orange, Vincent, *Park: The Biography of Air Chief Marshal Sir Keith Park* (London: Grub Street, 2010).
Orange, Vincent, *Churchill and His Airmen: Relationships, Intrigue and Policy Making, 1914–1945* (London: Grub Street, 2013).
Overy, Richard, *The Air War, 1939–1945* (London: Europa, 1980).
Overy, Richard, *Goering: The 'Iron Man'* (London: Routledge, 1984).
Overy, Richard, *The Battle of Britain: Myth and Reality* (London: Penguin, 2010).
Overy, Richard, *The Bombers and the Bombed: Allied Air War over Europe, 1940–1945* (New York: Penguin, 2014).
Owen, David, *Dogfight: The Supermarine Spitfire and the Messerschmitt BF 109* (Barnsley: Pen & Sword, 2015).
Parry, Simon W., and Postlethwaite, Mark, *Dunkirk: Air Combat Archive* (Walton-on-Thames: Red Kite, 2017).
Powell, Mathew, *The Development of British Tactical Air Power, 1940–1943: A History of Army Co-operation Command* (London: Palgrave Macmillan, 2016).

Prien, Jochen, and Stemmer, Gerhard, *Jagdeschwader 3 'Udet' in World War II; Volume II, II/JG in Action with the Messerschmitt Bf 109* (trans.) David Johnston (Atglen, Pennsylvania: Schiffer, 2003).

Prien, Jochen, Stemmer, Gerhard, Rodeike, Peter, and Bock, Winfried, *Die Jagdfliegerverbände der Deutschen Luftwaffe 1934 bis 1945: Teil 3, Einsatz in Dänemark und Norwegen, 9.4. bis 30. 11.1940,Der Feldzug im Westen 10.5. bis 25. 6.1940* (Eutin, Schleswig-Holstein: Struve´s Buchdruerei und Verlag, 2002).

Price, Alfred, *The Luftwaffe Data Book* (London: Greenhill, 1997).

Prior, Robin, *When Britain Saved the West: The Story of 1940* (New Haven, CT: Yale University Press, 2015).

Probert, Henry, *The Rise and Fall of the German Air Force, 1933–1945* (Poole: Arms & Armour Press, 1983).

Proctor, Raymond L., *Hitler's Luftwaffe in the Spanish Civil War* (London: Greenwood, 1983).

Radinger, Willy, and Schick, Walter, *Messerschmitt Me 109: Das Meistgebaute Jagdflugzeug der Welt. Entwicklung, Erprobung und Technik. Alle Varianten von BF (Me) 109A bis 109E* (Oberhaching, Bavaria: Aviatic Verlag, 1997).

Raven, Alan, and Roberts, John Arthur, *British Battleships of World War Two: The Development and Technical History of the Royal Navy's Battleships and Battlecruisers from 1911 to 1946* (Annapolis, MD: Naval Institute Press, 1976).

Ray, John, *The Battle of Britain, New Perspectives: Behind the Scenes of the Great Air War* (London: Brockhampton, 1994).

Ray, John, *The Battle of Britain: Dowding and the First Victory, 1940* (London: Cassell, 2000).

Sarkar, Dilip, *Bader's Duxford Fighters: The Big Wing Controversy* (Worcester: Ramrod, 1997).

Sebag-Montefiore, Hugh, *Dunkirk: Fight to the Last Man* (London: Viking, 2006).

Shenk, Peter, *Invasion of England 1940: The Planning of Operation Sealion* (London, Conway Maritime Press, 1990).

Sims, Edward H., *Fighter Tactics and Strategy, 1939-1970* (New York: Harper and Row, publishers. Inc., 1972).

Sinot, Colin, *The RAF and Aircraft Design: Air Staff Operational Requirements, 1923–1939* (London: Routledge, 2013).

Smith, Malcolm, *British Air Strategy between the Wars* (Oxford: Clarendon, 1984).

Smith, Peter C., *Stuka at War* (London: Ian Allan, 1980).

Smith, Peter C., *Stuka Squadron: Stukagruppe 77 – The Luftwaffe's 'Fire Brigade'* (Wellingborough, Northamptonshire: Patrick Stevens, 1990).

Smith, Peter C., *Stuka Spearhead: The Lightening War from Poland to Dunkirk, 1939–1940* (London: Greenhill Books, 1998).

Smith, Peter C., *Skua! The Royal Navy's Dive-Bomber* (Barnsley: Pen & Sword, 2006).

Peter C. Smith, *Dive Bomber!* (Mechanicsburg, PA: Stackpole, 2008).

Stewart, Geoffrey, *Dunkirk and the Fall of France* (Barnsley: Pen & Sword, 2008).

Taylor, Telford, *The Breaking Wave: The German Defeat in the Summer of 1940* (London: Weidenfeld and Nicolson, 1967).
Terraine, John, *The Right of the Line* (London: Wordsworth, 1998).
Thiele, Harold, *Luftwaffe Aerial Torpedo Aircraft and Operation in World War Two* (Crowsborough, East Sussex: Hikoki, 2004).
Thompson, Julian, *Dunkirk: Retreat to Victory* (London: Pan, 2009).
Thorburn, Gordon, *Bomber Command, 1939–1940: The War before the War* (Barnsley: Pen & Sword, 2013)
Turnbull, Patrick, *Dunkirk: Anatomy of Disaster* (London: Batsford, 1978).
Turner, John Frayn, *The Bader Wing* (Barnsley: Pen & Sword, 2007).
Van Creveld, Martin, *Supplying War: Logistics from Wallenstein to Patton* (Cambridge: Cambridge University Press, 2004).
Ward, John, *Hitler's Stuka Squadrons: The Ju 87 at War, 1936–1945* (St. Paul, MN: MBI, 2004).
Weal, John, *Jagdgeschwader 2 'Richthofen'* (Oxford: Osprey, 2000).
Weal, John, *Jagdgeschwader 52: The Experten* (London: Bloomsbury, 2012).
Williams, John, *The Ides of May: The Defeat of France, May–June, 1940* (New York: Alfred A. Knopf, 1968).
Willmott, H. P., *The Last Century of Sea Power, Vol. II: From Washington to Tokyo, 1922–1945* (Indianapolis: Indiana University Press, 2011).
Wilson, Patrick, *Dunkirk: From Disaster to Deliverance* (Barnsley: Pen & Sword, 2000).
Winters, Harold A., Galloway Jr., Gerald E., Reynolds, William J., and Rhyne, David W., *Battling the Elements: Weather and Terrain in the Conduct of War* (London: Johns Hopkins University, 1998).
Wood, Derek, and Dempster, Derek, *The Narrow Margin* (Barnsley: Pen & Sword, 2003).
Wright, Robert, *Dowding and the Battle of Britain* (London: MacDonald, 1969).
Zimmerman, David, *Britain's Shield: Radar and the Defeat of the Luftwaffe* (Stroud, Gloucestershire: Sutton, 2001).

Chapters

Alexander, Martin S., 'Dunkirk in Military Operations, Myths and Memories', in Robert Tombs and Emile Chabal (eds.), *Britain and France in Two World Wars: Truth, Myth and Memory* (London: Bloomsbury, 2013).
Bishop, Edward, Cox, Sebastian, James, Cecil, Probert, Henry, Richardson, Tony, Thornurn, Geoffrey, and Wood, Derek, 'Digest of the Group Discussion', in Henry Probert and Sebastian Cox (eds.), *The Battle Rethought: A Symposium on the Battle of Britain* (Shrewsbury: Airlife, 1991).
Boog, Horst, 'The Strategic Air War in Europe and Air Defence of the Reich, 1943–44', in Horst Boog, Gerhard Krebs and Detlef Vogel (eds.), *Germany and the Second World War, Vol. VII, Germany's Initial Conquests in Europe* (Oxford: Oxford University Press, 2006).

Corum, James S., 'Defeat of the Luftwaffe, 1935–1945', in Robin Higham and Stephen J. Harris (eds.), *Why Air Forces Fail* (Lexington, KY: University Press of Kentucky, 2016).

Deist, Wilhelm, 'The Rearmament of the Wehrmacht', in Militärgeschichtliches Forschungsamt (ed.), *Germany and the Second World War, Vol. I, The Build-Up of German Aggression* (Oxford: Clarendon Press, 2015).

Gray, Colin, 'Dowding and the British Strategy of Air Defence, 1936–40', in Williamson Murray and Richard Hart Sinnreich (eds.), *Successful Strategies: Triumphing in War and Peace from Antiquity to the Present* (Cambridge: Cambridge University Press, 2014).

Harris, Jose, 'War and Social History: Britain and the Home Front during the Second World War', in Gordon Martel (ed.), *The World War Two Reader* (London: Routledge, 2004).

Higham, Robin, 'Introduction', in Robin Higham and Stephen J. Harris (eds.), *Why Air Forces Fail* (Lexington, KY: University Press of Kentucky, 2016).

Jacobsen, Hans-Adolf, 'Dunkirk 1940', in H.A. Jacobsen and J. Rohwer (eds.), *Decisive Battles of World War II: The German View* (trans.) Edward Fitzgerald (London: André Deutsch, 1965).

Liddell-Hart, Basil, 'The Second World War', in C.L. Mowat (ed.), *The New Cambridge Modern History*, Vol. XII [2nd Edition] *The Shifting Balance of World Forces, 1898–1945* (Cambridge: Cambridge University Press, 1968).

Maier, Klaus A., 'The Operational Air War until the Battle of Britain', in Militärgeschichtliches Forschungsamt (ed.), *Germany and the Second World War, Vol. II, Germany's Initial Conquests in Europe* (trans.) Dean S. McMurry and Edwald Osers (Oxford: Clarendon Press, 1991).

Millett, Allan R., Murray, Williamson, and Watman, Kenneth H., 'The Effectiveness of Military Organizations', in Allan R. Millett and Williamson Murray (eds.), *Military Effectiveness, Vol. I, The First World War* (Cambridge: Cambridge University Press, 2010), pp. 2–4.

Murray, Williamson, 'The Luftwaffe against Poland and the West', in Benjamin Franklin Cooling (ed.), *Case Studies in the Achievement of Air Superiority* (Washington, DC: US Air Force, 1994).

Smith, Malcolm, 'The RAF', in Paul Addison and Jeremy A. Crang (eds.), *The Burning Blue: A New History of the Battle of Britain* (London: Pimlico, 2000).

Stegemann, Bernd, 'The First Phase of the War at Sea', in Militärgeschichtliches Forschungsamt (ed.), *Germany and the Second World War, Vol. II Germany's Initial Conquests in Europe* (trans.) Dean S. McMurry and Edwald Osers (Oxford: Clarendon Press, 1991).

Umbreit, Hans, 'The Campaign in the West', in Militärgeschichtliches Forschungsamt (ed.), *Germany and the Second World War, Vol. II, Germany's Initial Conquests in Europe* (trans.) Dean S. McMurry and Edwald Osers (Oxford: Clarendon Press, 1991).

Articles

Bond, Brian, 'Dunkirk: Myths and Lessons', *Royal United Service Institute Journal*, Vol. 127, No. 3 (February 1982).

Boog, Horst, 'German Air Intelligence in the Second World War', *Intelligence and National Security*, Vol. 5, No. 2 (1990).

Bradshaw, Peter, '*Dunkirk* Review', *The Guardian* (17 July 2017), [https://www.theguardian.com/film/2017/jul/17/dunkirk-review-christopher-nolans-apocalyptic-war-epic-is-his-best-film-so-far, accessed 23 February 2018].

Burls, Nina, 'RAF Bombs and Bombing: 1939–1945', *Royal Air Force Historical-Society*, Vol. 45 (2009).

Cairns, John C., 'Great Britain and the Fall of France: A Study in Allied Disunity', *Journal of Military History*, Vol. 27, No. 4 (1955).

Corum, James S., 'The Luftwaffe's Campaigns in Poland and the West 1939–1940: A Case Study of Handling Innovation in Wartime', *Security and Defence Quarterly*, No. 1 (2013).

Cummings, Anthony J., and Goulter, Christina, 'Ready or Not? The RAF and the Battle of Britain.' *BBC History Magazine*, Vol. 8, No. 11 (2007).

Daily Telegraph, 'Obituary: Wing Commander David Cox', 5 February 2004, [http://www.telegraph.co.uk/news/obituaries/1453460/Wing-Commander-David-Cox.html, accessed 25 May 2018].

Ferris, John, 'Fighter Defence before Fighter Command: The Rise of Strategic Air Defence in Great Britain, 1917–1934', *Journal of Military History*, Vol. 63, No. 4 (1999).

Goldrick, James, 'The Problems of Modern Naval History' *Great Circle*, Vol. 18, No. 1 (1996).

Hoch, Anton, 'Der Luftangriff Auf Freiburg am 10 Mai 1940' *Vierteljahrshefte für Zeitgeschichte*: Jahrgang 4, Heft 2 (1956).

Huan, Claude, and Marchand, Alain, 'La Bataille aéronavale de Dunkerque (18 Mai–3 Juin 1940)', *Revue Historique Des Armées*, No. 172 (1988).

Jacobs, W. A., 'Air Support for the British Army, 1939–1943', *Military Affairs*, Vol. 46, No. 4 (1982).

Jick, T., 'Mixing Qualitative and Quantitative Methods: Triangulation in Action', *Administrative Science Quarterly*, Vol. 24, No. 4 (1979).

Kirby, M., and Capey, R., 'The Air Defence of Great Britain, 1920–1940: An Operational Research Perspective', *Journal of the Operational Research Society*, Vol. 48, No. 6 (1997).

Koch, H. W., 'The Strategic Air Offensive against Germany: The Early Phase, May–September 1940', *The Historical Journal*, Vol. 34, No. 1 (1991).

Larew, Karl G., 'The Royal Navy in the Battle of Britain', *The Historian*, Vol. 54, No. 2 (1992).

Lee, Asher, 'Trends in Aerial Defense', *World Politics*, Vol. 7, No. 2 (1955).

Lee-McCloud, Chris, 'Spitfire!' *Journal of Museum Ethnography*, No. 17 (2005).

Mackay, Niall, and Price, Christopher, 'Safety in Numbers: Ideas of Concentration in Royal Air Force Fighter Defence from Lanchester to the Battle of Britain', *History*, Vol. 96, No. 3 (2011).

Marchand, Alain, and Huan, Claude, 'Dunkerque: Opération "Dynamo"', *La Fana de l'Aviation*, No. 248 (1990).

Neitzel, Sönke, 'Kriegsmarine and Luftwaffe Co-operation in the War against Britain, 1939–1945', *War in History*, Vol. 10, No. 4 (2003).

Orange, Vincent, 'Review, The Battle of Britain, New Perspectives: Behind the Scenes of the Great Air War by John Ray', *Journal of Military History*, Vol. 59, No. 2 (1995).

Saxon, Phillip, 'The Second World War', *Royal Air Force Historical Society Journal*, Vol. 17, No. 1, 'A History of Navigation in the Royal Air Force' (1997).

Schiavon, Max, 'Les Relations entre Hauts Commandements Français et Britannique en 1939–1940', *Revue Historique des Armées*, No. 264 (2011).

Sumida, Jon Tetsuro, '"The Best Laid Plans": The Development of British Battle-Fleet Tactics, 1919–1942', *International History Review*, Vol. 14, No. 4 (1992).

Summerfield, Penny, 'Dunkirk and the Popular Memory of Britain at War, 1940–58', *Journal of Contemporary History*, Vol. 45, No. 4 (2010).

Index

Alexander, Major General Harold 109, 111
Aircraft types (British)
    Albacore 234, 236–7, 241
    Anson 227–9, 231–2, 234, 238
    Beaufort 234–6, 238
    Blenheim 186–7, 205, 224–6, 238, 241, 251, 256–63, 265–7, 281, 297
    Defiant 174, 182, 186, 199, 202, 204
    Gladiator 205
    Hampden 253–4, 269–73, 276–7
    Hector 239
    Hudson 143, 224–6, 231–4, 238
    Hurricane 34–8, 48, 63, 174, 177–9, 182–3, 185–6, 195–7, 199, 202, 204, 208, 226, 295
    Lysander 239
    Roc 224
    Skua 106, 187, 224–7, 236–7, 240–1
    Spitfire 10, 34–9, 47–8, 63, 100, 122, 174, 178, 182–3, 185–6, 189, 192, 195–7, 199, 201, 204–5, 207–8, 226, 295
    Swordfish 230, 234–40
    Wellington 253, 268–73
    Whitley 253, 269–73, 276–7
Aircraft types (German)
    Do 17: 27, 31, 40, 80, 87–8, 178, 189, 194
    He 111: 40, 50, 56, 62–3, 81–2, 88, 124, 140–1, 186–7, 189, 224–6
    Ju 87: 27, 30–1, 39–40, 81, 86, 120–2, 128, 130, 137, 146, 148–9, 183–4, 187, 190–1, 194, 196, 225–6, 300
    Ju 88: 40–1, 45, 62, 81, 86, 119–20, 123, 125, 138, 148, 184, 186, 224–8
    Me 109: 27, 29, 32, 34–7, 39, 47, 49, 54, 63, 81, 174, 179, 183–4, 186, 188–9, 193, 199, 201, 205, 225–6, 240, 295
    Me 110: 27, 35–6, 54, 69, 137, 174, 178, 184–5, 187, 189, 192, 197, 201, 300
Air Superiority 9–10, 29, 83, 88, 127, 145, 173, 175–9, 181, 185, 188–91, 193, 201, 203, 209–10, 226, 256, 293, 295, 301
Air Supremacy 83, 184
Anti-aircraft guns (Allied) 123, 129, 142, 147–8, 179, 187, 240
    Ship-based anti-aircraft 8, 83, 86, 88, 90, 121, 124, 128, 138, 140–1, 148 179, 188, 190, 209, 295, 294, 298, 301
Anti-aircraft guns (German), Flak 101–4, 224, 240, 256, 263, 270; *See also* RAF Bomber Command, Attacks on German artillery and Flak batteries
Anti-shipping role 104
    Lack of 239, 271
Antwerp 29, 31, 268, 273
Artillery (German) 98–101, 103, 113 n.7; *See also* RAF Bomber Command, Attacks on German artillery and Flak batteries
    Firing from Calais 100, 104
    Firing from Nieuport 97
    Firing on Route X 8, 97–100, 102, 104–5, 107, 110–12
    Halting further evacuation 8, 97–8, 111

Battle of Britain 2, 4–6, 10, 36, 50–1, 56, 192, 194–5, 198, 200, 203, 208, 294, 301–2
Bergues 106, 263, 265–6, 271
Boulogne 27, 30, 102, 129, 163–4, 232, 236
Bray Dunes 82, 97, 124–6, 139–40, 159, 162
British Expeditionary Force (BEF) 1, 2, 4, 123, 137, 179, 199–203, 209, 239, 256–8, 266–7, 270–1, 295, 303

Calais 27, 29–31, 34, 35, 97, 100–4, 119, 120, 129, 163–4, 177, 193, 224–5, 227, 232, 238–9, 241
Charleville 30–1, 275

Churchill, Winston Stanley 1–3, 7, 9, 14, 79, 146, 174, 183, 200, 260

Den Helder 230, 233–5
Detling 33, 232
Douglas, Air Vice-Marshal Sholto 26, 58, 198
Dover 84, 86–8, 102, 107, 110, 112, 120–1, 139–40, 144, 161, 163, 165–6, 189, 225
Dowding, Air Chief Marshal Sir Hugh 10, 26, 38, 45–6, 49, 181, 195, 196, 199–204, 207–8, 255, 301–2
Downs, the 163, 165–6
Dunkirk
  As decisive battle 1, 200, 203, 208, 295
  Cover from smoke 53–4, 111–12, 122, 124, 127–8, 140, 142, 191, 267
  Daylight evacuations suspended 8, 14, 98, 102, 108, 110–12, 162, 298, 303
  Embarkations from beaches 81, 105–6, 122, 125–7, 130, 141–2, 162, 180
  Importance of Dunkirk Mole 105, 123, 129, 137, 141–2, 295, 299–300
  Number evacuated 1, 80, 85, 121–3, 126, 129, 137, 141, 147, 162, 177, 180, 189
  Route X 8, 88, 97–100, 102, 104–5, 107–8, 110–12, 164, 298, 304
  Route Y 82–3, 97, 100, 105, 108, 111, 114 n.19, 121, 123–4, 165, 224, 227–9, 235, 304
  Route Z 34, 97, 102, 105, 239, 304
Dynamo *See* Dunkirk

E-Boat 11, 223, 228–38, 242, 302–3 *See also* RAF Coastal Command, Anti-shipping operations
Eden, Anthony 1, 12, 144
Evacuation fleet 4, 7, 25, 56, 61, 85–90, 97, 101, 104–5, 108, 111, 119, 127, 138, 146–7, 161, 167, 180, 185, 188, 190, 209–10, 224–7, 229, 233, 236, 238, 241–2, 268, 281, 294, 300, 302 *See also* Luftwaffe, Vessels sunk; Royal Navy, losses
  Crews at breaking-point 84–5, 89, 93 n.59, 138
  Losses to collision or misadventure 2, 79, 161, 167

  Personnel vessels 79–80, 82, 84–5, 87–9, 93 n.59, 110, 123, 141, 173, 180, 228, 238

Fleet Air Arm 10, 14, 27, 223–42, 295, 302
Fleet Air Arm Squadrons
  No. 763 (FAA) 237
  No. 801 (FAA) 236, 240–1
  No. 806 (FAA) 106, 224–7
  No. 812 (FAA) 239
  No. 815 (FAA) 223, 237
  No. 825 (FAA) 239–40
  No. 826 (FAA) 33, 241
Flushing 276, 290 n.184
Frisian Islands 231–2, 235, 273
Furnes 260–3, 265–6, 271, 272, 280

Galland, Hauptmann Adolf 28–9, 51
Givet 30, 269–70
Gort, General Viscount John 106, 181
Grauert, General der Flieger Ulrich 30, 125
Gravelines 31, 103, 112, 122, 170, 225, 226, 267
Guise 30–1, 269–70

Halder, General der Artillerie Franz 101, 146, 177, 186
Hamburg 272, 276–7
Hamm 269, 272–3
Harris, Air Vice-Marshall Arthur 254
Hawkinge 33, 195, 240
Hazebrouck 260, 270–1
Hook of Holland 60, 227, 230–4, 273
Hondschoote 266, 273

Ironside, General Sir Edmund 1, 12
Ijmuiden 232–5

Kesselring, General der Flieger Albert 28, 36, 39, 55, 122, 178
Kleist, General der Kavallerie Paul Ludwig Ewald von 101
Kriegsmarine 61, 144, 164
Kwinte Bank 124, 164

La Panne 82–3, 97, 101, 105–6, 125–6, 139–40, 162, 164, 166, 241, 266
Lille 27, 101, 120, 146, 192, 253, 259
Luftmine *See* Luftwaffe, mine operations
Lufttorpedo 61–2

Index

Luftwaffe *See also* Luftwaffe training; Vessels sunk, Luftwaffe
   Air bases 5, 26–7, 28–35, 51, 124, 138, 147–8, 177–8, 205, 270, 295, 299
   Air crew (shortages) 42–3, 5
   Air Support for German Army 122, 125, 139, 144–6
   All-weather capabilities 299
   Bombing of beaches and dunes 82, 126, 138–140, 158, 183
   bombing of Dunkirk Mole 80–6, 121, 127, 130, 139, 142, 173, 183
   bombing of Dunkirk port facilities 119–122, 125, 127, 129, 157, 298
   bombing wrecks 87, 143–4
   Combat tactics 47–8
   effect of weather 31, 41, 54–5, 59, 80, 123–4, 127–8, 137–8, 141, 144–9, 157, 177–80, 182–3, 186–9, 197, 205, 209, 251, 259–62, 270, 272, 276–7, 294–300, 303
   experience 6, 41, 44–5, 48, 56, 64, 190
   Failure to stop evacuation 4, 8–9, 79, 167, 300, 303
   Failure to bomb Dover 144
   Fair weather force 6, 53
   Fighter operations 34–5, 50, 83, 86, 88, 127, 173–96, 198, 201, 209–10, 239, 296, 300–1
   Flight routes 35, 147, 299
   Formations 45, 47
   Fuel shortages 6, 30, 274
   Losses 28, 174, 201
   Mine operations 163–6
   Night flying 56–7, 157—62
   Norway 39
   Numerical Strength 26–7
   Objective 25, 129, 138
   Spanish Civil War 41, 47–8, 51
   Strafing 88, 123–4, 127, 138, 159, 189–90, 229
   Torpedoes (*See Lufttorpedo*)
   Vessels sunk 2, 79–90, 121, 124, 127, 139, 147
Luftwaffe Training 41–4, 51–2, 296, 299
   Anti-shipping 6, 26, 60–3, 141
   Blindflugschulen 55
   Fighter 48, 51
   Flying in poor weather conditions 41, 53–4, 296, 299

   Gunnery 50
   Instrumental 52–7
   Navigational 55–6, 296
Luftwaffe Units:
   Fliegerdivision 9: 166
   Fliegerkorps I: 30, 81, 120–1, 125, 137, 139, 147, 177
   Fliegerkorps II: 30, 121–2, 125, 137, 146, 148, 177–8
   Fliegerkorps III: 30
   Fliegerkorps IV: 56, 120, 125, 157
   Fliegerkorps V: 125
   Fliegerkorps VIII: 13, 29–31, 81, 84, 120–2, 125, 137, 139, 145, 148, 177
   Fliegerkorps X: 40, 62–3
   Jafü 3: 29–30
   JG 1: 29
   JG 2: 31, 47, 51
   JG 3: 30
   JG 20: 30
   JG 26: 187
   JG 27: 28–9
   JG 52: 28, 31–3, 45, 48, 54, 183, 277
   JG 54: 29
   JG 77: 277
   KG 3: 178
   KG 4: 31, 82, 121
   KG 26: 30, 62
   KG 27: 120
   KG 30: 63, 119, 125, 184
   KG 51: 56
   KG 54: 120
   KG 76: 27, 31, 80, 87, 188
   KG 77: 30–1, 56, 82, 184
   LG 2: p. 30
   Luftflotte 2: 6, 28, 81, 101, 120, 122, 140, 142, 178, 187, 189
   Luftflotte 3: 29, 145
   StG 2: 27
   StG 77: 30
   ZG 1:185, 192
   ZG 2: 45

Mardyck 103, 239
Menin 257, 259, 269, 271
Middelkerke 83, 241
Military effectiveness 1, 4, 40, 49–50, 52, 80, 130, 137, 146, 175, 179, 188, 197–9, 209–10, 293–4, 296, 301

Newall, Air Chief Marshal Sir Cyril 183, 270
Nieuport 81–2, 97, 100–1, 105–6, 112, 125, 140, 159, 163–4, 187, 224, 230, 240–1, 260–4, 266, 271–2, 282

Ostend 27, 31, 82, 120–1, 125–6, 163–4, 224–5, 227–8, 230, 233–4, 237, 260–2, 271

Park, Air Vice-Marshal Keith 26–7, 192, 194, 198, 207
Peirse, Air Marshal Richard 200, 203
Plunkett[-Ernle-Erle-Drax], Admiral Sir Aylmer Ranfurly 110, 228
Portal, Air Marshal Charles 253–6, 268, 273–4, 297
Portsmouth 163, 165–6

Ramsay, Vice Admiral Bertram 3, 8, 14, 85, 88, 106, 109–12, 122–3, 142, 158, 161, 165
Richthofen, Generalmajor Wolfram von 13, 29–31, 39, 84, 125–6, 148, 268
Robb, Air Commodore James 251, 256, 274
Rotterdam 232, 238, 242, 273
Roulers 261, 269–71
Ruhr, The 255, 270, 273, 276, 277, 281, 290
Royal Air Force 3, 26 *See also* RAF Bomber Command; RAF Coastal Command; RAF Fighter Command
  Air Intelligence 51, 120, 205–6, 302
  Anti-Aircraft Co-Operation Unit 237
  Battle of France 12, 208, 265, 274
  Claims of victory 2–3, 6–7, 14, 174, 260, 295
  Criticism of 2–3, 12, 106, 175, 181, 193, 294
  Expansion 43–4, 53
  Doctrine 175–6, 255
  Pilots attitude to radio equipment 198–9
  Volunteer Reserve (personnel) 45, 208
RAF Advanced Air Striking Force 275
RAF Air Component – BEF Rear-Headquarters (Back Violet) 239
RAF Air Tactics Branch 196
RAF Bomber Command 10–12, 257–9
  Air interdiction 251, 253, 257–63, 266, 269–75, 280
  Attacks on aerodromes 268–9, 273
  Attacks on German artillery and Flak batteries 102, 112, 258–9, 266–8, 281
  Attacks on industry and oil targets 275–9, 281, 297
  Close Air Support 187, 251, 261, 263–5, 272
  Critics of tactical role 251–2, 254–5, 273, 278
  Dunkirk perimeter 265, 271–3
  Effect on Luftwaffe 255–6, 275, 277
  Inexperience 45, 59, 254
  Limitations of bombs 264
  Limitations in poor weather 58–9, 259–62, 270
  Moon/illumination for night attacks 270, 272
  Navigation 58, 60, 64, 259, 297–8
    See also RAF training, Navigation and instrument
  Redistribution of German Flak batteries 11, 255–6, 278
  Sorties 251–2, 256–7
  Tons dropped 251–2
RAF Coastal Command 10–11, 27, 293, 295
  Air Cover of evacuation 223–7, 302, 241, 302
  Anti-shipping operations 223, 228–37, 242, 302–3
  Anti-submarine operations 223, 237–8
  Bombing operations 238, 242
  Close air support 187, 223, 238–42
  Flare towing operations 236–7, 242
  Reconnaissance 223, 227–8, 302
RAF Fighter Command 83, 176 *See also* RAF training
  Air cover, absence of 86, 112, 182–3, 185, 188, 193, 225–6, 301
  Air cover Calais 29, 177
  Air Cover of evacuation 86, 88, 122, 127, 175–205, 209–10, 300
  Air defence of Britain 10, 203–5, 207–8, 302
  Air cover, in front of Dunkirk 3, 9, 34, 223

Index

Airbases 5, 26, 30, 32–5
Aircraft shortages 207–8
Combat tactics 46–8, 51, 185, 193, 196, 210 See also patrol tactics
Luftwaffe aircraft destroyed 88, 122 (check), 174, 177–8, 184, 189, 300
Formations 46, 48, 64
gun harmonization 49
Inexperience 6, 25, 44–5, 47–50, 52, 64, 192, 194–6, 206–7, 296
Losses 127, 174, 177, 181–2, 186, 189, 196, 207
Numerical disadvantage 5–6, 25–6, 63
Patrol tactics 177, 182, 196, 209, 301
Pilot shortages 45, 208
Radio Equipment 186, 196–200
Resources committed 10, 45, 26, 122, 178, 181, 183, 196–207, 295, 302
Sorties 2, 178, 181–2, 201, 204, 209, 300
Squadron rotation 52, 201–2, 206, 301
Standing patrols 35, 241
Successes 300
View of Luftwaffe 41
Wing Patrols 9, 86, 88, 182–4, 186–7, 190–6, 210, 300
RAF Groups:
  No. 2: 251, 253, 256–7, 264–6, 274, 279, 281, 297
  No. 3: 58, 59, 253, 268, 272
  No. 4: 59, 253–4, 269–70, 272, 276–7
  No. 5: 253–4, 269–70, 272, 276–8
  No. 11: 4, 9–10, 26–7, 33, 39, 83, 182, 192, 195, 198–9, 201–2, 205, 301
  No. 12: 194, 201, 203
  No. 16: 239
RAF Squadrons
  No. 1: 50, 191
  No. 17: 186, 194
  No. 19: 36, 38, 46, 49, 185, 194
  No. 21: 259
  No. 41: 186
  No. 43: 45
  No. 48: 227, 229
  No. 54: 37–8, 192
  No. 56: 34, 47, 184
  No. 65: 40, 206
  No. 66: 195
  No. 72: 194
  No. 73: 36
  No. 74: 206
  No. 79: 206
  No. 87: 177, 197
  No. 92: 34, 193, 196
  No. 107: 253, 266–7
  No. 110: 266–7
  No. 111: 199
  No. 145: 37, 186
  No. 206: 234
  No. 213: 193
  No. 220: 224, 226, 231, 233, 238
  No. 229: 35, 41, 50
  No. 235: 224–5, 238
  No. 245: 39, 186, 194, 197
  No. 254: 224–5
  No. 264: 199
  No. 266: 206
  No. 500: 33, 227–8, 231
  No. 601: 174–5
  No. 605: 38–40, 47, 195, 206
  No. 609: 38–9, 49, 194, 199
  No. 610: 50
  No. 611: 39, 196
  No. 613: 33, 239
  No. 616: 48, 195
RAF Training 41–564
  Flight Training School 43–4, 53, 58
  Fighter 6, 42, 44, 47, 53, 206, 296
  Gunnery 49–50
  Navigation and Instrument 52–3, 57–60, 64, 298
  Operational Training Units 44, 59
Royal Navy 7, 52, 90, 111–12, 123, 125, 129, 130, 165, 181, 228–30, 294, 299
  Losses 2, 79–80, 84, 147, 294, 302
  View on RAF air cover 183, 193

Scheldt, Estuary 232, 234
Schnellboote *See* E-Boat
Socx 265, 272–3
Soest 273
Somme, the 28, 32, 62, 101, 103, 125, 145–6, 158, 253
Speidel, Generalmajor Wilhelm 6, 148
Spence, Wing Commander Edgar Henry Douglas 128, 159
St. Omer 258–60, 269–70, 280
St. Pol 29–30, 259

Tennant, Captain William 14, 85, 86, 109, 122, 142–3, 147, 183
Terschelling 233, 235
Texel 229, 231–5
Thourout 120, 260–1, 270–1

Veurne *See* Furnes
Vlissingen *See* Flushing

Weather Conditions 34, 64, 81, 129, 142, 185–7 *See also* Luftwaffe, effect of weather, Luftwaffe, Fair weather force; Luftwaffe Training, flying in poor weather conditions;
Causing errors 54, 56
During anti-E-Boat patrols 229, 233

Weygand, General Maxime 2
Willemsoord 233, 235

Ypres 120, 259, 262–3, 271

Zeebrugge 125, 163–4, 224, 235

www.ingramcontent.com/pod-product-compliance
Lightning Source LLC
Chambersburg PA
CBHW052143300426
44115CB00011B/1502